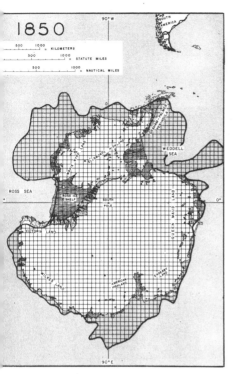

CROSS-HATCHED AREA INDICATES UNEXPLORED TERRITORY

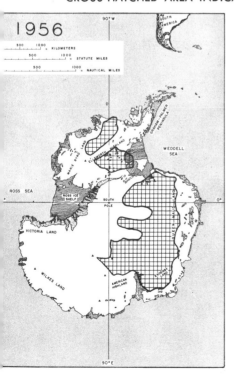

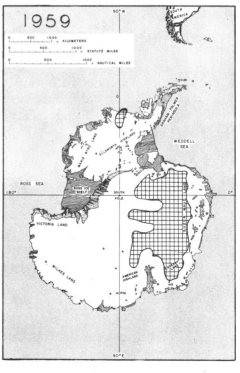

90° SOUTH

The Story of the American South Pole Conquest

Paul Siple

New York

90° SOUTH

*The Story of the American
South Pole Conquest*

G. P. PUTNAM'S SONS

Library of Congress Catalog Card Number: 59-11029

The color photographs in this book as well as that on the back of the jacket
and the double-spread illustration of the Station following page 192 are used
through the courtesy of the National Geographic Society, which published
Dr. Siple's articles "We Are Living at the South Pole" and "Man's First Winter
at the South Pole" in the July 1957 and April 1958 issues of the *National
Geographic Magazine.*

MANUFACTURED IN THE UNITED STATES OF AMERICA

VAN REES PRESS   •   NEW YORK

With Love to Ruth

ACKNOWLEDGMENTS

THE author is indebted to so many who played a part in making this book possible that he regrets being unable to mention more than a few. I must begin with a general group which starts with Admiral Byrd and extends to all who took part in the events which are here recounted.

I am especially indebted to: the Army that permitted me as their employee to have the opportunity of taking part in the venture; the Departments of Navy, Air Force, and Defense that established the station; the National Academy of Sciences and its associated committees under the United States National Committee for the International Geophysical Year.

More specifically I wish to express my appreciation to the following individuals for their assistance in the development of the book: Alfred Steinberg for technical assistance in the organization and styling of the story; Walter Minton, President of G. P. Putnam's Sons, for his encouragement and patient helpfulness; Steve Becker whose intellectual probing helped get the task of writing underway; The National Geographic Society for its assistance in providing the illustrations—especially Dr. Melville Bell Grosvenor, President of the Society, and staff members Thomas Abercrombie, David S. Boyer and Leonard J. Grant; Edward Remington for the use of his diary and illustrative material; John Tuck for critical review and suggestions; Lt. Col. Murray A. Wiener, USAF, for his personal assistance at the outset of the venture; Gerald Pagano for his many timely suggestions and research assistance; my daughters Ann, Jane and Mary for help with the maps and illustrations; last but not least my wife Ruth who bore with me through the ordeal of absence from home and family life and assisted immeasurably during the development of the account.

Contents

8 · CONTENTS

FOREWORD

by John Tuck, Jr., Lt. (jg), USNR, Navy Support Leader,
South Pole Station, 1957

W HEN I first left McMurdo for the South Pole with the Navy Advance Construction Party on November 19, 1956, I had no idea that I would later become an overwintering resident. I had requested a second year in Antarctica, to have an opportunity of observing the IGY in action, but since I felt that this request needed some concrete, practical justification, I based it upon the prospect of further work with the dog teams, at one of the other coastal stations. At the time I left for the Pole I'd had no definite reply to my request, but was expecting approval.

With this assumption that I would continue to work with the dogs, I was completely taken by surprise upon receiving at the Pole, several days later, a message from Rear Admiral George Dufek asking if I would volunteer to serve as Military Leader of the South Pole Station. I then had to completely regear my thinking and start again from scratch. I'd been looking forward to carrying on with the dogs, but on the other hand the Pole Station unquestionably presented a greater challenge, and to be offered this position was, I felt, a considerable honor.

The deciding factor, however, was the man with whom I would have to work most closely. The dual command system of separate Military and Scientific Leaders appeared to hold promise of trouble if there were not close co-operation and a spirit of give-and-take between the two leaders.

At the time I did not know Paul Siple well, but yet well enough to have formed a strong impression: I was absolutely certain that if I couldn't work constructively with him, and circumvent any potential difficulties of the dual command system, then there was something radically wrong—with me. I was confident that I could work with

9

him, and had full confidence in his abilities and experience. This was the deciding factor, and it was with firm anticipation of a successful year that I accepted Admiral Dufek's offer. The passing of time served only to strengthen and broaden my early impressions of Paul, and never have I for a moment regretted my decision.

Paul brought to the Pole experience in, and an understanding of, polar operations unmatched either individually or collectively by the other members of the wintering-over group. Positive effects of this were evident from the start, before construction even began, when with Dick Bowers he placed the physical layout of the station on a practical and livable basis. Such seemingly small details as placing the roofs of all the buildings at a common level can be easily overlooked by the unknowing, its importance unrealized except in later realization of the consequences of not doing so. Other examples could be cited *ad infinitum,* perhaps even *ad nauseam.* But time and again Paul's experience proved itself, though some of it can never be fully appreciated even by our group, for much was preventative in effect, and only through witnessing the results of inexperience can one adequately appreciate the value of its opposite.

Also, Paul's experience was coupled with an ability to make itself manifest through others rather than being dogmatically propounded, and discussion of problems and ideas as to their solution frequently led to someone else coming up with the answer which Paul could have given at the outset. This gave a greater sense of responsibility and achievement to less experienced men, and as by-products elicited both readier co-operation in implementing decisions, and, not infrequently, other worth-while ideas. The snow mine is a case in point. Harking back to it, it is difficult to recall the genesis of our snow mine *cum* glaciology deep pit, as the ideas of a number of individuals were incorporated in its development. But the basic idea originated with Paul Siple.

Invaluable as his abilities and experience were, however, it was as a *person* that Paul made his most signal contributions to the success of the South Pole Station's first year. His leadership was a grand thing to observe, and it was leadership by leading, not pushing. On any task, especially an unpopular one, he was first on the job and last to leave it. In the long and arduous process of digging the 1,000-foot tunnel to the seismometer pit his shovel was invariably the first set in motion and the last set down. In the snow mine also, Paul logged more hours' work than anyone else, and at an output rate matched by few and exceeded by none. He was by some years the oldest man in the camp, but the young bucks who initially figured that it would be easy to work this elderly gent into the snow found, to their great chagrin, that they had an ample challenge in simply endeavoring to keep up with him.

Some of the most prominent challenges of polar living fall in the provinces of mind and emotion, rather than muscle and matter. A man with breadth and depth of scientific background can, through intelligent understanding, questioning, and encouragement helpfully stimulate those directly engaged in the various programs at times when routine may tend to become a rut, and can engender renewed interest and increased scientific inquiry, thus thwarting potential stagnation. He may also need to bring technical competence to bear to bolster a flagging program. These attributes are all facets of Paul Siple, and ones in which he excelled. His basic initiative evidenced itself also in recreation programs, general and scientific lectures, and our Sunday religious services.

The less precise area of personalities and emotions is the most difficult to define and the one most fraught with potential stumbling blocks. Among a group of men living in close and unremitting proximity there are bound to be frictions. Many will resolve themselves naturally and without leaving any lasting trace. Others, however, are not self-resolving and may lead to serious consequences; these are a prime test of leadership. We were not free of these frictions, but none became permanent or had a serious effect; it is to Paul that the credit that this was so is due. His unvarying good nature, sincere interest in each man as an individual, and steady, patient impartiality won common respect and trust. His was an often-tapped well of common sense and sound judgment which placed problems in perspective and plumbed their causes for practical and workable solutions. With unruffled grace and humor he heard out grievances great and small, real and imagined, favoring neither scientist nor sailor but being governed by the realities of the situation at hand.

The question of human conflicts, in the main either omitted altogether or glossed over in polar accounts, is treated in this book as an integral part of the story of the first wintering at the South Pole. The year was certainly a happy and successful one, yet it was not without its emotional crosscurrents and occasional clashes. Paul examines these, not out of ill-will nor with any intent to belittle any individual— far from it—but to cite candidly the nature of these problems, their causes, and what was done to overcome them. Presented with honesty and integrity, this insight into the inner, generally taboo, life of a polar station is not the least of the significant contributions of this book.

I am confident that I can speak for each man of the South Pole Station's initial wintering party in according to Paul Siple the great credit that is his for the success and pleasure of that year. For myself, knowing and working with him, a grand friend, teacher, and solid inspiration, was indisputedly the most valuable aspect of my two years in Antarctica.

JOHN TUCK, JR.,
Lt. (jg), USNR

90° SOUTH

The Story of the American South Pole Conquest

Chapter 1

THE SOUTHERN JOURNEY BEGINS

*T*HE *Pole . . . Great God! this is an awful place.*

Thus scribbled Captain Robert Falcon Scott in his diary on January 17, 1912. Conditions at the South Pole were so horrible that even a properly reserved Britisher could cry out in anguish.

I was aware that since Scott's time no man had set foot at the South Pole. In fact, other than the ill-fated Scott party of five who perished before they could escape the sprawling Antarctic Continent, and the four-man party led by Roald Amundsen, the daring Norseman who beat Scott to the Pole by a mere month, no one in all history had tramped about at the Pole. And even Amundsen and Scott had left the Pole with little delay.

I thought of them that Wednesday afternoon of October 3, 1956, as I pressed the door buzzer at 9 Brimmer Street in Boston. I had come for lunch and a last talk with Admiral Richard E. Byrd before making my scheduled departure the next evening for the vast icy continent of Antarctica. Once there I would plane inland some 850 miles to the geographic South Pole itself. Here where Amundsen and Scott had so briefly trod, I had agreed to spend more than a year of my life guiding scientific research.

My trip to Boston from Virginia to lunch with Admiral Byrd, at a time when I was in the midst of frantic last-minute packing, was occasioned by several reasons. We were first of all old comrades at exploring. Though he was twenty years my senior, our relationship had mellowed through the years from an original father-son quality to that of equal friends. Then, again, an additional reason for my pressing his doorbell this day was that he was the Officer in charge of the United States Antarctic Program, named by President Eisenhower himself, and I was his deputy. It had been at his specific suggestion that I had extended my duties to include those of IGY Station Scientific Leader at the South Pole.

I had objected to this last assignment at first on grounds of my age, reluctance again to leave my family, and the press of other important duties. Just as important was the fact that I had doubts about the logistical planning which had gone into the Pole Station, the effect of the split command which would exist there and leave ultimate authority in question, and the fact that not only had the men who would man the station had no voice in its planning, but almost half of them had not even been selected as yet. All to no avail. "Now see here, Paul," he had said shaking his head, "we've been on five Antarctic expeditions together. You know the Antarctic from every angle and you've served various expeditions in just about every possible aspect."

The Admiral was a man of resolute will. "On or about 1 October 1956," he had written me officially, "you will proceed and report to the National Academy of Sciences, United States National Committee for the International Geophysical Year for temporary additional duty as Scientific Leader of the South Pole Station for a period of approximately eighteen months."

Of course I had been involved in the organization of the IGY almost from the start and knew that it was to run from mid-1957 to the close of 1958. Sixty-seven nations and roughly 10,000 scientists were committed to man 2,000 scientific stations around the globe. The South Pole Station, manned with a complement of eighteen, was to join the other stations in the simultaneous collection of data. It was hoped that with an assault of this size we would learn a great deal about meteorology, the aurora and airglow, glaciology, ionospheric physics, seismology, cosmic rays, gravity, geomagnetism and other physical phenomena.

But to some extent, Admiral Byrd's interest in establishing a South Pole base went far beyond the IGY. He wanted it said, as did I, that the United States had done the impossible. A fierce national pride burned within him. Scientifically, we both agreed that the base would provide a vital tie-in juncture for the three contemplated world chains of scientific stations. But science would have to wait a while under the circumstances, he insisted. "To put down a base at the Pole and keep men living there will tax all our ingenuity and will in itself be a great national achievement." For such was our decision.

"How are you, Paul?" the Admiral greeted me now. He did not look well. His face had a grayish pallor and there was a transparency to the flesh over his handsome features. But he still exuded his usual boyish enthusiasm and puckish humor.

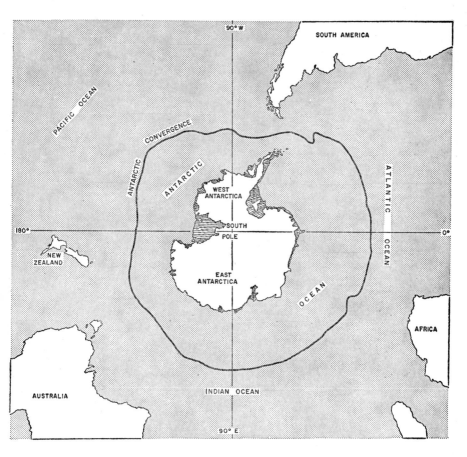

Antarctica in relation to the surrounding oceans and continents.

Over lunch we talked about my coming trip and the many vexing problems that had arisen during the planning and preparation of the broad American Antarctic program. There had been individuals who had not lived up to our best expectations. Others had failed to take advantage of experience that we had gained in the past. There had also been, as all too often is the case, too many individuals with strong voices in the planning who were unacquainted with the Antarctic and would have no responsibility for living at the Pole. "An opulent expedition," Byrd summarized the effort of the previous year, when we went along on the Navy's Deep Freeze I expedition to inspect the start of the American IGY program. I agreed and estimated that it would cost almost a million dollars to station each of the eighteen men at the South Pole.

Not all our time was taken up with my upcoming trip. We also reminisced about our various adventures over the past quarter century. Five times now we had gone exploring together to the Antarctic Continent. The first trip, though almost thirty years before, was still vivid. Then I had been the proud Boy Scout selected to accompany the Byrd Expedition of 1928–1930 to Little America on the sea edge of the Ross Ice Shelf. It had been on this expedition that Byrd became the first man to fly over the South Pole.

"Do you remember," Dick said, "our fright in that little boat when that herd of killer whales came after us?"

How could I forget! Just as those mean beady-eyed twenty-five-foot monsters reached us, we had leaped from the boat onto a jutting piece of ice. Byrd had pulled out a revolver in case they continued after us. Fortunately, they turned away. I say fortunately because a revolver bullet would have inflicted about as much damage on them as a mosquito bite. The entire incident had created enormous amusement back aboard ship. Only a few days before I had been appointed assistant to the scientific staff. "Why aren't you out there on the bay studying killer whales?" the others ribbed me for weeks afterward.

That day Byrd and I also talked about some of the men who had accompanied us on previous expeditions. Most were of the rough and tough school, on that first expedition from 1928 to 1930 and on the second Byrd venture to the Antarctic from 1933 to 1935. Their thoughts had centered chiefly on "wine, women and song."

Yet the Antarctic generally wields a profound effect on personality and character and few men are the same after a stay there. Many of the men on the first two Byrd Expeditions found purpose to their lives in the Antarctic and rose far in life. Yet it was surprising how many of the men later suffered violent ends either in the line of duty or still pursuing adventure in some far corner of the earth.

So the Antarctic conjured up a curious mixture of good and bad memories for us that afternoon. We knew it as both a hateful and fascinating place. It was cruel and heartless, yet its cold beauty, ominous silence and weird phenomena were haunting. In addition, we knew the Antarctic for its enormous scientific and strategic value.

Certainly neither of us would have disputed the fact that the Antarctic held the meanest environment on earth, or that it was at its center that its vicious hostility climaxed. In some areas winds of hurricane force were frequent, with gusts reaching up toward 200 miles per hour. On the million-square-mile plateau, upon which the geographic South Pole rests at an altitude of almost two miles above sea level, the cold could be expected to drop far below a piercing minus one hundred degrees Fahrenheit. To add to the discomfort, the sun would be gone entirely for six months and be ever-present the following six.

An ice-covered continent of more than five million square miles, its area approximated that of the United States and Europe combined. In some zones the polar ice crust is likely to be miles thick, and the land or rock beneath the ice in many areas is no doubt far below sea level. In a continuous assault, the ice advanced like the glacier it is from the high plateau surrounding the geographic Pole toward the distant seas. Along its relentless route, it filled valleys, rode over hills and plummeted between 15,000-foot mountains in awesome icefalls. At the continent's rim the ice moves headlong into the frozen seas, along the way producing dangerous crevasses on the land and huge icebergs on the sea. Should this vast polar icecap ever melt, it would raise the level of the oceans by eighty feet or more and flood out the bulk of the world's population clustered near the world's seacoast.

Along the outer boundaries of Antarctica you could, of course, see penguins and other birds, a variety of fish, seals and killer whales. But as you advanced into the interior, only by careful search would you find even the primitive lichens and moss, algae and fungi. At the continent's center, at Latitude Ninety South, chances were that at best only the simplest bacteria and molds would be discoverable.

This remote region was accidentally reached in the seventeenth century by mariners blown off their course. Evidence is that they apprehensively fought to move their barks northward against mountainous Antarctic seas and winds of hurricane force. A Yankee sealer

—Captain Nathaniel Palmer—was probably the first to sight the uninviting mainland in November, 1820.

The afternoon was fast disappearing by the time the Admiral signaled a maid by uttering a soft "now." She returned with a mail package on a tray. I saw that it was addressed to me at Byrd's address and that it had been torn open.

"Oh, I opened it accidentally," Byrd said, as he directed me to open the package in his presence.

Inside, I found a navigator's wrist watch. On the back of the case, there stood engraved—TO MY OLD COMRADE, PAUL SIPLE. FROM DICK BYRD.

We regarded each other silently.

"Paul," he confessed, "living at the South Pole would have been the high point of my life. But since I can't go, there is no one else I'd rather see taking my place than you."

It was a sticky moment for both of us, and I left him feeling saddened, rather than elated.

It was the last time I saw Admiral Byrd alive.

Chapter 2

SEARCH FOR A CONTINENT

THE decision to erect an American station at the South Pole was made sometime in 1955. Yet in a historic sense, this was merely the culmination of two centuries or more of probing the mysteries of the Antarctic. Without the spadework and inspiration of our many predecessors, plus the breath-taking advances in science, the South Pole Station would not have been possible.

Whether it was inevitable destiny or simply man's insatiable curiosity and eternal search for means of bettering his lot, the conquest of the South Pole has followed an astounding mathematical pattern. For it is apparent that there is an ever-accelerating pace in all human endeavor as time passes, population increases, and man's knowledge grows. The fields of communication, travel and exploration all show ever-increasing effort as time passes.

The advances of Antarctic exploration and man's movement southward toward the Pole illustrate this law of accelerating effort. In the Antarctic it came in spurts after each new technical innovation or during pioneer exploits. After Columbus dared cross the Atlantic Ocean it was easier for others to be less fearful. In 1502 Amerigo Vespucci followed the South American coast to about Latitude 50° S, and reported reaching an extreme southing of 54° S. In 1520 Magellan found the straits that bear his name and a passage around South America to continue the first circumnavigation of the globe. Drake, 58 years later, missed Magellan's passage in a storm and found clear passage around the Horn in Latitude 57° S.

The cold seas and occasional evidence of ice kept men from adventuring farther south, although occasionally storms blew sailing ships far off course—some never to be heard from again. But one, the Dutch ship *Blijde Bootschap,* translated *Good News,* survived to report that they had reached Latitude 64° S.

On the accompanying histograph you will note this accident to the *Good News* placed it ahead of normal schedule of man's rate of southward advance.

This one-dimension map with years substituted for longitude and drawn on semi-log paper to render a straight line out of ordinary exponential curves, shows the rest of the outline of man's southward movement at a glance. As you will see, it was no accident but sheer drive of daring pioneers like Cook, Ross, Shackleton, Scott, and Amundsen that kept man advancing toward the Pole on schedule.

I have included on this graph also the progress of man's houses in which he first wintered over at a new record southing. One might almost think we who were going to live at the geographical South Pole were predictably destined to do so in 1957. Finally, with the Pole attained, and nowhere farther south to go except straight up, I have brought my graph up to publication date to show that the apogee and perigee of the first pole to pole orbiting satellite launched in 1959 was slightly behind schedule. However, I have no doubt that by the time a safe high radiation-free path is assured, man in a satellite will be orbiting over the South Pole on schedule with the progression of events that began at least some four and a half centuries ago.

Let us return more leisurely to review man's southward advance, for it is wrought with more romance and fortitude than meets the

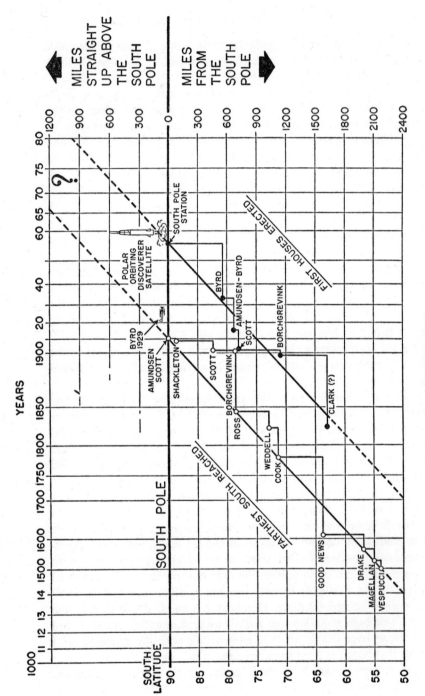

MAN'S SOUTHWARD ADVANCE

eye in a cold mathematical analysis of the events. In truth, our goal to set up a scientific observation station on the geographic South Pole had an awesome ring that made us fully respect the task that lay ahead.

Such prior exploratory efforts as were made came in three distinct waves and as the result of as many unrelated reasons. The first assault was chiefly a search for profits and wealth. This period ended roughly about 1840. Then followed a long romantic period of more than seventy years when brave souls fought the outrageous rigors of the ice continent solely in the interest of discovery. Men gingerly put foot on the continent. A group of men daringly wintered on the edge of the Antarctic. And finally in December, 1911, the Pole was reached. Once this was accomplished, the third period began: the age of scientific research.

The name Antarctic is derived from the Greek words *anti* and *arktos,* which means "opposite the bear," or the Arctic. That a Southern Continent might exist was a notion implanted by imaginative mapmakers of the Middle Ages. *Terra Australis Incognita,* they labeled their mythical continent, which they assured map readers contained riches exceeding those yet known to man.

Vessels began pushing southward from Europe past Africa in search of this Southern Continent and its rumored breath-taking wealth. When, to their dismay, they found only endless ocean, the search shifted in time to the area south of the Americas. Finally the quest moved across the Pacific to the vicinity of New Zealand and Australia. In 1772, the bold English mariner, Captain James Cook, set out on a voyage to circumnavigate the globe. He blasted with finality the hope that the mythical Southern Continent existed in a temperate zone.

If another continent existed at all, Cook proved that it would have to be south of the 60th parallel. Furthermore, he concluded from his own harrowing experience that any southern continent would lie farther south than man would dare to voyage. Three times he crossed the Antarctic Circle and penetrated on January 17, 1773, as far south as 71° 10', or less than nineteen degrees from the South Pole. On none of his ventures below the Antarctic Circle, however, did he sight land. All he met was the Antarctic ice pack, and not being able to find a path through it, he was forced to turn north. "I will not say that it was impossible anywhere to get farther to the south," he wrote, "but the attempting it would have been a rash and dangerous enterprise. . . . It was, indeed, my opinion, as well as the opinion of most on board, that this ice extended quite to the Pole, perhaps joined some land . . .

but if there is, it can afford no better retreat for birds, or any other animals, than the ice itself. I, who had ambition not only to go farther than anyone had been before, but as far as it was possible for man to go, was not sorry at meeting this interruption."

Despite Cook's pessimism, others continued into the Antarctic seas. Instead of seeking *Terra Australis Incognita,* however, they came in search of prize animals. Following the American Revolution, the assault on Antarctica came from American and British sailing masters who traveled southward in little sloops in search of wealth. Seals were known to spend their summers breeding on sub-Antarctic islands, and Yankee captains hunted them for their oil and especially their fur. Whales also abounded and were valuable for their oil and ambergris.

Destruction became the order of the day. The crew of a single sealer, for example, killed 60,000 seals in a four-month period. And as the slaughter continued without abatement, necessity forced further southern penetration in search of new sealing grounds. The sealers were totally uninterested in geographic discovery, yet they uncovered several hitherto unknown places, such as the South Shetlands, South Orkneys and Macquarie Island. For economic reasons a sealer would not tell another what he had found. Thus information about an island would not be divulged until the seals there had been slain.

It was only a matter of time before the Antarctic Continent would be discovered. This event seems to have occurred on November 17, 1820, when a tall, husky, twenty-year-old Yankee seal hunter, Captain Nathaniel Palmer, first sighted the Antarctic mainland at approximately 60° West Longitude. Though the ice kept him from landing, he followed the shore line "every where Perpendicular" and explored the north coast of West Antarctica.

Two months later Palmer chanced upon the *Mirny* and the *Vostok,* two ships of the Imperial Russian Navy under Admiral Fabian von Bellingshausen. The Russian admiral, then in the midst of an exploratory cruise in which he discovered a couple of Antarctic islands, was astonished by Palmer's success. "Among other things," Palmer wrote later to a friend, "I informed him of our Trip to the South in Lat 68° & the Discovery of a Land [never before seen] and it was him that named it Palmer's Land."

At the time of Palmer's discovery of the continent, the Monroe Administration, which then held office in the United States, had no interest in claiming the Antarctic. The United States was a relatively new nation and its own western frontier was thinly populated. Besides, Palmer was not an explorer in the traditional sense, but only a hunter of seals. Furthermore, most of his and others' notes which would have confirmed his discovery were lost.

Recent discovery of logbooks of various Yankee sealers have brought to light interesting accounts of Burdick and Davis, two Yankee captains in the course of several hunts on the ships *Huron, Huntress* and *Cecilia.* These mariners not only explored the northern coast of Palmer's new land, but John Davis sent a landing party ashore at Hughes Bay on February 7, 1821 which is the first recorded landing on the Antarctic Continent. It was to be another three-quarters of a century before the next landing would be made on the opposite side of the continent.

Captain Clark of the British sealer *Lord Melville* established the first shore party known to have wintered over in the sub-Antarctic South Shetland Islands. They established a hut on the northern shore of King George Island where eleven men resided over the winter season of 1820–21.

This account does not pretend to list the narrative of the many sealers and early explorers who bit by bit added to the uncovering of Antarctica. It does, however, attempt to show how man's insatiable curiosity drove him in quest of the South Pole.

The record southing of Captain Cook of 71° 10′ S in Longitude 106° 54′ W on January 30, 1774 was not broken until Captain James Weddell, a British sealer, pressed southward through pack ice along Longitude 37° 17′ W in his ship *June* and reached farther south than anyone had attempted, 74° 15′ S on February 20, 1822. The ice-filled sea from which he fled bears his name and is one of the two great indentations into the otherwise circular continent of Antarctica. Dense ice pack and the lack of seals caused him to turn back.

With the decline of the sealing industry came the second period of Antarctic activity. This was the era of purposeful and romantic exploration. In the mid-1830's, the governments of the United States, England and France took a direct interest in the Antarctic. Chief hope of the three governments was to locate the South Magnetic Pole, for by getting to this pole, mapmakers would be able to produce more accurate magnetic maps, so essential for accurate navigational purposes. Three government-sponsored expeditions set out: the Americans under Lieutenant Charles Wilkes; the British under Captain James Clark Ross; and the French under Captain Dumont d'Urville.

None of the three set foot on the continent, where the South Magnetic Pole was located. However, the exploratory contributions of the trio were highly significant.

Although his expedition was authorized by an act of Congress in May, 1836, Wilkes did not leave Norfolk, Virginia, until August of 1838. Captain D'Urville sailed first, heading for the Antarctic from Cape Horn with two corvettes, the *Astrolabe* and the *Zelee*. While he failed to land on the coast, he spent three years exploring offshore islands and discovered Adélie Coast, an ice-walled area that he named for his wife. Here D'Urville met with the now arrived Wilkes Expedition. Poor ship handling marred the greeting and they parted each thinking they had been snubbed by the other.

With the blessings of the Van Buren Administration, Wilkes had gone to sea with six vessels and a complement of 345 men, including a dozen scientists. Though Wilkes traveled in the *Vincennes,* the largest ship, it was in as bad a state of disrepair as the others. Only four of the vessels managed to reach sub-Antarctic waters.

Beset by scurvy, inadequate clothing and leaking ships, the Wilkes expedition nevertheless sailed fearlessly into the ice pack surrounding the continent in 1839. From the deck of the *Vincennes,* the American observed and charted the coast line of the Antarctic Continent between 160° and 97° East Longitude. This was on the Australian side of Antarctica, almost directly opposite the jutting peninsula young Palmer had seen in 1820.

An interesting sidelight to Wilkes' Expedition is that in 1838, Lieutenant William Walker, a junior commander to Wilkes who was in charge of the eight-man crew of the 96-ton *Flying Fish,* daringly approached a section of the continent close to what is now called the Thurston Peninsula. The significance of his enterprise is that no ship since then has reached that point. Also in the course of this expedition one of the seamen, William Stewart of the *Peacock,* commanded by William Hudson, died, making him the first American victim of the Antarctic.

The third of this period's great explorers, Captain James Ross, left England in September, 1839, with two sturdy vessels, the *Erebus* and *Terror.* Having got wind of the exploits of D'Urville and Wilkes, he stubbornly refused to follow their routes toward the continent. Instead, he headed southwest from Tasmania and turned toward the South Pole along the 170° East meridian. Early in 1841, he plowed into the dangerous ice pack, but with extreme good fortune he found a route through the seemingly solid ice-crusted sea and only four days later emerged into an open-water sea, that is today named Ross Sea in his honor. Pushing on due south, he came to the continent, only to find himself face to face with a vast snow-ice barrier, a mast-high cliff extending for several hundred miles east-west across his path. Said Ross: "As we approached the land under all-studding sails, we perceived a low white line extending from its eastern extreme point as far as the eye could discern to the eastward. It presented an extraordinary appearance, gradually increasing in height as we got nearer to it, and proving at length to be a perpendicular cliff, between 150 and 200 * feet above the level of the sea, perfectly flat on top, and without any fissures or promontories on its even seaward face."

The achievements of Ross were of great importance. Besides discovering the Ross Sea, Victoria Land, the Prince Albert Mountains, and Mount Erebus, the most active volcano in the Antarctic, he had found the Ross Ice Shelf, across which later proved to be the most accessible route to the geographic pole.

However, Ross was not satisfied with his honors. From whatever motives impelled him, he cast strong doubts on Wilkes' findings. Where Wilkes had reported land, Ross gravely asserted that he himself had come upon open sea. Naturally, a cry soon arose that Wilkes had perpetrated a fraud.

Certainly it was true that in some of his calculations, Wilkes had been off by as much as fifty miles. But what he described and what was later found in the general vicinity were certainly the same. Indeed, Ross also proved to be in error on many of his own calculations as is so often the case with the explorers who push back a frontier. But after his attack against Wilkes, Ross's own errors were glossed over.

Certainly the entire episode was beneath Ross's dignity. As for Wilkes, the outcry against him unfortunately led to a general discrediting of his exploratory work in the Antarctic by British polar historians. Even in the United States credence was given to Ross's statements, and later Wilkes was court-martialed for making false geographic claims and for being cruel to his men. But though he was publicly reprimanded for alleged cruelty to his crew, he was speedily and deservedly acquitted of the first charge.

After the important assaults on the Antarctic led by Wilkes, D'Urville and Ross, more than a half century passed before further gains were made. For a time the Civil War caused a lessening of American interest in the Antarctic. Afterward, polar interest built up to a crescendo in the vigorous effort to seek out the Northwest Passage and the North Pole.

However, a new burst of Antarctic activity came in the 1890's, im-

* Later estimates have shown the Barrier face to average nearer to 100 feet high.

pelled to a large extent by the Sixth International Geographical Congress in London in 1895. "The exploration of the Antarctic regions," this Congress declared, "is the greatest piece of geographical exploration still to be undertaken."

The race now began to reach the geographic pole. In 1894, a Norwegian expedition under Captain Leonard Kristensen and H. J. Bull made a landing on the Antarctic Continent when the men came ashore at Cape Mare, in about 71° South Latitude and 170° East Longitude. This landing was well publicized, unlike that of Davis's crew in 1821, and was long accepted as man's first landing on Antarctica. Then in 1897, Belgians under Lieutenant Adrien de Gerlache, commanding the *Belgica,* penetrated into the southern ice pack west of the Graham-Palmer Peninsula * until their ship froze into the pack. Drifting helplessly for months, the Belgians nevertheless became the first to winter in the Antarctic area. This expedition also achieved another "first," as a result of the ability of the ship's American physician. Dr. Frederick Cook, a picturesque character as his later career proved, was among the first to suspect the nature of scurvy (or "Polar anaemia," as he called it), the scourge of the seas. Cook rightly believed that if men ate fresh meat they would avoid the disease. Thus, when most of the crew came down with scurvy, Cook successfully entreated the young Norwegian first mate, Roald Amundsen, to help collect and experiment with a regular ration of fresh seal meat for all hands. Later, when the ice pack broke up, signs of scurvy had disappeared.

Another "first" came the following year. C. E. Borchgrevink, leader of a privately sponsored British-Norwegian expedition, determined to spend a winter on the continent. Having been a member of the Kristensen-Bull expedition that made the first landing on the mainland mass at Cape Adare, the daring Borchgrevink now pushed his way through the difficult pack ice to effect another landing there. Here, through a wild dark winter, he and nine others subsisted in a hut to prove that man could withstand the harshness of the continent. All emerged none the worse for their experiment except Nikolai Hanson, their zoologist, who died of an internal ailment, probably appendicitis. Hanson became the first man to be buried in the Antarctic.

Later, on his way home, Borchgrevink made a new record southing

---

* This name used here for perhaps the first time, combines the accepted British and American names. For years, a heated controversy has raged as to whether the American Palmer or the British Bransfield first sighted the promontory. (Biscoe, an Enderby whaler, applied the name of the British First Lord of the Admiralty, Sir James Graham, to it.) Commemoration of this controversy seems as worthy as the original discoveries.

in what was later to be named the Bay of Whales. This new record was only 40 nautical miles south of the record set by Ross in 1842, and it had required fifty-eight long years for man to take this tiny further step toward the Pole.

The accomplishments of courageous explorers, like Cook, Palmer, Bellingshausen, Wilkes, D'Urville, Ross, Gerlache and Borchgrevink, now made possible the greatest single exploit of all. For with their work accomplished, other men dared think of trekking beyond the rim of the continent into the unknown—to the South Pole. It was truly an age of monumental discovery that rose with the dawn of the twentieth century. And from this heroic Antarctic period, the names of Robert Scott, Ernest Shackleton and Roald Amundsen stand apart.

Captain Scott made the first foray when he headed the British National Antarctic Expedition of 1901–1904. Thirty-two years old at the time, Scott had amassed $460,000 for his venture as the result of grants from the British Government, the Royal Geographic Society and the Royal Society, as well as private donations. Scott entertained no real hope of reaching the Pole on this trip, his purpose being to make several sledge journeys inland as preparation for a further expedition when he would attempt to reach his prime goal. He hoped only to learn enough about the Antarctic from this first expedition to make a second one less hazardous.

His ship, the *Discovery,* with forty-nine men aboard, reached the pack ice close to the international date line on New Year's Day, 1902. A week later he was through the ice to the open Ross Sea. It was summertime in the Antarctic, and he proceeded down the coast into McMurdo Sound. Here he was able to set up a building on land to augment his ship at what he called Hut Point on Ross Island. His hut was about thirty feet square in area, with a pyramid-shaped roof and a small porch enclosing the wooden building.

Scott explored several hundred additional miles of the coast line, including the northern tip of the King Edward VII Peninsula and the eastern anchor of the immense Ross Ice Shelf. But his primary purpose remained to travel within the continent, and with this in mind he made three long sledge journeys, one of 380 miles, southward on the Ross Ice Shelf. On this longest journey he penetrated 207 miles closer to the Pole than had Borchgrevink only two years before. Buffeted by roaring winds, temperatures in the minus forties and dangerous underfooting, these were indeed risky undertakings. But to Scott they showed the feasibility of making his way to the Pole on some future expedition. Only one man had been lost, and this was Seaman Vince, who died not on a sledging journey but at Hut Point when his slippery boots carried him over the edge of the precipice.

At the outset of his voyage, Scott had remarked, "Not a single article of the outfit had been tested." Through the trial-and-error system, which was often costly, he learned through experience how to organize a necessary routine for his men and equipment. For instance, the sledging parties had been initially ignorant on such rudimentary matters as how to use cookers and lamps and how to erect tents in the field.

However, certain errors of judgment occurred during this first expedition that were to be compounded into tragedy on the second. For one thing, Scott did not understand the relationship between food and energy, failing to realize that a larger, huskier man required more food than a smaller man in order to maintain his strength. Share and share alike was indeed a democratic method, but it was unwise for the Antarctic. For another thing, Scott, who drove himself to physical extremes, had little understanding of physical weakness in others, and even less patience. This revealed itself when Ernest Shackleton, his heavy-browed, jut-jawed aide, developed signs of scurvy, and with it an attenuation of strength. Even so, he had man-hauled supplies over a great distance. But Scott took Shackleton's lessening of strength as a personal weakness. However, it is perhaps wrong to hold this particular act against Scott, for I have discovered in the course of several expeditions that when each man's role is vital it is almost inevitable for even the wisest leader to regard illness as a sign of weakness. A far more serious blind-spot in Scott lay in his lack of faith in dogs as a means of transportation. When most of the dogs on his expedition sickened and died, Scott concluded that it would be unwise to use them as sledge haulers on his next expedition.

Next came Shackleton as leader of his own expedition in 1907. Having been requested by Scott not to use his old base, Shackleton skirted the Ross ice barrier to the east in search of a suitable basing point. In time he came to a wide bay, which he called the Bay of Whales because of the numerous whales he saw there.* Unfortunately, Shackleton did not establish his base on the barrier here. Had he done so, he would have had the best and shortest route to the Pole.

---

* This bay had been seen by Scott and Shackleton five years before when they had called it Balloon Bight in honor of the first aerial flight by man in Antarctica. When Shackleton now saw it, it had changed greatly in shape, however. I later studied both Scott's and Shackleton's maps and concluded the change in shape was due to the fact that a large iceberg which had been lodged in the bay had floated away by the time of Shackleton's second visit.

Instead, he watched with horror as a piece of the ice barrier calved, or broke off, and ordered his ship, the *Nimrod,* away to search for a safer spot. Watching the calving of the barrier, said Shackleton, "made me decide then and there that under no circumstances would I winter on the Barrier, and that wherever we did land we would secure a solid rock foundation for our winter home." A solid rock foundation existed on Ross Island in McMurdo Sound, and here he returned to establish camp.

There were some side excursions during Shackleton's bold effort to reach the Pole. Two of his scientist-explorers, Douglas Mawson and T. Edgeworth David, with other companions, scaled the 13,200-foot-high Mount Erebus, the active volcano Ross had named for one of his ships in 1841. Professor David and Mawson also located the South Magnetic Pole far out on the Victoria land plateau, and found the Magnetic Pole to be not a point but an area that drifted continually. This launched the Australian Mawson in a lifelong career of Antarctic exploration.

As for Shackleton, he set off with three men for the geographic pole at Ninety South Latitude on October 29, 1908, having estimated that the journey would take ninety-one days and set a daily ration of thirty-four ounces for each man. Obviously Shackleton had been shaken by the failure of dogs on the Scott Expedition, for he took with him four Manchurian ponies, each to haul a 650-pound loaded eleven-foot sledge.

By November 26th, the small party passed the point of Scott's southernmost penetration over the Ross Ice Shelf. However, there was little cause for celebration because only one pony was still alive on December 1st. A few days later their last pony disappeared down a crevasse, almost carrying one of the men with him. Shackleton's party was now faced with the task of man-hauling its gear.

In their journey south across the deep ice shelf, Shackleton and his men had been skirting a high mountain range on their right. Now when they discovered that the mountain range was veering off to the southeast, they realized that they would have to cross it if they were to reach the Pole. On December 5th, they found the Beardmore Glacier (named for a backer of the expedition). Beardmore provided a route across the mountains, though hardly a safe passage, for the glacier was over a hundred miles long and replete with dangerous crevasses and deep snow. They ascended slowly, hauling painfully as they rose thousands of feet above the ice shelf. This grueling climb has always held a particular fascination for me, for while Shackleton was struggling up the Beardmore Glacier, my mother was struggling to bring me into the world. I made it on December 18, 1908, but it was December 27th before Shackleton fought his way to the head of the glacier.

They had come more than 500 miles and ahead of them lay the plateau that led to the Pole. A great optimism engulfed Shackleton when he realized that his goal was not far distant. But he soon changed his mind. Wind and weather on the plateau were much fouler than in the relatively sheltered glacier, while the high altitude of almost 10,000 feet produced shortness of breath. One day they progressed only four miles and gaspingly found themselves exhausted.

On January 9th, Shackleton wisely decided to call off his southward trek. The men were tired and food was short. "We have shot our bolt," he wrote in his diary. A blizzard raged, an "icy gale," as he called it, and the ground surface was hard, keeping them half walking and half running. They were at 88° 23′, or within 97 miles of the Pole, indeed a great tragedy to them after all they had come through. Shackleton looked longingly south through powerful glasses, but his reasoning told him that though they might cross the "dead white snow plain" to the Pole, if they did they might not return alive. "Whatever regrets may be," he wrote in his diary, "we have done our best."

In effect, Shackleton was the first man to reach the vicinity of the Pole. Had he gone on he would have found no change in the scenery save for the sun's achieving an even transit around the horizon. Shackleton's expedition had brought men 366 nautical miles closer to the Pole than Scott had ventured. The 97 remaining miles was actually less than any of the previous pioneers save Borchgrevink had advanced the frontier.*

The year 1910 saw the beginning of the final climactic quest to reach the Pole. Two expeditions got underway that year: one led by Roald Amundsen, the former first mate of the *Belgica* in 1897; the other led by the returning Captain Scott.

Originally, Amundsen had embarked with his ship, the *Fram,* for the North Pole only to learn en route that Robert Peary, the American explorer, had already reached it on April 6, 1909. Disappointed

---

* In view of the fact that as a member of Scott's sledging party in 1902 Shackleton took part in advancing man's farthest southing by 573 nautical miles (nearly ten degrees of latitude), he made the greatest progress since Cook in 1773.

but undaunted, Amundsen swung the *Fram* about and headed for the Antarctic.

Although Scott had a head start, luck was with Amundsen, and stayed with him throughout his expedition. Where it took Scott three weeks to get through the ice pack, Amundsen got the *Fram* beyond it into the Ross Sea in four days. This delay put Scott at his winter base on January 3, 1911, while Amundsen was only eleven days behind him in arriving at his own base site.

Essentially, Amundsen was not a scientist but a traveler. He had not come to observe scientific phenomena, but instead concentrated his efforts on the single objective of reaching the Pole in the shortest time possible. In excellent physical condition at thirty-nine, Amundsen was a fine skier, navigator and nautical man, as well as being a bit foolhardy and brave. With his objective stripped of the necessity of making encumbering scientific observations, Amundsen had only nine men in his shore party and each was geared to tasks designed to make a dash to the Pole possible. On the other hand, Scott's shore party numbered thirty-three and included twelve scientists who did outstanding work.

There were other advantages held by the Norwegian. Scott had landed his wintering-over party at Cape Evans, on McMurdo Sound, not far from his old camp at Hut Point. Amundsen, not insistent on wintering on a rock foundation, had gone to the Bay of Whales to winter on the ice shelf itself, since he did not agree with Shackleton's earlier warning that wintering on shelf ice was dangerous. It was his belief that the shelf at the Bay of Whales was firmly anchored to land, and that only its edges periodically calved. "This formation," he said, "with the exception of the pieces that had broken away, had persisted in the same place ... What, once, in the dawn of time arrested the mighty stream of ice at this spot and formed a lasting bay in its edge, which with few exceptions runs in an almost straight line, was not merely a passing whim of the fearful force that came crashing on, but something even stronger than that—something that was firmer than the hard ice—namely, the solid land." *

So in establishing his base away from the edge of the barrier, Amundsen had no fear that his camp would be carried away on an iceberg. And by putting his camp where he did, he was almost a

---

* Actually, Amundsen was wrong here, for I later proved that the shelf ice was moving at the rate of roughly four feet a day. Yet, Amundsen had fairly good reason for thinking that the ice was anchored, for opposite him was Roosevelt Island and this was snow-covered land.

hundred miles closer to the Pole than Scott, less than the distance by which Shackleton failed to attain the Pole, and faced a journey of roughly 800 miles.

He had yet another advantage. He planned to rely on dogs, the natural animal for polar travel, while Scott planned to travel with Manchurian ponies. Dogs could traverse the treacherously crevassed glacier passes through the southern mountains. They could also continue beyond to the Pole itself. On the other hand, ponies would have to be abandoned at the base of the mountains. They were also slower than dogs and sank deeper into snow. In addition, ponies were hay and oats burners, which supplies would have to be carried along for them to eat. Unlike them, dogs were cannibalistic and in an emergency some of the dogs could be killed and fed to those remaining.

Great irritation and anger spread through Scott's winter base at news of Amundsen's advance preparations. The leisurely atmosphere disappeared. Then the race began on October 19, 1911, when Amundsen and four others left his camp with four sledges, each drawn by thirteen dogs. Scott, however, did not leave Cape Evans until November 1st, by which time Amundsen was already south of 81° or more than 200 miles ahead. By November 15th, with his men riding on the sledges almost all the way, Amundsen arrived at 85° South. Now he decided not to cross the mountain range by way of the Beardmore Glacier, as Shackleton had done. Instead he went due south and sought his own pass. He skirted the range until he came to a valley glacier between two mountains which he called the Axel Heiberg Glacier, after a financial contributor to his expedition. Unlike the Beardmore Glacier, which was over a hundred miles long, this glacier, although far steeper for the dogs, ran on for only thirty miles before reaching the south polar plateau. On November 22nd, Amundsen's party had reached the head of the glacier and paused almost 11,000 feet up before gaining the polar plateau. Here, according to plan, they shot twenty-four of the dogs that had outlived their usefulness.

At that moment Scott and his party were approaching 81° South Latitude, just about halfway to the southern mountains and not yet 200 nautical miles from his camp. Here the first support party turned back. On December 9th, the Beardmore Glacier was reached and the second support peeled off; the weather had been unpleasant and the men were beginning to tire. The remaining ponies were shot and the ascent of the glacier began. At its summit another depot was established and the third support party left. On New Year's Day, 1912, the remaining eight men established a final depot beyond 87° South.

Now the final three-man support party left to make its way back to the coast leaving Scott and four companions—Titus Oates, Taff Evans, Birdie Bowers and Dr. Edward Wilson—to make the approximately 200-mile haul to the Pole.

Meanwhile, the Amundsen party found the going far easier and had coasted along to a point only 95 miles from the Pole, or closer than Shackleton's nearest approach, by December 8th. Amundsen's dogs were in excellent condition and his calculations had proved accurate. From this point on, the slope of the land was downhill. There was surprisingly little wind and the temperature ranged between −10° to −20°. On December 13th, as Amundsen wrote: "It was like the eve of some great festival that night in the tent . . . I was awake several times during the night, and had the same feeling that I can remember as a little boy on the night before Christmas." The next afternoon the Norwegian flag waved at the South Pole. And after a ceremonious dinner topped by a cigar for all hands, Amundsen and his four companions turned homeward on December 17, 1911.

Over a month later on Tuesday, January 16, 1912, Scott's party was in high spirits, for they had arrived close to the Pole in Latitude 89° 42′ S. That afternoon, however, as Scott wrote in his diary, Bowers "detected a black speck ahead. Soon we knew that this could not be a natural snow feature. We marched on, found that it was a black flag tied to a sledge bearer; nearby the remains of a camp; sledge tracks and ski tracks coming and going out and the clear trace of dogs' paws —many dogs. This told us the whole story. The Norwegians have forestalled us and are first at the Pole. It is a terrible disappointment, and I am very sorry for my loyal companions."

It was the next day that he uttered his painful cry of desolation: "The Pole . . . Great God! this is an awful place and terrible enough for us to have laboured to it without the reward of priority. . . . Now for the run home and a desperate struggle. I wonder if we can do it."

Of course, as is well known, they did not do it. They did fairly well until the middle of February as they plodded back. Then the weather turned bad, and the already weary men found their remaining strength ebbing rapidly.

The first tragedy occurred as a direct result of Scott's lack of understanding of the relationship between food and energy. Taff Evans was the first victim. A giant of a man, with enormous strength and endurance when healthy, Evans had been put on the same quantitative ration diet as Birdie Bowers, the smallest man in the party. Evans had been expected to use his great strength to more or less carry the group along, but on his meager rations he was the first to weaken. When he did, Scott showed critical disappointment. "Evans has nearly broken down in brain, we think," Scott entered in his diary as they tottered homeward toward their base. When he fell behind on February 17th, the four others skied back in search. "He was on his knees with clothing disarranged, hands uncovered and frostbitten, and a wild look in his eyes," wrote Scott. "His downward path was accelerated first by the shock of his frostbitten fingers, and later by his falls during rough traveling on the glacier, further by his loss of all confidence in himself." Evans died shortly after midnight that night.

Oates went next in a classic show of personal valor. By March they were past the Beardmore Glacier, but the temperature had dropped ominously beyond minus forty degrees. Suffering from a badly frost-bitten foot, Oates was unable to pull, and realized that his condition was a deterrent to the progress of the others. On Friday, March 16, Scott recorded, "It was blowing a blizzard." That day Oates turned to the others in the tiny shelter and said, quietly, "I am just going out-side and may be some time."

"He went out into the blizzard," wrote Scott, "and we have not seen him since . . . We knew that poor Oates was walking to his death, but though we tried to dissuade him, we knew it was the act of a brave man and an English gentleman." Indeed it was.

On March 19th, the remaining Scott, Wilson and Bowers reached a point only eleven miles from their depot, where quantities of food and fuel awaited them. They were now less than one hundred and fifty miles from their home base. But Scott's right foot was badly frostbitten and a blizzard had begun to blow.

They never moved beyond this point. On Thursday, March 29, Scott wrote in his diary:

> Since the 21st we have had a continuous gale from W.S.W. and S.W. We had fuel to make two cups of tea apiece and bare food for two days on the 20th. Every day we have been ready to start for our depot 11 miles away, but outside the door of the tent it remains a scene of whirling drift. I do not think we can hope for any better things now. We shall stick it out to the end, but we are getting weaker, of course, and the end cannot be far.
>
> It seems a pity, but I do not think I can write more.
>
> R. Scott

For God's sake look after our people.

So died the last gallant three.

When the bodies were found, a further message lay among Scott's belongings. It ended with these words:

> Had we lived, I should have had a tale to tell of the hardiness, endurance and courage of my companions which would have stirred the heart of every Englishman. These rough notes and our dead bodies must tell the tale, but surely, surely, a great rich country like ours will see that those who are dependent on us are properly provided for.

Thus ended the era of man's quest to attain the South Pole on foot.

Chapter 3

A BOY SCOUT WITH BYRD

SCOTT'S tragic story was one that touched the hearts of most boys of my generation. Both in its futility and bravery it conjured up visions of how we might have acted in similar circumstances. In this sense, it afforded an inspirational lesson in manliness.

Yet the cold truth was that it did not awaken me to any desire to become an Antarctic explorer. What was to bring me to travel six times to the Antarctic and spend years in a forbidding ice age started as mere happenstance.

Had I not remained an active Boy Scout at nineteen; had there been no Byrd Antarctic Expedition in 1928; and had there been no contest among Boy Scouts between the ages of 17½ and 19½ to select one who would accompany Byrd, I might never have gone to the Antarctic.

There were six finalists, including myself, who descended on New York City for a week of tests and inspections. My advantage was that I was taller, heavier and older than the others, though all impressed me as being excellent Antarctic material in respect to their personali-

ties, skills and aptitudes. The high point of that week was lunch with
the awesome hero, Commander Byrd, who turned out to be a soft-
spoken merry-eyed man. I had followed his legendary exploits with
more than passing interest and it was hard to believe that we were together in the same room. I must confess that the fact that I was finally
judged the winner found me joyful but also bewildered at the speed at
which events had moved.

That first expedition, which was to span a period from August,
1928, to June, 1930, had begun as an impulsive remark. As Byrd told
me and many others afterward, his plan originated just after his return
to Spitsbergen from the flight that made him the first man to fly
over the North Pole. Roald Amundsen, still seeking for "first," had
hoped to add to his South Pole luster with precisely Byrd's achievement. He was there at Spitsbergen on Byrd's return from the North
Pole, and he asked, "What shall it be next?"

"The South Pole," Byrd replied. And on that slight basis he began
his expedition.

For the past ninety years, the government had not been interested
in Antarctic expeditions, and support came from private sources, with
generous donations being made by the public and several business
firms. Chief among the many contributors were John D. Rockefeller,
Jr., and Edsel Ford. Byrd estimated the total cost of his substantial
undertaking at $750,000, and in order to raise this then substantial
sum, he was forced to spend a great deal of time pleading and explaining his cause. Beyond this, the task of planning and gathering the expedition together was immense. But Byrd, who was then a mature
forty years old, had unique drive, foresight and persistence. While his
special personal objective remained that of flying over the South Pole,
it was his intention to provide scientists with the opportunity to conduct scientific research into Antarctic geology, geography, biology,
physics and meteorology.

Only sixteen years had passed since the Amundsen-Scott treks to
the South Pole, but resounding scientific advances had occurred in the
interim. Hastened by World War I, the age of the airplane had come
into being. With this new instrument, the possibility for greater mo-
bility now existed, as well as the opportunity to explore broad and
dangerous sections of the Antarctic from the air. There was also the
radio, which was coming into general use. Where Scott and Amundsen
had been cut off entirely from the outside world, there would now be
almost immediate communication. Field parties were no longer left to
their own resources. They could call for help to fly to their aid.

However, all such advances remained for a long while academic subjects of discussion for me and the scientists, engineers, mechanics and dog drivers who were on our way to the Antarctic in August, 1928. Pinched as he was financially, Byrd relied on old sailing ships to transport us to our destination. The *City of New York,* on which I worked for my passage, was a bark built in 1882, and its billowing sails were reminiscent of pre-Civil War vessels. It had a steam engine which could generate only 200 horsepower, or the equivalent of a modern automobile. Its hull, however, was of three-foot-thick hardwood, built to withstand ice, and it was the nearest ship to a modern icebreaker then existent. But the *City of New York* was basically a sailing ship and thus my introduction to the seafaring life was made "before the mast" with all the hardships and discomforts this implies which even the toughest modern explorer finds difficult to even imagine.

The rigors of the trip to New Zealand, where Commander Byrd was to join our party, did much to separate the men from the boys. Luckily for me, I was nineteen, stood more than six feet tall and weighed one hundred and sixty pounds. Otherwise, I could not have competed for my place among the crew.

Thirty days passed before we sighted Panama, then another forty before we paused in tropical Tahiti, and finally another thirty before we docked in New Zealand. Eighteen-hour-a-day work schedules, short water rations and spoiled meat caused several would-be explorers to quit along the way. There was also a damaging flood in the engine room and a fire in the radio battery storage room. In addition, the heavy physical labor apportioned to each of us, as well as long watches that prevented anyone from getting more than five unbroken hours of sleep, caused many to lose their appetite to continue on to a place where conditions were expected to grow even worse.

In New Zealand matters grew more serious. The decks of the *City of New York* were jammed with houses, airplanes, gasoline drums and crates. On top of this mess, which was piled so high the mainsail couldn't be set, rode eighty-five sledge dogs who barked continually. Final business was attended to, for from here we were to leave for the unknown. At Dunedin, the men were told to go to a wharf shed for their winter clothes. When I was handed ship's crew clothing instead of ice party clothing, I was shocked. All along I had assumed that I would be a member of the Byrd wintering-over party and not simply one of the crew of the *City of New York,* or her sister ship, the tramp steamer *Eleanor Bolling.* Mustering up my courage I approached Byrd on the dock and rather disappointedly asked him if the clothing allotted to me represented a final decision. "Nobody knows who is going to stay on the ice," he said with fatherly sternness. "Everyone who does will have to have a reason. Besides, we do need crew members to bring the ships back for us at the end."

Old New Zealanders accustomed to seeing expeditions sail south gave the top-heavy *City of New York* little chance to make the trip to the continent 2,500 miles away. But Byrd would not be deterred. The *City* shook and pitched ominously as she plowed through heavy seas. On December 10th we passed Scott Island, which stands on a "corner of the earth," at the point where the 180th meridian crosses the Antarctic Circle. Scott Island, which most whaling vessel captains at the time were prone to believe to be a fictitious place, turned out to consist of two high rock peaks on which thousands of beautiful snow-white petrel birds sat between their sorties.

Navigation now became more difficult because the farther south we traveled, the more overcast the weather grew, while the closer we drew to the South Magnetic Pole, the more highly erratic our compasses became. Commander Byrd was much concerned because we were due to rendezvous with a Norwegian whaling factory ship, the *C. A. Larsen*, which was to tow the *City* through the ice pack. Fortunately, however, we met up with the *Larsen* shortly after spying our first whales and icebergs.

With luck we made it through the ice pack in a week, coming into the placid waters of the Ross Sea on December 21st. In the passage through the ice pack, we saw our first seals and penguins, including both the stately four-foot-tall Emperor penguins in their formal attire and the smaller comic Adélies, which skidded on their bellies across the ice.

Sailing on south we came at last to the awesome Ross Ice Barrier, the floating edge of the continent ice, a white cliff that rose more than one hundred feet above the sea. There was an eerie quality about the barrier that made the men fall silent. We did not attempt to visit McMurdo Sound, where Scott and Shackleton had established their winter bases. Instead we sailed 400 miles to the east to the site of Framheim, Amundsen's camp, on the Bay of Whales, a huge twenty-mile break in the face of the barrier. This bight extended inward about ten or fifteen miles, and the bay formed was filled with a solid sheet of low bay ice here or there bent or broken up into picturesque pressure ridges.

With great excitement now, we anchored to the bay ice by means of large iron hooks planted in holes dug into the ice. Supplies were carried off the ship while Byrd set off to find a suitable campsite. Before long he was back to announce that he had found an excellent campsite on level ice eight miles from the ship, to which he promptly gave the name Little America.

The first Byrd Expedition to the Antarctic was now in business. But as the supplies left the *City,* my concern continued to grow as to whether I would be a resident of Little America or a member of the crew which would take the *City* back to New Zealand. When the temperature dropped to minus thirty degrees, the *City* made preparations to leave and several husky men cried when told they could not remain at Little America.

I became a member of the winter party by coincidence of a Boy Scout skill. Byrd advanced Lawrence Gould, a geologist, to be second in command of the expedition. Larry had promised the American Museum of Natural History that he would bring back a barrel each of seal and penguin skins, and now with his advance in status, hard rock geologist Larry was quite anxious to turn over this messy job to anyone else who would take it. I was more than eager to do it for him. Even so, he apparently had to plead my case with Byrd before I was permitted to remain with the Little America contingent of the expedition as a taxidermist, dog driver and naturalist.

At Little America, we dug holes four feet down and set the lower sections of our houses in place. Later the wind drifted snow on top of the houses until they were completely covered. This served to keep us warmer in the period ahead when more frigid winds would blow. Commander Byrd christened the shack to which I was assigned The Biltmore. Eight of us lived within its ten-by-ten walls. We had double bunks against each of the four walls, which left barely enough free space for a door and a window. In front of the snowed-over window was a kerosene heater, while most of the center space in the room was occupied by a large box which we used for a table. Ice accumulated in the cracks in the floor, and the mattresses in the lower bunks froze to the slats early and remained in that condition.

As for food, half our meat was of Antarctic origin. On our trip down, the skipper of the whaling vessel *C. A. Larsen* had given us some whale meat which had cured in the funnel smoke as it hung in the rigging of the *City of New York*. Now, though it had turned a little green here and there from spoilage, we found it tasty by comparison to our rancid barreled beef. In addition, we also ate penguin and seal meat, which was black in color and had a unique gamy taste, to say the least. Our dehydrated vegetables, however, turned out to be inedible. In the first place, they were the leftovers from World War I, and second, they had apparently been spoiled vegetables to begin with.

Yet all these food problems were not of tremendous concern because this was an adventurous expedition. Everything was new and untried since few if any of us knew in advance what to expect in the Antarctic, for the literature was meager. We didn't really know how cold it would get, how hard the wind would blow, or what the condition of the snow would be. For example, Byrd had brought a pair of snowshoes along for each man and only a few pairs of skis. As it turned out he should have done the opposite, for the snow was so hard a walking man didn't sink into it.

Because of the publicity which attended my selection to accompany the expedition, Byrd insisted that I stay safely close to the base. As he told me, he could not take the chance of having anything happen to me. Looking back on this expedition with the hindsight of over twenty-five years, this must have been a strain for him, considering all his necessary duties. When one of the dog handlers suffered an unfortunate accident, Byrd permitted me to drive a team. Nevertheless, aside from a few trips twenty to forty miles away, he adamantly refused to let me go out on the unknown trails with other dog drivers only a year or two my senior, limiting my dog team travel to the trails from the camp to the bay and the surrounding ice shelf.

Even so, I had some close calls. My lead dog was Holly, a beautiful little gray husky that unfortunately I could never teach to turn off the trail to the right or left at my command. On one occasion she went plunging off downhill across the top of the shelf ice toward the precipitous edge of the barrier while I hung to the sled with all my weight on the brake. As we neared the edge of the barrier, my heart pounded wildly. With but twenty feet more to go before we plunged to oblivion, one of the men close by saw my plight, leaped among the dogs and threw them into a fighting, snarling mass within a few feet of the edge.

There was another time later on when I went exploring on the shelf ice to the west side of the Bay of Whales to the very brink of the barrier with Chips Gould, our carpenter. While he held me by rope I foolishly hung partly over the edge and dropped a plumb line down to measure the height of the barrier. When the line reached the 125-foot mark with much more to go, I suddenly became concerned, for I realized that if Chips let go it would be the end of me. With an effort he pulled me back and I vowed henceforth to use safer and more scientific ways to measure the heights of deadfalls.

The winter night at Little America lasted from April 22nd to August 22nd, which meant that we would have no sunlight for four months. Thus the scientific personnel began a frenzied effort to conduct some of their studies before they would be more or less confined to quarters. The meteorologists sent up gas-filled balloons to obtain data on winds in the upper atmosphere and took sun readings with their theodolite, a surveying instrument that has a small telescope and was used to measure vertical and horizontal angles. Larry Gould had flown to the Rockefeller Mountains in Byrd's Fokker plane, *Virginia,* in order to do some geological work before the winter night set in. The plane, piloted by Bernt Balchen and Harold June, was completely wrecked by being blown from its ice mooring, after reaching and setting them down at their destination, by a wind with a velocity of more than one hundred and fifty miles an hour.* Another plane was dispatched to rescue them after some of us got almost halfway to the mountains by dog teams.

As for me, my weight had risen above two hundred pounds. And now, in addition to my duties as dog trainer and taxidermist, I also became a longshoreman as did most of the party as the winter approached. Byrd asked that we lay in a supply of a hundred tons of seal meat, a task which meant going down on the bay slaughtering the lumbering animals and hauling their bloody carcasses back to camp. There was no sport in killing the big half-ton seals for they were kindly bovine-appearing mammals and they offered no resistance. We tried to assure each other it was sheer necessity that made us do it.

Blizzards began to blow in March, during the period when we still had part of a day of sunlight. The majestic Ford tri-motored all-metal monoplane, most modern plane of the day, which Byrd was to use for his flight to the South Pole after the winter season ended, was now surrounded by a huge snow-block wall and covered by tarps. Several of us also struggled to bring up the last caches of material from the barrier to Little America. On one such trip with my dog team I experienced my first combination of a blizzard and a white-out.

A white-out is the antithesis of darkness. A clouded sky reflects the white snow on the ground, and a white void results everywhere because there are no shadows and no horizon. A complete loss of orientation occurs, for there is no visible up or down. In a white-out,

* Actually, in 1934 I discovered that the plane had been moored to glare ice covered only by a thin layer of snow which blew away in the storm. The tie-downs were light cord. Thus even a lesser wind than that recorded could have moved the plane since there was little to hold it down.

objects darker than the snow as well as people look as if they are standing in the middle of nowhere. Now, however, the blowing snow erased everything beyond my lead dog with even more whiteness.

My first experience with the double white-out was disconcerting. After lashing fifteen cases of fifty-pound boxes of gasoline to my sled, I started back to camp running alongside my dogs. The route was laid out with orange trail flags set every hundred yards along the path, but suddenly I seemed to be in the middle of a milk bottle surrounded on all sides by whiteness. I had not only lost the trail but also all sense of direction. As I broke out in a proverbial cold sweat, I searched the omni-white that pressed in on me from all sides for a trail flag. None was in view, for though I did not realize it then, I was probably scanning neither the sky nor the ground. Luckily, instinct told me that the trail had to be upwind, and though I stumbled and fell like a blind man, I miraculously made my way back to camp with the team.

Others had similar stories to tell about white-outs. For instance, there was the occasion when Larry Gould was going down a mountain trail with a dog team. Mike Thorne was skiing ahead of the dogs, but when Larry suddenly glanced up he could not see Mike. He stopped his team quickly, turned back toward the other dog teams and yelled, "Where's Mike?"

Back came Mike's voice. "What's the matter? I'm right up here in front of the dogs."

Larry stared in the direction from which Mike's voice had come. There he spied Mike suspended high in the air. The explanation was that Larry had been walking along with his eyes focused on the white surface. He had thus lost the horizon, and when he thought he was looking ahead toward Mike, he was instead staring at the ground a few feet ahead.

With winter upon us, we stayed close to our base. There was little time to be idle, however. All the men were assigned tasks to keep the base in good repair, wait on table, wash dishes and fill the snow melter. For melted snow was our only source of water. The snow melter, however, was used only to provide water for galley and drinking purposes. For personal uses—bathing and clothes washing—we had to resort to melting buckets of snow ourselves. It was thus that in the cold of the winter the process we called "dry washing," or exchanging soiled clothes for almost equally soiled garments which had previously been set aside for laundering but which now looked somehow cleaner than those being worn, came into existence. And so the "Knights of the Gray Underwear" was born.

The scientists now continued their research and laid plans for the coming spring season which would begin late in August. My days were filled with housekeeping tasks, preparing for next spring's jobs, tending to my dogs in their icy tunnels, skinning penguins on the mess table (the cook took the meat for dinner), and reading the scientific books in our well-stocked library. The Biltmore's temperature was a cool minus thirty degrees when we climbed out of our bunks each morning, in itself an incentive to start heavy physical labor to speed blood circulation. Frequently the oil in the kerosene lamp congealed into a jellied mass and the flame went out before I reached the dog tunnels. We remained outdoors only a few minutes at a time, because the temperature, which reached a low point of minus 72.2°, resulted in frozen cheeks and noses.

With the coming of spring and the return of the sun, Little America sprang to life. Larry Gould took a geological party four hundred miles toward the South Pole to the Queen Maud Range of mountains while Commander Byrd and the aviators made ready the Ford tri-motored monoplane, the *Floyd Bennett,* named after Byrd's comrade on his North Pole flight. All hands set to work with snow shovels and after a long −40° day the plane came out of its snow-wall house, where it had remained all winter, and test flights began with a view toward a final flight over the South Pole. I was permitted to fly on one of the *Floyd Bennett's* test flights as well as on flights in the expedition's two smaller planes. What a place it was for one's first flight! From the initial test flights, the *Floyd Bennett* progressed to exploration flights to the mountains four hundred miles to our south. Every possible precaution was taken in case the plane was forced down on its chief flight and the men had to walk back to Little America. Byrd was a daring individual, but he was also a firm believer in careful planning. He preferred to return a live failure rather than a dead hero.

The excitement built up in the camp as the moment approached for the epic flight. Finally, at three P.M. on November 28, 1929, we were all on the surface to watch the take-off for man's first flight over the South Pole. Byrd was to navigate the plane; Bernt Balchen was the pilot; Harold June, the radio operator and co-pilot; and Ashley McKinley, the aerial photographer who would map the territory. After a round of handshakes, the four climbed into the plane, and at 3:29 the huge gray corrugated aluminum *Floyd Bennett* raced down the rough and drifted surface of the barrier and rose into the sky for man's first flight over the South Pole. As the plane dwindled to a mere speck in the southern sky, a mixed feeling of joy and anxiety overwhelmed all of us who were left behind.

Weary as we were from the long hours of labor spent preparing for the flight, few of us were able to go to sleep that night. Instead, nearly everyone sat huddled close to our radio listening to the continuous whining sound of the plane radio's carrier wave which told us everything was all right. Then for a while our spirits drooped as the radio went off the air. But then the radio began again, this time with a coded message that the plane had made the climb over the 15,000-foot mountains and was flying over the polar plateau. Eighteen hours and thirty-six minutes after the take-off we all cheered as the big plane circled the camp and gracefully touched her skis to the snow.

We carried all four occupants back to camp on our shoulders and the story of the flight was related in all its exciting detail. They had decided to fly up the Liv Glacier instead of Amundsen's Axel Heiberg Glacier as their route across the mountain range. Near the head of the glacier, the rate of climb had fallen dangerously low and they had circled and circled trying to get over the mountains. Finally Byrd had to make a vital decision. The plane had to be lightened if they were to clear the peaks. If he jettisoned gasoline, they would never make it to the Pole and home. But if he dropped their emergency food and they were forced down, they would suffer Scott's sad fate. "Harold, throw the food overboard!" he ordered June. Byrd's daring had overcome his safety precautions, and they made the plateau with five hundred feet to spare. The rest was almost anticlimax.

"What was the Pole like?" I asked, with little thought that I would one day live there.

"A white desolation and solitude," Byrd replied. At the spot where Amundsen and Scott had once stood he had dropped a flag weighted with a stone from Floyd Bennett's grave.

The expedition was not yet over, though its high point had been reached. Besides my other duties, I undertook the job of keeping records of the growth of baby seals in their early months of life. Mother seals measuring eleven feet in length frequently charged me and Dr. Coman or whoever gave me a hand as we made our daily measurements of length and girth and weighed the little fellows. At the age of one month a baby seal was almost as much of a problem as his mother, for his weight was now two hundred pounds. A wrestling match took place every time I tried to take a measurement. The babies had also cut their teeth by this time and enjoyed nipping our hands and seats.

As the expedition's taxidermist, it was also my duty to bring back specimens in the form of sealskins and skulls. Cleaning skins was a particularly greasy, messy job which in my case was made more difficult by a bit of overzealous physical exertion. While upending an eight-hundred-pound frozen seal, I tore some chest muscles attached to the collarbone near my left shoulder. For a long while, I was left with only one usable arm, for the other had to be bound tightly inside my shirt.

Despite this, other tasks developed due to my curiosity. One was to take soundings of the Bay of Whales. With one arm I chopped a hole about a foot in diameter through eighteen feet of solid ice and a several-foot-deep mass of loose, silver-dollar-sized ice crystals. Into the underlying water I then lowered a fine steel piano wire to the end of which was attached a clamshell scoop that would snap shut on the ocean floor. The ocean floor proved to be fifteen hundred feet beneath the ice. This was a startling discovery indeed, for it meant that the ice shelf on which the camp rested was actually afloat, and had there been more severe blizzards or storms at sea our camp might have floated out as an iceberg. As it was, Little America, which had been established eight miles back on the bay ice when we arrived in December, 1928, was only two miles back when we left in February, 1930. Of course these changes were due to the "thin" ten- to fifteen-foot bay ice breaking out, whereas the barrier edge of the shelf ice remained virtually unchanged.

Another job Commander Byrd wanted me to do was to catch some penguins and keep them alive. "Let's try to take back some live penguins to the various zoos in the United States," he said to me. "I think it can be done, even though no one has so far succeeded."

It was as a result of this experience that I got the best advice I ever had.

"Aside from using strips of seal meat and blubber, how am I going to feed them until our ships arrive with a supply of fish for them?" I asked.

"Get in touch with zoos," Byrd replied.

Ultimately I brought in fourteen Emperor penguins and six of the smaller Adélies. By radio I contacted several American zoos. Back came replies that I should feed them fish and cod-liver oil.

Of course, without any supplies of fish they could not be put on this diet and I soon found that my charges were dying. "Did you send the messages?" Byrd asked me when I reported this fact to him.

"Yes, I tried everything," I said sadly. "But the zoos in Philadelphia, St. Louis, Washington and the Bronx said I should feed them fish and cod-liver oil which we don't have."

He looked at me coldly. "Did you try Edinburgh and Hamburg?"

"No," I said.

"But you told me you tried everything," Byrd hammered at me.

As I walked away my cheeks were flushed and my eyes were lowered. I had quit before I was half through. I vowed never again to come to him or to anyone else for an answer to a problem before I had tried every possibility. Years later when a problem seemingly stumped me, Byrd's voice and words would suddenly appear: *Did you try Edinburgh or Hamburg?* And I would continue on to a solution.

I think this example is a typical case which reveals the reason for Byrd's great success in handling and inspiring the men he led. He was a master of the art of putting a question to a man which would not answer his problem but which would spur him on to new thoughts. Obviously the great advantage of this method was that when a man succeeded at a task where he had previously failed, he could be confident that it was the result of his own efforts.

Some of the penguins survived in spite of the seal meat and seal blubber. However, since they always ate under water and were either incapable of or disinclined toward picking food from the snow, we had to force-feed them. They were also a problem for another reason.

At first glance, penguins appeared to be rather foolish creatures as they stood idly about like huge bottles. But in an important respect they were smarter than we. We kept them in an open pit at the outset, but they chipped at the snow wall with their bills to form steps by means of which they escaped. When they were recaptured, I put a picket fence of split bamboo around the top of their pit. This proved no problem to them, for they simply pulled out the pickets with their bills. Next I set gasoline barrels on end, tied together all around the pit. Now to escape they stood on one another's shoulders like a tumbling team.

Finally, it became necessary to establish a penguin watch, with one man going out each hour to see if the penguins were attempting an escape. Again the penguins showed their ingenuity. They stationed one of their number on lookout to warn the others when the human watchman was coming. If I sneaked up quietly to the edge of the pit, I would come upon the penguins chipping the wall or huddled as if discussing some means of escape. However, when their lookout spotted me, he would let out a rasping squawk and his fellow prisoners would separate and walk nonchalantly away with an air of innocence.

We left Little America on the *City of New York* on February 19, 1930, but not before Byrd had discovered the Edsel Ford Ranges and Marie Byrd Land, named after his loving and patient wife. An interesting feature of Marie Byrd Land was that the immense Andean chain in South America appeared to be anchored here.

So the first Byrd Expedition came to an end. It had had more than its share of both successes and failures. But perhaps the most important achievement of the expedition was that because of it, Byrd had succeeded in turning American attention back to the Antarctic after ninety years. We had also begun to acquire new technology about living in polar areas. We had introduced airplanes, radio and mechanical vehicles to Antarctic exploration and this brought on advances which made modern polar exploration safer and more practical. And, for my own part, the expedition had given me my start and left me with an intense desire to return to the Antarctic as a scientist.

As we left the Bay of Whales, several men announced that this was their first and last visit to the Antarctic. But I, who had left home a boy and was now returning a twenty-one-year-old man, felt the continent of "white desolation and solitude" was now a part of me.

In fact, returning to civilization was a jarring experience. I recall the bewilderment I felt on returning to New Zealand. My hair was uncut and my clothing was ill fitting. It took a while before the way of life in the outside world came back into focus. And then with a rush I remembered the beauty of flowers. I spied some late summer varieties blossoming on the other side of a fence and I leaned over to inhale their fragile fragrance deeply. Then I hurried to a field where I flung myself on the ground and lay daydreaming in the soft warm breezes until my body cried out for a glass of milk and some fruit, foods I had longed for more than a year.

Chapter 4

ANTARCTICA REVISITED

WHILE we were returning from that first expedition, Byrd confided that he planned a second expedition in 1932 and that he wanted me along. In my work I had gone beyond the novelty of being a Boy Scout on a rugged expedition, he said, and when we returned again to the Antarctica, I would go as a regular member.

Elated by this, I returned to Allegheny College at Meadville, Pennsylvania, where I rushed through my remaining three years of college work in two years. My goal was to graduate as a biologist and geologist before the new expedition began.

I was greatly aided in my efforts by one of the most wonderful men it has ever been any budding scientist's good fortune to work with, Dr. Chester A. Darling, head of Allegheny's Department of Biology, who devoted far more time than he could afford to helping me to ready myself for the upcoming expedition. I owe him more than I can ever repay or even relate for the guidance and inspiration he offered me, not only during those three years, but for many years afterwards.

Meanwhile, with the nation mired in the worst economic depression in its history, Byrd was having difficulties in raising sufficient funds for his undertaking. As a result, the expedition had to be postponed a year. In the interim I went on what could best be termed a field trip abroad (my only piece of traveling luggage was a knapsack), designed to introduce myself to the populated areas of the world as opposed to the vast empty reaches I had already seen. I financed this jaunt, all too inadequately, with the proceeds of my first book, *A Boy Scout with Byrd,* and traveled through Europe, including the Soviet Union, and then through the Near East. It was here that a chance encounter with a young American geographer introduced me to the academic subject of modern geography which was to become my field of specialization. I traveled on to sample desert living by journeys on foot down the Jordan River and visits into arid wasteland south of the Dead Sea. Then, early in 1933, a message reached me in Egypt that Byrd wanted me to return to Boston posthaste.

By an act of Congress after his South Pole flight Byrd had been elevated in rank to rear admiral. Now I found him in the midst of hectic activities designed to nail down his minimum requirements. The expedition would cost a million dollars. Once again he would base his operations at Little America, from which he planned to make large-scale exploratory field trips into uncharted parts of the Antarctic, as well as extensive aerial surveys over new territories. In addition, there would be an inland station, the first in Antarctic history, from which unprecedented weather observations would be made throughout the four-month-long winter night. Shortly after my arrival at Boston headquarters, I learned that it would be my responsibility to assemble the supplies for this inland station and nurse them from Boston to whatever lonely spot on the Ross Ice Shelf they were to be assembled.

The raising of a million dollars in cash and equipment was a painful process. First Byrd had dropped into the kitty his own life's accumulation plus donations from others, all of which came to $150,000. Most of the men who were to go along on the expedition then agreed, as had we who went on the first expedition, to serve for one dollar a year, an act that reduced operating overhead considerably as compared with later expeditions where some personnel were paid considerably more than they might have earned at home. Byrd, with the invaluable assistance of Vic Czegka, our machinist on the first expedition on loan from the Marine Corps to serve as logistician on the upcoming expedition, had gone after many sources to obtain money and supplies. About $100,000 worth of scientific equipment was borrowed from colleges, private institutions and government agencies. A total of 30,000 letters went out to other possible contributors. There were successes and failures. For instance, one hundred and twenty-seven manufacturers of overalls were bombarded with letters requesting outfits. Certainly we expected that we would be flooded with overalls, for we were sure the manufacturers would see the advertising dividends that would accrue to generous firms. Yet not a single manufacturer would contribute denim wear, and in the end we had to buy them. However, Byrd's luck was better with oil companies, communication networks, manufacturers of precision instruments, meat packers, shoe manufacturers, coal and tobacco companies, and many others who contributed time, research and products to the expedition.

As for ships, Byrd wanted a seaworthy freighter and an icebreaker.

With the depression, ships were rotting in ports by the thousands, yet Byrd had no money to buy the vessels he desired. Fortunately, the United States Shipping Board let him have an oil-burning tramp steamer for an annual rental of one dollar. She was old and worn, but Byrd was overjoyed and rechristened her the *Jacob Ruppert,* after a sponsor. The icebreaker proved more difficult to find. The search finally narrowed to a sailing cutter, the *Bear,* an ancient Coast Guard veteran of Arctic expeditions which was owned by the City of Oakland, California. However, it could be sold legally only by auction. Thus, Byrd reached a gentleman's agreement with municipal authorities to bid only a token amount for the *Bear.* But a junk dealer showed up at the auction and put in a bid of $1,000. Words were exchanged with the junkman, who intended to buy the *Bear* for scrap. Finally, Byrd had to pay out $1,050 from his now almost nonexistent bank account before he could wrest the *Bear* away from her would-be destroyer.

It was not until the fall of 1933 that the two ships set off for the Antarctic. Aboard were more than five hundred tons of supplies, as well as the crews and the fifty-six members of the final ice party, including several who had adamantly insisted after the first expedition that they would never return to the Antarctic. Now they smilingly announced that nothing would keep them away from this second journey. Admiral Byrd and I were on the *Jacob Ruppert.* I was to be chief biologist of the expedition despite the fact that I was hardly qualified for the task professionally. I proceeded by staffing the department with good professional research men and serving largely as administrator. I was also named logistics boss for establishing the inland weather station, my first introduction to the problems of supplying the necessities to enable men to exist in the Antarctic. Slowly but inevitably Byrd was involving me in positions carrying increasing responsibility.

Dr. Tom Poulter, a physicist and a giant of a man, was to serve as second in command to Byrd, and Commander George Noville, Byrd's old companion of arctic and transatlantic flights, became his executive officer. Martin Ronne, who had been with us on the first expedition and whose Antarctic explorations dated back to Amundsen's era, had died, but his son Finn was along.

As compared with the first arduous trip down to New Zealand aboard the *City of New York,* a voyage of one hundred days, the *Jacob Ruppert* sighted the high peaks of North Island, New Zealand, after only fifty-five days. The *Bear* had almost foundered in a hurricane off Southport, North Carolina. But perhaps the worst of our voyage was pulling into Easter Island, some 2,000 miles off Chile. The large stone images were delightful, but the natives stole everything that was not nailed down firmly. Field glasses, hats, trousers and even oarlocks disappeared, as if a swarm of giant locusts had passed over us. As we left, Byrd put it bluntly: "Our call at Easter Island has almost ruined us." It would be good, we agreed, to leave the last of civilization—even primitive civilization—behind us.

New Zealand proved again to be no place for relaxation. There were far too many last-minute jobs to be done before we headed south into the ice pack. Many who had not gone along on the first expedition could not understand the need for the intensive effort now. But those of us who were veterans understood the importance of getting to Little America, establishing ourselves in camp and beginning our scientific work before the winter night began.

There was every reason to believe, when we pulled away from New Zealand on December 11th, that our time schedule was in good order. Sailing considerably to the east of our path to Little America in an effort to discover the uncharted coast of Marie Byrd Land we used a Curtiss biplane equipped with pontoons for exploration from our thin-skinned metal ship. However, as we approached this land we encountered tremendous numbers of icebergs, as many as 8,000 being sighted in a single day, and were forced to retreat without achieving much success in our mission. We then headed southwest for Little America through an untried entrance into the Ross Sea and were rewarded by not sighting a bit of pack ice.

On January 17th we sighted the Ross Ice Shelf, or the barrier edge of the continent. A vast sense of pleasure came over me at the familiar sight of the sheer 100-foot cliffs of this frozen sea extending nearly 500 miles at Antarctica's rim and 400 miles wide into the wasteland toward the South Pole. Hemmed in on two sides by gigantic, snow-covered mountain ranges, and on a third by lofty snow plateaus, it opened on the fourth side to the Ross Sea, which was in reality the southern extremity of the Pacific Ocean. The Great Ross Ice Shelf is not solid ice, but actually somewhere between snow and ice, or what the glaciologists call névé. It is snow that has lain for years until it has been packed by driving winds, partly ablated by the sun and then subjected to crystallization under the sub-zero temperatures. It has gone through an endless number of such cycles. This great floating weight of accumulated snow bore down into the sea until in places it actually rests on the floor of the ocean, attaining a thickness of hundreds of feet. Of course, this great mass of ice ends abruptly at the open Ross

Sea in a precipitous cliff which rises from fifty to more than two hundred feet above the water.

And it was this that I now saw as we skirted the eastern edge of the ice wall toward the bay that was nothing more than a great complex niche cut back into the great barrier. When we reached the Bay of Whales, we found Little America where we had left it, though snow had drifted high over the camp in the four intervening years so that only the radio towers, smokestacks, ventilators and a few poles marked our old home.

Elatedly we brought the *Ruppert* into the bay to within two miles of the camp. We rejoiced for we were certain our haul would be simple compared with the eight miles required on the first expedition. Little America lay in a wide, sheltered basin on top of a forty-foot-high barrier and was surrounded by higher and more ancient barrier ice on three sides. The fourth or western side gave way immediately to a narrow inlet of the bay, Ver-sur-Mer Inlet, a half-mile-long, narrow, pie-shaped section cut from the eastern wall of the Bay of Whales which served as the gateway to Little America.

But our initial joy gave way to deep concern when we saw the condition of the ice guarding the mouth of Ver-sur-Mer Inlet. Slow but constant closing of the barrier walls of the bay had produced a vast amount of pressure ice in the inlet. Like frozen waves, the pressure ice now had crests that rose fifty feet and made unloading dangerous. Another danger lay in the calving, or breaking off, of large chunks of the barrier edge, which were dropping, each with a thunderous roar, too close to the *Ruppert* for comfort. Among the pressure ridges and the icefalls we found telltale evidence of plane tracks and the moving bay ice that had wrecked the plane of Lincoln Ellsworth, another American explorer who had been here recently, planning a flight across the continent to the Weddell Sea. Unfortunately, an accident to his plane thwarted his plans, and he had already departed.

Our only alternative route for bringing supplies to Little America lay in a wide detour from the west, or far side of the bay, going around the pressure ice and bearing north again for Little America. This would mean a forty-mile round trip to and from a camp that squatted only a few miles from our ship! But there was nothing else to do except take "Misery Trail," as we called this route.

There followed a nightmare of unloading, shuttling, returning and unloading again, fortunately made easier this time as compared to the first expedition by the presence of four successfully operating tractors. Even so, our timetable was knocked awry and the condition of the men and dogs, who still did roughly half of the work, deteriorated rapidly. I had charge of one unit of the landing party and my own dog team was hauling a ton of supplies at a time over twisted pressure ice. For two and a half weeks the men kept relentlessly at this task, averaging only three or four hours' sleep a day. Often necessity kept us going thirty-six hours without stop. Blizzards and heavy fog hit us as if to test us further and we cried out in rage at the perversity of the elements. Hardly an hour passed that didn't bring news of some imminent danger. Ice was breaking up along the route; the ships would have to abandon their moorings; men were marooned on the bay; a dog team was running wild, fighting and snarling; exhausted men were found who could not remember what they were supposed to be doing, let alone guess what time of day it was in the continuous light.

But we had more to do than bring supplies onto the barrier from the bay. Little America, which we had hoped would still be useful, lay buried under drift snow. Roofs and support beams had been crushed by the heavy load, and regular entrances were no longer usable. For example, when the Administration Building was found, we could enter it only headfirst. After several hundred tons of snow had been shoveled off other roofs, we found inside a helter-skelter of clothing and supplies abandoned at the close of the first expedition. However, on the mess table, as if placed there that very day, was a big pork roast which our cook had set out before we left four years previously. As he put it, the roast was for "whoever might come back here . . . you can't ever tell."

In the end, it was necessary to build eight new buildings on top of the old ones and make connecting passageways between the two camps. There was also the Mountain House, or the prospective inland weather station, which I erected temporarily at Little America II for testing purposes. "Now the worst is over," we said wearily, when the new city had come into being.

However, we were mistaken. "Let's take a stroll, Paul," the Admiral said to me one day. We left camp for a walk across the neighboring ice shelf. "What's this?" I pointed to cracks in the barrier surface. "How much bad luck can we have?" Byrd asked.

Deep cracks had appeared with the ice on both sides moving freely up and down, and we soon found that they virtually encircled Little America. In several places we actually lay prone on the snow and watched the cracks closing and widening. Here was peril indeed! Little America was rising and falling with the movement of a storm out at sea and was in danger of floating out to sea. If more ice should break out of the bay, Ver-sur-Mer Inlet, too, could drift out. Then our camp would be left hanging on the edge of the sea and in time might become the only city adrift on an iceberg. Despite its apparent safety in years gone by, Shackleton's misgivings about the Bay of Whales weighed heavily upon us at that moment.

Hurrying back to camp, Byrd hastily assembled all the men and discussed our dilemma. Many of the men were weary enough to suggest that we take a chance and remain where we were. Others argued that we must tear down Little America II and move the camp farther back on the barrier. Groans rose at this. Finally we compromised. Men and dogs, almost sleepwalking by now, moved supplies for a six-month emergency to "Retreat Camp," about a mile and a half farther southeast on the solid shelf ice.

This precaution later proved unnecessary. For as the sun gradually sank lower in the sky, temperatures dropped. The bay froze, the ice along the cracks ceased to move and finally the cracks themselves froze over.

But our troubles were not over. One of the planes cracked up; fire broke out in the doctor's storehouse; and one of the men required an emergency operation for appendicitis.

Fortunately no one died, and with the coming of a new season, the past was quickly forgotten. We could now turn our attention to grumbling about minor inconveniences and suspicions. For instance, Byrd had brought three Guernsey cows to the Antarctic so we could have fresh milk, an interesting if somewhat debatable experiment. We still had to use a lot of powdered milk and soon several of the men were, only half seriously, I confess, suggesting that the men in the cow barn were drinking the cream and diluting the remaining milk.

As a result of our many mishaps, time was growing short for carrying the portable inland weather station to its final resting place. Originally, Byrd had wanted us to erect the Mountain House at the foot of the Queen Maud Mountains, or about halfway from camp to the South Pole. But a shadowy twilight was already settling upon us. In the complete darkness of the Antarctic winter, we might never make it back to the base from the four-hundred-mile journey to the mountains. We might go a hundred miles inland, I agreed to Byrd, but it would be dangerous to venture beyond that point. Besides, weather observations made even that short distance from the coast would be of considerable scientific value. Somewhat disappointed, Byrd nevertheless decided to go inland as far as the crevasse zone near Latitude 81° S would permit.

As we made ready to depart inland, another question arose. How many men would occupy Advance Base during the long winter? Byrd had already pondered this. If alone and isolated, he felt that two men would be at each other's throat in a few weeks. One man might seethe at the way the other dropped a boot or chewed his food. As for a larger party, this was more than the base required, he said. Besides, the chances of cabin fever were only slightly less than with two. Byrd announced that he would stay alone.

Nine of us left Little America the midnight of March 16, 1934, in four tractors, each pulling one or two sledges. Each tractor unit carried 60-day rations for each man, a tent, sleeping bags, a stove, fuel and assorted camping equipment.

The temperature quickly dropped into the minus fifties as we left Little America behind. At times when we could bear the pain of the cold no longer, some of us jumped from the tractors and ran alongside until we became winded and started to cough and even spit blood.

With the route crisscrossed with tricky crevasses, travel was necessarily slow. Even with a careful watch, an occasional tractor found crevasses the hard way and had to be dug out and backed to safety. Luckily none fell into the monstrous crevasses which abounded in the area, for this probably would have been the end of the tractor and its occupants.

Our plan was to travel steadily, day and night, and stop only for necessary repairs. Thus we made camp and pitched tents only when a tractor broke down or when a blizzard obliterated our vision. At fifty miles one of the tractors failed and had to be ditched. No attempt was made to maintain regular mealtime! To stave off hunger we munched hard Eskimo biscuits. It was not to my liking when we finally did stop to eat, for I was more experienced with trail life and had been elected trail cook, and there was little satisfaction in cooking for nine men on two small primus stoves at a temperature of fifty below zero. Even so, the cold produced such ravenous appetites that the men demanded more than my kettles would hold.

Our instructions had been to erect the parts of the Mountain House just short of the bad belt of crevasses 123 miles south of Little America. We reached that point on the 21st, and after a night's sleep in our tents, set to work in frozen boots and ice-covered parkas to hollow out a hole in the barrier surface to hold the Mountain House. After several hours of strenuous excavating, we heard the hum of an airplane motor. A few minutes later Byrd comfortably stepped onto the barrier, after an hour's flight from Little America. "How is the shack coming, Paul?" he greeted me.

"Slowly," I told him. All our faces were blotched yellow with frostbite. We worked steadily all that day and far into the next night laying timbers and spiking the sections of the house. I barely managed to bolt together the stove, which was the only way that we could get relief from the chill. Even more difficult was my task in erecting the delicate meteorological equipment, the reason for Byrd's stay here.

Before we departed on the return trip, we had a farewell dinner with the Admiral. Later our parting with Byrd was a sad occasion. His face evidenced his regret that he would soon be left alone in this forsaken spot during the next several months of winter darkness. He stretched out our departure until it was embarrassing. "Good-by and good-by and good-by," he called after us.

Like many fine moments, the drama of that moment was spoiled by an unspectacular event. One mile homeward from Advance Base a tractor broke down. Soon we were hurrying back to the Mountain Shack to spend another night with Byrd. By the time we pulled out the next day, flashes of annoyance crossed his face that we were still there, and his farewell to us was more perfunctory.

Once back at Little America the expedition spent the winter keeping house, preparing for spring journeys and scientific work and worrying about the Admiral. And we had good cause for alarm.

For almost five months Byrd survived in absolute solitude, in polar darkness. And during more than half that period he was desperately ill as gas fumes thrown off by his radio generator and the oil stove he used for cooking poisoned him. The stovepipe froze above the roof of the shack, preventing adequate ventilation, and the house filled with poisonous fumes. His condition was made worse by the fact that he did not maintain a proper diet, a fairly common affliction of those living alone.

I have known few men as brave as Admiral Byrd. Fearing that we would launch a danger-fraught rescue attempt, he had kept his illness a secret. His weight had steadily decreased until he became so weak he could scarcely drag himself up the ladder to make his weather observations, and his entire body was wracked with pain. When a tractor party finally reached him in mid-August, he had to remain at Advance Base for two months to regain sufficient strength for the trip back to Little America.

"Was it all worth while?" was my first question when I saw him again in October.

"Yes," he replied earnestly. "I learned much, but I never want to go through that experience again." I knew that what he had learned was only partly the result of his weather observations. He had learned much more about himself.

Before he had left for Advance Base, Byrd had agreed to let me lead a summer trail party into the virgin east. Three exploratory trail parties left Little America during the Antarctic spring. My own left on October 14, 1934, and included three men: Alton Wade, the expedition's geologist, Olin Stancliffe and Steve Corey. Some days howling blizzards kept us in our tents. Other days our three dog teams, consisting of nine dogs each, covered more than ten to twenty miles. For food we ate chiefly pemmican hoosh, a brick formed from concentrated, dehydrated dried meat, fat and cereals. The bricks were melted with snow in kettles and made into a sort of stew.

We were gone for three months, exploring and making scientific observations in unknown Marie Byrd Land, where no man had ever trod before. There was something about the Antarctic that I found exhilarating on the trail. Its quiet was so profound that one could spend hours on end in satisfying contemplation. It was my job to break trail for the dog team, a task which meant skiing alone in front, with no one to talk with for hours at a stretch. Except at rest periods, one was alone with his thoughts and had time to do the thinking he could not do in the bustle of civilization.

At the age of twenty-four I was now getting my first taste of real firsthand exploration on this three-month traverse party into virgin unmapped territory, a form of exploration not far removed from that experienced by the early men who had sought to achieve the Pole on foot. From the top of Mount Grace McKinley we saw a vast array of brick-red, black, gray and brown mountain peaks. These had to be mapped because they had never before been seen by man. I served as surveyor and navigator and tried to run a set of angles on the major peak each day as we took our sun sights. These mountains were only heads and shoulders poked up out of the ice which flowed down off the continental plateau rising 6,000 feet behind it to the south and east.

This Edsel Ford Mountain region we found to be quite ancient geologically. The black mountains were thick-folded sedimentary layers without fossils which had been largely eroded away to expose granite and metamorphosed rocks that had welled up as molten masses ages ago. We even found an extinct volcano in the region, which implied that changes were still going on beneath the surface.

At Mount Haines, Al Wade ferreted out a quartz vein with a pocket of lead ore and some pyrite, an ore of iron and sulfur. Our excitement was great at this discovery, but not as high as when another member of the expedition had returned from the Queen Maud Range with a small nugget of gold. With wild shouts, many of the men were ready to go on a new Gold Rush. Only under pressure did our "prospector" admit that the gold was a filling that had dropped from his teeth when he had attacked a tough Eskimo biscuit.

Before we returned to Little America, I had found 94 species of lichens, including 86 which proved to be new species never before seen. I also found five different kinds of mosses which I had to chip off rocks with the help of an ice-ax blade and a geologist's hammer. Nor were plants all I found. At one point in the Edsel Ford Mountains, I gathered some specimens of pinkish ice, the coloring of which resulted from the abundance of red rotifers, minute multicelled aquatic animals. I also found evidence of skua gull rookeries, some small open "lakes," actually melt water ponds containing microscopic life. On Mount Helen Washington in the Rockefeller Mountains, I also found a snowy petrel rookery, a full thirty-five to fifty miles from the open sea.

Chapter 5

EXPEDITION LEADER

WHEN I returned from the Antarctic with the men of that second expedition, I felt that while exploring was fun, it was time I chose a career which would provide a salary in excess of a dollar a year. The following year I married Ruth Johannesmeyer, whom I had begun courting six years earlier at Allegheny College. Ruth joined me at Clark University where I earned my Ph.D. in geography in 1939. Specializing in physical studies of the earth as they affect man's activities, I studied climatology under the eminent Dutch professor Samuel van Valkenburg and received my training in physiography from the late Wallace Atwood whose textbooks introduced so many young Americans to the subject of geography. My dissertation concerned the "Adaptations of the Explorer to the Climate of Antarctica."

Meanwhile interest in the Antarctic was stirring again. Politics as well as scientific exploration had come to the frozen continent, and various countries had begun marking on maps parts of the Antarctic which they claimed belonged to them. Among the nations making such claims were Great Britain, France, New Zealand, Australia and Norway. Later, even without having attempted any explorations, Chile and Argentina joined the claimants. Charles Evans Hughes, Secretary of State under President Calvin Coolidge, had first stated the position of the United States regarding the Antarctic when he said in 1924: "It is the opinion of this Department that the discovery of lands unknown to civilization, even when coupled with a formal taking of possession, does not support a valid claim of sovereignty, unless the discovery is followed by an actual settlement of the discovered country."

So the American policy became one of not recognizing the territorial claims of other nations in the Antarctic.

By 1939, when some of Hitler's explorers landed on the far side of Antarctica from Little America, the Roosevelt Administration decided that the American policy regarding the Antarctic must be further implemented. The seed of an avenue of approach to a new program came first from Richard Black, who had been a member of Admiral Byrd's second expedition. It was Black's suggestion that the National Government, through the Division of Territories and Island Possessions of the Department of the Interior, establish a permanent agency to deal with the Antarctic. This agency, under Ernest Gruening, would maintain permanent settlements in the Antarctic and thus meet the sovereignty requirements laid down fifteen years earlier by Secretary Hughes.

"Fine," said President Roosevelt, when the idea was first broached to him. "But let's get Byrd to run the program."

So in the summer of 1939, one hundred years after the Wilkes Expedition, the Government of the United States came to support an Antarctic expedition. This time, however, Americans under government auspices would remain in the Antarctic.

The first I knew of the government's venture came in the spring of 1939, when Admiral Byrd called me. "There is going to be a government expedition to the Antarctic," he said, "and I want you to take charge of the logistics for the expedition."

I accepted this responsibility, and he added, "We are planning three or four bases this time and you will be the leader of one."

President Roosevelt set up an Executive Committee of representatives of the Departments of State, Interior, Navy, War and the Treasury to run the government's Antarctic program, with primary responsibility for the program's execution resting with the Departments of the Interior and Navy. The venture was called the U. S. Antarctic Service, with Admiral Byrd as Commanding Officer.

Formal instructions for the U. S. Antarctic Service's field activities later came to Byrd from the President. Upon examination of this long letter, I found among its many sections the following pertinent clauses:

6. When in all respects ready for sea, you will proceed to the Antarctic by routes chosen by you and there establish two continental bases, to be known as (a) East Base, and (b) West Base.

(a) It is desired that the East Base be established in the vicinity of Charcot Island or Alexander I Land; in the event that a suitable site in those areas cannot be reached by ship or by ship-based parties, alternative sites on Marguerite Bay should be investigated.

(b) It is desired that the West Base be established on the east shore of the Ross Sea in the vicinity of King Edward VII Land; in the event that this area cannot be reached by ship, or a base established without undue hazard, an alternative site in the Bay of Whales at or near Little America should be investigated.

(c) The principal objective in the field is the delineation of the continental coast line between the meridians 78 degrees W, and 148 degrees W and the consolidation of the geographical features of Hearst Land, James W. Ellsworth Land and Marie Byrd Land. It is desired that long-range aerial flights, equipped with mapping cameras, consolidate these areas; if practicable, supply caches to extend the cruising range of planes should be established. Flights so far as possible should be planned to supplement previous flights which have been made along the 75th, 101st, 116th, 134th, 160th and 162nd meridians of West Longitude.

(d) Secondary geographical objectives are the delineation of the unknown west coast of the Weddell Sea between Cape Eilsen and Luitpold Coast, and the determination of the eastern extremity of the Queen Maud Range and the William Horlick Mountains and their relationship to the Sentinel Range.

(e) It is desired that you investigate by air the area in the vicinity of the South Magnetic Pole and the unknown areas between the Weddell Sea and the South Pole.

(f) The United States has never recognized any claim to sovereignty over territory in the Antarctic regions asserted by any foreign state. No member of the U.S. Antarctic Service shall take any action or make any statements tending to compromise this position.

Members of the Service may take any appropriate steps such as dropping written claims from airplanes, depositing such writings in cairns, et cetera, which might assist in supporting a sovereignty claim by the United States Government.

This was indeed a sweeping order. Yet we found that of the million dollars we believed necessary to inaugurate the work of the U.S. Antarctic Service, Congress was willing to appropriate only $350,000. Again the job called for Byrd's untiring effort to raise the rest of the money. Eventually the War Department donated $107,114 in supplies and equipment, and the Navy Department $219,352. Through donations of his own equipment and money and through contributions from several private institutions, Byrd was able to raise an additional $239,945.07. For one dollar, he turned his icebreaker *Bear of Oakland,* which he had overhauled at a cost of $120,000 over to the Navy for use on the expedition.

For the first time I was now part of a government expedition, and a change it was from the free and easy days of the first two Byrd expeditions. First indication of change came to me as supply officer of our colonization project. Preparations crept along because of the need to write specifications for everything wanted and because all ordering had to be done through channels. I knew what we needed, but I could not buy equipment directly. All purchases had to be made through exacting bidding procedures which often, in the end, did not bring us what we needed. At times this drove me frantic. On one occasion, the men in our radio department overspent their budget, and items were actually delivered and accepted before I realized what had happened. As overseer of expenditures and allotments, I considered transferring funds from other segments. However, before I could take any action, the Department of Interior sent out telegrams canceling all purchases of supplies not yet delivered. In the emergency, I rushed from Boston to Washington to straighten out the matter only to be greeted by an order to balance the overspending, which meant we had to make sharp cuts in our food, equipment and household budgets. Another time it was necessary to call out expedition members on a Sunday morning to unload coal from railroad cars because we lacked money to pay others to do the job. This was particularly disheartening since many of the men had signed up for salaries of one dollar a year, while others had agreed to work for the government for ten dollars a month.

Problems with the Navy also came to the fore. There was, in some quarters of the Navy Department, I learned, resentment of Admiral Byrd partly because of his various successes and the publicity he had amassed, partly because his spectacular promotions (he had risen from commander to rear admiral) had come without his having been in the active list. In actual fact, his rank on the retired list meant that other officers on active duty would not have their chances of promotion blunted. Then, too, Byrd had powerful friends in Congress, as well as being a personal friend of President Roosevelt.

Despite occasional efforts to thwart the Admiral's progress or spiteful denial of his requests, nothing could swerve him from his outspoken loyalty to the Navy, and he ignored all incidents. Yet in this quiet war, I now found that I, as a close associate of the Admiral, was also a target.

Another problem developed in the late spring of 1939. Captain Cruzen, who had just taken over command of the *Bear*—which together with the *North Star* would carry the expedition south—insisted in Boston that he would have to abide by Navy regulations which required cash payment for the meals of all civilians riding on a naval vessel. Even had we wished to abide by this reasonable request, we could not have done so for the simple fact was that we did not have sufficient money left. "I'll give you food," I told him firmly, "and all you'll have to do is have it prepared, but there won't be any other payment." What began as a minor argument turned into a knockdown-drag-out fight before Cruzen withdrew his demands, apparently after realizing the only way his demands would be met was if he went to Congress to get money appropriated to meet them.

But despite a number of such frustrating and unpleasant experiences there was a larger objective before us. And on November 21, 1939, the colonizing expedition was packaged and I left Philadelphia with the Admiral and other members of the expedition aboard the Interior Department's old vessel, the *North Star*. Aboard the ship were 65 howling dogs, a giant Condor plane, a small Beechcraft and an enormous vehicle on wheels, the Snow Cruiser. Byrd's plans were to come to the Antarctic briefly, do a bit of exploring personally from the *Bear*, which was also traveling down, and then return to the United States. Dick Black was to be in charge of the East Base, some 1,200 miles from the West Base, where I would function as leader, aerial navigator and geographer. My old trail companion, Dr. F. Alton Wade, would serve as senior scientist and leader of the snow-cruiser unit. Aboard were also American flags, claim sheets and bronze benchmark monuments in support of American sovereignty. Our primary activity was to be exploration and execution of a scientific program, yet the official aims of the U.S.A.S. were nationalistic. The idea proposed by the State Department was that if the U. S. maintained continuing bases in the Antarctic, our claim on Antarctic territories if and when we made one would be upheld by any international court, or by international law.

Our trip down was swift and uneventful, except for two experiences. At Pitcairn Island, Richard Christian, descendant of the *Bounty* mutineers and the chief magistrate of the island, boarded our ship for a talk with Byrd and me. The war in Europe had broken out two and a half months earlier and since then no British ships had come to Pitcairn Island. The islanders were growing panicky over their dwindling food supply, and we agreed to give them some of our staple provisions.

While a majority of the ship's crew visited the fascinating island and bartered for wood carvings and knickknacks, a few of us sweated down in the holds shifting cargo to get at the flour, sugar and other items the natives wanted most. The ship was stowed for polar discharge and not for selective withdrawal. From time to time we who were laboring cast envious eyes at the mountainous island, thinking of our carefree shipmates ashore. Although Admiral Byrd didn't take an active part in the stevedoring, he steadfastly refused to take the pleasure of a visit ashore until we were free from our duty and could join him. As we weighed anchor later that day the native song of thanksgiving which floated up to us from the small boats alongside filled our hearts with pride.

On the other hand, an event at the very start of our voyage between Philadelphia and Panama provided us with one of the most unhappy moments of the whole journey. Byrd's own orders and the government's instructions to expedition members were not presented to those going south until we had actually sailed.

Provision 9(c) of the government's orders provided that all expedition members would surrender to the government at the first port north of the Antarctic, upon their return "all journals, diaries, memoranda, remarks, writings, charts, drawings, sketches, paintings, photographs, films, plates, as well as all specimens of every kind, collected or prepared during their absence from the United States." For a while, I expected a full-scale mutiny over this unfair and stupid ruling. For a majority of the civilians were being paid at most ten dollars a month, and several came hoping to benefit themselves academically or indirectly at the termination of their service.

Smoldering antagonism flared suddenly when Byrd asked on behalf of the Executive Committee that our civilian personnel sign a statement agreeing to abide by this ruling. Many insisted they would leave the ship at the next port rather than submit. Finally they signed a statement indicating that they had "read" the order. When Byrd rather unhappily insisted that they had to add "and will obey," our civilian members retaliated with a private meeting at which they decided unanimously to resign in a body when we reached port. It was a determined group who met in Byrd's cabin with the Admiral. But he put it to the men as an act of faith that he would do his best to have the order rescinded, and on this basis the crisis ended.

We reached the Bay of Whales on January 9, 1940, and were soon busy erecting Little America III about six miles north of our earlier bases and one mile east of the edge of the barrier. Two winterings over were enough for Admiral Byrd, who did not plan to come ashore, but instead went off on a bit of serious exploring on his own before returning to the United States. Traveling on the *Bear of Oakland,* whose captain was Lieutenant Commander Richard Cruzen, Byrd took off on a seaplane that was let over the side and discovered the Thurston Peninsula, a hitherto unknown section of the Pacific coast line of the Antarctic lying almost due south of Dallas, Texas.

Life as an expedition leader differed radically from my previous status as an ordinary member under the guidance of a superior. There were daily decisions to be made on matters affecting morale, work routine, and scientific and exploring activities. My group consisted of thirty-three men, part of whom were civilians while the rest were members of the Army, Navy and Marine Corps.

Except for three crises, life proceeded fairly smoothly. Tom Poulter, who had been Byrd's second in command on the previous expedition, had constructed a $150,000 mammoth Snow Cruiser, which was donated to the U.S. Antarctic Service by the Armour Institute of Chicago. It was a tremendous machine, measuring 55 feet long, 20 feet wide and 15 feet high, with wheels ten feet in diameter weighing three tons each. Power was supplied by Diesel generators. Nestled on the roof of the Snow Cruiser was a small Beechcraft plane equipped with skis. Inside the vehicle was a regular camp complete with bunks, galley, darkroom, laboratory and machine shop.

Under the command of Al Wade, geologist of the second expedition, the Snow Cruiser was to function as an independent roving base. It was intended that the Snow Cruiser would even go to the South Pole, with its Beechcraft acting as reconnaissance eyes. But unfortunately, although the Snow Cruiser could ascend hills, on the level, by some oddity, it sank into the snow six inches deep and then could not climb over the curb of the higher snow in front of its wheels. When the Snow Cruiser failed to travel more than three miles, the unhappy Wade Party was forced to remain at West Base with us. This was an unfortunate arrangement for capable Al Wade, who had come to the Antarctic fired with lofty ambitions for his Snow Cruiser, which was to have made its way to and wintered at the South Pole.

But the Snow Cruiser failure was not the worst of our problems. During the evening of the forty-eighth day of our long winter night, on June 7th, Dick Moulton, in charge of our Chinook kennels, came dashing into my room with the loud scream: "Fire!" Our blubber house, where we rendered out fat, had gone up in a blaze which endangered the lives of our dogs in adjacent tunnels.

A blizzard raged and the temperature was minus fifty. But we could not let anything happen to our dogs, for without them I would have to call off all trail operations next summer. Out we scurried into the dark, half dressed and armed with axes and shovels. A red glow, diffused by the drifting snow, served as a beacon which enabled us to reach the point of the fire a hundred yards from the camp exit, where flames from the furiously burning building below were leaping up through the snow. Cheeks and noses froze as we frenziedly tried to find the adjoining buried roofs of the dog kennels, which we knew were filled with smoke. In the midst of this search our electrical system shorted out and all the lights of the camp went out. It was only by sheer luck that the tunnel top was located and broken and the men dropped through to rescue the dogs, some of which were already unconscious.

Yet now, even with this timely rescue, our own danger was great, for we could not find our way back to camp in the darkness. We undoubtedly all owe our lives to Buck Boyd, our mechanic, who located an emergency generator, put on a spotlight and thus guided us back safely.

But this incident was minor compared with our greatest scare. One of the men, who had been the butt of frequent jokes, did not show up for dinner on July 26th, the ninety-seventh day of the winter night. A search of the base did not find him. Then someone remarked that he had once mentioned a compulsion to commit suicide. Aghast at the thought that a man was wandering off on the ice in the dark in the minus 20 degree cold and twenty-to-thirty-mile wind, I organized five search parties.

One went in each direction while the fifth probed the area close to camp. All efforts were to no avail and at length we returned to camp. Although I was concerned that this would be the first instance of a life lost on any of the three expeditions I had been on, I was more concerned for the would-be suicide. A check of his belongings showed that he had gone out wearing little clothing. The men grew moody at the sight of his gear, so after all probabilities of survival passed, I ordered his belongings packed for eventual shipment to his family.

Then came the miracle! After almost two further days during which blizzards made renewed search impossible, I went up onto the snow surface, that buried our camp, with two other men to check the visibility for further search. Off in the distance I spied a stumbling figure. With a rush we made for him and came upon our missing man. Incoherent and with his white frozen nose protruding from the front of his parka, he had somehow made it back to Little America after spying our beacon light in a lull in the storm.

Willing hands ripped his frozen clothing from his body. Then reaction set in and he shivered violently. Having gone without food and water for three days, he was completely dehydrated and no amount of hot coffee, bouillon and cocoa seemed to slake his thirst. But outside of losing a few frozen toes, he recovered.

He had gone out to die, and yet he could not die. Had he gone out comfortably dressed, the gradual reduction of body heat would certainly have killed him eventually. But being poorly dressed, he soon found himself convulsed by wracking shivers. The pain was so great that he had decided to find his way back. By luck or by accident, he had.

I am certain those viewing polar expeditions from afar wonder how we poor shut-ins manage to while away our hours. The truth is that the winter nights pass so rapidly that I for one never seem to get all the things done I expected to accomplish. I always bring home some of the books I take along for winter-night reading, unread. The first half of the winter usually moves along leisurely in contrast to the exhausting pace maintained during the period of camp construction. Then by midwinter, the tempo picks up and becomes more frantic as sunrise approaches and everyone strives to be ready to make the most of the short summer season.

The midwinter has special compensations of its own. Except for a few routine tasks and observation, there is nothing much that has to be accomplished on any specific day. Once one starts a task he can, if he chooses, continue on uninterrupted. There were times when some of us would get so absorbed in an interesting problem, such as perfecting the design of an instrument, the calculation of a formula, or research on natural phenomena, that we would hardly go to bed for a period of a week or so. Then once a goal was reached, we'd sleep most of the time for a couple of days afterwards to make up for it. My longest siege this winter came when I discovered some fascinating physical relationship among features on our table-model globe. I felt certain I had found concentric patterns of very specific shapes and sizes which seemed to repeat themselves over and over around the globe. I tried to search among our meager books and maps for other geographical relationships without much success. I was possessed with a notion that they were the "footprints" of former locations of the earth's poles.

However, there were more serious things to be worked on during the winter night. Things to accomplish which had to do with our presence at this spot so far from home. . . .

The scientific activities we were able to carry out included studies of weather, climate, glaciology, mapmaking, magnetism, aurora, and physiology. The coldest period came as usual in the spring, when the sun was on its way back up. This year the temperature hit −74° F. the week after the sun rose. Our meteorologist Arnold Court made the first Antarctic upper-air radio-balloon soundings which showed upper-air temperatures aloft to be as low as a chilling −130° F.

Throughout most of the winter night several of us slaved over a batch of aerial photographs we had taken the fall before in an effort to make a detailed field map of the Edsel Ford Mountain region of Marie Byrd Land. This map would be used as a base map by the field parties invading the region by dog team the next summer for the purpose of studying the geology, glaciology, and biology of the region. It covered an area equivalent to the State of Connecticut. My survey five years earlier served as ground control.

Al Wade and Larry Warner spent much of the winter studying the ice layers under our camp by means of a 30-foot shaft dug down into the snow and thermometers placed in much deeper holes drilled down to depths below sea level but still within the shelf ice. An almost constant temperature of about −10° F. existed most of the way down except near the surface. This temperature agreed quite closely with the mean annual temperature for the year as calculated from our surface observations. Meanwhile, Leonard Berlin, our surveyor, and I discovered that, as I had suspected since our first two expeditions, the ice shelf on which our camp rested was moving steadily westward day by day. Using both celestial observations and actual measurements, we found that the movement was of the order of a third of a mile per year. No wonder that the seasonal bay ice in the Bay of Whales was wrinkling up into great pressure rolls which were becoming as thick as the flanking shelf ice itself. The west side of the bay wall was moving north while the east side was charging broadside into it. Some day, we realized, a catastrophic event would occur when one wall would have to give way to the irresistible force of the other. The thrust began, we realized, hundreds of miles back where the shelf ice was being itself pushed by ice flowing off the continental heights.

While these studies went on, Roy Fitzsimmons and Murray Wiener were carrying on studies of the magnetic storms and aurora. The South Magnetic Pole was about a thousand miles north and west of us, so that our compass needle was drawn off about 105 degrees from true directions. Once during the winter Wiener and others made a journey by tractor several miles over a measured course so that radio-synchronized simultaneous photographs could be made of the aurora from both ends of the baseline. Pictures of the same aurora would appear to have different stars back of the aurora luminescence. From these pairs of photos it would be possible to measure the approximate height of the aurora, which was often two or three hundred miles high. On one of these journeys the temperature fell to about −70° F. and the spirit of scientific adventure nearly froze within the trail party. Indeed, they lost all enthusiasm for the gorgeous draperies of light arranged in tier after tier as though great curtains hung down from heaven. The bottom edge tinted purple contrasted with the bright yellow-green of the major portion of the display. It ruffled constantly as though a wind were disturbing it.

Doctors Frazier and Lockhart studied the effects of the cold on our bodies and our diet. Russell Frazier was our medical officer and he tried an experiment on some of us one day to see how fast our noses, cheeks, or ears would freeze when exposed to −60° F. and a 15-mile wind. Most of our faces frosted in 45 seconds or so. But some whose faces flushed didn't freeze after five minutes' exposure, at which point Doc had to quit, for his hand on the stop watch started to freeze.

It becomes apparent to anyone subjected to cold that a windy day feels much colder than a calm day on which the thermometer may actually register a considerably lower temperature. I adopted the word "wind-chill" to express this factor, recognizing that it was in reality a rate at which the body was cooling. Earlier, during the research involved in my doctorial thesis, I had developed a trial index by multiplying wind speeds times degrees below freezing. However, on this expedition when the index was put to test, we found that the scheme didn't work well. Although light winds had decided cooling effects, the cooling effect of heavier winds did not increase proportionally to their velocity. During the winter I set up an experiment to try to measure the rate in time it took for a cylinder of water to freeze. Charlie Passell helped me measure accurately the exact length of time that the cylinder remained at the freezing point while it was giving up its heat of crystallization under nearly 100 different combinations of wind velocity and temperature.

We soon found that our personal hunch about wind-chill had been correct. The chill—or cooling rate—doubles when wind velocity increases roughly from one mile per hour to about three miles per hour. The rate increases two and a half times at nine miles per hour and triples by the time the wind increases to twenty miles per hour. However, when the wind blew greater than forty-five miles per hour, there seemed to be no further increase in the rate of cooling of either the cylinder or our own exposed flesh and at this speed the cooling rate was only three and a half times the one mile an hour rate. Although we tried to assess the actual calories of heat that would be removed from a man, we later realized that there are so many variables in a man's size, shape, health, and rate of heat output during various activities, not to mention his control over selection of position and clothing, that an index of wind-chill numbers was all that we could hope to derive. For example, according to our (dry shade) wind-chill index, at a value of 1,000 (no matter by what combination of temperature or wind it is produced), the cooling rate feels bitterly cold. At values of 1,400 or higher, bare flesh is apt to freeze after prolonged exposure. As far as we knew then the wind-chill value of about 2,500, the worst we experienced at Little America, was a world's record. We were later to find that the South Pole in winter would get much, much chillier.

Throughout the winter our mixed civilian and military group got along surprisingly well. This was partly due to the fact that everyone was so absorbed in getting ready for the big events to take place during the approaching summer. The camp was a beehive of activity, getting food rations, camping gear, and sledges ready for the projected cross-country journeys.

When summer came with the sun up twenty-four hours a day, five separate field parties headed east to explore the Edward VII Peninsula and Marie Byrd Land. Those few who remained to carry on the science program and the summer exploratory flights were indeed taxed for manpower. Once when our planes were both off on flights, the camp crew was reduced to about seven men—the cook, radio operators, meteorologist, ground crew, and one or two helpers.

I acted as navigator on the longer flights of exploration. And several times, when our biggest plane, a Curtiss Condor, was not flyable for want of repairs, Ted Petras and I flew east as far as we could in the little Beechcraft belonging to the Snow Cruiser. To increase the distance we could fly, we landed to refuel at pre-established gas caches three times going outward and as many times on the return. We were rewarded by finding and photographing many new mountain features off to the eastward.

In mid-December, as navigator in our two-engine yellow Condor, I was on a flight where I discovered a 15,000-foot mountain which Admiral Byrd later proposed should be named Mount Ruth Siple, after my wife. In mid-air on a later flight, one of the Condor's engines caught fire and blew up, and we had an uneasy few minutes as we coasted down for a "landing" which left the plane a total loss.

Unfortunately, with the deterioration of the international scene and the spread of World War II, our plans for maintaining our Antarctic settlements ended suddenly. When Congress would not approve a further tiny appropriation of $250,000 for the next year, we had to pack and head for home. It was a sad ending to an ambitious program, made even sadder by the fact that the tendency of the American press to refer to the expedition as if it were a private undertaking of Admiral Byrd's instead of a quasi-government-sponsored operation, resulted in its being unjustly criticized. Yet even so, Byrd and a number of private citizens had contributed several hundred thousand dollars.

As we evacuated our base in February, 1941, we could point to several major accomplishments, as could the distant East Base, even though we had not achieved permanent occupancy. We had delineated 800 miles of a coast line never before, or since, approached by ship, found fourteen new islands, seven new mountain ranges, and two large peninsulas. In all, we had investigated some 150,000 square miles of new territory and conducted a number of valuable scientific studies.

And all this we had accomplished in the face of great odds. For instance, we had often been disgusted with many half-thought-out orders dispatched to us from Washington for fulfillment. These were still coming to us until our time of departure. Then too, being an agency of the government, we were constantly harassed by the amount of paperwork required. There was also the baffling requirement that at the expedition's end we return all supplies. Actually, this was exceedingly wasteful instead of being a saving, for it cost a great deal of money to bring the supplies back and most of them proved to be valueless after they were returned.

This was the modern beginning of Antarctic exploration by the American Government, and certainly I felt that there was much still to be learned. But this would have to wait, for in the years immediately ahead the United States would be faced with a struggle which threatened its very survival.

Chapter 6

OPERATION HIGHJUMP

IT WAS a rainy day in April, 1941, when the *Bear* arrived in Boston, and I found a man waiting for me on the dock who identified himself as France Fraze of the Army's Quartermaster Corps. If we were involved in the war, Fraze said, shortly after introducing himself, fighting might take place in all climates. "That's why we want you to consider helping us as a cold weather expert," he concluded.

The Army lacked such specialists and I was asked to assist in the development of special cold-weather clothing. At first I worked as a civilian, but when Pearl Harbor came I was commissioned a captain. At the conclusion of World War II, I was mustered out as a lieutenant colonel.

During the European fighting, the Eisenhower Command asked me to investigate and propose a solution for the rampant trench foot that was crippling our American forces all along the western front. This malady caused by too long exposure to wetness and temperatures within ten to twenty degrees above or below freezing had afflicted 50,000 of our front line officers and G.I.'s—with too many losing one or both feet and sometimes hands. My investigation took me into front line units from the Free French fighting along the Italian border up through France into the Low Countries. I crossed the Rhine with General Montgomery's British First Army. The results of my studies showed that in addition to excessive length of exposure, inadequate footgear and clothing, the commanders had not been taught their responsibilities to make up for a physiological failure in the body's warning system. When the feet get cold fast, as they do in the polar regions, the pain becomes so intolerable that a man must attend to them by exercise or warming. In the case of trench foot where freezing itself is not a danger and cooling is very gradual, the pain reaction is not triggered off by the nervous system. The man can go on for hours with only a feeling of mild discomfort easily overlooked in the excitement of battle. The body mechanism trying to reduce heat loss from the body reduces the heat flow to arms and legs to such an extent that if temporary relief is not occasionally provided, not enough oxygen reaches the tissue to permit it to go on living. The northern British who suffer chilblains, a kindred disease, in their underheated homes in winter had little if any trench foot, while we were having so much of it. Fighting was less mobile in the northern British sector that winter than for U.S. troops and the British rotated their men in and out of the front line every 48 hours whereas U.S. commanders, continually advancing, kept our fighters going until they became casualties for one reason or another. There was no time or place to return our men for thorough body warming and dry clothing and footwear. Yet if we had not kept pressing, the war might have lasted longer and more would have been killed than those crippled by this subtle cold injury.

With spring advancing and victory assured in Europe, I was returned to Washington and then on to the Philippines, the headquarters of the Pacific war theater. My task was to advise on winter clothing and protection of forces preparing to invade the main islands of Japan. When the dropping of the two atomic bombs made this unnecessary, I flew to Japan with the first waves of the occupation forces to assist with sudden new problems of training and equipping for winter activities men who had been living for many months in the tropics. Then in the spring of 1946 I entered the Army Chief of Staff's Office of Research and Development as a civilian scientist. My new career was to involve the application of my environmental research concepts to Army equipment and personnel in any environment they might be called upon to fight to preserve the free way of life. In due time my interest was to broaden to the entire aspects of basic research and the segment with which I was a charter scientist eventually developed into the Army Research Office.

Of course, during World War II, I had had little time to think about the Antarctic. In addition to my work, there was my growing family, which was now about to reach its full complement of three daughters.

Nevertheless, Admiral Byrd, whom I saw frequently in Washington, kept me abreast of disquieting events that were taking place in the Antarctic where German submarine raiders were using Antarctic waters to facilitate easy and quick movement from ocean to ocean. In the Atlantic Ocean sector, the Germans at one stroke captured fourteen excellent vessels of the Norwegian whaling fleet, thus obtaining valuable fuel supplies. Later, in the Pacific, they came up to Australia where they mined the harbors of a number of major cities and ports. Freewheeling from one Nazi base to another in the Antarctic, the German raiders captured or sank many thousand tons of Allied vessels, including the *Sydney,* an Australian light cruiser, and the *City of Bayville,* an American ship.

Worried by these marauders, the British in 1943 dispatched Lieutenant Commander J. W. S. Marr to set up two radio bases to ferret out the presence of German raiders. This was of special interest to me because Marr had been the Boy Scout with Shackleton in 1922, as I had been with Byrd in 1928, and was probably the inspiration for Byrd's decision to take a Scout to the Antarctic. Marr set up his bases quickly, one on Deception Island and the other at Port Lockroy on the west side of the Graham-Palmer Peninsula. Soon German depredations had fallen off markedly. The British, however, remained there to establish permanent settlements. Thus began British colonization in the Graham-Palmer Peninsula, which was vociferously opposed by the Argentinean and Chilean governments that, sight un-

seen, claimed the peninsula and the land to the South Pole for themselves. Taking a leaf from the discontinued U. S. Antarctic Service, the
British began to seriously approach the requirements of territorial acquisition in the Antarctic.

With the war's close, I had hoped for a resumption of American
efforts to establish permanent bases on Antarctica. However, Admiral
Byrd's old friend and supporter, Franklin Delano Roosevelt, was dead
and the new Administration was too busy with other mammoth immediate concerns to be bothered with the Antarctic. Furthermore,
defense interest had again swung out national attention to the Arctic.

As a preliminary to further work in the Antarctic, I suggested in
early 1946 that the blank map areas in the Arctic Basin be filled in.
This suggestion was readily accepted and a hectic aerial photo reconnaissance program was soon underway. Yet, despite the claims of war-
time aerial navigators as to the accuracy of their science, it was obvious to many who flew north in that program that there was much
to be learned if a similar effort to erase the blank spots on the map
of Antarctica was to be successfully accomplished. I thought of this
later in the year when, on October 8, 1946, I rode with a B-29 crew
over the North Pole as a civilian with the first USAF crew to attempt
this. The flight took twenty-four hours for the simple reason that we
kept straying off course. We had started to fly to the Pole on the
150th meridian. But after long wandering in an area where the maintaining of direction was difficult, we finally made our way to the Pole
on the 90th meridian. This flight was notable too because it was the
first nighttime flight. The sun was below the horizon by 6 degrees.
Moonlight made it possible for us to see the open leads in the sea ice
at the Pole. The long period of twilight flying added greatly to the
navigator's difficulties.

While this Arctic effort was going on, Admiral Byrd succeeded in
reaching the ear of Fleet Admiral Chester W. Nimitz, then Chief of
Naval Operations, and Secretary of the Navy James V. Forrestal. In
late August, 1946, Nimitz approved a program which was to dwarf
all previous Antarctic explorations. "Operation Highjump," it was
to be called.

In a directive of August 26th, Nimitz ordered Highjump to attempt
to establish an air base on the ice surface of Antarctica and conduct
various scientific programs in the course of which the Navy would be
able to train men and test equipment under polar conditions. There
was also one more interesting provision: An additional task assigned
Highjump would be that of "consolidating and extending United

States potential sovereignty over the largest practicable area of the Antarctic Continent."

Operation Highjump was to be chiefly a Navy undertaking with Admiral Byrd serving as Officer in Charge and personal representative of Nimitz. Captain Richard Cruzen, who had commanded the *Bear* on the third expedition, was made Commander of the Operating Task Force, and, at Byrd's urging, was elevated to rear admiral shortly before leaving on Operation Highjump, since Byrd felt the program would run more efficiently if the Commander of the Task Force had flag rank. I was named Byrd's Scientific and Polar Advisor as well as being Senior War Department Observer, heading a group of sixteen observers.

The plan was to break the task force into three subcommands. Cruzen, while remaining in charge of operations of all three, personally directed the Central Group. He was to lead four ships to the Bay of Whales where Little America IV would be established, and an air strip would be built so that planes from the 35,000-ton aircraft carrier *Philippine Sea* could land there. The Western Group under Captain Charles Bond was to explore along the coast of Wilkes Land and continue until it met the Eastern Group. This group, led by Captain George Dufek, whom I had known as a lieutenant on the *Bear* on the third expedition, was to deploy its ships off the Walgreen Coast and the Palmer Peninsula and then move forward until it met Bond.

With thirteen ships, including a submarine and an aircraft carrier, nineteen planes, four helicopters and four thousand men, Byrd hoped to photograph and map all of Antarctica's 16,000-mile coast line, and with this in mind, the East and West groups carried three PBM flying boats, capable of long flights and equipped with a battery of three-lensed cameras which would take three-directional pictures of the land beneath. If all the pictures were taken at uniform elevation, mapmakers would then be able to draw contour and elevation lines. In addition to coastal photography, several photo-reconnaissance aerial trips were planned for the interior of the continent.

I sailed with Cruzen on his flagship, *Mount Olympus,* in early December of 1946.

When a man starts off to the ends of the earth, cutting himself off from the normal flow of life, there is always a lurking concern over the important events of a family life at which one's presence is essential. And since Ruth had presented me with our third daughter in October, my thoughts were with my growing family even more than on earlier occasions.

Then, as we were fast approaching the Antarctic, Dick Cruzen called me into his cabin to give me a brief radiogram informing me of the death of my father. It was the first death in my immediate family, and the pangs of sorrow I felt were increased by the distance which separated me from those whom I would have liked to help comfort. A few weeks later another message from my sister explained how my gallant mother had fallen and broken her hip. Twice in a row I was half a world away from my mother's side when she needed the comfort of her wandering son.

After a particularly trying trip south, marked by extreme difficulty in getting through the Antarctic ice pack due to a decision to proceed along the ice-choked regular path down along the 178th meridian instead of probing for an ice-free passage, we arrived off the Bay of Whales in late January with considerable ship damage.

One of the purposes of Highjump was to establish a new Little America and build an ice strip for reconnaissance planes. When I had left the Antarctic in 1941, the entrance to the Bay of Whales had been a mile and a half wide. Now, six years later, the entrance was less than three hundred yards wide. The two separated barrier walls had moved slowly toward each other and all but wiped out what had once been the southernmost harbor in the Antarctic. The west wall was now moving northward at the rate of four feet each day while the other was progressing westward toward it at a similar speed. My earliest studies had shown that about every fifty years the two ice walls came together, temporarily ending the usefulness of the Bay of Whales until later enormous pieces of both walls broke off and floated to sea as huge icebergs. From the appearance of the bay when we came on Highjump, the barrier walls were due to collide in six months.

Little America III had moved almost two miles to the northwest since I had seen it last. Near to the edge of the barrier, Little America IV now went up two miles north of Little America III as a tent camp for 300 men. Our plan was to remain here only six weeks. It was with sentiment that I accompanied Marine Major Buck Boyd and Lieutenant Commander Jim McCoy, old comrades from our previous expedition, in a search for the buildings of snowed-under West Base. After digging away about four feet of snow, we finally came upon the skylight of our old science building. Lowering ourselves into the building, we found we could hardly recognize our old quarters. It was as cold, dark and dank as the inside of an icebox and yet we could almost feel the presence of our former comrades who had spent so many months here with us. The walls and ceiling were ornamented with ice crystals that glittered with all the colors of the spectrum in the light of our oil lamp. On the table we found meat, bread and butter still in excellent condition and we had lunch to commemorate the old days.

Then Admiral Byrd flew in some 600 miles from the carrier *Philippine Sea* to the hastily marked landing strip at Little America IV on January 30, 1947, and the exploratory phase of Operation Highjump was officially underway. By April, we were back in the United States, but not before a great deal of work had been done on the continent.

In a general way, the periphery of the entire continent was delineated and many of the interior features were roughed in by 70,000 aerial photographs. The exercise was highly useful as a training venture, though many of the photographs later proved puzzling to precision mappers accustomed to a high degree of accuracy, since the planes were largely flown by pilots who did not know the polar regions and whose crews were unfamiliar with aerial mapping, for although they were enthusiastic volunteers, their training had been basically for normal military flying. In addition, there was an almost complete absence of ground control, with the result that many of the crews were unsure of what they were photographing. I could appreciate the problem, for I joined in some of the flights. The ever-changing features of the continent plus the difficulty in determining distances from the air presented a plaguing dilemma. For instance, while I had located Mount Ruth Siple on the third expedition, from a distance of nearly 80 miles away, I now found that my calculations of location and height were somewhat off. Shades of poor Wilkes back in 1840, I thought, who had been off as much as fifty miles in his charting.

Yet certainly the inaccuracy of early charts should not be too surprising, for the explorers who go into an unknown area to uncover the existence of a land are primarily concerned with giving a first approximation of *what* exists rather than precisely *where* it exists. It is the duty of those who come later to locate precisely what is there and where it is. Unfortunately, the almost inevitable poor positioning of the first explorers is invariably the target of criticism of these latecomers, concerned with filling in the details of geology and geography. Both groups are vital to the progress of exploration!

Many scientists had accompanied Highjump. Cruzen, however, considered them superfluous, choosing to emphasize the exploratory aspect of his orders at the expense of the scientific, and they were given so little opportunity to pursue their work that many of them vowed they would never return to the Antarctic with a Navy expedition. The result was that many of the best scientific opportunities were left to the plane pilots, most of whom unfortunately did not recognize them. The classic case was the young flyer who flew in past the Shackleton Ice Shelf on the continent's west coast and discovered a three-hundred-square-mile area of ice-free hills. This oasis lay in pristine beauty near the coast line and contained several blue and green lakes of open water set among barren, brown rock hills. To his credit, the pilot conscientiously landed. But he had no technical tools to examine his find. Lacking even a thermometer, he put his hand in the water and observed that it felt "comfortable." Fortunately, he had a bottle and filled it with the water before his return. There was great excitement in the Western Group that the first true lake in the Antarctic had been discovered. Unfortunately, the water in the bottle turned out to be brackish, a clue to the fact that the "lake" was actually an arm of the open sea. But this was not determined before the eleven press representatives aboard the *Mount Olympus* had fired off dispatches to the outside world describing the oasis as a "Shangri-La" and implying that it was warmed by a mysterious source of heat and might be supporting vegetation.

The bare land was startling to newcomers in a region of so much snow and ice. It was, however, by no means unique, for there are numerous areas of ice-free land in the Antarctic where glaciers have parted and left an open space. One such area exists near the head of the Beardmore Glacier, about 300 miles from the Pole. I discovered similar areas in Marie Byrd Land. And most celebrated of all these ice-free areas is, of course, the Taylor Dry Valley in the vicinity of McMurdo Sound.

Whatever its deficiencies, Operation Highjump represented an important step forward in Antarctic exploration. Not only did Highjump reveal a renewed interest by the American Government in the Antarctic, but the Operation also ushered in the era of photographic exploration of the continent by technicians who did not necessarily recognize what they saw as opposed to the earlier efforts of men who had to rely on their own eyes. In addition, plane crews gained technical first experience in high-latitude flying and landing on snow, invaluable training for coming American bases in the Arctic. And despite the deficiencies in Highjump, aerial reconnaissance proved its vast importance in uncovering the Antarctic by providing the first nearly complete outline map of the coast of Antarctica.

These were all reason enough for a second Highjump. Fanning out in all directions in a series of flights and with new navigational tools, a Highjump II, Byrd and I knew, should have little difficulty filling in the details of the interior of Antarctica not covered by Highjump I. World War II had left the United States as the only nation capable of doing this job, and success would establish a pre-eminent American claim over the entire continent. For by mapping all of the Antarctic and being the first to sight the still unseen two-thirds of the continent, the United States could be in a unique position to claim Antarctica for its own, should it so desire.

Highjump I was followed up by two American expeditions. Navy Operation Windmill, carried out by Task Force 37 consisting chiefly of two new wind-class icebreakers, pinpointed landmarks along the Wilkes Coast in order to make Highjump I's aerial photography more useful. And a private American expedition, headed by Finn Ronne and using a small Navy vessel and Air Force planes, wintered over at the USAS's partially supplied East Base, which Ronne found now flanked by a brand-new British base situated only a few hundred yards away. Ronne's expedition carried out a goodly amount of useful scientific research along the Weddell sea coast. One of the interesting things about this expedition was that two American women, Edith Ronne and Jenny Darlington, accompanied it and became the first women ever to winter over in Antarctica.

Unfortunately, Highjump II itself never left the ground. Set for 1949–1950, political considerations brought about its sudden demise. Supplies for Operation Highjump II had already been purchased, the money spent and the logistics carefully laid out when it was called off in the name of economy. Yet Defense Secretary Louis Johnson wanted to seize upon something spectacular to eliminate so that his postwar economy drive would appear politically significant.

President Truman was engaged in a completely unrelated squabble with Admiral Byrd's brother, Senator Harry F. Byrd of Virginia. "There are too many birds (Byrds)," newspapers quoted the President. Unable to take adequate retaliatory action against the Senator, the Administration took revenge on his brother, the Admiral, even though he was in no way involved in the controversy.

This was a matter of deep regret to Byrd and me. For we realized that Highjump II represented a great lost opportunity for the United States to gain the major voice over the Antarctic's future. Now the future of the continent lay in another direction, fraught with deep-seated international complications.

Chapter 7

PLANNING THE IGY

BY THE time the 1950's arrived, the political situation in the Antarctic had grown chaotic, as overlapping national claims had carved the continent into an inedible pie with all slices meeting at the geographic South Pole. Oddly enough, little if any of the territory had even been seen by the vociferous claimants. On the other hand, the United States, whose Antarctic explorations had uncovered more of the continent than the sum total of all claimants, had not raised its voice to demand a single foot of Antarctica.

The Australians claimed the largest slice, an area running up almost to the edge of the Ross Ice Shelf on the 160th East Meridian to the 45th East Meridian far west past Wilkes Land largely on the strength of the explorations accomplished by the expeditions headed by the already mentioned, extremely able, Sir Douglas Mawson. The French disputed part of this claim with a smaller one of their own between 142° East and 136° East. New Zealand claimed a sector extending from the eastern limits of the Australian stake-out to the 150° W meridian which included the Ross Ice Shelf, and thus the sites of the four Little Americas. This was a most interesting claim, considering that I was the only person who had ever seen the entirety of the Ross Ice Shelf in a combination of trail traverses and air flights. The Norwegian Government claimed Queen Maud Land, a broad section beginning at the western limits of the Australian claim and ending on the opposite side of the continent from the Bay of Whales.

The worst controversy among the various claimants came over the Graham-Palmer Peninsula, first sighted by Connecticut Captain Nathaniel Palmer in 1820, landed on by Davis's crew the next year, and later the site of East Base in the 1939–1941 expedition of the U. S. Antarctic Service. Here where British Lieutenant Commander Marr had established World War II bases to thwart German raiders, and a number of other British explorers including Sir Vivian Fuchs had got their start, the British, Argentineans and Chileans claimed the Peninsula as their own. As has been mentioned, the British called it Graham Land, while the Argentine Government called it San Martin Land and the Chileans, O'Higgins Land, after their own national heroes. None in turn accepted the American name of Palmer Peninsula.

The antagonism among the three claimants almost came to bloodshed following World War II, with all three establishing bases there. At one time prior to the IGY, seventeen bases sprouted on the Palmer Peninsula: Britain had seven; Argentina, six; and Chile, four. Once when a British landing party attempted to reach shore at Hope Bay, an Argentine military force fired machine-gun bullets over the heads of the men. At times Chileans, Argentines and British all had stations virtually within sight of one another. In time a pattern jelled. As soon as the nationals at one base departed, watchful claimants of another nation scurried in, destroyed the station and erected their own buildings with their flag unfurled on top. Some of the incidents, serious to the nations involved, were so amusing to an onlooker they rivaled the machinations of a Gilbert and Sullivan operetta.

At the time of Highjump in 1947, I had unofficially sounded out New Zealand and Australian polar officials regarding the possible establishment of an international condominium over a part of the continent and found their interest high as long as it was restricted to essentially English-speaking lands. In fact, they favored an even more inclusive arrangement which would encompass the entire Antarctic. This I was reluctant to push since it might be considered as coming into direct conflict with the Monroe Doctrine in those areas claimed by South American countries.

By the early 1950's, Britain, Norway, New Zealand, France and Australia had reached agreement and recognized each other's claims in the Antarctic. Though the United States did not recognize any of these, or other claims, these nations expressed a willingness to permit an American claim on the sector including Marie Byrd Land and a part of Ellsworth Highland, an area along the Pacific Coast that no ship had ever approached. For unlike the quiet Ross Sea that sits between the ice pack and the Ross Ice Shelf, the waters along those coasts are almost perpetually frozen. This appears to be the result of the Easter Island Ridge, a vast mountain range or even a continent

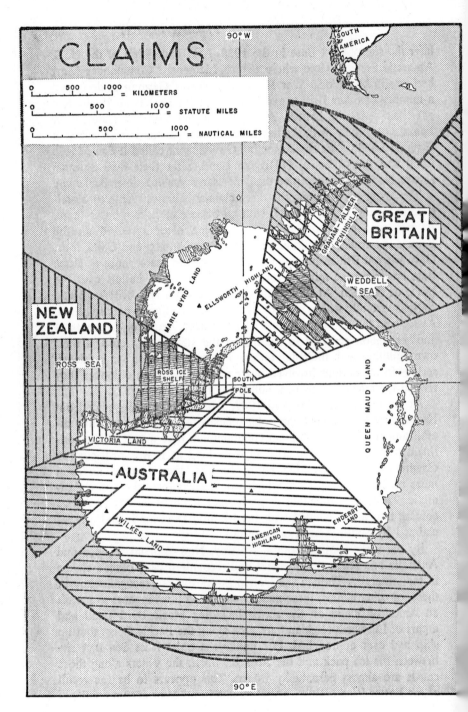

Sovereign claims by various nations in the Antarctic.

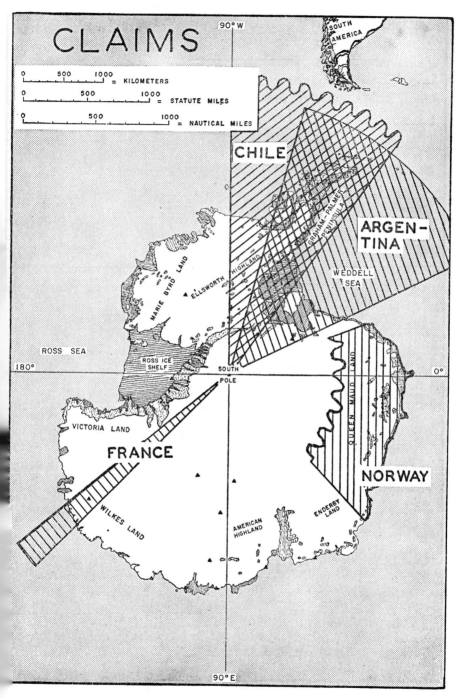

Sovereign claims by various nations in the Antarctic.

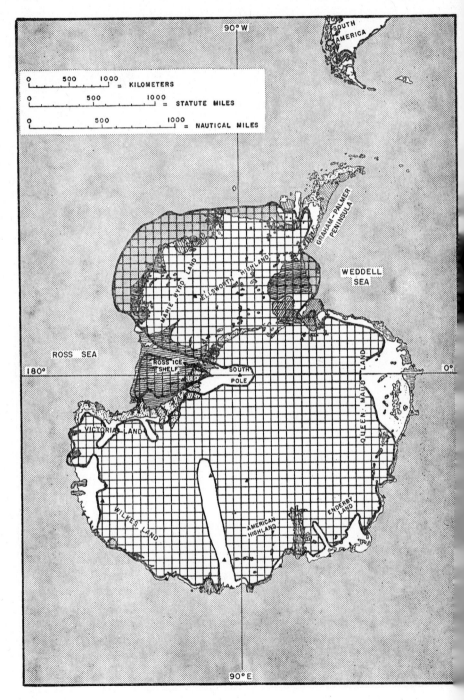

Clear areas are those actually viewed by air and land expeditions of all nations other than the U.S. prior to the start of the IGY in July, 1957.

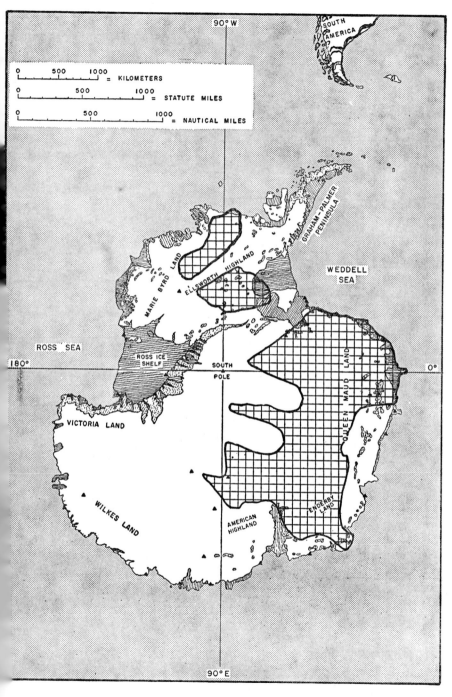

Clear areas are those which had been actually viewed by U.S. air and land expeditions prior to the start of the IGY in July, 1957.

beneath the sea, which deflects the warm waters of the Pacific Ocean away from that portion of the Antarctic coast.

All of these national activities in the Antarctic were most disquieting to Admiral Byrd and me. We had devoted so much of our energies to exploring both the surface features of the Antarctic and its scientific phenomena that we looked askance on an Antarctica which excluded the United States.

Then, rather late in the game now, about 1950, the Department of State awakened suddenly to a desire to reconsider the question of establishing American claims in that continent. "But you haven't got a single document in your files to show what the United States has done," I argued in unison with other Antarctic specialists. This was true because the American Government had never officially drawn together factual information which would readily show where Americans had gone in the Antarctic, and, particularly, what they had accomplished. All that existed was a mass of personal literature in the form of a number of books and scientific articles, diaries, letters, specimens and photographs, none of which had been examined and authenticated officially. Even the vast amount of data gathered by the U. S. Antarctic Services had not been collected and printed, because Congress had ended that agency before reports could be written.

"All right," said State Department officials, "let's put things in order now." A note of urgency hung in the atmosphere.

"Everything is going forward at an ever-accelerating rate," Admiral Byrd said and smiled.

Thus began a renewed national interest in the Antarctic. And as time passed, the program broadened. Laying out a ten-year schedule, the government's first decision was to consolidate all American rights in a written history. A further step planned was to accomplish the mapping and exploration task originally set for the ill-fated Operation Highjump II in 1949. With these in mind, the government established several committees devoted to American interests in the Antarctic.

For instance, the mapping committee, of which I was a member, had two subcommittees: a Where and a How subcommittee. The Where group worked on such matters as what parts of the Antarctic needed mapping and which sections should be done first. The How subcommittee devoted itself to the technology of mapping and how we were going to do the job. Since the problem of logistics could best be handled by the military, the Navy again gained the leading role here, for only on ships could men and equipment be delivered to the Antarctic.

I well remember the day when George Dufek came into the picture. The Korean War had begun and I had gone to Korea to roam the full length of the ever-changing battle lines to check on winter equipment for the Army. Upon my return, I encountered Captain Dufek in the Pentagon one afternoon in 1954. I had known George first as an energetic and brash lieutenant who served as navigator aboard the *Bear* on my third expedition to the Antarctic. It was George who had replied to Admiral Byrd's query off the Ross Barrier: "What do you think of it?" with "It's a hell of a lot of ice. But what good is it?" Later Dufek had commanded the Eastern Group in Operation Highjump in 1947. Here he had performed well, though he had perhaps had more than his fair share of accidents. On one occasion, a helicopter in which he was riding misjudged its landing aboard a seaplane tender and plunged him into the icy sea. Fortunately, he was pulled out within a minute, since a man can survive only a few minutes' immersion in Antarctic waters. Another time, when he transferred at sea from the destroyer *Brownson* to his flagship the *Pine Island,* in a stormy sea, the breeches buoy broke and his airborne chair plummeted into the freezing water. Obviously the possessor of a charmed life, he was again rescued none the worse for his experience.

Yet despite these mishaps, there was something about the Antarctic that still intrigued Dufek. He had just flown in from the West Coast where he served as commanding officer of the Naval Air Station at Whidbey Island, Washington, near Seattle. "There's something going on in the Antarctic, Siple, isn't there?" he asked me.

When I nodded, he went on, "I'd like to get into it. What are my chances?"

I told George the details of the planned national program. "I'll speak to the Admiral about finding a place for you," I said.

"I'd appreciate that," said George. "I'm going to be retired soon and I'd like to get into it until I am."

Later I asked Byrd about adding Dufek to our group. He pondered on this a short while. Actually, Byrd was only adviser to the Chief of Naval Operations, but he had no intention of taking a back seat to others in the general planning phases of the over-all national program for the Antarctic. He would need someone to deliver the forthcoming expedition to the continent. "What do you think of putting George in command of the task force when the time comes?" he asked. "Of course, this will mean that we'll have to get a special bill through Congress so he'll have the right to command as a retired officer."

Shortly afterward, Dufek joined the How subcommittee dealing with logistics. "Now that I got what I want," he said to me gleefully, "what do you want?"

"Nothing," I said with a smile.

One of the rules of life is that no public activity can continue for long without running headlong into another. At the same time that the national program was moving forward, another development had crept into the picture. This was the program devised by geophysicists throughout the world for an International Geophysical Year. The IGY was to be the third massive attack on the geophysical aspects of the earth.

The activities of the two previous geophysical "years" were confined to the polar areas. In brief, they involved the following:

In 1882–83, ten nations, including the United States, engaged in the First Polar Year. The time period selected resulted from good reason, for this was a period of peak sunspot activities. Sunspots are caused by gigantic storms on the sun. Since geophysics is the physical study of the earth and its atmosphere, and since the sun is assumed to be the chief source of all energy reaching the earth, periods of peak sunspot activity constitute the best time for studying their effect on phenomena such as weather and earth magnetism. It was because the effects of sunspot activity are most noticeable on the weather and magnetism at the ends of the earth that the program centered on the polar regions.

The First Polar Year found meteorology, astronomy, magnetic and mapping stations established throughout the Arctic region. The only station outside this zone lay at South Georgia in the Antarctic region, under the direction of a German expedition. Chief results of this First Polar Year were the discoveries made in the field of geomagnetism. Of personal interest to me was the fact that the *Bear of Oakland,* which had carried part of the men on my second and third expeditions to the Antarctic, had been involved in the First Polar Year during which it had rescued survivors of the Greeley Expedition in 1884, the ill-fated American group taking part in the "year."

A fifty-year gap separated the First and Second Polar Years. Despite the world-wide depression, more than thirty nations participated in this second geophysical attack during 1932–33. Again the emphasis was on the Arctic region, though the British and Norwegians accumulated some information in the Southern Hemisphere. The second Byrd Antarctic Expedition of 1933–35 had been a fringe participant of this Second Polar Year. Chief among the gains resulting from the Second Polar Year were a greater awareness of the ionosphere and its effect on radio transmission, and the acquisition of an understanding of the need for conducting aerometeorological observations in order to predict weather.

Those, then, were the two Polar Years which demonstrated the advantages of nations working together on scientific programs. A Third Polar Year was projected for 1982–83.

However, by the close of World War II, scientists were aware that a revolution had occurred in most of their fields. Those gains could readily be put to use to make further advances in science. But those of us who were in the geophysical sciences realized that we were in dire need of additional geophysical information which could best be acquired by a massive international program if we were to capitalize on our recently acquired theories to make major break-throughs.

Credit must go to Dr. Lloyd Berkner for making the proposal in 1950 to hold another polar year at the next period of peak sunspot activity, scheduled for 1957–58. I had known Berkner first as a radio engineer aboard the *City of New York* on the first Byrd Expedition of 1928–30. Now his proposal to the International Council of Scientific Unions (ICSU) contained a note of urgency. The thirty-two years to the next scheduled polar year was too long to wait for information we needed now.

Events moved forward quickly. The ICSU, a private organization tying together a host of international scientific groups, accepted Berkner's plan enthusiastically. In short order, it set up CSAGI (Comité Spécial de l'Année Géophysique International) to co-ordinate the "year."

But CSAGI decided to study more than the polar regions, for the phenomena needing study were world-wide. Information was needed not only from the extremes of the earth, but from *all over* the earth. For this reason CSAGI selected the name International Geophysical Year (IGY) instead of Third Polar Year. Furthermore, instead of a year of making simultaneous observations throughout the globe, IGY's "year" would consist of eighteen months, from July, 1957 through December, 1958, to allow observers a good seasonal overlap of sunspot activity.

Since scientists were expected to conduct observations within their own national boundaries, in 1952 CSAGI turned to the science academies in various nations to establish their own national committees for the IGY. In the United States, this meant the National

Academy of Sciences, the quasi-national voice of science in America. Dr. Detlov Bronk, head of the Academy, named a group of about twenty-five persons to meet with him in Washington. I was one of those Bronk asked to become a member—because of my work as a polar geographer, rather than the fact that I was then serving as director of the Army's basic research program. Following our first meeting, our group became the United States National Committee for the IGY, or USNC-IGY.*

Dr. Joseph Kaplan of Cal Tech was named as chairman, and we began a loose probing of the phases of earth sciences we felt should be considered as the American contribution to the IGY. It all seemed an ephemeral undertaking to us then. Few expected that it would result in the major program that ultimately resulted. The organization had no money and there were grave doubts that the Administration and Congress would provide financial backing for whatever program we devised.

Yet we realized the importance of having the United States make an outstanding contribution to the IGY. For it was vital that each nation fulfill its capabilities in the necessary geophysical research. With the United States a world leader in science, it was essential not only that we engage in a major program, but also that we offer to aid other nations needing scientific instruments and training for their personnel. If not, there might be serious gaps in the information needed to draw fundamental conclusions.

In an atmosphere of enthusiastic confusion, we began by holding meetings every few months. Then with the ending of the Korean War, the pace increased.

In 1953, we selected a number of scientific disciplines in which we would develop our program for the IGY providing funds became available. For instance, my assigned area in this planning task was glaciology. For this discipline I outlined a preliminary program and made rough estimates of what I guessed it might cost to conduct it. Others did the same in other fields, and we then moved ahead to set up technical panels for each discipline.

In time we settled on twelve geophysical disciplines: aurora and airglow, cosmic rays, geomagnetism, glaciology, gravity, the ionosphere, longitude and latitude determinations, meteorology, oceanography, seismology, solar activity, and rocket and satellite studies of the upper and outer atmosphere.

In addition, we set up various *ad hoc* committees, where all the

* See Appendix II.

disciplines were considered together within a geographic area. These area committees included one for the Antarctic, another for the Arctic and a third for the tropics. Coincidental to the disciplines and the areas, the IGY also planned three world-wide chains of observation: one to run through North and South America to the Graham-Palmer Peninsula; a second chain of stations to slice through Europe and Africa and to the edge of the Antarctic; and a third chain to pass through Japan, the Philippines, New Zealand and Australia before reaching the Antarctic.

Pressure for scientific bases in the Antarctic began building up early at the international level, for it was easily apparent that without such bases one-fifth of the earth's surface would not be included. After all, a gap of several thousand miles existed between South Africa, Australasia and South America. Unless simultaneous scientific observations were also made in the Antarctic, scientists would be hampered in trying to draw knowledgeable conclusions. Thus the United States joined with ten other nations in expressing an early interest in establishing IGY bases in the Antarctic.

I was of course doubly interested in whatever IGY programs were to involve the Antarctic, since I was also taking part in the American Government's national program. Thus when a USNC Antarctic Committee was established, I became a member, even though my duties with the Army precluded my devoting more than a portion of my time to it.

Independent of any government agency, the USNC-IGY Antarctic Committee began sifting through various proposals to determine what we could do in the Antarctic. And now I was amused to find that while I was accepted as a scientist, I was not accepted by some as an Antarctic authority. Instead it seemed to be generally accepted that "old-timers" knew less than untried newcomers. It was an eye-opening discovery to learn that though I had been on four Antarctic expeditions, I was considered by some to be full of old wives' tales unrelated to the modern scene.

And yet this attitude should not have come as a surprise to me, for I had written six years earlier in the Army Observers Report of Operation Highjump:

> Veterans quickly become obnoxious when they are in the minority. They speak boldly of conditions to be met and frequently in a changeable place like the Antarctic the unexpected usually happens. A veteran of more than one previous experience

generally becomes more cautious, for he realizes the times he has been wrong and may be embarrassed by the braggadocio of one-time veterans. In short, new men resent being told what to expect and quickly lose faith when the predictions prove wrong or are interpreted wrongly. Soon there builds up a disregard for the veterans and they may become almost ostracized. Neglect of warnings are sometimes unfortunate in consequence and even the innocent veteran is identified with false predictions he did not make. But he is branded because he is a veteran. Veterans are important on an expedition as a link with the past as long as they are not tied to it. Extreme tolerance is required on both sides to prevent misunderstandings. The veteran is prone to step outside his field of personal knowledge and may make unusual circumstances of the past seem like usual or common experience. Each man who goes on an expedition becomes a veteran and if he goes twice he may find his whole outlook changed and soon has to realize that he didn't learn everything the first time. An expedition which fails on the other hand to heed some of the advice of its veterans has strong critics close at hand, a circumstance frequently justifiable.

Certainly this attitude of the uninitiate toward veterans was to haunt both Admiral Byrd and myself as well as all the old-timers continually in the operations ahead.

In November, 1953, Dr. Lawrence Gould, who had last been in the Antarctic twenty-five years earlier as Byrd's second in command on the 1928–30 expedition to Little America I, was named chairman of the IGY committee. At one meeting Dr. Harry Wexler of the U. S. Weather Bureau quoted a statement made over forty years earlier by Simpson, meteorologist with Scott's last expedition, which suggested that Antarctic weather might possibly fan out from the region now known as Marie Byrd Land. Wexler's enthusiasm for Antarctic weather stations in this area led to his being appointed Chief Scientist of the Antarctic Program, although he had never been to the Antarctic and did not plan to go as a member of the expedition for a prolonged period.

Chief business of the committee soon narrowed down to talk of establishing a single station in the Antarctic. Captain Finn Ronne, who had served with the American expeditions of 1933–35 and 1939–41 and later led his own expedition to the Graham-Palmer Peninsula and the Weddell Sea, was now a consultant to the committee. Ronne pleaded the case for erecting the station on the Weddell Coast.

I proposed returning to the Bay of Whales area where we could take advantage of the knowledge already accumulated at the various Little Americas, a course which would give us a head start for adding to what we had already learned. Even more important, that area lay under the doughnutlike ring of greatest auroral activity and would serve as a vital location for corollary studies of other nations. In the end, the committee decided on Little America.

All the while the USNC-IGY's Antarctic Committee was in existence, I was associated with the entirely unrelated Antarctic program of the National Government. Under the National Program to map the continent as preparation for any possible American territorial claims, we were considering establishing several permanent bases in the Antarctic. It occurred to me early that the two separate ventures of science and national interest could be loosely linked by a marriage of convenience. Other countries, such as Britain and Argentina, planned to do just this, while the Norwegians, the French and the New Zealanders made a point of planning their IGY bases in territories they claimed. For instance, while British scientists planned geophysical studies under the Royal Society, another branch of the British Government, the Falkland Island Dependency, continued their national mapping of the Graham-Palmer Peninsula in order to strengthen their claim to it.

We, on the other hand, had a scientific group that did not know whether it would acquire government backing and funds, and an exploring and national interest group already operating as a government agency.

Some of the scientific group would have been aghast at any suggestion that the dedicated international program join hands with the nationalistic interests. On the other hand, the national program mapmakers were reluctant to consider IGY as of any possible value in their own programs and goals. Yet I knew there were elements in both that could be joined while retaining an essential separation of authority.

My opportunity came when the USNC-IGY Antarctic Committee began considering how to deliver and establish the Little America Station. Some suggested hiring a commercial vessel to transport scientists to the Antarctic, a glib and easy display of optimism considering what was involved in setting up a station and surviving in the Antarctic. Even if money were available to deliver the scientists to the

Ross Ice Shelf, how were they to proceed expeditiously once they dragged the scientific equipment onto the ice?

There was only one solution. "You will have to ask the Defense Department for ships and logistics aid to carry out an expedition," I argued.

"But do you think there is a chance that Defense might help us out?" they asked.

"Let's ask and see what happens," I replied.

Meanwhile, on the other side of the Antarctic ice fence, the National Program personnel were not certain of what use the science program would be to them. "They'll just clutter things up with their pipe-smoking and phony theoretics," some argued.

However, I took the view that the National Program would ultimately benefit from aiding the scientists. In the first place, the National Program contemplated establishing several permanent bases in the Antarctic. What harm would befall the program if American scientists were to live at these bases? Furthermore, as I pointed out, if the USNC-IGY's Antarctic work was not undertaken, we would still have to do that identical work eventually, and it would be more expensive when we did. And we would be held back ten or fifteen years unless the gaps in the Antarctic geophysical sciences were filled as they would be if we co-operated with the international effort.

So a marriage of sorts came into existence between the USNC-IGY and the Defense Department. And with it came a new development.

Once the Defense Department agreed to erect the proposed Little America V for the USNC-IGY, the appetites of the eager scientists were whetted. If they could have one Antarctic scientific station, why not more? Though Little America would be the chief scientific station, they argued, other stations elsewhere on the continent might have unique and correlating advantages of their own.

The Defense Department responded to this USNC request with surprising warmth. For Defense now thought that the National Program

The South Pole Station under construction. The builders had already mov from survival tents into the two Jamesway huts and were at work erecting t powerhouse and garage to the right of the larger hut. Crates of IGY equipme and steel trusses lie scattered nearby, while behind the camp lies a dark mou of fuel drums. White strip at top of picture is a portion of the 10,000-fo runway used by ski-equipped planes. The American flag in the lower left corr flies from pole erected to mark the spot tentatively identified as the actr South Pole. © NATIONAL GEOGRAPHIC SOCIE

Scott's 1902 hut at Mc-Murdo. It stands only about a half mile from the Navy's base, which was behind the camera. This picture looks out over ice-choked Mc-Murdo Sound.

Admiral Byrd (left) revisits Little America I & II in January of 1956 on his last trip to the Antarctic. To his left stand Paul Siple. Major Murray Wiener, USAF, and IGY representative Edward Goodall, all three veterans of one or more earlier Byrd expeditions. Behind the group is the top of one of the steel radio towers which originally reached 70 feet above the snow surface when erected in 1929.

Ships of Task Force 43 at McMurdo Sound are dwarfed by Mt. Erebus, Antarctica's only active volcano, in the background.   U. S. NAVY PHOTOGRAPH

Aerial view of Mt. Erebus, showing the volcano cone.   U. S. NAVY PHOTOGRAPH

A Globemaster wings its way over the Queen Maud Range en route back from the South Pole where continental Antarctica rises to an altitude of almost two miles. Here, frigid winds blowing down a funnel-like tributary of the Beardmore Glacier (left) *have stripped these mountainsides bare.* © National Geographic Society

The D-2 tractor driven by CM/3 John Randall of the construction crew hauls a load of fuel barrels to camp from the drop area. U. S. NAVY PHOTOGRAPH

With the temperature in the minus 30's Willi Hough rides on skis behind a 24-foot parachute. Strengthening winds as the polar summer waned soon put an end to this exciting, if chilling, sport.

The foundation for the garage, the first permanent building to be erected, showing how some buildings were sunk into the snow to maintain a uniform roof line for the entire camp. In the rear a paradrop of supplies is coming down.

Front view of the almost completed garage in mid-December. The big Jamesway used by the construction crew can be seen to the left behind the garage.

Above: *Paul Siple* (left) *and Lt.* (jg) *Richard A. Bowers, USN, who supervised station construction examine the mirrored globe later set atop the striped "South Pole."*

Below: *Jack Tuck with the then ten-month-old Bravo.*

might be enhanced by the mere existence of American scientific stations. And with this show of receptiveness, requests for additional stations began moving across the desks of the national programmers.

Before long there was agreement to erect a Byrd Station about 600 miles in the interior of Mary Byrd Land. Defense agreed to activate Finn Ronne's proposal for an American IGY station on the almost inaccessible Filchner Ice Shelf, on the edge of the Weddell Sea. Both stations would require a most exacting effort, for there were enormous complications involved. The Filchner Ice Shelf Base would be under Ronne's command and be called Ellsworth Station, in honor of Lincoln Ellsworth, the American explorer who had made a memorable first transantarctic flight in November, 1935. Another base, named the Wilkes Station after the American discoverer of Wilkes Land, was to be erected on the Clark Peninsula near the Windmill Islands in Vincennes Bay and would be in the charge of Carl Eklund, a scientist who had been at East Base in 1940.

It was inevitable that we IGY scientists would try to push our luck even further. "Wouldn't it be nice to put up a station at the geographic South Pole at Latitude Ninety South?" a scientist mused one afternoon. At once silence fell over the room.

The thought of such a station was enough to inspire awe in any scientist. Only Scott and Amundsen had reached the Pole by land, and even from the air only Admiral Byrd and his crews had on two occasions gazed down upon the frozen plateau. The first time for Byrd had been in 1929 and the second, almost twenty years later, during Highjump. Certainly the meager literature on the Pole showed it to be one of the most desolate spots on the globe.

All of us who were veterans of the Antarctic were concerned about the dangers in establishing a South Pole Station. True, such a station would provide the cornerstone for the planned three world-wide chains that would cut through the continents and end at the Pole. True, such a station would also provide welcome information on Antarctic weather, since little was known about weather conditions in the interior of the continent. And true also that since the South Pole was enveloped in darkness for six continuous months it offered, more than any other place on Antarctica, a splendid opportunity to learn whether the absence of sunlight in the ionosphere played a significant role in influencing radio signals. Yet the undeniable fact was that the path to the South Pole was fraught with great dangers, as I pointed out to the National Academy of Sciences, which was sponsoring the American aspects of IGY. The glaciers along the way were filled with dangerous crevasses. Even if tractors were to make the traverse along the routes taken by Amundsen, Scott and Shackleton, their payload would be meager, perhaps a drum or two of oil or a few hundred pounds of food. This would hardly constitute an adequate means for constructing and supplying a scientific station. Furthermore, if delays occurred, tractors were certain to find their antifreeze frozen in temperatures that might well drop to more than one hundred degrees below zero, a temperature man had never lived in before.

No decision regarding a South Pole Station was reached by the time the CSAGI Conference for the international IGY effort met at Rome in September, 1954. Here representatives of the various IGY nations first made public their proposed location of IGY observation stations. And in the course of the meetings, the question arose whether any nation proposed to erect a South Pole Station. Smiles crossed the faces of the delegations at this question. Then suddenly the American delegates popped up with, "We cannot commit ourselves. But we'll ask our government."

A radiogram to the Defense Department evoked an evasive reply to the effect that while they were not certain they could, we should tell the assembly the United States would try. Of course this was a noncommittal answer, but without the knowledge of what might be entailed in the construction of such a base, the American Government was unwilling to be more positive.

The conference did not push the matter further and gave no additional thought to constructing a South Pole Station. Then the next July the First Antarctic Planning Conference of the IGY was held at Paris. I attended these week-long sessions as a member of the American delegation which had no intentions of discussing the proposed Pole Station.

The chief function of this conference was to establish the ground rules for the eleven nations expected to erect stations in the Antarctic. These countries were Argentina, Australia, Chile, France, Japan, New Zealand, Norway, South Africa, the United Kingdom and the United States. There was also talk that the U.S.S.R., whose delegates had not arrived when the conference got underway, planned to erect IGY stations in the Antarctic.

Here, in a continual rush from one meeting room to another, we discussed such matters as methods for communicating between stations, mutual aid among all the stations, and we told of the kinds of equipment, such as planes, dog teams and radios, we would be able to make available in case of emergency. But far more important than these were the discussions as to methods of making simultaneous standardized scientific observations in our various fields of activity.

However, the chief purpose of the Paris conference was to enable each participating nation to outline its aims on the continent and disclose where it planned scientific stations. The British and Argentines could not understand our desire to erect Ellsworth Station in an area they claimed as their property. Other claiming nations revealed a similar distaste for "foreign" IGY stations. In the region centering in the Graham-Palmer Peninsula, the bitter rivals—Britain, Chile and Argentina—planned to name their already existing cluster of more than twenty stations as IGY stations. Evidence later pointed to the fact that some of these stations sanctioned by the IGY employed few, if any, qualified IGY observers.

The question of a South Pole Station was not brought up as the conference proceeded. But then fate intervened in the guise of the Soviet Union. Russian scientists arrived late to the Paris meeting, and shortly after their arrival startled the assembly by several suggestions. They first suggested including mapping surveys and geological studies, a plan which was quickly ruled out by countries with claims in the Antarctic who wanted no "foreigners" mapping territories they considered their own.

Hardly had this proposal died away than the Russians dropped a bombshell. The Soviet Government, they said, planned to erect a station at the geographic South Pole. All eyes turned to the Americans for argument. However, we of the American delegation realized that the attitude of the American Government had not changed essentially since its noncommittal statement at the previous Rome meeting.

Taking up the reins, Prof. G. Laclavère, the French chairman of the conference, turned toward the Russians and shook his head. "I'm sorry," he told them, "but we have accepted the offer of the United States to erect and man a South Pole Station. We don't think there should be two stations there." Actually, we had not gone anywhere near that far, but now we were committed, especially so since the Russians subsequently accepted the chairman's alternate suggestion that they build a station at the Geomagnetic Pole.

I remarked, as we left the conference, that there could be no backing away now from "doing the impossible." Somehow we would have to erect a self-sufficient village at the Pole to house and support a group of Americans. It promised to be the most difficult construction job in history.

Chapter 8

OPERATION DEEP FREEZE I

ONE morning in early spring of 1955, an Army official dropped a memo on my desk blotter. "You'll be interested in this, Paul," he said with a smile. "But don't you dare agree—we need you here."

The memo was from the Navy to the Army requesting assistance in the construction of American IGY bases in the Antarctic. One paragraph that caught my eye was the request for "some Weasels, helicopters and Dr. Paul A. Siple."

Flattering though it was to be put in the same class with essential vehicles, especially the Weasel which is a polar-type Jeep, my primary obligation lay with the Army's basic research program. "Besides," I argued, "I've already spent a lot of time outside the office on IGY and National Antarctic Program matters."

Of course, the Army agreed with me. However, the deciding desk in the Pentagon Building did not. I was informed shortly afterward that the Department of Defense considered my temporary change of assignment a small enough investment for the Army to make in the Antarctic program. "You will phase out your present work and report as early as practical to Rear Admiral George J. Dufek, Commander of Task Force 43," came the order.

True to his word, Admiral Byrd had recommended Dufek's selection as head of the Navy's logistics force to construct the USNC-IGY's Antarctic stations. When George had gone on the retired list as a rear admiral, Byrd and others besieged Congress to pass a special bill permitting him to command as a rear admiral, even though he was on the retired list.

Headquarters for Task Force 43 were in the decrepit old Post Office Building in the heart of Washington, D. C., where business was not only being conducted in offices there but also in corridors. Desks were piled high with notebooks, memos and stubs of pencils, and phones jangled continually when I joined Dufek for duty. A note of frenzy hung heavily about the ancient building, for Task Force 43's assignment was to have all the American scientific stations erected and operating in the Antarctic by early 1957—less than two years away. This meant planning the entire job, purchasing the supplies, carting them to the Antarctic, delivering men and materials to station sites and constructing the camps so the scientists could live undisturbed and in safety while they made their geophysical observations.

There were several slots where Dufek could have utilized my services, for by now I was experienced in all phases of Antarctic living, from logistics, to exploring, to scientific work. Thus, when George gave me the post of Director of Scientific Projects for Task Force 43, it was with the understanding that I would be called upon to help out as a consultant on all other phases of this gigantic undertaking.

Unfortunately, when George assigned me to my work with his task force, he was unable to provide me with desk space. The few offices he had managed to commandeer were already crowded with naval personnel, and I found myself walking up and down hallways in discussing work projects. This ludicrous situation lasted several weeks and must have been a matter of considerable perplexity to staid officials who had to pace the floors with me in order to conduct their business. Working conditions improved somewhat when I had at last found a desk jammed against the wall of a small room occupied by eight others. However, this presented its own problem for not only did the desk have no phone, but was also shared by two other men. When all three of us showed up at the same time, we were faced with quite a dilemma.

It required the unwitting aid of President Eisenhower before I was able to rest my weary legs. When the President appointed Admiral Byrd as Officer in Charge of the U.S. Antarctic Program, Byrd acquired an office in the old Post Office. "Use my office, Paul, when I'm not here," he told me. Working without salary or expense payment, Byrd arrived and departed as he saw fit. He would come to Washington for two or three weeks at a time and then would be away about an equal period. Later on, when he put in more time in Washington, he had another desk brought into his office so I would not suddenly be back again in the hall or the crowded little room.

By the time I returned from the Paris IGY Antarctic Conference in July, 1955, a further expansion in American Antarctic planning was in progress. For with the decision to erect a South Pole Station, Task Force 43's job broadened. Despite the hot humid summer that lay like a wet blanket over Washington, the Task Force's activities now acquired the appropriate name of "Operation Deep Freeze."

There would be a series of Deep Freezes, we agreed. During Deep Freeze I, which would operate during the Antarctic summer lasting from about November, 1955, to March, 1956, we would establish the Little America Station and a tractor scouting party would stab its way 600 miles or so into the Marie Byrd Land to find a suitable site for the Byrd Station. Locations would also be scouted for the Ellsworth and Wilkes Stations. Also during Deep Freeze I, the materials necessary for the South Pole Station and Little America would be delivered to the Antarctic. The Navy planned to establish a South Pole support base at McMurdo Sound, on the smoking volcanic island which Ross had discovered and from which the renowned Captain Scott had begun his ill-fated trip to the South Pole forty-five years before. It was hoped, but only hoped, that the bay ice at McMurdo would support heavily laden planes flying in from New Zealand some 2,000 miles away.

Deep Freeze I would also include phases of the National Program, as well as some preliminary IGY work. For instance, there would be the various science programs that I was co-ordinating, plus an extensive aerial exploration of more of the still unseen portions of the continent.

Deep Freeze II would come into existence the following July at the beginning of the government's fiscal year and the field operations would begin approximately in October of 1956. During this operation, the remaining stations would be constructed from supplies gathered together at McMurdo and Little America. Once these stations were up, plans called for them to be manned by the science observers so they would be in full swing when the International Geophysical Year began on July 1, 1957.

The enormity of the task was at once apparent. For somehow between mid-1955 and the fast-approaching fall season, Deep Freeze I had to be put together if the Task Force were to maintain its tight time schedule. Once its ships left American ports there could be no turning back for items inadvertently omitted. As a result, the tempo of our activities gained speed like an onrushing train as the days relentlessly passed. Daily course charts outlined dozens of vital meetings, almost all of which affected the outcome of the operation. There were often as many as a half-dozen meetings proceeding simultaneously, and by rushing here, then there, one might encompass several minutes of each, though a few weeks at this pace brought one close to physical collapse.

In a single phase of the work, as Director of Scientific Projects for the Task Force, I found myself involved in a host of scientific proposals from various government agencies. For example, the Hydrographic Office wanted to conduct oceanographic surveys, to make sonic observations in order to improve the information available to officers who would later take ships to the Antarctic. The Army Quartermaster Corps wanted to study the polar clothing in use, with a special project involving a new insulated boot I had helped invent. A university research contractor for the Office of Naval Research planned physiological studies of the effect of the cold on men working in the Antarctic. Still another project was one planned by the Army Signal Corps, which involved studying radio wave propagation across ice and through snow. There was also an Air Force project to study ice landings and take-offs.

Although the Navy was responsible for freighting in all material and constructing Antarctic stations, the USNC-IGY as the customer of the station had many decisions and tasks of its own to complete for Deep Freeze I. As a member of this group I was also heavily involved with these. At times I found myself figuratively sitting on both sides of the conference table at once. There were science buildings to be erected at each station. What were they to look like? Which types of scientific equipment would go to which stations? Where should the science buildings and meteorological balloon inflation shelters be erected within the camps? How many men would be needed at each of the planned stations and what science programs would they conduct? Where should the ionosphere antennae be located so that they would not interfere with radio operations? Where would certain buildings designed for making visual observations be located so they would be free from interference from snowdrifts and from the smoke and vapor created by the rest of the camp? These and other questions required sensible and swift answers.

Unlike Task Force 43, which had to consider all expenditures in the light of how they would look to the Navy's comptroller, the IGY, perhaps because they did not actually control their own funds but only told the National Science Foundation how to spend earmarked money, took a more casual view toward its financing. The IGY did not let contracts directly for the material, equipment and research it was undertaking. Appropriations came from Congress to the National Science Foundation, which then used this money, after deducting a

part for overhead, to finance contracts with other government agencies
and with universities and research institutions, which in turn hired
personnel, provided services, and bought scientific equipment under
the National Academy's USN-IGY. In the process the money was
subjected to further attrition as each agency through which it passed
deducted a generous amount for its own overhead.

Besides handling the National Program's scientific work and meeting with the IGY on its varied problems involved in Operation Deep
Freeze, I had sufficient calls on my remaining time to keep me occupied almost around the clock. A series of incredibly difficult problems had to be solved even before construction or fabrication contracts
could be let. There were questions of transportation, housing, clothing,
food, and a host of other matters which had to be answered without
delay. Part of one of my days might be spent in a meeting to determine the design of the Antarctic houses, another on materials and
tools; still another on headgear. Housing had to be simple for construction purposes, yet able to withstand the violent jolts of the wild
Antarctic winds.

The normal routine established by Dufek was to place a senior
naval officer in charge of each meeting. This meant that since only
three or four polar specialists at most were available to participate
in the meetings, the majority of the men in attendance had little
knowledge of cold weather requirements. Initially this brought on a
problem, because the naval chairmen conducted the meetings on the
Hellenistic principle of a single vote for each participant. Fortunately,
a majority of those who did not know the Antarctic voted with the
Antarctic veterans, on most important matters at least. However, it
was sometimes difficult to find the proper solution because the Navy's
logisticians wished to supply the most readily available gear, without
due consideration as to what was best suited to actual conditions.
Thus it was not enough to know the answers to problems which one
had learned through long and hard experience. One also had to have
the patience of Job to spell out the details.

For example, there was the matter of hand gear. At one meeting
I argued that we required three types of mittens for different situations.
"Why not only one?" others asked disapprovingly.

"Because one type will be too heavy and the other too light under
most circumstances." A glove was best for the period aboard ship and
for the Antarctic summertime when dexterity is important. From freezing to somewhat below zero a leather work mitten with removable
wool liners became the proper hand gear. And in extreme cold a

special mitten with a maximum thickness of 1½ inches was best. "Why not a thicker mitten than that?" I was asked.

"Research shows," I replied, "that a thicker mitten will actually do little if any good. A thicker mitten means one with a larger surface area and this soon runs into the law of diminishing returns because the rate of heat loss over the larger area increases faster than the rate of conservation provided by increasing the thickness of the insulation."

The enormity of the task involved in Operation Deep Freeze I can perhaps best be illustrated by enumerating some of the supplies we had to take with us. Besides 1,800 men, 30 dogs, three icebreakers, two cargo ships, one oiler, one auxiliary cargo ship and nineteen planes, we also had to plan for and procure household supplies, lumber and millwork, tools and hardware, building supplies, scientific equipment, heavy equipment and trail gear—a listing of which filled literally hundreds of pounds of order sheets. To mention the larger items, we required Weasels, tractors and Sno-Cats, more than 15,000 drums of fuel oil, jeeps, fork-lift trucks and 30-ton rollers for leveling snow. Among the smaller items, we had to keep constantly alert to make certain, for instance, that we had brass and copper nails because steel building nails would interfere with magnetic readings. Then, of course, there were problems of screening out a certain number of items well-meaning individuals had solicitously added to the lists—such as the electric floor-waxing and polishing machines someone suggested buying for each base.

Problems of logistics required more than planning and collecting materials. There was also the job of making delivery. For instance, when Task Force 43 first considered means to deliver equipment, men and material to the Geographic South Pole, the initial thought of the inexperienced was to use tractors. However, this notion was quickly discarded as impractical in view of the distances involved and the crevasses lining the route. Then others raised the bizarre possibility of using blimps.

The inevitable conclusion was that the task could be accomplished only with planes that could either land at the Pole or drop more than 500 tons of materials including ton tractors to construction crews on the icy plateau below. Altogether it would be a feat of enormous proportions, considering that the planes would first have to fly more than 2,000 miles from New Zealand to a manufactured-ice runway at McMurdo before traveling the next hitch of 850 miles to the Pole. Thus, as a precautionary measure, the plans which were developed called for a way station between New Zealand and McMurdo Sound.

Ultimately, this developed into a joint American-New Zealand station at Cape Hallett, a place nestled at the foot of towering mountains and teeming with penguins, on the direct flight route from New Zealand to McMurdo. There would also have to be a refueling and weather station between McMurdo and the Pole during the summer period for the smaller planes which would freight in personnel. This station, manned by only three or four men, was first established near the foot of Liv Glacier, close to the spot where Byrd had set his gas cache for his first flight to the Pole. Subsequently it was moved out onto the Ross Shelf nearer to the foot of Beardmore Glacier, the mountain pass Shackleton and Scott had traversed to reach the polar plateau, since this was more in the direct air route to the Pole.

As the preparations for Deep Freeze I neared their climax, Admiral Byrd requested me to devote more of my time to his over-all assignment. Byrd's authority concerned all phases of Deep Freeze except the direct command of the Task Force 43 in its actual operations. Operational command of ships, equipment and men belonged to Dufek as Task Force Commander.

Byrd's request proved disquieting to me, for I was officially attached to Dufek's office. I did not want to offend the Navy, which had assigned me to Dufek, but at the same time I had strong ties to Byrd.

For a time I attempted a compromise by working with Byrd as much as I could while continuing with my regular assignment. However, serving two masters is not the best of arrangements, and in short order the situation disintegrated further when Byrd insisted I work with him full-time. He could not understand it otherwise, because our lives and interests had been linked together now a quarter of a century. And though our relationship had changed to partnership over the years, I could not bring myself to point out to him the situation he was creating between me and Task Force 43.

Gradually Byrd was absorbing my energies to serve him. Now as his Deputy Officer in Charge of the U.S. Antarctic Program, one of my functions became that of keeping tabs on the activities of the Task Force. However, since most things operational reported directly to Dufek, little information came my way. In addition, Dufek had three far-flung elements in his command. At Davisville, Rhode Island, the actual logistics for Deep Freeze I were being assembled. There was also the air station at Patuxent, Maryland, where the planes and air crews of Deep Freeze I were being tested and trained. Only on a single occasion did I manage to visit Patuxent with Dufek. And then, of course, there was the Task Force's main office in the old Washington

Post Office, where I had never even managed to acquire a desk of my own.

Byrd and I were especially concerned that the Task Force obtain the use of the best airplanes. For Byrd's first flight over the South Pole in 1929, he had diligently procured the most modern plane then available. Now for Deep Freeze I we wanted the Task Force to invite the Air Force to use their very long-range reconnaissance aircraft or some B-36's. However, the Navy preferred to try to do the job itself, using its own R5D's, which had a much smaller range, but could operate from ice strips in the Antarctic.

Byrd was far from well and this fight did his health no good. The stout heart that had carried him through so many dangerous adventures was weakened, his hair had turned white and he had lost much weight, but only once would he admit that he was not the Byrd of old. This occurred one day in the office when he spoke to me about the future. "Before long," he said, "this Office will become a permanent government agency." He stared at me. "And when it does, I want you to be in charge."

This was his first intimation that his health was failing. And it ended as swiftly as he had mentioned the future of our Office. "As for now," he said, "let's get on with Deep Freeze One."

Chapter 9

DEEP FREEZE I IN OPERATION

B Y November of 1955, Task Force 43 had completed its arduous planning and preparatory tasks in record time and we were ready for the job ahead.

"All set," came the word, and three cargo ships loaded with an array of equipment ranging from rubber bands to tractors set off from Davisville, Rhode Island, for the rendezvous in New Zealand. About the same time two icebreakers, the *Glacier* and *Edisto,* left from Norfolk and Panama on their mission to tow fuel barges laden with about 550,000 gallons of fuel across the Pacific to New Zealand. Later the icebreakers were to deliver the fuel barges to McMurdo Sound off the Antarctic coast, where they would purposely be frozen into the ice for the winter.

I was apprehensive about several aspects of this highly complex affair. In the rush we had made many decisions without an adequate check. Surely we would discover many necessary items were missing. Men who were full of confidence in the system by which we were proceeding would be damning it soon. But I knew from experience that makeshift materials were often adequate substitutes and that where some men faltered, others whom one hadn't really counted on would step into the breach. Even on his expedition that had carried him all the way to the Pole, Amundsen had forgotten to take along snow shovels. And on Byrd's first expedition to the Antarctic in 1928, we had hit the ice pack with barrels of rancid meat and lowest-grade vegetables. Yet not only had we survived that two-year stay, but most of us had actually emerged no less robust that when we had left home.

Early in December Admiral Byrd and I left by commercial plane to meet the Task Force in New Zealand. The strain the past several months had placed on the Admiral was revealed by the many deep lines on his pale face. But once we were in the air, the promise of new adventures relaxed him. When we stopped at Dallas, he was highly amused by girl pickets, aspiring to the right to explore Antarctica, parading up and down the airport carrying signs that read: BYRD UNFAIR TO WOMEN. This demonstration was obviously inspired by a news story which had quoted Byrd as saying that the reason Little America was the quietest place on earth was because no woman had ever set foot there. Later on the West Coast, where we made another stop, his spark was momentarily dimmed when a newsman interrogated him rudely during a press conference.

But once we were over the Pacific his spirits revived. With a broad sweep he reminisced about his early life and talked about the Virginia Byrds and the trio of brothers who had been amusingly named Tom, Dick and Harry by their parents. His marine-blue eyes shone as he recalled his adventure in traveling around the world alone when he was only twelve. He told about his consuming interest in active sports, though he never particularly enjoyed watching others at play. At the Naval Academy he had broken a leg twice: once while playing football against Princeton and again when he fell from the flying rings preparing for a gymnastics contest. These accidents had left him with a bad leg that had forced his retirement from the Navy shortly before World War I because he was judged medically unable to stand watch. Nevertheless, he had talked his way past the Medical Examining Board in 1918 and returned to naval aviation.

A modest man, Byrd did not talk of his twenty-two citations and special commendations, nine of which were for bravery and two for extraordinary heroism in saving the lives of others. Nor did he boast of the medals he had amassed, which included the Congressional Medal of Honor, the Congressional Life Saving Medal, the Distinguished Service Medal, the Flying Cross and the Navy Cross.

Instead, his talk was of minor matters, of adventures that went awry or did not turn out as expected. There was the accident to his plane that had enabled Lindbergh to become the first man to fly the Atlantic nonstop to Europe in a land plane. Later, Byrd had made the trip with Bert Acosta, George Noville and Bernt Balchen, though they had almost failed to reach France. They had crashed into the sea off the coast and had had to swim for their lives.

"How did those early years go for you, Paul?" he asked.

"Not so adventurous or romantic as yours," I said, waving off his query. Born in 1908 in Montpelier, Ohio, I had moved to Erie, Pennsylvania, at ten with my parents and sister Carrol when my father went to work as a machinist with General Electric. In those early years, we had moved almost annually, perhaps a harbinger of my later exploring career. We had been a religious and necessarily frugal family.

"Where did you learn so much about sailing ships?" Byrd asked. "The crew on the *City of New York* on our first expedition said you knew more about running that old bark than many of them did."

"Sea Scouts," I said. "We had a replica of the flagship *Niagara* which Oliver Hazard Perry commanded in the War of 1812. It stood in our harbor in Erie and we Sea Scouts used it for training. That's where I learned the nomenclature and seagoing knots."

"How did you actually decide to enter the competition to be the Boy Scout to go with me?" asked Byrd. "Of course, mind you, I'm glad you did—that is, in a way."

"I remember it well, because it almost started a furore in the family," I said. "My sister was to get married on a Monday in June, 1928. That previous Friday I had gone with several other Scouts to begin setting up tents for a summer camp at Camp Thomas, about twenty miles west of Erie on Lake Erie. Although I was only nineteen, I was to direct the camp that summer.

"When my father drove out over the dirt roads in our 1913 touring car to bring me home, all the other boys except one insisted upon returning home for the weekend. I could not leave that single boy in camp alone, nor could I agree to totally desert our unguarded equipment. 'But I'll be home on Monday in plenty of time for the wedding,' I promised my father. He took the load of boys back to Erie.

"And that night when Sandy McGavern and I prepared for bed, Sandy suddenly turned to me and said, 'Are you entering the contest to be the Boy Scout who's going along with Byrd?' I had never heard of your contest."

"Heaven protect those hard-working public relations people who had been rushing up and down the country publicizing it." Byrd shook his head. "But what was the family furore it caused?"

"Well, on Monday I was back in Erie learning that I was barely eligible to send in an application. You wanted a Boy Scout between the ages of seventeen and twenty and fortunately I was still nineteen. Then I rushed to the public library, where I forgot my sister's wedding and began reading about the Antarctic. That's where my father found me, an hour before the scheduled time for the wedding."

"I'm sorry I upset your household," Byrd said politely.

"What was your reaction to me when you saw me in New York as one of the six finalists?" I asked him. In all our years together I had never known.

Byrd laughed. "The minute I saw you, I knew you were the one. In fact, so did your opponents. Don't you remember that Dr. West asked each of the boys to list which of the others he thought most worthy to go with me? Well, all of them picked you." He drummed on the window. "It's funny the picture some people carry in their minds of the way a Boy Scout should look. I told George Noville, my exec, who was to have gone with us, that he would have to look out for your welfare and he wailed, 'But I don't want to be a nursemaid to a little tyke. What did I do to deserve this?'

"Of course, he didn't know then that you were over six feet and built like a brick wall. A thin brick wall, that is. I remember," Byrd laughed, "the sport the doctors had giving you your physical examination before we left. Especially the stop watch incident."

"Oh, that," I snorted. The doctor had asked me to hold my arms out. Then he had put a stop watch in one hand and left the room. I didn't know what to do, so I continued to hold my arms outstretched.

Finally, he returned, retrieved the watch and muttered, "Thirteen minutes. Hmmmm."

My mind went back over the various expeditions. "The men on that first expedition were the most adventurous," I said. "They were real soldiers of fortune."

"McGuinness most of all," said Byrd. "Did you know he had British flags tattooed on the soles of his feet? Few things gave him more pleasure than to stamp hard as he walked."

The British Empire had had a price on Charlie McGuinness' head, for he had run arms for the Irish and on another occasion had deserted the British Army to fight for the other side. There was hardly a war during his time in which he did not participate. Besides the Irish Revolution, he had fought on both sides during World War I. And after our Antarctic expedition, he had later fought on the Loyalist side in the Spanish Civil War in the mid-thirties. Then he went to Russia from whence he sent his wife a post-card Soviet divorce and reportedly became an admiral, though his individuality shone through so brightly that he ended up in jail.

"But McGuinness was certainly naïve for a man who got around the world the way he did," I told Byrd. "Why, do you know that he actually believed albatrosses carried their eggs under their wings? 'They're always at sea, aren't they?' he yelled at me one time when I scoffed, 'and name anyone who has ever seen an albatross sit down on anything but water.' "

On the way back from Little America I, McGuinness had regaled us with tales of his fantastic adventures with Count von Luckner, the daring German raider of World War I. His tales were so wild and woolly that most of us enjoyed them as fiction and doubted that he'd ever met Von Luckner. When we came into New York Harbor on the dirty, unpainted tramp steamer, the *Eleanor Bolling,* we were shunted off like orphans while the colorful *City of New York* was surrounded by harbor craft. Suddenly a dazzling speedboat had come roaring across the harbor and circled us. "Ahoy, Mac!" a voice boomed. It was Von Luckner looking for his friend.

"And what about the crowbar on that first expedition?" Byrd clapped his hands. "Vic Czegka's crowbar."

"Oh, *that.*" I laughed. We had had a snowmobile on the first expedition, a Ford mounted on caterpillar treads. Sverre Strom, the strongest man in camp, George Black and Jim Feury took the snowmobile out one day to lay depots far from camp. Before they left they asked Vic Czegka, our machinist, if they could borrow a crowbar.

"Take good care of it," he bellowed threateningly at them, "and don't come back without it." A former Marine master sergeant, Vic was as tough as they come, and was known especially for the way he guarded our precious tools as if they were made of gold.

Only eighty miles from Little America, they were caught in soft snow on the Barrier. A raging blizzard howled and they could not move the snowmobile. Finally they abandoned the machine and headed back for camp on foot. It was a dangerous trip, yet Vic's words rang in their cold ears.

So it was that three weary, chilled, stumbling figures arrived back in camp dragging a 20-pound crowbar on their survival sled. "Here it is, Vic," Strom gasped. "We brought your damn crowbar back."

Vic had laughed wildly and taken the three men to his bunk. Under his mattress he showed them six other crowbars!

Subjects changed rapidly and later Byrd and I talked about the decision of the Navy on Deep Freeze I to permit liquor on the Antarctic Continent. We had both opposed it, I most strenuously as a member of the "Liquor Committee" of Task Force 43. In the past we had always forbidden liquor on expeditions, not because we were teetotalers but because there was no way to know how men already keyed up would react under its influence, and a group of isolated individuals battling the elements had sufficient problems without adding to their burden. "Remember on the second expedition when Tom Poulter discovered that our doctor had smuggled in about thirty cases of liquor?" I cut in. After Tom had confiscated the whole supply, he wasted little time emptying the bottles in the snow.

"The way that poor doctor groaned when he found out what Tom had done," Byrd said, "was enough to make anyone sorry for him. Of course, I didn't think so when he declared himself unfit to remain on the expedition and demanded to be evacuated at once."

The doctor had actually left us and for a few days Byrd had considered calling off the entire expedition. For how could an expedition get along without a doctor? Fortunately the British oceanographic vessel, the *Discovery II,* had heard about our problem and picked up a doctor in New Zealand for us. Later this second doctor transferred to the *Bear* in the ice pack and arrived at Little America II just before the Ross Sea froze up and the dark winter period began.

Our reminiscing aboard the plane over the Pacific had been so pleasant that it seemed no time at all before we were landing in Hawaii. We were to remain here only a short while before resuming our flight to New Zealand, and here Byrd pulled a practical joke that was in reality a typical warm gesture. We had gone for a walk on the hotel grounds when he left me to enter a phone booth. "Paul," he called out to me, "I have a friend on the other end of the line I'd like to have you talk to."

I took the receiver from him and cautiously said "Hello." The voice on the other end turned out to belong to my wife Ruth in Arlington, Virginia. She hadn't known when the operator got her to the phone that she would be speaking to me. I glanced over at Byrd and found him beaming like a proud uncle.

The weather turned hot and uncomfortable by the time we touched down at the Fiji Islands. Byrd was tired now and much of the joy of the trip had evaporated. It had been so hot in his berth that he had been unable to sleep. In addition, the Navy had assigned him an aide when we left the States and the aide had been drinking steadily all the way across the Pacific, to Byrd's great annoyance.

When we finally arrived at Auckland, New Zealand, Byrd needed a day or so to recuperate. But the entire press corps was on hand for an interview and the New Zealand Air Force put on a dress parade in his honor. Then after we spent the night at the Governor General's Mansion in Wellington, I accompanied Byrd on a rigorous round of speechmaking, dedicating and laying wreaths. Soon the Admiral was all but completely exhausted. Nor was his temper improved when he learned that the naval aide had fallen victim to the D.T.'s and could not handle any of the ceremonial duties or the necessary official liaison with the Task Force and the press.

The plans for Deep Freeze I called for two of our icebreakers, the *Glacier* and *Edisto,* to depart from New Zealand on December 10. Byrd and I were to travel on the *Glacier,* the largest and most modern icebreaker in existence, on her maiden voyage through the ice pack. Dufek, en route to New Zealand aboard the cargo ship *Arneb,* was to leave for the Antarctic when we sent back word that we were through the ice pack and on our way through the Ross Sea to McMurdo Sound at the continent's edge.

I had hoped that Byrd would get a rest on the trip to McMurdo, but this was not to be the case. In fact, we were off to a bad start as soon as we boarded the *Glacier.* When we came up the gangplank, a roomful of reporters was already assembled to interview Byrd. However, the Admiral wanted to be shown his quarters first. Through an unfortunate blunder, Byrd's cabin proved to be an all but unfurnished room below the water line. Abandoned personal effects of the former occupant still littered the cabin. Adjoining rooms of the ship's junior officers were luxuriously carpeted and equipped by comparison. I watched Byrd's face as he took in the ill-equipped room he was supposed to occupy. Admirals just are not quartered below the water line and beside the engine room, but he did not protest although I could see he was almost speechless with rage. Even later, though he held a superb press conference, I could see that it still required an obvious effort on his part to control his temper.

Immediately afterward I sought out a captain and Byrd was transferred to better quarters, if not the proper ones. Nevertheless, the memory of the indignity remained, even though Dufek sent Byrd a wire saying: YOUR PRESENCE WITH THE TASK FORCE IS AN INSPIRATION TO ALL OF US.

Nor was the *Glacier*'s voyage to the Antarctic a quiet interlude. The *Glacier* had been christened only the previous June. Measuring 310 feet in length, the ship displaced 8,300 tons and her top cruising speed was nineteen knots. Her fourteen diesel engines developed 20,000 horsepower and she could crush her way through a fifteen-foot thickness of ice.

Unfortunately, the *Glacier* had a round bottom and did not roll normally from side to side the way most other ships do. Instead, she lurched erratically and unpredictably, tossing men and gear about with abandon. The result was that with few exceptions seasickness was common and there were accidents galore. On one wrenching lurch, Admiral Byrd was thrown across his cabin and cut his forehead and nose. "How did you make out in the war?" I asked him when I saw him.

Those who travel by sea from New Zealand to the Antarctic for the first time later speak of their voyage as one passing through the "roaring forties," "furious fifties" and "screaming sixties." This would aptly describe the maiden voyage of the *Glacier*.

And yet I spent many enjoyable hours renewing acquaintanceship with this part of the world that I had not seen since 1947. Until we reached the Antarctic convergence, where the cold water from the Antarctic meets the warm water from the tropics, we were followed by an enormous number of birds, chiefly albatross and mutton birds. On December 14, as we neared basaltic Scott Island, we saw our first ice and experienced our first night of continuous daylight. Then five miles east and south of Scott Island, we met the ice pack.

Fortunately the *Glacier* brought us through the pack by December 16. Through the Ross Sea we steamed and it was not until we were within fifty miles of the continent off McMurdo Sound that we began again to hit thick ice. Now began a careful poking about until we found an open lead on the east side of the Sound and we came to halt on the 18th only two miles off the earth and rock shore, past many seals and close to three Adélie penguin rookeries containing several hundred thousand penguins. Great numbers of skua gulls inhabited the area, big brown hawklike birds that feasted on penguin eggs and youngsters.

It was good to quit the ship for the ice, especially since the temperature in my quarters aboard the *Glacier* had never fallen below eighty degrees. With the aid of a pair of skis I made it to shore, while the men aboard ship put together our Otter, a single-engine plane equipped with fixed skis. Our initial jobs were to set up a preliminary land station and to find and mark an ice landing strip for the planes that would be flying in from New Zealand. With feverish haste the latter job began. As a first precaution we used a chain saw to cut seven feet into the ice, and when we did not reach water at this depth, we concluded that the bay ice would support the big planes. By the 19th, a message went off to Dufek that an 8,000-foot airstrip was ready to receive the eight planes planning to make the flight, and another message went out to six ships of the Task Force fleet to station themselves along the route the planes were to fly.

Admiral Byrd wanted to be present when the historic flight was completed. However, Captain Ketchum, the Task Group Commander, who had the icebreakers under him, announced early on the morning of December 20th that he was sending *Glacier* out a distance of forty miles since it could maneuver well in the ice should a plane be forced down close to shore. Ketchum felt that the other icebreaker, the *Edisto,* which would be arriving in a day or so, had better radio equipment and might be of more use to the incoming planes. Thus Byrd stayed on the *Glacier* and left McMurdo Bay. He said nothing, but I saw the disappointment in his eyes.

Byrd, however, first asked me, because of other duties I had to perform, to be on hand to welcome the planes as his representative. I got off the *Glacier* onto the fast ice with others about thirty-five miles from the site that had been picked for the shore station. We could see the *Edisto* out in the ice, but we had to wait on the ice several hours until she made her way to us. But the time sped past rapidly as a pack of killer whales approached and eyed us hungrily. Their size and appearance were disconcerting to those in the party who had never seen killer whales before. But the whales did not prove to be as big a problem as a single fifteen-inch-high penguin that wandered into our midst and tirelessly bit at and slapped away at some of the men. Finally our adventures ended when the *Edisto* arrived.

Of the eight planes that took off from New Zealand on the 2,250-mile trip to McMurdo Sound, four twin-engined R4D's encountered such strong headwinds that they had to turn back. The other four, two P2V's, long range twin-engine Neptune patrol bombers with ski-wheel landing gear, and two R5D's, four-engine Skymasters with wheel landing gear, touched down safely. However, the pilots of the P2V's failed to spot the runway because a thin skin of snow had covered the surface and thus landed at the camp miles away. Of the R5D's, one had already landed before I reached the airstrip, so I could only report to Byrd having seen one of the planes land.

Nor did I care much by this time because I had gone forty hours without sleep. Quite late at night with the bright sun shining, I joined the pioneer party who had pitched four tents on top of Hut Point, the site of Scott's first expedition. The floors were snow and they had no stoves, but crowding into one of the tents and tumbling into a sleeping bag, I slept until the following noon when I was roused to lend a hand in setting up more tents.

I found the thirty-foot-square house that Scott had erected in 1902 to be in excellent condition, except for the fact that the interior of the building was filled with snow right up to its pyramid-shaped roof. Abundant evidence of that early expedition and others that had later come here lay strewn about the outside of the hut, in the form of tin cans and rope ends.

Later I trudged to Vince's Hill, a small ridge of black volcanic rock about forty feet high right at the end of Hut Point and a few hundred feet away from Scott's hut. Here in honor of Seaman Vince, who fell over the nearby cliff and drowned on March 11, 1902, stood a cross set in the volcanic rubble and held in place by old food boxes. On brown eight-hundred-foot-high Observation Hill south of Scott's hut, I paused before a larger cross erected in memory of Scott's party of five who were lost on their polar venture in 1912.

All of these sights I viewed reverently, for they lent mute evidence to the heroism of those early-day explorers.

But there was little time to dwell on the past. Within a few days our tent camp had grown until it held fifty busy men. A galley tent had sprung up, followed by a mess hall tent where soup became available three times a day to supplement our combat rations. Supplies and equipment were beginning to arrive now, and one of the first things

I saw was a pile of snowshoes which had been brought in as a priority item for snow country, although as long ago as Byrd's first expedition we had found them to be virtually useless in the Antarctic's hard-packed snow. Meanwhile evidence was accumulating that cracks in the thick ice rendered it relatively unsafe for the tractor hauls between Hut Point and the *Edisto,* which lay at the edge of the ice thirty-five miles away.

It was here at Hut Point that I spent my seventh Christmas Eve in the Antarctic. Huddled about a small stove in our drafty tent, we took time out while a few of the men opened packages they had lugged the thousands of miles from home for the occasion. I recall that Dick Bowers, then a young Seabee lieutenant there to carry out the actual construction of the camp, had almost two dozen small packages which his wife had packed and which, when he opened them, proved to contain an assortment of puzzles and games which he distributed to his less fortunate mates. Ike Taylor, our Navy doctor who had five young children back in the States, set the tone of the affair by the obvious joy he got out of watching Dick open his parcels. I also recall that it was that evening that I first met a tall, thin, taciturn young lieutenant named Jack Tuck. With the parcels all open, Captain Dick Black, my companion on former expeditions and now camp master, and I contributed some carefully hoarded cheeses and crackers to the festivities, which concluded on a high note as a group of enlisted men serenaded us from outside with a selection of Christmas carols.

I had remained ashore because Dufek had requested me to select the site for Little America V, which would function as the American IGY's chief scientific station in the Antarctic. The year before, the icebreaker *Atka* on an exploratory trip to the Antarctic had reported that the Bay of Whales and the old Little America sites 450 miles eastward were unsuitable because the two bay ice walls had collided and large portions of the west wall were gone, ending the bay's usefulness for the time being.

My plan was to use the Otter plane to fly to the Bay of Whales area and pick out an appropriate site nearby. But on December 23, the Otter had taken off from a cache of supplies left out on the edge of the sea ice by the departed *Edisto* with a heavy load and had crashed. Fortunately, no one was killed, but the plane was a total wreck and one officer's knee was damaged for life.

This necessarily brought a change in plans that reached me on the 26th. In the meantime, I joined in the local exploratory effort to find a permanent site for the McMurdo Naval Base which was to support the establishment of the South Pole Station.

On December 26, I reported back to the *Glacier* and found both Admirals Byrd and Dufek aboard. The decision now was to head the *Glacier* eastward along the Barrier to the vicinity of the Bay of Whales. From here I would use a helicopter to find a suitable site for Little America V. Byrd was as happy as a boy on this trip, though I warned Dufek and his staff that I had been confidentially informed the Admiral's health was not good and might be endangered if he was aroused emotionally.

As had been reported, the old familiar Bay of Whales was no more, and the walls of the Barrier were sheer perpendicular uprights more than one hundred feet high. Moreover, Admiral Byrd wanted to see the site of Little America I and we went ashore by helicopter. We found the three steel radio towers I had helped erect at Little America I barely protruding above the surface, although they had originally stood some seventy feet high. All that remained of the Second Little America were the tips of five once-high telephone poles, while the tent village we had established as Little America IV on Operation Highjump in 1947 had partly disappeared as a result of the Barrier's calving.

Though I had spent so many years of my life here, there was little time for regrets. "Let's go," I told Lieutenant Colonel Murray Wiener of the Air Force, who had been a member of my West Base in the 1939–41 Expedition. Our helicopter was soon high over the Barrier, roaming the area in the search for a new Little America.

We roamed a hundred miles to the east to the edge of the Edward VII Peninsula, but it was in the Kainan Bay region only twenty-odd miles east of the other Little Americas that I finally found what appeared from the air, at least, to be a good spot for the base. Landing, we made an extensive reconnaissance of the area we had seen from the air. Then after reporting back to the Task Force, I led a trail party inland on skis on a 24-hour trip to make sure that the area I had selected was not full of crevasses. My final camp choice was a flat surface 150 feet high from which one could see the headlands of the bay. Yet it was far enough removed from the edge for safety and was not in the path of gravity winds blowing down into the bay.

It was December 30th when I returned to the ship after pinpointing the site of Little America V. After receiving the thanks of Byrd and Dufek, I fell into bed quite exhausted. Nevertheless, I was up and about by noon the next day and able to help with the unloading of the first tractors and equipment for the IGY Station. And that night, with ships of the Task Force lined up alongside each other under the bright sun, we celebrated the arrival of 1956.

This was perhaps the last show of conviviality between Byrd's and Dufek's staffs. Somehow the feeling had now become rampant among the men of Dufek's large staff that Byrd's mere presence threatened the ascendency of Dufek as "Admiral of the Antarctic." Byrd, who was above such pettiness, ignored the snowballing minor acts of discourtesy both to himself and to all who were veterans of earlier expeditions, but they continued to occur.

Fortunately Byrd had always said, "My peers will never insult me; my inferiors cannot insult me." But other members of his staff were not able to control their feelings as was the Admiral.

It was with a sense of relief that we left Little America V and returned to McMurdo Sound. Byrd's consuming interest in the whole operational activities lay in the exploratory flights the Task Force was to make as part of its Deep Freeze I execution of the National Program. Unfortunately, the Task Force completed seven of its contemplated twelve flights without even informing either Byrd or myself. By the end of Highjump I, about 40 per cent of the continent had been viewed from the air. The program called for Deep Freeze I to fill in 75 per cent of the Antarctic.

We learned after the fact that one of the Deep Freeze flights had created a serious problem in the minds of many in the Task Force. A Marine Corps pilot had returned from an early January, 1956, flight to the South Pole with disturbing "news." The snow at the Pole was so soft and deep, he declared, that planes and men would fall through and disappear. To the inexperienced Task Force officers, this was positive proof that no base should or could be established at the South Pole.

He hadn't landed at the Pole, the officer said, but he had done the next best thing before reaching his conclusion. As his plane circled the Pole, he had cast out three objects: smoke flares, ink, and cardboard. All had ominously disappeared.

Although the planning group was greatly disturbed by the pilot's story, Byrd and I found it highly amusing. In the first place, Amundsen and Scott had both walked over the Pole and had not reported soft snow. Nor had they disappeared in drifts.

As for the scientific investigation made by the pilot, it was as if he had deliberately attempted to be as unscientific as possible. For it was obvious what had happened. The smoke flares he had thrown from the plane had given off white smoke that could not be distinguished from the white surface. As for the ink he threw out, investigation revealed that he had put it in a white balloonlike rubber container which undoubtedly hadn't broken. Nor had the penguin-shaped pieces of cardboard he had tossed overboard helped his testing either, because they were white on one side and must have landed with that side facing up. Finally, at the speed at which the plane was traveling, it would have been most difficult to spot objects of the size of the ones employed.

Nevertheless, when doubts still lingered as a result of the Marine pilot's findings, Byrd and I decided to fly to the Pole and examine the area ourselves. This flight in itself was unusual, for it was the first time Byrd and I had ever flown together. From the second expedition onward, we had operated under a firm rule: we would not fly in the same plane. Byrd always wanted me to check his plane's survival equipment and give my approval before he would fly. Then he wanted me to remain behind to come to his rescue if his plane developed trouble. In return he did the same for me when we were on expeditions together.

However, with a doubt now cast on the feasibility of a South Pole Station, Byrd decided that we should fly together. In fact, he proposed to the Task Force that we should land at the Pole where we would take the deep snow temperature, which would be an approximation of the average winter temperature at the surface, and make other scientific observations that would be useful later in planning the construction of the South Pole Station. Our R5D plane was not ski equipped so we could not attempt a landing at the Pole at this time, and we had to be content with only inspecting the Pole from the air.

Byrd was excited as we took off from the bay ice at McMurdo early on January 8. "Let's take a look at the spots where the Russians are planning their inland IGY stations," he told Lieutenant Commander Henry P. Jorda, our pilot, and Squadron Commander Gordon Ebbe, thus putting into execution an intention he had long nursed privately.

After learning at the Paris IGY meetings that the United States would build a South Pole Station, the Russians had agreed to set up their main base close to the Shackleton Ice Shelf, directly opposite the geographic South Pole from the Graham-Palmer Peninsula. They planned to call this base the Mirny Station after one of the vessels used by Bellingshausen, the Russian Antarctic explorer, in 1820. In addition to this land-based IGY Station at Mirny, the Russians planned another smaller coastal one on the ice-free area discovered during our Operation Highjump in 1947 and named Oasis, and two inland stations: one at the Geomagnetic South Pole, or at the axis of the earth's magnetic field, to be named Vostok Station after the second of Bellingshausen's ships; the other at Sovietskaya, or the "Pole of Inaccessibility," the spot in Antarctica farthest from the sea at Latitude 82° 30′ S and Longitude 56° E.

Now we flew over toward the Russian IGY inland area and examined both the high terrain and air weather conditions. The general area in which Sovietskaya would some day be established proved to be more than 11,000 feet high. From this Pole of Inaccessibility the continental icecap seemed gradually to slope toward the sea, tending to confirm my earlier supposition that Antarctica has two major ice-drainage systems, one emanating from the heights in Marie Byrd Land and the other from a long ridge in the neighborhood of the Pole of Inaccessibility.

However, we did not quite reach the Pole of Inaccessibility itself because thick black clouds loomed up and we had to climb to higher altitudes from which we could no longer see the surface. Thus we turned at the 80th Parallel and flew directly toward the Geographic South Pole along the 90th Meridan East. As we rose to higher altitudes, I glanced toward Byrd and saw that he was in obvious distress. Traveling with a weakening heart at 15,000 feet had made him airsick and he appeared to be suffering from the diminished supply of oxygen which had affected the other passengers as well. "Don't bother, Paul," he said to me when he caught my look of concern. "It must be something I ate for breakfast. I'll be over it in a minute," he added reassuringly.

Looking down from the plane, I suddenly caught sight of the central polar plateau, which Shackleton, Amundsen, Scott and Byrd himself had previously described. Unlike the Ross Ice Shelf, which was like a second home to me, the polar plateau seemed permeated with an aura of deep mystery. Below there lay only snow and more snow. I had to admit to myself that if any place on earth one could find a spot that seemed filled with nothingness, this was it.

Jorda overshot the Pole by forty miles before he realized his position. Then, returning, he circled the Pole three times. So this is where Amundsen and Scott almost met, I thought. And here brave Shackleton had yearned to stand, boss of the Antarctic just as he was "Boss" to all his associates.

"The South Pole doesn't look any different from the way it did on my 1929 and 1947 flights," Byrd said, interrupting my thoughts. I watched as he stared transfixed at the plateau beneath us.

As we hovered over the Pole area, I busily mapped and compared the snow surface with that of other areas with which I was familiar. The Pole snow was obviously hard packed and broken only by *sastrugi,* or snow ridges on the surface formed by the wind. Carefully I sketched the direction of the sastrugi patterns. The sastrugi were shaped like fantail fish with definite heads and long wriggly tails. Their direction indicated that the prevailing winds blew from the general direction of the unexplored portion of the continent lying toward Africa and generally referred to as the African Quadrant. Altogether, the picture of the surface was that of a hard-top area broken spasmodically by sastrugi. "It's quite safe for planes to land here if they have ski landing gear," I commented to Byrd, who nodded agreement.

We returned to McMurdo some 800 miles away by way of Beardmore Glacier. And as we dropped in altitude over the Ross Ice Shelf, Byrd began to feel better. The speed at which we crossed the Barrier reminded me of the long week of torture we had gone through in 1934 to set up Byrd's Advance Base one hundred miles from Little America II. By the time we climbed down the ladder at McMurdo, Byrd was his usual smiling self again. "There is no danger of encountering deep snow at the South Pole," he assured the Task Force planners. "You can go ahead with plans to establish a Pole Station this coming fall. In fact, maybe I'll be there."

A few days later the Soviet ship *Ob* arrived in Antarctic waters to explore the areas where the Soviet bases would be situated. Hardly had they landed when Byrd sent a message to them:

> WELCOME TO WILKES LAND. HOPE YOU ARE HAVING GOOD LUCK FINDING YOUR IGY BASE SITE. WE RECENTLY FLEW OVER INTERIOR IN VICINITY OF YOUR PLANNED INLAND BASES. SURFACE DOES NOT APPEAR ROUGH, BUT GLACIAL PLATEAU RANGES BETWEEN 11,000 AND 13,000 FEET ELEVATION. WE WOULD LIKE TO EXCHANGE WEATHER INFORMATION. SIPLE JOINS ME IN SENDING OUR BEST WISHES FOR SUCCESS IN OUR INTERNATIONAL EFFORT IN SCIENCE.

All through early January of 1956 an atmosphere of gloom hung over McMurdo. On January 6, the supply ship *Wyandot* had unloaded a mammoth 30-ton D-8 tractor on the bay ice for delivery to Hut Point about 40 miles away. Along the trail a young Navy driver named

Richard T. Williams attempted to take the tractor across a narrow crack in the ice. Suddenly the ice broke and sent the tractor plunging into the water below. Williams had no chance to escape and perished with his machine. In his memory the McMurdo supply base adopted the name of "Williams Air Operating Facility."

After Williams' death concern grew lest there be more accidents. This concern reached the always safety-conscious Byrd a few days after our South Pole flight when his son, Dick, Jr., Murray Wiener and I went by helicopter to Cape Royds to visit Shackleton's camp and then on to Cape Evans to Scott's second base. It was a leisurely excursion on which we intended to soak up the atmosphere of those early expeditions. I had assumed that our pilot would maintain contact with Williams A.O.F. during our seventy-mile round trip. Unfortunately, he did not and when we returned Byrd was considerably upset. In fact, I learned he had requested Dufek to send out a search mission.

As January ebbed, Byrd grew anxious to leave. We had achieved our main goals in Deep Freeze I, he pointed out, and there was little need to linger. His attitude was in sharp contrast with that which he had exhibited on Operation Highjump. I recalled that when departure time came in 1947, a striking sunset had turned the sky into a Kodachrome world. Even as the last call had been shouted, Byrd had kept his eyes fixed on the iridescent sky. "But I don't want to go yet, Paul," he had said, shaking his head.

But times had changed. The small discourtesies exhibited toward Byrd by Task Force officers who felt Byrd represented the past had continued without abatement, and the strain of ignoring them had grown wearing to a man whose temper could be Wagnerian when he was provoked. Time after time I could see the anger creep along the entire length of his body and then subside as his words came out steady, even casual.

The beginning of February, Byrd asked me to arrange for our departure from the Antarctic. I realized that my leaving with him would create a problem, since technically I was on Dufek's staff and subject to his orders. However, I soon learned that the Task Force had no particular desire to have me remain but was almost insultingly willing to have Byrd and me take our leave.

Fortunately, Commander John Cadwalder, a good man and officer, could be entrusted to carry out the co-ordination of scientific work of Deep Freeze I which I was overseeing through to completion.

And so on February 3, Byrd and I pulled out of McMurdo Sound and headed for home. For Byrd it was his last departure from the Antarctic. His wisdom had been responsible for bringing about the great new era of Antarctic activity. Others would carry on his work of exploration, making even greater use of the scientific and mechanical tools of the modern world. None could live long enough to hope to make a greater contribution than he had.

Chapter 10

TIME FOR DECISION

IMMEDIATELY upon our return to Washington, Admiral Byrd sought a clarification of his position as Officer in Charge of the U. S. Antarctic Program. The behavior of Task Force 43 had cast strong doubt on the role of our Office, and Byrd now insisted that the intent of President Eisenhower's original order be spelled out.

Even before we left McMurdo, the Task Force had taken upon itself the authority not only to write plans, but also to approve and carry them out without consulting the Program office. Since it was only Byrd and his staff against the entire Task Force, it was best that the matter be threshed out now in Washington before plans for Deep Freeze II jelled.

It was preposterous that we should have to waste precious time and energy on this matter, especially since so much work had to be accomplished before the fall of 1956. Yet there was no alternative if the hard-won information we had gathered in the course of all our previous expeditions to the Antarctic was to be made available to the program ahead.

Fortunately, Admiral Arleigh Burke, Chief of Naval Operations, was well aware of the indignities Admiral Byrd had suffered during Deep Freeze I, and he was quick to clarify Byrd's status. In a memorandum for the record, on April 19, 1956, Admiral Burke reported that Byrd "was not getting forceful backing in all the matters that are his responsibility, and in some instances he was either bypassed or not kept informed. . . . I expressed to Admiral Byrd the Navy's appreciation of his continued valuable effort in assisting the Navy, not only in polar work but in many other things as well. I told him I had just signed the directive covering our Antarctic operations for the coming season, and hoped that it would clarify responsibilities."

In a later clarifying operation order to the Commander, Task Force 43, Admiral Burke wrote:

> The Secretary of Defense letter of 21 October 1955 to Rear Admiral Richard E. Byrd, USN (Ret.) designated him as Officer in Charge, U.S. Antarctic Programs. In this capacity, Rear Admiral Byrd is considered to be the senior U.S. representative charged with maintaining effective monitorship over those political, scientific, legislative and operational activities which comprise the over-all U.S. Antarctic Programs. *In respect to specific operations and expeditions in the U.S. Antarctic Programs,* of which Deep Freeze is one, the Officer in Charge, U.S. Antarctic Programs will provide technical and scientific advice, including advice on the technical suitability of plans and projected operations, to Commander Task Force FORTY-THREE. . . .
>
> The OinC AP and his staff have wide Antarctic knowledge and broad scientific and technical contacts. Under his assigned responsibilities for monitorship of political, scientific, legislative and operation aspects of the over-all program, it is expected that recommendations made by him will receive full consideration by CTF 43 and also by CINCLANTFLT and the CNO. If these recommendations are of such broad nature that they should be considered by the Operations Coordinating Board and the National Security Council, the Chief of Naval Operations will take necessary action, in Washington, to assure such consideration.

Obtaining this clarification had cost Byrd a part of his ebbing strength. With a heavy heart I watched him grow thinner despite his inauguration of a heavy-food diet. Yet despite his loss of weight, his spirits gained an enormous boost from the return of personal dignity he had lost during Deep Freeze I. Now the decks were clear for attending to the many problems involved in Deep Freeze II.

Under Deep Freeze II, five IGY stations were to be constructed and manned during the 1956–57 season. These were to be in addition to McMurdo and Little America V, where a total of 166 men were wintering over in order to be ready for the gigantic construction task that would begin when the sun rose again late in August. Everything had to be in readiness for the International Geophysical Year which would begin on July 1, 1957. By airlift and tractor trail parties, construction supplies and equipment, as well as scientific gear, would be brought to the various sites and prepared for use. To insure that there would be no slip-ups in our timetable, this time twelve ships carrying almost 4,000 men would head for the Antarctic, as compared with the seven ships and 1,800 men of Deep Freeze I. A total of 500 tons of equipment for the South Pole Station was already awaiting airdrops at McMurdo, while 530 additional tons for the Byrd Station lay at Little America.

All this we assumed was to be in addition to our National Program of continued geographic investigation of the continent. But unfortunately, our National Program fell to pieces early in 1956, to our great surprise.

Our How subcommittee had been assigned the task of mapping the Antarctic. During Deep Freeze I our pilots had viewed more than a million square miles that had never been seen before. Now the How group proposed a $56 million additional mapping program, which would map the Antarctic on a scale more detailed than had ever been done in large areas of the United States.

"But this program is not justified at this time," I argued. A proper mapping approach would have been to proceed with a series of approximations of positions. Later, as more details were actually needed for scientific purposes, these approximations could be refined accordingly. Such a mapping program would at most have cost $10 million.

Instead, the reaction to the $56 million Antarctic mapping proposal proved fatal to the entire National Program. Aroused by its high cost, the President reportedly asked, "What are we actually committed for down there?"

Alan Waterman, head of the National Science Foundation, which was functioning as the USNC-IGY's fiscal agent, assured him that we were committed only to the IGY. And when no one contradicted Waterman, the President said we would carry out the IGY program and nothing else.

And with this decision, we who had worked so long and hard on the National Program watched it collapse. The budget sent to Congress contained no provision for the mapping program.

"It's a blow," Byrd told the National Program's personnel, "but let's see what we can save from the wreckage."

There was little optimism among us at the time that Byrd's dream of permanent American settlements in the Antarctic could be revived. But undaunted, he began from scratch, as he had so many times in the past, to plan for future long-range Antarctic bases and further exploration of the continent. He would certainly support the IGY, but this would not be the end-all of our efforts. The national interest must not be abandoned, Byrd declared. Since I was an active member of the IGY as well as Byrd's deputy, this put me in an odd position, for Byrd's nationalistic approach conflicted with the internationalism of the IGY program. The USNC-IGY refused to accept that American interest in the Antarctic went beyond the scientific. For instance, when Byrd met with IGY officials and spoke of possible American national rights in the Antarctic, I watched some of the IGY men shudder as though he were saying something obscene.

Left with the IGY program as our only official planning function under Deep Freeze II, we realized that the stations we would construct on Antarctica strictly for geophysical observations could prove useful later as an opening wedge for a renewal of the National Program. "Let's make the IGY a great success," Byrd told me.

Now the time had come to select the scientists who would man the IGY stations in the Antarctic. I was soon involved in this task as chairman of the Personnel Selection Subcommittee of the USNC's Antarctic Committee. For Little America, we planned a scientific complement of about twenty-five; Byrd Station, twelve; South Pole Station, nine; Hallett Station, three or four; Wilkes Station, fourteen; and Ellsworth Station, fourteen.

My subcommittee followed a complicated technique. In the first place, only volunteers were considered for Antarctic duty. No one would be forced to go to a station, but could instead volunteer for a particular place. The effect of this ruling became clear when surprisingly few volunteered to carry out scientific observations at the South Pole. Most intimated they felt this to be too risky a proposition. The stations along the coast where one was close to an ice bay or water looked more inviting.

Another odd feature of our Personnel Selection Board's procedure was that we did not meet an applicant personally. First his name was proposed by a panel representing the scientific discipline for his field of science which judged his technical qualifications. Next my selection board, which consisted of ten experienced polar men, passed on the applicant's suitability in other respects. Finally each volunteer underwent a detailed physical and psychological examination.

Usually the leading candidates were young men just entering graduate work in their fields. There were several reasons for this. In the first place, those who had already attained high standing in their specialty among the geophysical sciences had little desire to go to the Antarctic for the required year or two. It was their conclusion that the necessary observations could be taken by less experienced persons, while they remained in the United States and wrote the final reports from the accumulated records—and were accorded just as much recognition.

Second, presumably older men tended to shy away from exposing themselves to the difficult Antarctic environment. Third, an older person's personality was set and fairly rigid, while a younger man was more pliable and could more easily adapt himself to changing conditions.

Under the final planning arrangement, each IGY station was to contain two groups. One would consist of the scientific detail; the other, a Navy assortment of housekeepers, including cooks, carpenters, machinists and electricians, radio operators and doctors. Although our IGY Personnel Selection Board controlled the selection of IGY Station personnel, the Navy selected its own complement to man the scientific stations.

The Navy also restricted its Antarctic station personnel to volunteers. These men came to Davisville, Rhode Island, where they underwent a variety of similar tests which were not, however, so complex as those given the scientific personnel. Nor were the Navy's medical examinations apparently as intensive with regard to its own personnel as to the civilian scientists, as the later outcropping of physical ailments among its IGY Station personnel was to prove.

While the Navy undertook a physical program to toughen its volunteers to withstand the rigors of the Antarctic, the IGY began an orientation program for its successful candidates at Davisville. Dick Black, my old Antarctic comrade, became "foster mother" to the Pole Station IGY contingent.

Almost as soon as the decision came to have separate IGY and naval groups at the IGY stations, the question arose regarding who would be the station leaders. A long series of meetings followed. It was my opinion that there should be a single man in command and that he should be a civilian. However, Dufek countered with a proposal for a split command. If Navy men were put into the IGY stations, he argued, they should take orders solely from Navy officers and not from any civilian scientist. It could not work out otherwise, he went on, even though I pointed out that as West Base Leader from 1939 to 1941 I had had no such trouble with a contingent of Army-Navy-Marine Corps men under my jurisdiction.

"What if the two leaders in a split-command situation did not get along?" I asked. "The station would be split straight down the middle and there is no telling what might happen during the winter night." From long experience I knew that where men live in crowded isolation, the probability of trouble between two such groups is great. And where the men would be separated from the rest of the world, there would be no opportunity to appeal to the outside for decisions to settle disputes.

This was one battle I hated to lose. But the Navy was adamant in its decision to have a split command at the IGY stations, and the Academy of Science ultimately accepted the Navy's position.

I had given little thought to returning to the Antarctic during Deep Freeze II. In fact, I was considering returning to my post with the Army, and in June, I took a month off from Byrd's office at the request of the Army to go to Germany to advise on the research and development program of the new German army.

However, upon my return, pressure to return to the Antarctic was brought to bear on me from several quarters. I learned that it had been assumed all along by the IGY that I would become the scientific leader at the South Pole Station. Larry Gould, head of the USNC Antarctic Committee, wrote me several letters imploring me to go and Hugh Odishaw, executive secretary, called repeatedly to ask me to accept.

At first I turned a deaf ear to these urgings. I had already spent more than six years in the Antarctic. I had been away when my first daughter was born in 1940. Now I could not countenance missing out on my three daughters' remaining teen years. In 1947, I had left my sick father to go on Highjump and had returned to find my father long buried. Then too I was forty-eight now, well past the age to consider taking an active physical role such as that of expedition leader.

My family and my age were my primary considerations in rejecting the pleas put to me to go to the South Pole. But there were others, too. I had until recently been the director of a $90,000,000 Army research program covering all fields of science. My friends called it scientific suicide to desert my work entirely to spend a year guiding a handful of scientists making geophysical observations. Then too, my scientific work at the Pole would not even be of an independent nature in keeping with my status as a scientist. Nor did I think I could possibly emerge with an enhanced reputation in the world of science.

Then there was the serious problem of a split command, which would put me in charge of only half the Station's personnel. In addition, I did not know the actual details concerning the personnel and equipment going into that station. And the logistics having been left to the final discretion of the Task Force at McMurdo, I feared that preparations might well prove to have been all too inadequate.

All these totaled up to sufficient reasons why I should not go to the South Pole to live for a year. "It is out of the question," I said.

But I did not reckon with the Department of Defense and Admiral Byrd. "No one has ever tried to live at the Pole before," Defense officials pounded at me. "We are worried about putting people in there and trying to keep them alive. We'd only dare attempt it if we had someone with your experience directing it."

"You must, Paul," said Byrd. "And if you are not satisfied at the Pole that it is safe to live there, you'll have the authority to call it off."

Late in August, as a member of the American delegation, I attended the IGY conference at Brussels where the member nations made firm, final agreements regarding their Antarctic activities. Upon my return to Washington, the time for procrastination was gone. Within a few weeks the Task Force was to leave again for Deep Freeze II. Defense officials and IGY officers converged on me now to insist that I agree to go to the South Pole.

At length I made up my mind to accept, as Admiral Byrd apparently had known all along I would. For only days after I had made my decision I received a memo from him.

FROM: Officer in charge, U.S. Antarctic Programs
TO: Dr. Paul A. Siple

SUBJ: Temporary additional duty; orders for

1. On or about 1 October 1956, you will proceed and report to the National Academy of Sciences, United States National Committee for the International Geophysical Year, for temporary additional duty as Scientific Leader of the South Pole Station for a period of approximately eighteen months. In addition to your duties as Scientific Leader of the South Pole Station, you

will act as the Deputy for the Officer in Charge, U.S. Antarctic Programs, for such matters as are within the purview of the Officer in Charge, U.S. Antarctic Programs.

2. Upon completion of these duties you will return and resume your regular duties.

There was no turning back now—the decision was final. First I went to my own physician and then to a heart specialist. Both declared me sound. Then to strengthen muscles that would be needed in the months ahead, I proceeded with renewed energy at the task of excavating a family swimming pool adjoining my house in Arlington, a task that my enthusiastic daughters had been imploring me to complete for months. Here began nighttime and weekend pick-and-shovel digging, with Ann, Jane and Mary carting off mountains of dirt in wheelbarrows.

There was a last-minute rush now because my departure was set at midnight on October 4. I had to get my Antarctic clothing together in one place. There was a passport to renew, a contract to work out with American IGY authorities—and dozens of other odds and ends to handle. The Army would continue to pay my salary while I was working for the IGY and the Navy had agreed to transport me to the Antarctic and home.

The day before my departure, despite my hectic packing, I traveled to Boston for the farewell lunch with Admiral Byrd of which I have written earlier. His eyes were moist as we parted. Ours was a friendship of three decades now and it hurt to say good-by. Yet I felt that my absence would not be too important to Byrd in a business sense because he now had capable Captain Charles Lanham as his aide, as well as excellent staff members such as John Roscoe, Murray Wiener, Dick Black, Commander Viola Sanders and Dr. Harry Dater.

A steady downpour drenched Washington on the 4th. It is a silly superstition, perhaps, but many of the important days of my life seem to have featured heavy rains. There was a lunch with six old friends, then a visit with Melville Grosvenor and John Oliver LaGorce regarding some articles they wanted me to write at the South Pole for the *National Geographic,* then a visit at IGY headquarters to sign my IGY contract.

Late that evening Admiral Byrd called me twice to say farewell. Then it was time to go. Ruth, Ann, Jane and Mary, and my mother, too, accompanied me to the airport. Nine others were there to see me off, including Dick Chappell, a fine young man who was to go to the Little America Station as the Boy Scout with the IGY.

We passed through the airport and I kissed my family farewell. It was an emotional experience as it always had been. "Write me often," I called out. "We should get mail until next March."

And then the plane was in the air and once again I was on my way to the Antarctic.

Chapter 11

FAREWELL TO CIVILIZATION

THE plane squeaked to a jolting stop at Auckland, New Zealand, on October 9th. Murray Wiener, the only member of Admiral Byrd's staff in New Zealand, was on hand to greet me and accompany me on to Wellington. "You look shipshape," he said with a smile, after he caught sight of the calluses on my hands that had resulted from digging out the hole for my family swimming pool.

All the way across the Pacific, my mind had kept returning to the fears expressed by Defense and IGY officials regarding the proposed South Pole Station: "We might be sending men to their deaths." I did not have this fear, though it had been annoying to listen to this redundant comment. Probably the coldest spot on earth, a high altitude area of rarefied air, six months of sunless existence without possibility of outside aid in case of emergency, eighteen men crowded together for an entire year—the chances for serious troubles were considerable. Yet I felt certain that with all my polar experience and the lessons I had learned in the years I had spent with the Army specializing in environmental research, especially into the effects of living under extreme conditions of climate and terrain, we would get through the South Pole year without mishap, God be willing.

Sir Edmund Hillary, the conqueror of Everest, was also in Wellington, where he was planning New Zealand's Scott Base which would be established close by our station in McMurdo Sound. Ed wanted to renew our acquaintance and asked me to visit him to talk over mutual problems. I found him sitting on his desk in shirtsleeves, swinging his long legs, and we were soon throwing questions and answers back and forth regarding Antarctic and mountaineering techniques and equipment. Above all, he was concerned with getting sufficient money for his expedition. Nevertheless he bubbled with enthusiasm, for late in 1957 he was going to participate in the Commonwealth Transantarctic Expedition patroned by Queen Elizabeth. Vivian Fuchs, whom both Ed and I knew best as "Bunny," was to leave from the Shackleton IGY Station, near our American IGY Ellsworth Station on the Weddell Coast, and travel by American-built Sno-Cat tractor in a 2,000-mile dash across the continent to Scott Base. Hillary was to lay final leg depots for him from Scott Base to Depot 700, which lay west of the mountain range adjoining the Ross Ice Shelf, about three-quarters of the distance between Scott Base and the South Pole. There would be only limited IGY gains from this trip, but there would be considerable adventure and it looked like fun. "So you'll see Fuchs when he comes through your South Pole Station," Hillary said.

From Wellington, I took the overnight ferry to Christchurch on South Island, the air take-off point for the Antarctic. I had first seen Christchurch when it was a small town in 1930. But it had now grown into the largest city in New Zealand, though it still maintained the atmosphere of an English town with its small neat houses and floral parks. Surrounded by high hills and mountains, Christchurch lay in a wide pastoral plain, all of which had erupted into the full bloom of spring with seas of flowers, lovely tree ferns and other exotic trees. Bicycles were everywhere in the city dashing in and out among the buses whose front and rear were hung with perambulators belonging to passenger mothers.

The city was agog with goings-on preparatory to the coming IGY expeditions, and the press gave the Antarctic coverage worthy of a major world event. Only a few articles criticized our intention to erect and man a South Pole Station, intimating that such a man-made monstrosity would sully the memories of Scott and his intrepid party. Directly outside my window in the Clarendon Hotel, I could gaze upon Scott's statue in the park below and conjecture on his standing with the citizens of Christchurch. I could also conjecture upon his excruciating, seemingly unending, experience of dragging sledges to that forsaken spot where soon I would land after a swift and comfortable airplane ride.

Admiral Dufek was in the city and the local press had been carrying on a detailed account of his every move and thought. "How are you?" Dufek greeted me when I went to see him, then asked pointedly whether I was on his staff or Byrd's.

"Byrd's," I told him, and handed him a letter of instructions from the Admiral which, among other things, requested that I be on the first flight in to the South Pole. Byrd wanted me to be among the first group to land at the Pole. Dufek stuffed his copy of the letter in his pocket without comment.

"Incidentally, I want to get the barracks building included among the buildings to go up at the Pole," I told Dufek. "If we don't have this, we'll have to sleep in the mess hall or the science building and that would be unfortunate both for morale and work purposes."

"It's coming on one of the ships," he said matter-of-factly, "but we've got about everything scheduled for this year that we can. Maybe we'll be able to get it next year if everything goes well and we stay on at the Pole."

Dufek was planning on flying in the first Navy R5D Skymaster to Williams Air Operating Facility at McMurdo Sound on October 18. The bay ice was reported to be almost fifteen feet thick. Ever since the sun's return, the men left at McMurdo had worked in twelve-hour shifts around the clock on a seven-day-a-week basis to bulldoze the snow to form a new ice runway. They had also equipped the ice strip with a Ground Control Approach system (GCA) to prevent accidents due to poor visibility. After Dufek's Skymaster reached McMurdo, a second wave of P2V Neptunes and four R4D Skytrains would take off from New Zealand. I was to be in the third wave of C-124 Globemasters of the 18th Air Force, which was co-operating with the Navy to drop equipment at the South Pole.

Dufek left two days ahead of schedule on the 16th. The next day the second wave left for McMurdo and while I awaited departure, I completed the long list of chores I had listed before going to the Antarctic. One of the things I did was to arrange for the purchase of two large silvered balls that I wanted for a photographic experiment. One of them ultimately was to adorn the top of a flagpole as our first symbolic Geographic South Pole. The balls actually were good-sized street lamps which would be shipped from Australia and be mirrored in New Zealand.

While the Navy planes were en route to McMurdo, reporting back frequently on their progress on their radios, I paid a visit to the large contingent of American Air Force personnel stationed at Harewood

Air Field close to Christchurch. Colonel Crosswell, in command, and Major Ellen, his deputy, had asked Murray Wiener to arrange to have me give their air and ground crews an orientation lecture. I gave the earnest young airmen a brief rundown on Antarctic history and then went on to discuss the art of surviving and living on the pack or icecap in the event a plane was forced down.

After lunching with the Air Force officers who would fly the materials, equipment and personnel for the South Pole Station into the Pole, we checked again with the Air Weather Officer for the Task Force. There had been no recent radio reports from the planes, and the weather was deteriorating at McMurdo.

But by the time I got back to the Hotel Clarendon, there was news of the planes—bad news! One of the P2V's had crashed at Mc-Murdo in a near white-out, killing three members of the crew including the pilot and seriously injuring five others. The pilot had been on GCA until he sighted the runway; then he had called over his radio that he could see the surface and was going to make a usual approach. Thinking himself to the left of the runway, after spying a nearby hill which stood out against the total whiteness everywhere, he banked right and flew directly into the ice with a shuddering crash that demolished his plane.

Of course, I willingly gave up my place in the first C-124 so that extra Navy medical men could fly to McMurdo in my stead. Death always brings on gloom, and now the carefree spirit of the C-124 Air Force pilots at Christchurch gave way to caution. All this was accentuated by Dufek, who sent a message:

VISIBILITY ZERO, TOTAL WHITE-OUT BLIZZARD COVERING RUN-WAY AND WORKING AREA. DO NOT SEND ANY PLANES UNTIL FURTHER WORD.

Finally at 5:45 A.M. on Sunday the 21st, I left Harewood Airport outside of Christchurch right behind the first C-124 on the second of six Globemasters flying to McMurdo, some twelve hours and 2,000 miles away.

As we took off, I looked back on the sprawling city. My eyes took in the lush greenery, the paved streets, the shops and houses. It was good-by to civilization and on to the unknown center of Antarctica after a short stay at McMurdo. Not for more than a year would I see Christchurch and civilization again—if all went well.

Chapter 12

McMURDO JUNCTION

W E'RE coming in to McMurdo!" someone yelled.

I had spent most of the flight in the bunks in the rear of the cock-
pit, dozing, writing letters to Ruth and the girls and to Byrd, and
watching for familiar landmarks.

At approximately Latitude 62° 30' we sighted the first pack ice,
its menace barely apparent from the safety of an 8,000-foot elevation. From this height it appeared to be similar to slush and brash
with small floes. Only the icebergs farther south, many of which measured miles in all directions, belied the simplicity of the Antarctic seas.
As we neared McMurdo, I could see the landmark of Mount Erebus,
Antarctica's only continuously live volcano, as it expelled plumes of
smoke.

Dufek met my plane as it taxied to a halt on the ice airstrip beside
which lay the wreckage of the P2V, a grim reminder of the horrible
accident on the seventeenth. His unsmiling face gave evidence of the
tense anguish this misfortune had inspired in him. An additional
crew member had since died, bringing the death total to four. Nor
was this all the bad news. The U.S. Air Force C-124 Number 4, a big
77-ton Globemaster, which came into McMurdo two planes after
mine, landed at too high a speed on the less than perfect runway. As
a result, its nose wheel collapsed and the plane skated a thousand
feet on its nose sending up a cloud of snow and ice particles before
stopping. Fortunately, no one aboard was injured, though the $2,700,-
000 plane was apparently a total loss. The cost of Deep Freeze II in
men and equipment had thus become very high even before it was
officially underway.

Dufek drove me over the ice on his Weasel to my quarters at the
base, but there was little elation with the big job ahead in view of the
unhappy events of the past few days. Our laconic conversation was
accentuated by the harsh, blowing wind and the cold weather.

During the next few days the temperature rose, the wind died off considerably, and the village at McMurdo became a lively and busy place. Instead of the few tents which we had hastily erected at Hut Point the previous December, thirty-four houses now lent a substantial appearance to the base, overlooking the point from a high shelf of volcanic rubble a half mile east of Scott's 1902 base. Streets were named after political figures, admirals and puckish characteristics, as were the individual buildings.

My own temporary quarters amounted to a comfortable half room measuring 7 x 15 feet in total, in a flat-roofed eight-foot-high building made of Clements panels. This was one of the so-called "Deep Freeze" houses I'd helped approve in the blueprint stage so many months ago. It was a choice residence compared with the Quonset Huts and little Jamesways, the latter being mound-roofed cloth structures shaped like Quonsets. Ye Olde Sack Inn, as my building was named, stood at the corner of Forrestal Avenue and Honey Bucket Lane, the road down which the base's toilet refuse was regularly hauled for dumping.

McMurdo had blossomed quickly into a summer village of 300 men, a village self-contained in most ways. Because the mess hall was essentially built to accommodate the 93-man winter party, the men now had to eat in three shifts. Being on the first shift, I had to eat breakfast at what seemed the unearthly hour of six A.M., lunch at eleven and dinner at five. Trucks with scoops mounted in front brought snow to be melted in tanks for the water supply, but a large powerhouse made possible the use of several washing machines, dryers, showers and heated bathrooms, a far cry from the rigors of the early expeditions when we had to melt a few buckets of snow and then heat the water for a meager body scrubbing without even a tub.

Every Antarctic camp has its own characteristics and McMurdo was no exception. One of McMurdo's unique features was "Big Eye." The overheated barracks plus the never-setting sun had produced widespread insomnia and a Big Eye club functioned almost to rising hours for those afflicted. Then, exhausted, some of the men would sleepily drowse away most of the day—and be all ready for the Big Eye the next evening. Another feature of McMurdo was the Saturday evening "Happy Hour." As I have mentioned before, on previous expeditions we had made certain that little if any liquor was brought along, a practice that was looked upon by some as being prudish and ridiculous for the modern Navy. The new theory was that alcoholic beverages helped the men relax and forget the problems of living in the Antarctic, with the result that "Happy Hours" were arranged weekly so the boys could let off steam.

Perhaps the most striking feature of McMurdo to the newcomer was the deleterious degeneration of the language used by the men. All the Antarctic expeditions I had been on had been characterized by strong, colorful language, but at McMurdo the use of profanity had been developed into a fine art. One curious aspect of the language used at the base seemed to have been developed by a morale officer who, although he was a man of undeniably high morals, was a poor psychologist. It was his theory that if he talked as the men did, the boys would be shamed into correcting their own language. Unfortunately, his experiment served only to encourage others to use even worse talk.

Interestingly enough, no set place for religious worship had originally been included in the plans for McMurdo. But the men had devoted a large share of their free hours to erecting an attractive chapel and the majority now flocked there for Sunday services.

But if one were sometimes disappointed in the ways of man, there was always the backdrop of the Antarctic itself in which to find comfort. Out in the bay were the corpulent Weddell seals, a source of constant curiosity as they basked lazily on the snow, unmindful of strangers. Standing close to them, in their bovine contentment, I could not help thinking of the nightmarish polar winter night they experienced each year. For there is evidence that the hairy Weddell seal spends the dark winter season under the ice.

Certainly this would not be much of a feat for a fish. But consider that seals have to breathe fresh air at regular intervals and one's respect rises for these creatures. Picture yourself underwater with a ten-foot lid of ice between you and the surface. Perhaps here and there you might locate cracks that extend to the surface or some upward arching domes of ice where air pockets exist. Then picture yourself spending four months or more of each year in darkness, continuously in the water and always facing the hazard of losing track of a vital breathing hole while off searching for food in the dark. At the same time you must keep constantly alert against wandering into open water where marauding killer whales with teeth as large as bananas may snap you up in an instant. This, incidentally, is a problem that the Weddell seal's smaller cousin, the ice pack habiting crab-eater seal, has to contend with to an even greater degree, since he lives out in open water. One seldom finds a sleek silvery adult crab-eater that does not bear ugly scars—or two-foot-long parallel slashes

—on each side of its body, received when it managed somehow to wriggle out of the jaws of a killer whale that had seized it.

Yet when the polar winter ends, the huge seals enlarge cracks with their teeth, literally biting large chunks out of the ice, so that they can hunch their way to the surface to bask bovinely as if they were without a care in the world.

An unsolved riddle was still the subject for considerable speculation at McMurdo when I was there. The dehydrated remains of dead seals had been found high on the glaciers on the far side of McMurdo Sound, a great many miles from the nearest water. Could they have climbed laboriously with their awkward hunching movement to elevations so high above the sea to die? Were they mummified relics of an age many centuries ago when open water might have lain close at hand? I theorized that they had simply gotten lost. Seals and other Antarctic creatures often seem to find their way over snow and ice fields by moving toward water sky, the dark shadows from open water on the underside of a relatively solid cloud cover, much as polar skippers use such sky to navigate when they are looking for leads in heavy pack ice. I had noted that dark rocks cast the same dark shadows up on the clouds in overcast weather, and now I reasoned that these seals found mysteriously so far inland had been laboriously and erroneously making for what they thought was open water. But, alas, it had proved a mirage and the unfortunate creatures had perished pursuing the Antarctic sirens.

It was thus as I watched the seals on the bay ice that I realized how many mute counterparts man's struggle to survive had in the animal world.

Then there were the Emperor penguins, living on the far side of Ross Island. For some unfathomable reason, the Emperors always lay and incubate eggs during the coldest and darkest period of the year. Possibly this primitive bird in its breeding habits reflects seasonal behavior patterns belonging to an age less rigorous than the present.

These biggest of all the penguin family normally stand nearly three feet high, although with neck extended to full length they are a good four feet tall. Their average weight is about fifty pounds, although occasional specimens may be found weighing twice that. For so large a bird to attain its full growth in a single short summer season, it appears biologically necessary for it to start its egg-hatching task before the break of the Antarctic dawn. This is an approach similar to our own effort to stretch the short summer season at McMurdo by flying in planes far earlier than ships could reach the base.

With a dignity befitting its regal name, the Emperor penguin lays a single large egg without benefit of a nest. The site it selects is generally snow-covered. An Emperor lays its egg when the temperature in the rookery drops to below $-70°$ F. This is the dead of winter when it is almost continuously pitch dark except when the moon, aurora and star light are not obscured by clouds. The Emperor's egg would freeze quickly if laid on the snow. Therefore, the adult places the egg on top of its feet and holds it against a feather-free spot on its lower abdomen. But Mother Nature adds another burden for this majestic creature, for the cold snow would freeze the bird's toes if they remained long in contact with the snow. Thus nature has fortunately provided the big birds with large calloused heels which are less susceptible to freezing, and they simply curl up their toes and rock back and forth on their heels while utilizing their stubby tails for a third point of support. To conserve body heat in the miserable cold, the Emperors crowd tightly together with heads tucked down. The French reported that at one rookery a vehicle's headlights disturbed a tight knot of thousands of penguins, causing the startled birds to raise their heads. Immediately there rose a great cloud of vapor representing the community body heat which the birds had managed to blanket in with their bodies.

Penguins, which Anatole France so colorfully personalized long ago, entrance all visitors to the Antarctic. They waddle about on their apparently short legs in a most amusing manner, although actually their legs are quite long. However, since long legs would chill in such a frigid world if not kept inside their feathery overcoat, the birds normally keep their knees folded up under their wings. Thus they literally shuffle about while sitting down. In the water they use their wings to swim as other birds employ them to fly, driving themselves through the water at high speed. When they wish to leave the water for an ice pan, they dive deep and swim rapidly to the surface, emerging from the water with a suddenness as if they had been fired from a gun—and attempting, not always successfully, to land upright on their feet on the ice. Another curiosity is the square pupils of their eyes which close down to a tiny diamond shape in the brightest glare of the sun on the snow.

Rookeries of the little Adélie penguins were easily approachable along the shore at McMurdo and I visited them, too. These little fifteen-pound birds are lively and amusing, but they have their problems. Hungry sea leopards seek out the penguin rookeries and swim ominously about waiting for the birds to enter the water. The Adélie penguins fully realize the price the first bird must pay if a sea leopard is close by.

As a result, they play a quaint game of tag designed to force the loser to be the first into the water. The object of this deadly penguin tag is to make one of their members lose his balance and tumble into the water. The birds chase one another with wild enthusiasm, each trying to topple someone else overboard and still remain on the edge of the shore or ice floe. When at last one bird falls in, the game of tag ceases immediately, and the birds excitedly rush to the water's edge to see whether the loser falls prey to a sea leopard or whether he swims off unmolested. If the latter results, the watching penguins dive in and "go fishing."

There was something else about the ice area of McMurdo Sound that caught my attention. Because of confusing reports by pilots and an increasing concern about the ice, Dufek asked me on October 25 to make a helicopter reconnaissance over the Sound. If too much of the ice was breaking out prematurely, this would, of course, affect air operations vital to the scouting of the South Pole plateau where the IGY Station was to be established.

At nine A.M. I took off with two pilots and a photographer and we flew to dark rock Cape Royds, Shackleton's old base, which formed a mid-point along the west side of Ross Island well north of Hut Point. We then turned west along a wide open lead and found that the area rumored to be open had considerable coverage of field ice which had either blown in or was newly formed with a layer of unbroken snow on top. The weather was ceiling and visibility unlimited (CAVU), but it was cold as we traveled because we had to leave the helicopter's door open in order to take pictures. We covered most of the Sound, flying far enough north so that we sighted a ten-by-ten-mile-square iceberg I'd flown over the year before which was still wedged between Beaufort Island and the north tip of Ross Island. Its virgin whiteness was marred now by soot which had fallen on it from Mount Erebus. I was certain this was one of the pieces of the 2,250 square miles of Ross Ice Shelf which had broken out between 1948 and 1955. Next we flew to the west side of the Sound to within a mile of the entrance of Dry Valley and the 35-mile-long Ferrar Glacier that flowed from the plateau of Victoria Land to New Harbor in McMurdo Sound. Then we headed back toward camp. Here on the return flight, I checked the long cracks that ran east-west across the Sound, took pictures over the camp and airstrip and finally circled over the heavy pressure zone around Pram Point, where the Ross Ice Shelf collides with Ross Island in a series of rolls and pressures. "The bay ice is still safe. You can send the planes up," I informed Dufek. "There is no ice breakup across the entire Sound north of Cape Royds to the mouth of the Ferrar Glacier."

With this observation of the bay ice, the planes that had been grounded ever since their initial landings at McMurdo could now take off on their necessary flights. My estimate to Dufek and to visiting Major General Chester McCarthy, Commander of the 18th Air Force which was providing Globemaster planes for the coming equipment drop at the Pole, was that it would be a month, or perhaps two, before the airstrip would be endangered by a breakup of the ice in the Sound.

That afternoon the Task Force sent its first planes on missions. One Navy R4D Skytrain set off to scout a site for the small support air base at the foot of Liv Glacier along the southern limit of the Ross Ice Shelf, about 400 miles from the Pole. Other air parties flew a group of Army specialists over to Little America V, where they were to begin pioneering a safe route through the crevassed edge of Marie Byrd Land so that the gigantic D-8 tractor trains could move the IGY Byrd Station supplies to an inland-marked spot at 80° S on the 120th Meridian West. We wished these men lots of luck for they would need it. Silently we thought of Max Kiel, who'd lost his life the year before while driving a tractor into this perilous region. The next morning, on the 26th, Dufek told me that he was honoring Admiral Byrd's request that I go along on the first flight to the Pole.

It had been Byrd's intention, of course, that I should be in the first party to land at the Pole. However, since Byrd's written request was loosely worded and did not directly say "land," I found myself flying that afternoon in a C-124 Globemaster that toured the Pole without landing and then returned to McMurdo. Inadvertently this flight gave me an unusual Air Force distinction. Ten years earlier in October, 1946, I had flown in the first USAF plane to cross over the North Pole. Now, oddly enough, I was aboard the first Air Force plane to reach the South Pole.

The South Pole did not look at all inviting. I could tell from the appearance of the surface that the winter winds had been far stronger than the sastrugi had indicated the previous summer. Did the battered condition of the surface now mean that the winter would be far stormier than we anticipated? As a token salute to the future station below, the pilot dropped eighteen drums of fuel by parachute, as well

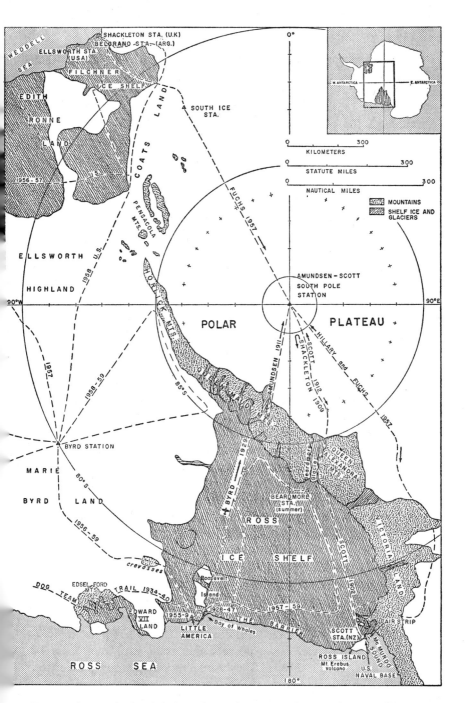

Routes taken to the South Pole and on other major traverses showing relative positions of McMurdo (lower right), Little America (center bottom), Byrd Station (left) and South Ice Station (top center).

as a "Grasshopper," an automatic weather station with batteries that would last six weeks.

Amusingly enough, none of the plane's forty-five passengers could spy these bigger objects on the surface after they were dropped, although the plane circled several times looking for them. Small wonder the Marine Corps pilot who had expressed dismay at not being able to discover his smoke flares, ink, and cardboard penguins had not been able to spot them.

As matters turned out, Dufek and his all-Navy crew pioneered the first of our many landings at the Pole. On October 31, he and a crew of six set down at the Pole in a ski-wheeled Navy R4D, the twin-engine Navy version of a DC3, piloted by Lieutenant Gus Shinn. No one with Dufek was familiar with cold weather procedure and they stepped from the warmth of the plane into a temperature of −58° F. and a wind accentuated by the blast of the plane's propellers. Had they been able to do no more than dig a hole in the ice and take the temperature, it would have been highly useful to those of us who were to live at the Pole; for the undersurface temperature would have allowed us to make a rough estimate of the average winter temperature on the surface. Instead, they hurriedly planted an American flag, took pictures, and horrifiedly discovered growing patches of frostbite on each other's cheeks. For the fifteen-mile wind made the −58° temperature nearly thrice as bad in its effect on human flesh.

"Let's get the hell out of here," Dufek ordered the pilot. But this was easier said than done, because by now the plane's landing skis were frozen to the snow and the windshield was completely frosted. And in addition to the frozen skis, engine oil was leaking badly.

The plane had fifteen propulsion bottles of JATO (jet-assisted take-off) attached to its underside, and these were what stood between take-off and being marooned. With the thrust of four JATO bottles about equaling the power of a single plane engine, the pilot fired off a group of four. When the plane did not budge, he exploded four more. Fortunately, this time the skis broke away from the ice's grip. Another four JATO's blasted off and finally the last three. The plane reeled drunkenly across the plateau and wobbled into the air.

This incident typifies the transformation that modern polar exploration has undergone. How different this coup was from those of Amundsen, Scott and Byrd! They were men who planned years ahead for their strike, familiarized themselves with the Antarctic and spent a winter's night to harden themselves before starting off. None of

Dufek's crew had ever spent a winter in the Antarctic and none had ever before experienced −58°.

It was little wonder, then, that Dufek returned to McMurdo shaken from his polar experience and suffering from a bad cold. "It's too cold to operate at the Pole," he said, "and it would be humanly impossible to do outside construction work there. I'm not going to put men up there until conditions are better."

And so the success of IGY South Pole Station appeared an unlikely enterprise as he flew off to New Zealand to recuperate.

Chapter 13

WAITING AT THE ALTAR

DESPITE Dufek's unfortunate experience and his reaction to it, there was little point in halting all preparations for a South Pole Station. Now that we had come this far, it was necessary to see the job through to completion. Besides, my curiosity was aroused to the point where there was no turning back.

Yet there remained a mountain of labor before we could plan on sending men safely to the Pole. For one thing, I did not know for certain, except in a general fashion, what the South Pole Station living facilities would consist of. Nor did I know precisely what equipment for the IGY Station had actually been delivered to McMurdo the year before. Byrd and other old-school explorers frequently summarized polar explorations with the words: "The poorer the planning, the more adventures there will be on an expedition." It was my intention to examine and re-examine the planning, for "adventures" really meant trouble caused by slipshod planning before the expedition got underway.

Fortunately, Howard O. Wessbecher of the IGY, a young man with a curly black beard and a ready smile, had wintered at McMurdo preparing the Pole Station equipment for airdrop. All winter long

Howard and the riggers had worked preparing packages and putting the boxes into 4-foot cubic canvas containers on pallets, each of which held up to a ton of equipment. Each of these so-called A-22 containers was felt-padded and equipped for a hooked-on parachute 65 feet in diameter so it could be airdropped by the big Air Force C-124 Globemasters.

When I arrived at McMurdo, Howard had already prepared one hundred drop containers, which lay stacked about the base ready to have their parachutes attached. These made a formidable tonnage, though they were a mystery to me because I did not yet know what they contained. As a result, I made a complete check of the supplies, listing them alphabetically and by classes of equipment and then comparing my list with one made by the IGY the previous year.

It was disquieting to discover that fifteen closely typed pages of equipment had either been left out or were in short supply. If we acquired nothing further and merely accepted what had been packaged, life at the Pole could certainly have turned out to be a grim affair. Quickly I prepared three lists of additional items by priority and went over these lists with the Task Force. List A contained items I considered so essential that I would fight for them; List B, those that were highly desirable or had been provided in too limited quantity; and List C, those that would be satisfying to acquire. For instance, List A included such things as raw stock material for emergency construction of instruments and gadgets, shop equipment, haircutting outfits, a sewing machine, steel wool, mops, and individual radios with headphones. List B contained such items as aluminum foil, calipers, spare drills, window glass, paraffin, sandpaper, paper towels, safety pins and turpentine. List C included darning cards, disinfectant, paper cups and napkins, etc.

Fortunately, the Navy granted me permission to requisition whatever items I needed if they were readily available at the base. So Howard and I went on a scrounging rampage, aided by the Seabees who would erect the base, scouring the mountain of equipment strewn about McMurdo. It turned into a game, discovering one item and then another, and little by little we found many of the things we sought. What we could not find, I itemized in a list that I sent back to IGY headquarters for their aid. I remember that we were particularly elated when we acquired a set of the Encyclopaedia Britannica, for I knew that during the winter night men would argue about various factual questions and it was important that they have source books to settle their disputes. I was also pleased when we were promised radios and headphones for the men of the South Pole Station; but our joy here was short-lived, for after the Navy went out and specially purchased them, all but a few were subsequently stolen from our cache.

While Howard and I were so busily concerned with adding to the South Pole Station's equipment, others at McMurdo were also concentrating on matters pertaining to that station. Certainly the man most immediately concerned was young Lieutenant (jg) Richard A. Bowers of the Navy's Civil Engineer Corps, who was to have charge of the building of the South Pole Station. Dick was only twenty-eight, a graduate of Yale and the holder of Master of Arts degrees in two subjects. Dick was tall and slim, possessed a scraggly beard, and was seldom seen outdoors without a brown hood over the top of his orange parka.

Bower's job seemed almost more than any man could handle. With five chief petty officers and seventeen men, he would have to construct a base into which eighteen men could then move to eat, sleep and work at the bottom of the earth. He and I knew that construction of the base would have to be carried out under wretched working conditions that would include bitter cold, possibly strong winds, thin atmosphere, deep but hard snow, and would offer little opportunity for his construction crew to relax, rest and blow off steam.

However, Bowers was not going into this task blindly. As far back as Davisville before leaving the United States in the fall of the previous year, he had hand-picked his men. Later he had worked with them on the construction of McMurdo Base, a job entrusted to him by the Task Force. His men would go any place with him; in fact, they were planning on going to the end of the earth with him.

Over the winter, from March to September, Bowers had winnowed down his McMurdo construction crew of Seabees until he emerged with a hardened core of thirty-five men including alternates. All winter long he had presided over weekly meetings at McMurdo, in the course of which he discussed every possible contingency involved in constructing a South Pole Station.

Actual construction would be only half his concern; the other half was to keep his men alive and get them out afterward without casualties. With survival at the Pole so basic a subject, he divided his men into six teams of four Seabees, each team designed to be self-sufficient during the first few weeks at the Pole. Thus each group was issued equipment necessary to permit it to survive for forty days under optimum conditions, or for fifteen days of heavy labor.

During the winter, Dick had also put his men through rigorous physical training. He also sent his men on several overnight trips to practice travel and camping techniques, relying on his only other officer assistant, Jack Tuck, as training officer. They also practiced erecting Jamesway huts exactly like those proposed for the Pole. In addition, Dick and Jack subjected their men to lectures, at which I took part after my arrival, stressing the polar experience of previous traverse parties and the essentials of cold weather living. The men were also taught the rudiments of navigation and cold weather first aid, as well as how to prepare their own survival rations and how to derive a maximum of comfort and warmth from their cold weather clothing.

Bowers also had the task of cornering the equipment and supplies he would need. Through the Supply Department, he gathered his equipment and sorted it for use in the following categories: advance party, subsequent personnel, construction camp equipment, camp equipment, and support material for Deep Freeze II. His Seabees also managed to pick up many items for me that were on my critical lists. As a matter of fact, they also rounded up a number of useful items that I had not considered for the Pole Station.

The fact that Dick, Jack and I shared the same house at McMurdo made our liaison simpler. Nevertheless, Dick was more than a trifle reserved in dealing with me at the outset because he was aware of the Task Force's attitude toward me. But he was a friendly sort and we soon became good friends as we discussed the myriad preliminary problems facing both of us.

For instance, Dick was confronted with the puzzling task of doing things from a pile of blueprints that in many cases just weren't going to work. As an example, the metal beams that went across the South Pole houses at the roofs and under the floors were supplied fully fabricated in twenty-foot lengths. However, the massive C-124's, despite their size, were not capable of throwing anything from their dropwells that was over twelve feet long. As a result, every metal beam had to be cut in two and drilled with holes. Then splice plates had to be made so that the divided beams could be joined again for use at the Pole. There were a tremendous number of such beams as well as large amounts of timber for tunnels and buildings. This, too, had to be cut in half, for most were about sixteen feet long.

There seemed no end to the preliminary problems. In fact, compared with the work that had gone into the planning, the actual job itself began to look relatively simple. A priority system had to be devised for the parachuted material so first needs would be handled first and others as they arose. Bowers also had to evolve a site storage plan which covered warehousing and traffic management techniques, so there would be a minimum of double handling of the parachuted material.

Nevertheless, despite all these besetting problems, as October drew to a close Bowers was fully convinced he was ready for the South Pole. His men were fully trained and hardened, the gear packed except for last-minute odds and ends, parachutes for the airdrops and extra splice plates were on their way from New Zealand, and reconnoitering over the Pole area had begun. By October 28, the Navy had already selected its South Pole auxiliary air station at the foot of Liv Glacier, and planes had landed there with the first equipment. Tests had also been made by R4D's which landed and took off from various points on the polar plateau. On this point, Dick showed me his diary entry:

> Upon ascertaining that the R4D's are able to take off from the polar plateau (Captain Hawkes and LCDR Frankiewicz have already taken off a 29,000-pound R4D with three JATO bottles at 10,600 feet), the Advanced Party will be landed. A camp will be set up immediately and sun lines taken. Within twenty-four hours, the Advanced Party should be within two hundred feet of the true Geographic South Pole. At this time, the additional construction teams will be called in. The airdrops can commence simultaneously. There seems to be no question that the planes can take off and land at the Pole.

So the moment we all anticipated tensely had arrived. But now, despite my natural desire to go in at the start of the expedition, Bowers asked me to wait until a bit later. "Dr. Siple will be brought in as soon as accommodations are available," he informed newsmen at a press conference at McMurdo. However, Dick agreed that I should arrive at the Pole before actual station construction began. "Give us a few days to set up tents and stoves and break out rations," he told me, as though I were a delicate fossil.

By October 31, excitement among Bowers and his men had reached a peak. But on the following day I noted a great change in the advance party. For in the interim, Admiral Dufek had made his landing at the Pole and had returned ill and doubtful that the South Pole Station should or could be constructed. What Dufek did not appreciate was that November would bring a steep rise in the temperature at the Pole, so that conditions would be greatly different from what he had experienced. In addition, the advance party had been rigorously training to acclimatize itself to cold weather living, whereas Dufek and the men in his party had not.

Bowers was as dismayed as I by Dufek's decision to hold up the Pole Station for a few weeks. I could fully appreciate his disappointment in view of his year of intensive preparation. Nor was our state of mind improved when on November 4 the Air Force followed up Dufek's decision by moving its personnel back to New Zealand and took ten members of the South Pole construction party along for ten days of rest and relaxation. "The rest of the camp," Bowers informed me, "has fallen apart at the seams."

Temporarily, we were out of business and Pole Station activity ground to a dismal halt. All the hectic work seemed for naught as the men awaited further word from Dufek. One bright Sunday, to relieve the pressure of waiting, I went for a walk with Bowers, Murray Wiener and a few others out through the pass to the southeast between Observation and Crater Hills to Pram Point on the Barrier side of Ross Island where we could spy mother seals sunning with their pups and Mt. Erebus smoking serenely. Here, in a couple of months, the New Zealanders would erect their IGY Scott Station. By the time we had climbed a thousand feet or more toward the northern rim of Crater Hill, we could see the Sound, the camp and runway as well as most of Ross Island. For a moment the tensions of waiting were erased. But they returned once we were back at McMurdo where other members of the advance party greeted us with long faces.

Then suddenly things began to stir. During the evening of the 8th, Bowers burst into my room with the information that three R4D's were ready to fly to the Pole. He also reported that Pole Station plans were apparently still on since he had received a message from Commander Herbert Whitney, the officer responsible for all Antarctic naval station construction, to the effect that under no circumstances was he to make any changes in South Pole construction plans without going through channels. Of course, this order was obviously aimed at me, but at the moment this was forgotten in the light of renewed interest in the polar station.

A few days later word came of the imminent arrival of the C-124's from New Zealand, and then on the 13th they began landing on the ice runway. South Pole construction was on again. Bowers' face wore a smile when I saw him again and the morale of his group was again high. "We're going to take off on the fifteenth," he told me.

"Good," I said.

But on the 15th, a communications blackout forced cancellation of the departure. This condition continued through the 16th, 17th and 18th of November to Bower's disgust. And then on the 19th, we woke to find the weather good and communications clear. The day for departure for the Pole!

Plans called for delivering a preliminary party of eight to the South Pole. I was to come in on Thanksgiving, the 22nd; then on the 26th, a further contingent of the advance party would arrive. Bowers' preliminary party would consist of himself, Jack Tuck, Chief Bristol and five Seabees: Montgomery, Woody, Nolen, Randall and Powell. They would carry along eleven dogs and be delivered to the Pole in two R4D's. The twenty-four-year-old Tuck had a silky brown beard that was the envy of all would-be beard growers at McMurdo. A recent Dartmouth Phi Beta Kappa graduate, he had come down on Deep Freeze I as a dog handler and had remained throughout the winter night busily involved with many other matters where his keen intelligence was needed.

At five P.M. that afternoon I was down at the airstrip where Bowers and Tuck were loading their eleven sledge dogs on the two aged ski-equipped R4D's. "I hope we don't have a hairy time down there," one of the Seabees piped up, as though he had read my mind.

"You won't," I told him.

Propellers spun; engines roared. I shook hands all around and the men climbed into the R4D's. Air Force Globemasters were also on the airstrip ready to take off and rendezvous with the R4D's at the Pole to help them determine the location of the Pole and to drop the first equipment and material for the Pole Station. "So long," I called out and waved as the advance party took off on its journey with destiny.

Chapter 14

THE ADVANCE PARTY DIGS IN

THE test had now begun. Could Bowers and his men dig in at the South Pole and secure a foothold?

All that night I stayed awake waiting for the first word. Then came the radioed information that the R4D's had landed at 12:45 A.M. in bright sunshine on the polar plateau. The men had climbed out with their dogs and a Globemaster parachuted sleds, a Weasel and a variety of equipment to them. The R4D's had a great deal of difficulty taking off, but they finally succeeded with the aid of their JATO bottles. The returning pilots told me that they had not been able to taxi normally because the high elevation produced an attenuation of power due to the lack of oxygen for the engines and their skis did not slide easily on the coarse, granular snow surface.

Left to their own devices, Bowers and his men began to suffer from the altitude and cold almost immediately. All the men felt dizzy and were seized with a strange feeling of exhaustion, some were frostbitten, and one almost passed out due to anoxia, or lack of oxygen. In addition, bad luck had floated down with them. The Weasel had landed hard from its parachuted drop and its batteries and transmission case were broken.

Despite their own tired condition and a temperature of −29°, by six-thirty in the morning the men had pitched three trail tents, retrieved most of the dropped gear, made their equipment secure and tethered the barking dogs. Then Bowers sent a message back to McMurdo reporting events and requesting a new transmission and batteries. A truly exhausted group climbed into sleeping bags about seven o'clock and slept so deeply that when a C-124 returned the following morning the plane had to buzz the tents six times before rousing the men.

Nor did Dick rise with any real feeling of satisfaction. Before the planes originally took off for the South Pole, the pilots and navigators had insisted they could navigate their way exactly to the Pole. "With all due respect, you can't do that," I told them. "If you get within five or ten miles of the Pole, you'll have done fine."

This statement had not gone down well with them. Later, over the polar plateau, the navigators reached agreement that they had arrived at the precise dot where all meridians met, and here the two R4D's had proudly put Bowers' party out onto the snow. Unfortunately, Bowers' report back to McMurdo after the planes had departed included his theodolite reading of the sun, which placed him and his men eight long nautical miles from the true South Pole. Actually the process of landing had exaggerated the error.

When the Air Force C-124 Globemaster returned the following morning, it brought batteries and a new transmission for the Weasel. However, the Weasel parts fell from the plane prematurely and landed about two and a half miles from the tents. And though the transmission landed safely, the batteries were all broken, a matter of keen disappointment to the men who had rushed pantingly across the ice to retrieve the drop. Obviously, the Weasel was in no condition to travel.

Later that day Bowers reported back to us an event that had frightened all of his hardy explorers. At 0800, a great tremor had roared through the camp, shaking the tents and then culminating in a roar like a clap of thunder. The noise and shaking were so great that the men had rushed from the tents certain that a C-124 had crashed near the camp. Outside, however, they had found only a puzzling, quiet nothingness that merely added to the eerie quality of the tremor.

"That was 'Antarctic Hush,' " I told him later. Antarctic Hush is a snowquake caused by a dropping of the surface due to hollow layers that form underneath, probably as a result of vapor transfer. After dropping the batteries and transmission, the C-124 had flown to the Pole where it had dropped "mogas" (gasoline for vehicles) and heavy construction lumber, the latter by intentional free fall. As a result of the lumber drop, layers of virgin snow had collapsed and this had precipitated successive snow surface cave-ins for miles around, in much the way a row of dominoes goes down. On many occasions on a previous expedition, I had been out on the trail with a dog team, moving along into virgin unexplored territory on skis, when suddenly the surface would jar beneath my feet. Then would come a rumble that picked up momentum as it moved away from me in all directions until far off in the distance a diminishing roar died once again into peaceful quiet.

Though the Antarctic Hush had produced widespread alarm among the men, Bowers was determined to move quickly to the Pole. He planned to start the 22nd, when he, Tuck, Bristol and Powell would set out by dog team, leaving the other four men behind to repair the Weasel. The new transmission had been installed in the Weasel, but the men would have to wait until more batteries were dropped to them.

Bowers' desire to reach the Pole quickly stemmed from two facts. The first was that the Air Force was beginning to drop construction material and equipment there and it was desirable to be on hand to retrieve, store and arrange the dropped supplies. Secondly, I was scheduled to arrive at the Pole on that day.

However, there was no need for him to hasten to the Pole on my account. I started off that Thanksgiving day from McMurdo after a long series of last farewells, only to have the weather turn bad so that when we got to Beardmore Glacier, the plane returned to McMurdo. After undoing all my fond farewells, I was put back on stand-by status, on the alert for future calls on short notice.

My comfortable but unsuccessful flight that day was in sharp contrast to what was occurring on the ground in those eight miles between Bowers' first camp and the Geographic Pole. Dufek, a ship and aircraft specialist, had on several occasions ridiculed the inclusion of dog teams on Deep Freeze I and II as a costly $40,000 concession to antiquated Antarctic expedition practices. However, as I had pointed out, the dogs might one day prove to be good insurance compared with the hundreds of pairs of useless snowshoes the Navy had brought to the Antarctic despite evidence of their lack of utility.

Jack Tuck later described the short trip to the Pole:

> The trip was a grueling one, and possible only because of the dogs who were pulling about a 900-pound weight, about two-thirds the normal load, at a steady two miles per hour pace. For the men, it was all we could do to hike the eight miles. A dog team is normally given a five-minute rest every hour, however for the men's sake much more than the dogs' it was necessary to rest much more often. I confess I was extremely proud of that bunch of hounds and their performance—I'd worked with them for over a year, and this was their first real test, which they passed with flying colors. Our admiration for Scott and Shackleton, man-hauling across the plateau, increased tremendously.

The high altitude and the sastrugi-strewn path to the Pole had winded the not-yet-acclimated men so that they arrived gasping for breath. All suffered severe headaches. Nevertheless, they set up a camp near the equipment dropped by the C-124. They were to be out of their parkas and windproof pants only when they crawled into their sleeping bags inside the cold tents they had erected.

They arrived at the Pole none too soon, for Globemasters whose pilots were impatient to get their mission over with were already overhead dropping food, building panels and more lumber. The Air Force had developed a special mechanism for its drops so that the men on the snow would not be excessively burdened in retrieving the fallen gear. This was a "quick release" gadget which was supposed to disengage the pallets from their parachutes as soon as they hit the snow surface. Such a mechanism seemed essential because with the expected winds at the Pole, if a parachute remained attached to a package once it reached the surface, the package would take off like a powered sled and disappear over the horizon.

Unfortunately, for reasons we never determined, many of the quick-release mechanisms went off as soon as pallets cleared the Globemaster dropwells and the parachutes jerked open. Other parachutes failed to open and streamed in. As a result, Bowers was faced with a major problem that threw his schedule completely off.

On the same day he reached the Pole, he informed us at McMurdo: "Two critical chutes streamed in—one Jamesway section and one aurora section." The loaded pallets had plowed so deeply into the snow that they were extracted with difficulty. The loss of the sections intended to be used to construct the aurora tower, which was eventually to sit atop the observatory building, was especially costly, for Bowers had intended to utilize these 4 x 8-foot panels to erect a generator shelter and workshop until the permanent South Pole Station had been constructed and the aurora tower could be set where it was intended to go.

On November 24, Bowers added to his sad list of stream-ins when reporting back to McMurdo. A priceless mechanic's box full of tools lay buried where no one would ever find it. So did another replacement set of aurora panels. In addition, a 24-barrel pallet of mogas had been lost, as well as a container of fuel oil, avgas (aviation gasoline) and lumber. Of the gear that was successfully located, Bowers reported that he and his three companions had to chase some of it two and three miles. But in several instances they had found burst or crushed packages that had fallen from poorly lashed containers.

Because of what was occurring, I was most anxious to reach the Pole and help Bowers. On the other hand Dick sent word back that he wanted me to wait until I (the elderly gentleman) could be received into a warm and comfortable temporary shelter. Nevertheless, after my first futile attempt to reach the Pole on the 22nd, I made daily attempts to join Bowers' party. However, poor weather conditions forced me back at McMurdo airstrip each time. Perhaps this was just as well, because I thus had further opportunities to locate other items that would come in handy at the Pole. I also had a chance to argue further with the Task Force about fulfilling my request to Dufek regarding the barracks building I wanted for the South Pole Station. One earmarked for the Pole was on its way to McMurdo, I further confirmed, though the Task Force staff continued to insist it would not be transhipped to the Pole until a year later.

Besides wanting me to postpone my arrival, Dick sent back messages protesting the Air Force's desire to parachute a man into his tent camp. Sergeant Richard J. Patton was the man the Air Force wanted to drop in to the Pole to check on the arrival of the Globemasters and the airdrops. Once he was on the ground, "Airdale," as Patton was nicknamed, would talk with the pilots by "Handie-Talkie" and give them directions regarding the timing and placing of the drops. Bowers objected to Patton's parachuting onto the Pole as an unnecessary stunt and requested that he be landed on the snow by an R4D.

Despite Bowers' protest on the 25th, Patton floated down on the polar plateau, the first man in history to do so. However, instead of landing with Bowers' party, he came down at Weasel Camp eight miles away. There he and the four men who had been left behind installed new batteries that had been dropped with him and managed to get the Weasel in operation. Then they set out for the Pole and arrived shortly before midnight. Patton immediately went to work on his ground-to-plane walkie-talkie radio as controller for air deliveries, for more food, fuel, building panels, lumber and radio equipment which came pouring down from the sky.

At three A.M. the following morning two R4D's touched down at the Pole with ten additional construction members of Bowers' advance party. This brought Bowers' total to nineteen with five more to come besides myself. I was supposed to reach the Pole in another plane at approximately the same time as the arriving ten, but again my plane did not take off from McMurdo because of mechanical trouble.

My enthusiasm rose the following day when Dick reported that his party had erected its first Jamesway hut, a 32 x 16-foot insulated-fabric structure 8 feet high, the first semipermanent habitation ever erected at the South Pole. They had worked all night long at a temperature of −25°, and by the time they were finished all were exhausted, cold and hungry. It was eight A.M. when the building was completed and since they were living in continuous sunlight without a rigid schedule, they tore into a meal and then headed into the Jamesway for a long sleep.

Ironically, all were up and out of the Jamesway five hours later. The heat had been so stifling that they yearned for fresh air, no matter how cold or rare.

Two other events of significance occurred that day. One was the first mail-drop delivery at the Pole in history. The second was an offer from Dufek to name Jack Tuck as Officer-in-Charge of the military personnel at the Pole Station during the coming IGY year. Jack had originally requested to be sent to the Knox Coast after the Pole Station construction job was completed, and Dufek's offer of the command of the military contingent at the South Pole Station came as a complete surprise to him. Dick Bowers would remain to complete the construction of the Pole Station and then fly home to his wife and children.

Back at McMurdo I learned of Dufek's offer to Tuck. It sounded like a good idea for I had liked what I had seen of Jack, who'd been in charge of the expedition's dogs before going to the Pole. I recall that shortly after this I went to visit old Air Force Sergeant Dutch Dolleman, a veteran of the USAS, in his dogtown shack. He, too, had heard the news about Jack.

"You're mighty lucky," he told me. "Jack's a good boy, as fine as they come." I'd known Dutch for years both on and off expeditions, and his high opinion of Jack set my mind at ease once and for all.

"And another thing," Dutch went on. "This pup Bravo you've been eying as a mascot for the Pole Station will be all yours now. He's really Jack's dog, and Jack will insist on having him."

"Fine," I agreed, reaching down to pat the three-month-old ball of fuzz yapping playfully at our feet.

With the increase in his party and the return of the Weasel on the 26th, Bowers could now proceed to complete the construction camp preparatory to erecting the South Pole Station. A D-2 Caterpillar tractor floated down on the 27th, and though it landed on its side, the men soon had it upright and in operation leveling snow and recovering airdrops. The second construction camp Jamesway, a larger structure 56 feet long, also went up that day. Bowers sent all the men to live in this second Indian-like lodge, while he and Tuck took quarters in the smaller Jamesway after allocating most of its space for use as the camp galley and for the Army TBW field radio gear.

On the 28th, while I was pleased with Bowers' progress in building his construction camp, I fretted over other matters. My arrival at the Pole seemed as far off as ever. And in addition, the Air Force had disquieting news to report. The Eighteenth Air Force was running out of drop equipment and usable Globemasters. This last matter was cause for mounting concern. Of the original eight Globemasters three of them, worth more than $8,000,000, sat crash-damaged on the ice runway.

The temporary loss of the three Globemasters as well as the P2V, which had crashed with four fatalities just before I had arrived, meant we were paying a severe price for putting a South Pole Station into operation. It made me apprehensive that the sum total of what might be accomplished at the Pole would never equal its cost in lives and dollars. Yet the play had begun, the first actors were on the scene, and the second act was ready to begin.

A tremendous task still lay ahead and I thought of the valiant deeds Bowers and his advance party had already performed in the past ten days. Nothing must keep him from completing his task. Certainly the fact that three of the eight Globemasters could no longer travel to the Pole was disheartening. So was the loss so far of 15 to 25 per cent of the airdrops due to stream-ins. Yet most of the losses to this point were in materials for Bowers' construction camp and not for the permanent South Pole Station. And much of this could be replaced from stock on hand at McMurdo.

The plane losses and stream-ins were not the only reasons for the Air Force's mounting concern. There was also the assertion that the IGY had raised its tonnage requirements for the South Pole Station, and that the Air Force had not planned on moving so much cargo. There had been little in the way of communication between the IGY in Washington and me to correct this misunderstanding. In fact, the IGY had been able to maintain little contact with me in their frantic rush to get the men and equipment selected for the other IGY stations. "It's as if I were far off at the end of the earth," I told Murray Wiener half-jestingly. What had happened was that no allowance had been made for the requirements of Bowers' advance party of twenty-four who were to construct the South Pole Station. They alone required some sixty tons of equipment that had not been included in the initial IGY estimate. This meant more flights, more drops and more drop equipment.

Despite all these factors working against it, the 63rd Troop Carrier Group of the 18th Air Force planned no diminution of effort until the job was done. I was again impressed with Colonel Horace A. Crosswell, commander of the 63rd TCG, a man of sterling character who was always co-operative despite his many problems. "We'll do our best," he assured me.

Yet roughly a hundred tons of food, medical gear and operational equipment for the South Pole Station was still on the ships which had not yet arrived at McMurdo when I was again put on the alert to depart on Friday, November 30. Dufek had not realized that there was this much still to come and was appalled when I brought it to his attention. "And I want my barracks building," I told Dufek again.

This time there was no false alarm of the sort I had grown so accustomed to expect since Thanksgiving. The R4D's were warming up on the airstrip when I arrived. I was to fly in one with a great deal of gear, including a field radio transmitter for the Pole Station, while the final five men of Bowers' advance party—Seabees Chaudoin, Roberts, McCrillis, McCormick and Tyler—were to travel in the other plane.

I had the feeling that we would reach the bottom of the world this time. And I was right. As we flew to the Pole, I wondered how Bowers and the others felt, those rugged volunteers alone there on the white nothingness. Would they be able to handle their mammoth job?

I would soon know.

Chapter 15

FIRST WEEKS AT THE POLE

THE flight to the Pole from McMurdo took five hours in good weather. We climbed slowly at first as the Task Force Center disappeared quickly from view.

We encountered an interesting phenomenon on the flight to the Pole. "What's that?" the pilot asked, pointing down to a large slightly dark area on the snow surface. "It looks like a cloud shadow," he said, "but there isn't a cloud in the sky."

This was something I had encountered frequently while flying during the third expedition in 1940. I could remember day after day flying over one area above which an odd-shaped cloud continuously lay close to the surface. Then one day I flew the same route and although there was not a cloud in the sky in that area, outlined on the surface was a distinct image of the former cloud.

"That's a photo image of a cloud that recently lay close to the surface," I told the R4D pilot. He stared at me as though I were pulling his leg. Actually, the physical explanation of the cloud image was that the sun's rays had created a different temperature in the areas adjacent to the cloud than existed in its shade. The moisture of the cloud combined with the lower temperature beneath it to cause fresh ice crystals that had a different appearance from the surrounding snow. Thus when the cloud was gone, its impression still remained on the surface.

Weather was poor for flying when we arrived over the South Pole and the pilot had to be talked down to a landing. As we swept in low, bright-hued dots on the snow turned out to be Bowers' advance party hustling about in orange, black, red, blue, green and brown parkas, or Windbreakers, and flags marking caches, trails, the outline of the camp and sundry other things. The parachutes from the airdrops strewn on the snow brought to mind a Chinese laundry that had been hit by a hurricane. The ground looked fairly smooth from the air, but it felt mighty rough in landing and consisted chiefly of hard sastrugi bumps with soft spots between. We were well shaken up by the time we climbed out.

Dick Bowers and several others came out with the Weasel from camp and greeted me warmly. "Well, you finally made it," he laughed. I noticed that even though swathed in heavy outer garments, he and the original members of the first landing party looked thinner than I remembered them.

"What, haven't you got it all built yet?" I asked him in mock dismay. "What have you been up to since I saw you last?"

"Not much," he said, sweeping an arm toward his construction camp.

A few hundred yards from the ice runway dark mounds of 400-pound fuel drums created a somber fence of a sort. Beyond them, amid a crazy quilt pattern of vehicle treadmarks, squatted Bowers' construction camp. In one group were Bowers' two olive-green Jamesways, an orange-colored box made from the aurora tower panels and a makeshift shelter covered by parachutes, while to one side were the two survival tents, mute evidence of the advance party's first days at the Pole. Off to the other side of the camp lay several of the large packages dropped by the C-124's, while beyond the camp steel beams and timber lay in a tangled mass. The air was full of the noise of the growling tractor, the zing of saws, the pounding of hammers and the yelping of the tethered dogs. In the distance I could make out the tractor hauling airdrop pallets. The place was busy as a bee hive.

"Quite an establishment you have here," I told Dick. And in all truth it was. For when one considered that everything here had to be carried 850 miles from McMurdo and from sea level on the coast to an altitude of more than 9,000 feet in the center of the continent, it was indeed an awesome sight. Dick's embarrassed mien upon hearing my words gave indication that he considered what he had accomplished to be in the day's work. But that, I knew from experience with Byrd and others, was a common characteristic of fearless men of action.

We walked through the camp to the smaller Jamesway where I was to live while the South Pole Station was being constructed. One of the first things I noticed as we passed the fuel drums was that I was moving a little slower than my usual pace. The altitude had slowed me and I knew there would be no running about in a place like this, at least not until my lungs had grown accustomed to the rarefied atmosphere. I was sufficiently warm at −25° in my mohair-lined parka, though I wondered how effective that covering would be during the extreme cold that would come the following March. We were now approaching the height of the South Pole summer during this month of December, a thankful prospect considering the heavy outdoor work that lay ahead.

Jack Tuck was to return to McMurdo on one of the two R4D's that had brought me and the remaining five Seabees to the Pole, and I was to replace him as Dick's roommate in the corner of the smaller Jamesway. "Here's port," said Dick, as we entered the Jamesway, a noisy spot indeed since it served also as the galley, radio shack, weather station, office, first aid station and a host of other odds and ends activities.

Jack was getting his gear together in the far end above the cacophony of voices, banging pots and crackling radio static. Dufek wanted him back at McMurdo for a while for briefing and to attend to our needs from the sending end of the program as well as to prepare his own gear for the winter ahead. After that, he would return as a "permanent" resident at the Pole while Bowers and his men would leave to be replaced by the eight Navy men who would be under Tuck's supervision in handling the housekeeping and radio duties of the IGY Station, and the eight IGY men under my charge.

I was still not reconciled to the notion of maintaining a split command among the Pole personnel, though I warmly shook Jack's hand. And Jack quickly disabused me of any idea I might have entertained that he might take into consideration my greater experience in the Antarctic. For he immediately quizzed me rather sharply about some of the changes in the South Pole Station layout I had earlier proposed to Bowers. "Why do you want to turn the powerhouse and garage around to face the leeward side?" he asked. "Why do you want a barracks building?" Patiently, I replied to these and other questions and our conversation ended on a friendly note.

"I'll be talking to you from the air," he told me before departing, "because I'll be flying overhead with some of the C-124's when they make their drops."

We walked to the ice strip together.

"I'll see you about Christmastime or perhaps New Year's Day," I told Jack just before he scrambled aboard the R4D.

"Be sure to bring Bravo when you come," I called after him.

I watched as his plane blasted into the air with the aid of its JATO bottles and headed toward the rim of the Queen Maud Mountains. It would fly over the mountains and then drop down to the gas cache manned by a half-dozen men at the foot of Liv Glacier. After refueling here, the plane would then fly the remaining 500 miles back to McMurdo.

As Tuck's plane took off, billowing white smoke from its JATO bottles enveloped us, and within five minutes the entire construction camp was enveloped in dense white clouds. Inside of minutes the entire sky was overcast, and with the disappearance of the horizon a white-out condition prevailed for a few minutes, forcing the men to grope about the camp at their tasks. I was to see this man-made white-out every time a plane took off from the Pole.

After Jack departed, I made a tour of the construction camp and examined the area where the permanent Pole was to rise. The 56-foot Jamesway housed all the men except Dick and me and was crowded with the Seabees' colorful clothing gear. Beside the smaller Jamesway stood a 35-foot radio antenna. Of the two survival tents, one was serving as camp toilet or village outhouse, and its packing-box furnishings and icy floor made it appear most primitive. The "aurora tower" shack presented its own problem in logistics. After three towers had streamed in, Bowers' carpenters had constructed one themselves from salvaged panels. It served now as a line shack for a little gas generator which provided lights for the camp and power for the radio. A quick check of the A-22 containers revealed that only a trifling amount of IGY gear had arrived at the Pole as yet.

That night when I wearily climbed into my sleeping bag and closed my eyes to the endlessly circling sun, I felt as though that first day at the Pole had contained a hundred hours instead of just twenty-four. A strange peace was settling over me when suddenly two men began working on a generator outside the corner of the Jamesway, and continued to do so all night long. From the other side of our sleeping quarters came the continuous squeaking and squawking of the radio. Its racket never let up, since the receiver was on stand-by night and day—though weather reports were transmitted back to McMurdo only on a three-hour interval.

"You'll get used to the generator and radio noise," Dick told me the next morning when I shook my head to clear my mind.

Even though this was only my second day at the Pole I had an insatiable curiosity to find out what the temperature was deep in the snow. Dufek's landing at the Pole had produced no physical information except the report that the snow was stubbornly hard when the men attempted to jam a flag into it.

I went out to the area which would adjoin our upwind snow reserve, that second day, and began digging a hole with an access ramp leading down into it. After going down a few feet, I had to cut out ice blocks with a small snow saw and dig them out with a shovel, a difficult task for someone not yet acclimated to the high altitude. Down six feet the temperature read −54° F. But I was not yet at the isothermal layer and I wasn't certain how far down it would be. However, it did confirm my belief that the weather would be extremely cold during the coming winter. I also learned what Dufek's trouble had been in trying to stick a flag in the snow. At a depth varying from one to two feet, I encountered a singularly resistant layer about one-half-inch thick. This hard layer was probably the result of a heavy windstorm at the Pole some four years or so earlier.

That first day of digging I moved about five tons of snow, and in four days I had created a pit eighteen feet deep. My thermometers showed −62° F., or what I believed to be a close estimate of the Pole's annual mean temperature. Similar diggings on earlier expeditions to Little America had produced a comparable −10°. Thus I reasoned that we could look forward to a temperature fifty degrees colder than Little America. Since the winter night at Little America got down to −70°, then −120° was a reasonable guess for the coldest winter temperature we might expect at the Pole. I checked my conclusion by another line of reasoning. If −60° was the mean temperature and 0° the highest summer temperature, then if the South Pole was like most other places the coldest winter temperature would be displaced equally below the mean. Again the answer was −120° F. The world's record was −89.7° F., set in 1933 at Oimyakon, Siberia. But this would be mild if my calculations were right, for we would have to endure temperatures a disconcerting thirty degrees colder! Even at −60° I had seen men spitting blood because the capillaries of the bronchial tract frosted. What would happen to men outdoors below −100°? We would find out in time, I told myself, half in apprehension and half in excitement.

My snow pit had another purpose besides that of delving for annual and cold temperatures. I had brought along equipment to check the density of the snow as well. Colonel Crosswell, commanding the 18th Air Force Globemasters delivering our supplies, was wondering about the possibility of landing those largest operational transport planes in the world on the polar snow. Was it hard enough?

My instruments showed that though the snow got harder and harder as I went down, it did not seem to increase proportionately in density. The ice blocks seemed heavier but this was illusory, for the specific gravity was .3 at the surface and only .4 twelve feet below the surface. "No. Your freight shipments will have to continue coming by airdrop," I notified Crosswell. It would have been a godsend to land the planes and call a halt to the costly stream-ins and the wasting of even more expensive drop equipment and especially parachutes, some of which cost far more than the items to which they were attached, but this was not to be. Dick Bowers and I made ramsound hardness tests, which amount to driving a bar into the snow by the uniform force of a weight dropped from a measured height. This confirmed our conclusion that it would take positive compaction of the surface before wheeled aircraft could land safely.

I made still another use of the snow pit. Before I quit working in the hole, I put 40 oranges into it for a treat during the coming winter.

The day after my arrival the tractor operator began bulldozing out shallow foundations for the Station's buildings and running the tractor back and forth in the resultant holes to beat down the snow preparatory to laying down timber. Drops were also coming in with more material for the Station. The schedule called for the erection of the garage and toilet first. After these would come the mess hall and the other buildings.

South Pole Station plans had been laid out in Washington by the Navy with IGY concurrence. They were considered firm by the beginning of Deep Freeze II, and Bowers had orders not to make any changes in the blueprints without going through the Navy chain of command. However, he was intelligent enough to realize that there were areas where the blueprints did not take into consideration what previous expeditions had learned the hard way about survival in the Antarctic, and that to hold to ill-advised prior decisions could cause difficulties later. He was therefore willing to accept the fruit of the experience I had gained in previous expeditions to the Antarctic. On my part, I gave only suggestions and never orders, which would have antagonized him. Yet I shudder to think what might have occurred later had someone less understanding than Dick been in charge of construction.

As I have mentioned earlier, one of the changes I wanted was to turn the garage and powerhouse around so that the garage doors would open to the leeward side and not the windward side as originally planned. My reason for this was to keep the windward side free of any traffic in order to keep the snow which we would have to melt for our water as pure as possible. Also it was essential to maintain the windward side of the Station free for our many sensitive scientific instruments and the installations which were to face in that direction. We had to put in a geomagnetic and seismographic tunnel and a snow mine for glaciology studies on that side and I wanted that yard unmolested by other activities. In addition, it was my belief that there would be less snowdrift and trouble on the leeward side and that the garage doors should open in that direction. If they opened on the other side, we would have cold wind and snow entering the camp proper during the long winter night, which would mean considerable heat loss.

Bowers accepted my points unhesitantly to my great satisfaction. He also agreed to other changes. For instance, the original plans called for snow around each building up to its roof, a requirement ordered by the Navy fire marshal. "If the Navy fire marshal will come and live with us," I told Dick, "then I'll agree to this."

I proposed a firebreak about the width of a Jamesway hut to divide the camp in the middle. Roughly half our food, fuel and gear would be distributed in each section, in case half the camp burned. In addition, I asked Dick to build an enclosed chicken wire and burlap insulated passageway encircling the Station so we could fight fires, if necessary from all sides of any building. This passageway would also make it possible for us to go from building to building without going outdoors during the winter. "And if we bulldozed snow on the outer side of the passageway on the windward side," I suggested, "it would keep the Station warmer and cut down on our fuel needs." We had computed that it cost ten dollars to deliver a gallon of fuel to the South Pole.

There was one other essential change that Dick accepted. As at the other IGY stations, the Navy had planned to put our fuel barrels out in the open. I, however, could not picture leaving the Station in the dark at minus one hundred degrees to wrestle in a 400-pound barrel of fuel. It would have to be done by hand, for no vehicle we had could operate at such low temperatures. And even if we did so, the fuel would be frozen and would take an interminable time to thaw. Bowers saw the impracticality of this and agreed to pile barrels three or four high along "Main Street," the enclosed passageway running the length of the camp, and also to create a main fuel cache alongside the garage facing the midway snow-wall firebreak.

Specifications called for four different height Station buildings. This created a problem. If the foundations were made at the same depth, the buildings would protrude at varying heights and cause dangerous snowdrifts to build up. Therefore, the foundations had to be at different depths so that the roof levels would be identical. In this fashion, the snow would blow over all tops. In some cases, this would mean digging three or four feet down before starting construction, and in other instances foundations would sit on platforms above the snow. But when winter came and the winds blew snow against the Station, all the buildings would be safe from drifts and none would protrude except the crownlike Rawin Dome for tracking weather balloons and the box-shaped aurora tower for observing the southern lights. Since these two structures had to be above the expected snow that would wash over the tops of the buildings, they would stand on stilts: the Rawin Tower above the mess hall at one end of the camp, the aurora tower above the science building near the other.

Even with all these alterations, I realized that there might prove to be other awkward and uncomfortable features in the completed Station. But these would have to reveal themselves by usage.

When I first arrived at the South Pole, I knew only a part of the construction crew by name. I was a stranger in the midst of the Seabees and it was difficult to get acquainted with them. They were a closely knit team because they had wintered together and had shared the rigors of the Antarctic, and I was an outsider. Their jokes and conversations were not things I grasped easily, especially single words or phrases that conjured up entire thoughts to them but left me bewildered as to their meaning. Yet I recalled how on earlier expeditions we had coined a similar jargon of our own with words such as "ob" to describe the art of taking off "to make a scientific observation," usually at the mess hall, when the work got too heavy, and "flag waving," which signified the fine military skill of apple polishing. The Seabees were always courteous and kind to me personally, yet it was obvious that I didn't belong to their set.

Of course, Dick Bowers was always courteous and the chiefs proved friendly on longer acquaintanceship and gradually the crew thawed out toward me.

The Seabees had proved themselves to be among the toughest during World War II, and these men of the construction crew were the cream of the Seabees. They groused, as do all military personnel, but this never affected their work. In fact, they worked as though they were trying to set some sort of a record: hauling, pounding, sawing, lifting and scrambling about the construction field like whirling dervishes.

If there was something abnormal about these Seabees, it was their language they used among themselves. It was descriptive, imaginative, forceful and absolutely unprintable. In all my experiences on merchant ships, on the battlefield or in the Antarctic, and this included my recent stay at McMurdo, I must admit that I never heard so many four-letter words applied to perfectly common objects and situations. Perhaps it permitted them to let off steam, or perhaps it was merely a means by which youthful, physically minded men attempted to add to their stature with their fellow workers. And yet perhaps they too had reason for complaint about my language, for once, after a lengthy explanation of a natural phenomenon, one of them said to me, "I hear you, Doc, but I don't read you."

But there was no denying that these men were doing a monumental job. As fast as the material dropped from the sky, we uncrated it or dragged it to camp, and the men kept busy utilizing it. And as the days passed, instead of the nameless individuals they were to me at the outset, they became men whose widely varying personalities I came to recognize and appreciate. This was so even though outdoors we were with few exceptions similarly attired in heavy boots, colored parkas, blizzard-proof trousers, mittens, gloves and anti-snowblindness goggles that made us resemble deep-sea divers. Dick Bowers and Chief Petty Officer Charles M. (Slats) Slaton wore unique costumes that distinguished them from the others. Outdoors Dick dressed in orange windproofs and wore a hood that had a vestlike attachment and a fur ruff over the outside of his parka. Slats, who functioned as Dick's straw boss, or the whip who kept everything going smoothly, most often wore no parka, but only a sweater over his underwear. How he did so without freezing was a subject of speculation among the men.

Because of the need to dovetail camp operations with the airdrop schedule, we operated on an odd work schedule. We usually did not get up in the "mornings" until noon, for the first C-124's generally arrived at one in the afternoon and the last one made its drop about five P.M. And if we worked well past midnight we could drag in the material before turning in for the "night."

Actually, often the dropped equipment wasn't all retrieved till long after midnight. For several days after I arrived I woke up at 6:30 A.M. by habit, even though the grinding generator and squeaking radio had kept me half awake most of the night. We took breakfast between twelve and one, a coffee break after three hours of work, then a heavy lunch between six and seven, another coffee break at nine and then supper between eleven and midnight. The food was none too palatable, for Spiers, our cook, admitted himself that he was a better mechanic than a cook. With his long blond beard and waxed mustache, he reminded me of a medieval philosopher, though his colorful language and wealth of humorous anecdotes classified him more as a "character."

On an average day, the roar of the first arriving plane brought most of us hurrying out to our drop zone that lay stretched before us like a great front yard. In circling the Pole as it made its drops, the red-trimmed silver Globemaster was actually flying around the world and every time it crossed the 180th Meridian, the world's date line, it left today to fly into tomorrow. "Well, here it is Tuesday," the pilot would call out to us waiting below in the Monday time zone. We could generally expect this sort of conversation four times during the afternoon, since we averaged four drop sessions a day.

Before I left McMurdo, Colonel Crosswell had offered to assign Air Force Sergeant Richard "Airdale" Patton to work with me full-time on guiding airdrops. However, after Patton parachuted in to the Pole, Dick Bowers, faced with problems of his own which demanded he make full use of every available man, assigned him to various other duties, though Patton still attended to "Handie-Talkie" guiding of airdrops with the plane pilots. As the only Air Force man at the Pole, Patton was an outsider like myself, and he underwent a great deal of kidding from the Seabees, all of which he took in good grace.

As the lead plane of the day flew overhead, Patton would make his way to the drop zone, followed by a group of us onlookers, where he soon had his radio tuned to conversation inside the plane:

"Cargo doors open!"

"Cargo doors open, sir!"

"Twenty seconds . . .

"Fifteen seconds . . .

"Ten . . .

"Five, four, three, two—drop!"

Then out from the belly of the Globemaster packages hurtled into space, often to be lost to our sight below momentarily because of the bright sun in the background. Then they returned to view as their parachutes struggled open.

For what seemed like an age we plane watchers stood motionless and prayed for the parachutes to open. For if they did not, the packages would stream in and bury themselves deep in the snow, some of them never to be seen again, others to be damaged beyond repair. We were also concerned that the streamers might hit some of us men as they plummeted earthward. And even when parachutes opened, a light wind could drag the packages off across the snow unless we could catch up with the chutes and cut the shroud lines to collapse them. The lumber came in via a free-fall drop without parachutes and occasionally a metal-strapped bundle of planks burst apart on the surface like a bomb, exploding wood for hundreds of yards.

Three different size parachutes were employed depending on the size and weight of the dropped packages. Small packages came down with a 24-foot chute and one-ton drops were under a 64-foot chute. A fuel platform measuring twelve feet by six feet and containing 24 drums—each weighing over 400 pounds—floated to us strapped to three white parachutes, each of which was 100 feet in diameter and had cost in the neighborhood of $1,200 each.

Streamers were always a heartache. The damaged and lost items meant either deprivation or additional expense for replacement—if similar items were fortunately available at McMurdo. For instance, for a few days fully half of the 24-fuel-drum platforms streamed, causing concern as to the ability of the Pole Station personnel to survive the coming winter night. When the fuel platforms streamed in, they disappeared completely from sight as the snow piled in the fifteen-foot hole they created. The only way they were discovered was by searching for fresh holes among the increasing maze of other pits where other items had been dug out. Even so, when they had penetrated ten feet or so below the snow surface, we had to dig laboriously to retrieve the drums because the undersnow hardened above them quickly. And after hauling the drums to the surface so Slats Slaton could drag them back to camp with the tractor, we often found the effort had been useless because the salvaged drums had been smashed or had sprung leaks. As an experiment, barrels of diesel oil were free-dropped, but they burst their seams and sprayed the area with fuel. Either the drops were made from too high an altitude or the drums were too weak or the surface too hard, for this system had previously worked well on the Greenland icecap.

The sticks, boards and pads that hurtled down on us from faulty drops were always a menace, but though the men had to remain perpetually alert, our thoughts centered more on the actual streamers than on this danger. For would we be able to find the stream-ins? And if we did, what essential equipment would be damaged or ruined? Our precious set of Encyclopaedias, which I had planned to use to settle minor factual disputes bound to come up during the coming winter, was one lost stream-in I could not replace. We dug in many spots but never found the volumes. This also happened to a ton of food airdropped in one box. Another box containing our entire supply of tomato juice streamed in and splattered the snow blood-red over a wide area. In several instances, steel beams were bent by the impact of landing and the builders had a great deal of trouble straightening them. The first building to be erected was to be the garage and on one early occasion we stood horrified as part of the garage walls streamed in. Fortunately, because they landed on end, they went only nine feet down and were salvageable.

I was the only person in the construction camp with vested interest in the IGY science gear. The more delicate instruments were to be delivered by landing ski-equipped planes, while the rest was to be airdropped. Thus I went to the drop zone each day to drag IGY gear back to camp on a little plastic sled and care for it until it could be installed. I took responsibility for storage of the IGY gear and South Pole Station living needs. At McMurdo, Wessbecher and I had labeled the containers by code number, so that when the air crew radioed WE ARE DROPPING NUMBERS 6, 9 AND 17, I would know what to expect.

This had seemed an orderly system for the IGY gear drops, and I had prided myself for having devised it. But by mid-December serious flaws became apparent. By then a significant amount of our material had been lost in stream-in airdrops, and still more had been damaged, including material for all phases of the scheduled program. Then, too, whoever packed the material which had arrived after my departure had not always bothered to invoice and label the containers so that after many a successful drop I hauled in a container of equipment with no idea of its contents. While Bowers reported to Tuck, who was now conversing with us regularly from McMurdo by radio contact, on discrepancies and shortages in construction material, I did likewise for IGY equipment.

My diary entries for this period show the following:

December 9   The three drops today were much poorer than usual. They dropped several water tanks which clobbered in, four out of seven coming loose from their harnesses. What hurt most were stream-ins of our Collins Radio gear and IGY material. We are still not certain whether we found it all. The retrievers are still at work.

December 10   One "H" harness on Plane 992 lost its entire load. Fortunately, most of the items recovered appear usable. Pibal * tripod cracked; ice chisels bent; snow stakes broken open. I made inventory and inspection and moved the boxes as close as possible to where they will eventually be used. The two built-in items, the Ionosphere Chassis and Hydrogen Generator, arrived safely. I prepared a message to go back to Howard Wessbecher at McMurdo concerning arrival material, especially the many discrepancies. I had no shipping manifests on the "H" harness and an A-22 container, with the result that I do not know what might have been lost.

December 11   When the radio announcement reported IGY gear to be dropped, I went out to watch each pass. A P.O.L.** platform came down properly under billowing para-

* Tripod legs for theodolite used in measuring meteorological pilot-balloon ascents.
** Military short name for items in the class of petroleum, oil or lubricants.

chutes. But one of the first A-22 containers with IGY gear streamed in. I went to the drop zone to determine by a process of elimination which one it was. It was container "13" that was missing.

While I stood at the drop zone, several more packages came down. Then two more planes appeared and still another A-22 container streamed in, landing with such force that it snapped the unopened parachute in and after it. Patton went out to sight the two loads but couldn't find them. Then Bowers and I trudged out and located both after long search. One was down ten feet and "Randy" Randall, Bowers' man in charge of all vehicles, cut out the container with a tractor and pulled it loose. The top of the second container was in sight only a foot below the surface. Then Slats drove out with the Weasel and we towed everything back to camp. Quick inspection shows considerable damage to both containers. Aurora-3 looks worse. Seismology-1 seems all right even though the boxes are bashed in. I had to use a jack to pry open Ionosphere-8, a large steel chest which itself weighed 100 of the total 204 lbs. Most of its items were crushed—two 35 mm. film magazines, transformers, glass plates, etc., though amazingly three pyrex glass measuring cups were undamaged. This was another container that did not conform to manifest. Aurora-3 on second examination was a sad sight, with four electric clocks, a pair of binoculars, two developing tanks, etc., damaged. I made out a long radio message concerning details of the loss and asked for replacements. I also made a plea again for a Barracks Building.

December 17   Another big job today was to move a 300-lb. Ionosphere box to the science cache I have prepared. My back feels broken tonight from this effort because I had to move it without help.

But this was not my only arduous task today. A large quantity of caustic soda spilled out of the A-22-13 container when it streamed in, and I had to get rid of the soda. If the caustic gets into the snow, it will menace our snow-water supply because it is extremely poisonous. I struggled so hard at this task that I popped a button off my new underwear. And even though I took every precaution in handling the soda, I burned my wrist. I have put powdered vinegar on my wrist, but I don't know which burns me worse—the vinegar or the caustic soda.

Thus went my troubles with IGY gear that was airdropped. Fortunately the more sensitive IGY equipment presented no vexing problems because it was delivered to the Pole by landing planes. However, the pilots took a dim view of these landings on the polar plateau. A few days after I reached the camp, Slats and Randall dragged parachutes filled with snow over the sastrugi-strewn landing strip and smoothed out a 10,000-foot ice runway. Slats worked almost ceaselessly at this task. In fact, he came in one night four hours after the camp was asleep and this was the conclusion of a day that had begun the previous morning. We had long given up conjecturing why he did not freeze wearing only a sweater. Nor did he seem to have any need for snow glasses. However, while working outdoors one time, snow blindness overtook him, and some of the men were thankful that he showed the environment affected him in at least one way. Yet many stared at the bandage that he had to wear over one eye for a while as if CPO Slaton had betrayed them.

Slats' and Randall's smoothed-out snow strip acquired the name of "Ike's Pike," and we were ready for visitors early in December. I noted in my diary on Thursday, December 6:

> The big event of the day was the arrival of the P2V Neptune at 2300. At least it was a big event for me because thirteen boxes of non-drop IGY gear were aboard, and these were mostly MET (meteorological items).
>
> The plane crew, however, did not share my excitement at getting an entire shipment without any loss or breakage. For the plane skis froze to the surface and all the JATO available was insufficient to free it. Everyone felt the altitude in carrying the spare bottles 100 feet from the plane.
>
> Later, after an hour or two of effort, the pilot tried a take-off, but the jet engine failed to work properly. Finally he gave up after a long effort at outdoor repair because new ailments due to the cold occurred faster than the repairs to the engine. We absorbed the eight-man crew into the camp, with Captain Cordiner sleeping on crash pads on the floor of the 6 x 10-foot

room already occupied by Bowers and me. The crew inaugurated our only just finished "head" * by using it as their bunkhouse for the night.

Actually, they stayed all the next day and part of the one after that, removing a frozen pump from the jet engine, repairing and replacing it along with repairing several valves. Just before six P.M. on the 8th, the P2V was warmed up for the fourth time that day, and with the aid of jet bottles and props the plane staggered into the runway. Now sixteen JATO bottles were fired off but as far as we could see, the plane was still on the ground when the JATO died out. In the blowing snow and smoke we were all certain that our guests were here to stay for a long time, when through the dim, thick atmosphere I spied the plane in the air. The cloud of JATO smoke and vapor trailing behind it reminded me of a Navy destroyer squadron laying a white smokescreen.

Chapter 16

CONSTRUCTING THE SOUTH POLE STATION

IN a complex national operation each individual participant and each organization has a participating right to believe his is the key operation without which the whole mission would fail. The establishment of the IGY South Pole Station is a good example. The taxpayers, the President, Congress and the government staff agencies directing the mission had a vital stake. So too the National Academy of Sciences, the National Science Foundation and the IGY, both nationally and internationally, as well as their array of committees and directors, had proprietary interest, for it was their scientific program that was to be carried out. The Navy and its Task Force

* Navy name for the latrine or toilet.

43 knew that the Pole Station was theirs. The Army felt a special interest because one of their civilian scientists had been furnished as a leader for the Station. The Air Force obviously transported virtually everything the last 850 most difficult miles. The VX6 Air Squadron delivered the Seabees and the wintering party. The Seabees at the moment were doing all the work on the site. Later the winter party would feel that they alone were doing the vital payoff task. I could go on, enumerating down to individuals, who could well say "If it weren't for what I did, the Station wouldn't exist." Yes, it certainly was an interdependent enterprise.

Naturally, the Seabees and I at the Pole looked with a jaundiced eye upon each of the contributing elements if it faltered, stumbled or failed to deliver a 100 per cent performance. Thus we were quick to grumble and chide the Air Force's stream-ins or the Navy's packaging or the IGY casualness, and forget the superb effort, the conscientious work and the fatiguing hours the crews put in to do their job. I wish I could justly record the gallant part each person and each organization played to make this unique community a reality.

So it is that I continue to recount in this narrative the happenings from my vantage point; revealing knowingly biased criticism and praises where another observer might well have reversed the roles of the hero and villain.

Despite the difficulties occasioned by stream-ins and faulty drops, it was obvious to me that Bowers' crew meant business in constructing the South Pole Station. The McMurdo estimate was that if no untoward events occurred, these highly trained and skilled Seabees could complete the job in two or three months. However, without any swagger the crew talked among themselves of packaging the task within a month and flying off for home by Christmas.

They had several things in their favor. First, these men knew their business because of the intensive training to which Bowers had subjected them. Second, they were adept at improvising adequate substitute materials to replace those lost in airdrops. For instance, when the principal tool chest streamed in and disappeared, they were forced to use inadequate tools but still managed to accomplish their tasks. Where insulating materials vanished, cardboard and broken panels could be used to insulate floors. And third, back in McMurdo the winter before, the Seabee builders had gone over every panel meticulously to assure that each was uniformly able to fit so that here at the Pole later they could be certain that the parts would swiftly and accurately fit together.

As much as I had been in snow country I learned lessons from these Seabees in the use of bulldozer and snow. They lacked a crane to lift heavy roof panels to the top of the wall sections. Within minutes a ramp of snow was pushed up at one end and the builders could carry the panels to the roof with ease. Job done, the ramp was expeditiously 'dozed away.

Then there was the matter of the design of the buildings themselves. Prefabricated 4 x 8-foot modular panels designed for the Antarctic's paralyzingly cold climate made swift construction possible. The walls, floors and roofs were made of four-inch aluminum and plywood sandwiches filled with mats of Fiberglas. These panels came tongue and grooved and equipped with a device which enabled them to be readily clipped together. The buildings had the aluminum sheathing on the interior surface of the wall panels, while the plywood exterior was painted bright orange, a striking feature to help both planes and ground parties sight the Station. Within the buildings, plywood was used for partitions, since the design of the buildings eliminated the need for internal load-carrying walls. The buildings were to have few interior doors, thus cutting down construction time. Exterior doors only at each end were the refrigerator type.

The Seabees had not contracted to produce a finished camp either indoors or out. They were to go far enough, however, so that the wintering-over party could finish the necessary outdoor work before winter set in. Indoors, the Seabees had even less to do. The essential factor was to have firm, closed-in buildings which could be heated and occupied. The winter party could put in partitions, shelves, and conveniences after they arrived. So the Seabees concentrated on constructing first the shells of the houses and the basic caches and tunnels surrounding them. Inside, they had to erect the stoves, install the electrical system, complete a snow melter and a water-storage system, as well as a toilet and sewage-disposal system. Then they could leave with a clear conscience, feeling the job well done.

As I noted earlier, my agreement with Bowers prescribed uniform roof levels, a factor that added to the construction time since the buildings had to be set at various levels to achieve this effect. Fierce wintry blizzards might bury the camp to the eaves, and I suspected they would, but also the howling winds would keep the flat rooftops swept clear of snow. With solid panels for our walls, our only windows would be sealed triple-pane skylights. As an added safety feature escape hatches offering quick access to outdoors were to be constructed at strategic points along and up through the roof of the burlap and the chicken-wire-covered tunnel system which was to enclose the entire Pole Station. How much of all this the construction party could complete before their departure was uncertain. Yet it was obvious that there would be much left for the wintering party to complete.

Dick Bowers was, of course, construction boss, and Slats Slaton, the senior CPO, kept everything moving as construction whip. But Chief Charles A. Bevilacqua, a twenty-six-year-old Seabee from Woburn, Massachusetts, was actually in charge of the building of the houses and tunnel construction. That it should be understood who was doing the building, Bev early erected a sign at the Pole which read: CITY LIMITS OF WOBURN.

Bev sported a set of Irish-style black chin whiskers without a mustache that lent his appearance an extremely salty air. I found him an especially likable individual and at times we would sit down and converse. Dressed in orange-yellowish windproof trousers and olive-drab windproof jacket and headgear, Bev led his team of men in leveling snow, putting down the snow sills, setting the trusses in place beneath the buildings that required them, laying down the floor, raising the sides, snapping in place roof trusses and covering the structures with the roof panels.

Bev's team consisted of Parry R. Williamson, Howard A. Hisey, Richard Prescott, Patrick D. McCormick, Gordon Tyler and occasionally Robert L. Chaudoin. These men were so expert that once the foundation was laid they were able to put up the shell of a house in slightly over a day's labor. They could easily erect a house in two days on a twelve-hour-a-day work basis.

I grew very fond of the builders as I watched them in operation. I did not attempt to interfere with their work, however, though I made certain to my own satisfaction as future occupant of the buildings that the contractor was meeting specifications.

Williamson, who along with our cook "Sperocious" Spiers had the most luxuriant beards in camp, was an extremely capable carpenter. However, Willie remained somewhat of a mystery to me because he was not easy to engage in conversation. Hisey was known as "Kiwi" because he had become engaged during his recent R and R to a New Zealand girl he'd met earlier while on his way to the Antarctic. He always wore a Tam o' Shanter with a big pompon on top. Dick "Poodle Pusher" Prescott had served with the dog handlers at McMurdo and now took care of the eleven dogs in the construction camp as well as serving with the builders' team. Dick was well liked by the

other men and with his long, year-old heavy beard, he looked star-
tlingly like an Amish elder. His dogs, poor creatures, led a neglected
life. Tethered to a line, they could expect little attention from busy
Poodle Pusher, whose activities with the builders precluded him from
taking them out on runs. The result was that they led a typical dog's
life, though they did not complain too much.

Of the others in Bev's crew, "Red Iron" McCormick was an ambi-
tious lad of twenty-one and an effervescent individual who resembled
the college-boy type in his speech and loud dress and was often the
butt of the jokes played in camp. Red Iron was usually the man sitting
on top the house parts and swinging a mallet when the frame was
being assembled. "Tiny," as his co-worker Tyler was called, was a
burly young giant. The biggest and strongest man in camp, Tiny had
a wonderful smile that lit up like a spotlight. He kept up a running
line of light chatter. Tiny was the powerhouse of the builders' team
and also had charge of the inventoried lists of the airdrops. The last
of the builders was Bob Chaudoin, a soft-spoken Mississippian who
also doubled as postmaster, typist of Bowers' official log and assistant
meteorologist. Bob, with his distinctive movie actor features and
heavy black beard, was also well liked. It was Bob's hope that he
would be permitted to stay with Jack and me at the permanent Station
during the coming IGY period. But as a Navy man this decision was
up to Admiral Dufek, I told him.

Bevilacqua's builders were backed up by Slats, who also took personal charge of the power boys handling the tractor and Weasel
transportation and all the heavy machinery. With a group of three,
including the part-time service of Air Force Sergeant "Airdale"
Patton, Slats accomplished veritable miracles in output. His crew not
only did the drop retrieving including the digging out of the stream-ins,
but they also did the bulldozing in camp and kept all the vehicles and
generators running. Such maintenance proved to be a major problem
because our master toolbox was an early stream-in victim. In addition,
it consumed precious time. For instance, on one occasion when the
tractor was hauling some drop packages into camp, one of its tracks
broke. With only a minor curse into the wind, Slats was soon undoing
more than 400 bolts to make the change.

Another time Randall, who was in charge of vehicles for Slats,
went out to work with the Weasel in near white-out blizzard conditions
with a 20-mile-an-hour wind blowing swirling snow. In the resultant
white-out, Randy was nearly blinded by the eddying ice crystals and
failed to spy a bank of snow. As a result, the Weasel turned over on

its side, fortunately without injuring Randy. Then, in a flash, Slats was on the scene, righting the Weasel quickly with his D-2 tractor. Luckily the Weasel suffered no damage beyond a cracked window. We would have been in difficulty indeed had it become inoperative.

Randall was a most interesting young man of twenty-one who had come from a large family in Massachusetts. He gave off a surface impression of being tough, but underneath this armor I suspected that he was highly sentimental. For long periods of time he would be extremely quiet, and then suddenly out would pour bursts of highly emotional comments. As with many of the others I felt I would have liked to know him better. Lean and strong, Randy had a tremendous appetite. I recall once when I entered the mess late, he was in mid-meal. But before he left the table he devoured four large steaks in addition to whatever he had eaten before my arrival.

Bill Goodwin, who also worked with Slats, took care of the engines and was a careful and accurate Weasel driver. Goodwin was not easy to know because he seemed to shy away from officers and civilians. But I was fully aware of his powers of persistency. Late one night we had generator trouble, a serious problem since we were dependent on the generator for our lights and radio. At four A.M. I heard Goodwin announce that if he didn't start the generator on the next crank, he was going to try for a half hour; and then give up and go to bed. Yet at six A.M. he was still cranking and a short while later I heard him shout with joy when the generator finally started.

The last permanent member of Slats' power crew was Colin H. Roberts, also the welder and ironmonger, a very likable juvenile. He typified the young sailor who feels that he must impress everyone with his capacity for drink and his worldly knowledge. In time he would mature, but I feared that he had suffered rather than gained by his year in Navy-Antarctica. Sergeant Patton also helped Slats with some of the heavy jobs when he was not on the drop zone serving as ground contact for the Globemasters. Patton did himself and the Air Force proud with his ever-conscientious efforts, and even found time later on to assist the radio group in assembling the radio station for the permanent settlement. Altogether the efforts of Slats' small crew were herculean. In one two-day period they moved about 500 diesel drums into permanent position.

By December 6, Bev and his builders had already finished the garage-powerhouse shell and had begun work on the mess hall foundation.

Perhaps the most striking difference between these young titans of modern Antarctica and myself from the old school of explorers came to light in our attitudes toward conservation of materials and tools. These youngsters were accustomed to the opulence of the military services. Their philosophy, if they had such, was an outgrowth of World War II practices, to get the job done and to hell with conserving supplies. They would reach for a new board for some secondary purpose and never think of substituting an altogether adequate board which happened to have a few nails in it. The latter would be burned as trash like yesterday's newspaper. In the rush they would drop their tools unmindful that snow has a way of swallowing them in a matter of minutes if there is even a tiny breeze blowing.

I had been taught on the frugal expeditions of the past that every board should be saved, for even in a million years a tree wouldn't grow in Antarctica. Old Vic Czegka taught me well to preserve tools and never, never lay one down on the snow and walk away from it.

Thus I suffered in silence as I watched the builders scatter tools and building materials about wantonly. The men were not mine to command but the tools and salvage materials after the job was done would be all we would have for the following year at the Pole Station.

In addition, there was another little problem caused by the fact that all the bundles of panels came heavily wrapped to withstand the shock of the airdrops. The individual bundles contained wood between the panels and were surrounded by cardboard and four-foot pieces of wood crating, all of which was strapped securely by several 1½-inch metal straps. Moving along at their tremendous speed, the builders would pull out the panels and throw the rest of the bundle on the snow.

I was disturbed when I found that the bulldozer operators seemed to delight in grinding the salvage material into the snow. I realized that if the Station was to be occupied for several years to come we did not dare get the snow full of debris. Future digging for foundations would be troublesome if we started off carelessly adulterating the snow. Slats also enjoyed building huge bonfires to "clean up the yard." Some of those early fires contained only slightly battered boards with nails, for the Seabees seemed to have an actual contempt for old boards.

The result was that I acquired a new job and became the official camp "picker-upper." The fast-moving crews had no responsibility or even concern for neatness or conservation. I foresaw a possible use for every chunk of wood debris, every length of wire and every stitch of canvas. This was an attitude that bemused the Seabees, but sometimes, it seemed, I spent ten hours of my twelve- or fifteen-hour workday stooping to pick up scraps and then sorting them and placing them in neat piles for future storage. Some days I collected as much as three tons of junk and my back felt as though it would never stop aching. It was soon easily noticeable where I worked and where I did not, for as I wrote in my diary for December 8: *I tried to keep up with the builders but they can strew debris around faster than I can pick it up!*

When the building shells were up, the utilities specialists moved in. Chief Edward A. Hubel ran this crew and his aides included Charles A. Wagner, Donald J. Scott and Harold C. McCrillis. Hubel, who was an extremely capable specialist as well as a likable and considerate person, drove his crew just as fast as the builders. Wagner was a quiet but powerful man who kept up a strong pace, but who was so closemouthed about personal matters that even his close associates were never able to discover his home address. In this respect, he brought to mind one of the men on the first Byrd expedition who came with us under an alias. We didn't learn his real name until several years after the expedition was over. Donald Scott, or "Scotty," took care of the stoves and brought in the fuel, and was a man I should have enjoyed knowing better. Scotty was exceptionally clean-cut, yet he managed to retain the complete respect of the other men because he was one of the hardest workers among the Seabees. Digging in a hole with others, for instance, he would keep on working effortlessly when the rest were panting from exhaustion. McCrillis, or "Squirrel," was the construction electrician whose task it was to wire all the buildings. He was easy to converse with and revealed himself to be a most thoughtful person.

Hubel's crew did not have to take a back seat for the builders. Over a period of a few days I wrote in résumé in my diary: *Hubel's group has made amazing progress. They put in the galley cookstove; also jet heater and space heater located in the mess hall; fuel tanks, water tanks, fans in the toilet as well as regular toilet seats on a box erected over a 15-foot pit and the washstands, waste tanks, hot-water-heater tanks and the basic wiring.*

Of the other five men in the whole crew, William W. Bristol's sole task was to photograph operations. With two movie cameras, several still cameras and a wide-angle, board-screen camera lent him by Walt Disney, "Beel" made a Navy historic record of the Seabees and was out taking pictures almost constantly. Floyd A. Woody, called "Doc," was our first-aid man and had a fairly good layman's knowledge of medicine. Woody was also the assistant cook, helping Spiers who was a better mechanic than a cook himself, and also tripled in duty as our barber. On one occasion after several meals of thinnish, anemic and tasteless mashed potatoes, several of the men voiced loud disgust and I asked Spiers and Woody if they minded if I tried my luck with them. The mashed potatoes were made from dehydrated, powdered mashed potatoes, but that was not the reason they were unpalatable. My potatoes turned out pretty well and I discovered that they differed from Spiers' simply because I had carefully followed printed directions.

Dale L. Powell served as our daytime radioman and Thomas T. Montgomery took the night radio watch. When I first came to the Pole, Powell rode about in the radio-equipped Weasel and handled all radio contacts until the main field station came into operation. I had known Montgomery back in Washington where he had been on the staff of the Task Force. Monty had an effervescent personality and was also a good operator and radio technician. He was particularly fond of working the construction camp's ham band and saw to it that every man made his share of personal calls back to the States. He did this even though it meant that he often had to put in an eighteen-hour day.

The last member of the construction crew was Jerry L. Nolen, who was also the meteorologist. He was one of our hardest workers. For instance, the 20-foot steel girders had been cut in half at McMurdo in order to fit them into the Globemasters for airdrops at the Pole. Working through an entire night, Jerry rebolted the girders for one house. This may not seem to be much of a feat, but consider that there were twelve girders below the house and twelve above, and each girder required no fewer than thirty-six bolts which had to be threaded in sub-zero air.

As for Jerry's meteorological work, there were a number of points on which I raised questions. We were getting strange diurnal, or daily, temperature cycles containing a puzzling high point at "noon" when the sun was in line with the 180th Meridian. A carpenter had helped Jerry build an instrument shelter from scrap after they got to the Pole. It had a dark single-ply door facing that meridian, and I suspected the dark door to be the reason why the temperature readings were illogical. Theoretically this could not happen when the sun was the same height all day long. To check this Jerry and I hung a thermometer from his Pibal tripod in free air and shaded it with white parachute cloth. And sure enough, we obtained a series of temperature readings that varied considerably from those inside the ersatz instrument shelter. Of course Jerry was a weather observer and by no means a full-fledged meteorologist. As a young sailor he had not been given much scientific theory beyond his high school physics course a year or two back. Therefore he found himself in a unique position of taking first weather observations at a remote spot on earth with a minimum of equipment and experience. He was eager to do a good job, however.

I also questioned the readings of Jerry's hand-held anemometer, which measured the speed of the wind. This anemometer registered a good stiff wind as a rather mild affair. I suggested that he check with the Task Force aerologist who was at McMurdo, to determine what correction factor we should make for elevation.

We were told emphatically that the instrument required no correction factor. Still I felt certain from the way the snow drifted that our wind velocities were off by about 10 per cent. Later on we found the altitude correction card for the instrument and substantiated the need to increase the wind speeds we had recorded to compensate for the altitude at the Pole.

With the garage finished except for its doors, Bevilacqua's builders began the mess hall on December 7 and completed it late the next night. Then the next morning they began work on the science building 200 feet away at the opposite end of the South Pole Station. They bulldozed down and made a firm foundation, then put in the sills and what floor girders they had available. Then all the next day they spent opening panels and straightening out beams. Some of the trusses were a complete loss because they had been bent originally during the big hurricane of the preceding year in New England. By the 12th the walls and floor were up for the inflation shelter set another 50 feet beyond the science building; and on the 13th the science building itself was completed. The inflation shelter was to measure 20 x 24 x 12 feet and was to be used as a place in which to manufacture hydrogen as well as to inflate and launch meteorological upper-air sounding balloons.

But there was no time to gloat, for on the 13th of December came disturbing news. McMurdo was running low on aviation gas and we were informed that we should expect no further airdrops until the 27th. However, even this was not half as disturbing as the rumor that last year's Seabees at McMurdo would be flown home to the U.S. on the C-124's before the Pole Station builders were returned to Mc-Murdo. There was an added hint that the pole construction crew would come out too late to take advantage of the C-124 flights and would therefore have to travel back to the States by ship, which meant arriving home months later.

This rumor caused an immediate drop in morale, for the men grumbled that while they were doing the big job in the Antarctic, they were to be penalized and left holding the sack.

Wisely, Bowers called a Happy Hour that evening so his men could let off steam. *The men have worked unceasingly since their arrival and deserve this small break in routine,* he recorded in his log. For almost a month the men had not rested as they performed prodigious feats of heavy labor under Antarctic conditions. Yet I was happy, when the Happy Hour ended, that we had not held others before. It was easy to understand why only a half-dozen men put in a full day's work the next day, the 14th.

News arrived that day that the Air Force after all planned two more flights before the 24th. This was indeed heartening because we were still some 130 tons short of what we needed, including food, vital IGY equipment, 300 drums of fuel and acetylene for the builders.

In an effort to give morale a boost, I decided to erect a "South Pole" that same day. Chief Hubel gave me a hand. It was a bamboo pole, which had been painted with ascending alternate orange and black stripes in barber-pole fashion. Many of the McMurdo inhabitants had signed the pole in white paint for good luck before it was sent in. To the top of the pole we affixed one of the 16-inch mirrored glass balls I had purchased in New Zealand. The ball was literally a gift from the heavens, for when it was dropped from a Globemaster I had watched it come shooting down to within a few feet of the ground, when its parachute miraculously opened. Besides being an ornament we hoped that the sunlight flashing off the mirrored ball would help make the campsite more easily visible from the air.

We put our symbolic "South Pole" on top the garage, even though we knew this was not the true Geographic Pole. Ever since his arrival Dick Bowers had kept taking sun sights in an effort to determine the more precise location of the true Pole. He used a Swiss precision theodolite which we had borrowed from the Army for the purpose. The operation required almost a dozen corrections for a variety of matters including altitude, pressure and temperature. He would take a series of elevations and bearings on the sun, following procedures to eliminate instrument errors, and then check his findings with his nautical almanac, which records for any time of day the altitude and bearing of the center of the sun. Then he would scratch his chin whiskers and say, "Now if I were actually at the Pole, the sun should be here. Hmmm. Here is where I probably am."

Then the following day Dick would take further bearings and discover that his earlier readings did not exactly check. The amusing result was that he kept moving the South Pole around. To mark the Geographic Pole he built a little plywood shack, 4 by 4 by 8 feet, on a metal airdrop platform which he would drag to his latest "Pole." The first time, he placed his little shack about 4,000 feet from my barber pole atop the garage. Later after staying up most of a night to perfect his observations, he dragged it to a spot bearing 145° Grid East from my pole at 2,400 feet. His final best estimate placed the shack about 1,200 feet from camp, which would have meant that we were lying on the 58 Meridian West. This was as close as one could come by using the low elevation sun and a theodolite. Possibly star shots would later perfect the location still more.

The airdrops came as announced and among the items were nine bags of philatelic mail that swamped us. Stamp collectors had sent us nearly a quarter million letters to which an estimated $15,000 worth of stamps were affixed. Bob Chaudoin, our postmaster, dragged the bags into the barren science building where he set up his hand-turned cancellation machine and laboriously canceled the stamps and imprinted each cover with POLE STATION, ANTARCTICA. The first-day covers were dated *15 Dec. 1956*. "Now we are officially on the map," I told him.

On the 15th, the Seabees began the tunnels that would encircle the base, beginning first with the tunnel framing for the food storage side of the mess hall, our "westernmost" building. Then they began on Main Street, moving down past the big Jamesway, the toilet and garage, the firebreak dividing the camp in two, the space for another sleeping quarters and on to the science building. They then returned around the rear of the Station. They did all this while at the same time completing work on the buildings. To hasten the deepening of the latrine pit, for instance, they ingeniously hung a Herman Nelson heater into the hole. Slats bulldozed down all tunnel areaways with such rapidity that I had to keep an eye on him to make certain that in his haste he didn't bulldoze IGY gear I had already stored in caches close to the science building.

This watchfulness paid off on one occasion when I found he had heaped my valuable science cache space with snow. Because all other hands were occupied I undertook to clear the snow away all by myself, a backbreaking job since it was equivalent to shoveling three feet of snow off a hundred-foot sidewalk.

On the 17th I had my first bath since arriving at the Pole to celebrate my birthday on the 18th, the ninth I would celebrate either in the Antarctic or on my way there. My beard, which was over two weeks old, had the start of white points at the chin, and I realized that when it was full grown I might have the appearance of a Biblical patriarch. Truly time had passed swiftly since I was the fuzzy-cheeked boy who had first come to the Antarctic with Byrd twenty-eight years before.

At midnight on the 20th, Bowers thought work had come along so well that a ceremony was in order. He would transfer the Stars and Stripes from the pole hastily erected on arrival to the garage top "South Pole." Spiers, the cook, and Williamson, one of the builders, won honors for the longest beards in camp and were given the privilege of raising the flag. The men assembled in two rows and saluted as the flag went up. It was an impressive ceremony, though the Seabees were rather quiet. Obviously they had begun to realize that their work was almost finished. This was the eve of midsummer day when the sun stood at its highest altitude. The frequent halos about the sun 22½ degrees in radius came tangent to the horizon and a brilliant false sun appeared on the horizon just beneath the sun.

Word came on the 23rd that the first eight Seabees would leave on the next landing planes. The meteorological Rawin Tower platform was now up on top of the mess hall roof and Slats and Randall were slaving almost round the clock dragging the long and short runways in anticipation of the first planes for over two weeks. "We're going to hold our Christmas Party tonight, a day early," Bowers told me. "All of us might not be here tomorrow night."

He looked rather wistfully about at the camp he had constructed.

The Air Force had airdropped an Oregon Christmas tree some time ago and now the men trimmed it outdoors and then set it up in the science building. With an air of mystery Dick produced several bottles of liquor he had cached for the occasion. And when Scotty, Chaudoin and some of the other men began singing carols, there was every indication that this would be an occasion long to remember. Unfortunately, alas, a few of the men worked as hard on the punch bowl as they had on the camp and carried on until eight the next morning.

Oddly, every eye was relatively clear by the next noon and scanning the sky for the two R4D's and the P2V which were to land. They came that afternoon though the P2V, piloted by Captain Cordiner and Jack Torbett, got lost and arrived over an hour late.

During the time that we were sweating out the tardy P2V, I received my Christmas present. It was the most spectacular halo about the sun I had ever seen. The magnificent phenomenon took up most of the sky and was caused by refraction of sunshine by ice crystals floating in the atmosphere. There were two great circles of rainbow hues around the sun. The inner one was about equal to the midsummer height of the sun (22½ degrees) so that the rim came tangent to the horizon. Below the sun was a brilliant white glow that nearly rivaled the sun in brightness. Above the sun on the circle was a complex yoke shape like the cupid lips along the edge of a cup of fluid under a bright light shining from one side. Also on the same inner circle on either side and equal to the height of the sun were brilliant iridescent sundogs like jeweled settings of a ring. The second circle around all this grandeur was nearly ninety degrees across, occupying a quarter of the sky. Two brilliant half rainbows came up from the horizon tangent to this circle like great outward-pointing horns. Tangent to this outer circle above the sun was the upper tangent arc of another inverted bright rainbow. What made this optical phenomenon all the more unusual were the white bands of light forming a cross with the sun at the center. The vertical arms joined the sun to the bright spots below and above it, whereas the horizontal arms of the cross not only joined the sun to the sundogs on either side but kept on arching around the sky above the horizon. Opposite the sun a delicate six-pointed star of white light formed in the sky reminiscent of a huge star sapphire. For nearly an hour this spectacle awed us and nearly made us forget the tenseness of our worry over the overdue plane.

After all the planes were safely down and we had unloaded the cargo of non-drop IGY material, we held a long conference and enjoyed a hearty Christmas supper of two steaks apiece and three canned ears of corn. Then the eight Seabees picked up their gear and I said good-by to Prescott, Chaudoin, Scott, Tyler, Hisey, Goodwin, Williamson and Roberts. It was difficult for some of them to utter a nonchalant farewell. Bob Chaudoin in particular who had sought unavailingly to be allowed to stay on as part of the Station's permanent party had tears in his eyes when I pressed his shoulder.

This was the beginning of the end of Bowers' great venture, though he and his remaining Seabees worked hard up to the very day when they flew off to McMurdo. Even when the winds rose on Christmas and a white-out enveloped us, work did not flag. McCrillis finished all the basic wiring; the others continued to cover the tunnels. On the 28th they completed as much as they could do on the Rawin Tower and the platform that set it six feet high above the mess hall. And now at the very end of their ordeal, some of the men developed jangled nerves from overwork.

At three A.M. on the 26th some of the men decided to stage an impromptu steak-cooking late snack party. When the sound of their voices came booming from the galley into the other end of the little Jamesway where Bowers and I slept, Dick got up from his sleeping bag and requested them to be a little more quiet.

Burly Slats, with a patch over one eye as a result of an attack of snow blindness and obviously exhausted from the strain of the past weeks, turned on him and gave vent to some well-selected adjectives and adverbs. Sagely Dick did not reply but came back to bed, and shortly afterward the fun must have disappeared from the steak party for the men left for their own quarters in the big Jamesway.

Dick did not sleep any more that night. "I'm going to have to put him on report and send him back on the first flight," he said angrily. This was his prerogative, of course, and I said nothing, though I realized that Slats had done a superb job as construction crew whip. But he had broken the traditional respect for a superior officer.

I was thankful when an hour before breakfast, Slats appeared. He tugged on his sweater and offered a loud and forceful apology. There was no getting around it, Slats was a real man in all respects. Happy to have the incident closed, Bowers beamed and quickly accepted the apologies. An hour later the men were working together and the incident forgotten. Bowers had once again shown why he was a fine leader.

There was more news now. Big news. Eight more men were to leave when the next P2V arrived. More important for me, Tuck and the eight men of the Navy's permanent support party were to arrive at the same time. The eight others of the IGY party under my charge would come at a later time.

Our ham radio was in operation and all Bowers' Seabees had an opportunity to talk with their families back in the States before leaving. On the 27th, Sam Newman, a ham operator in Bethesda, Maryland, arranged a phone patch for me. I was able to speak to Ruth and our daughters Ann, Jane and Mary, my mother and my sister Carrol. With a seventeen-hour time difference, it was midnight in Washington and poor Janie, who had been roused from a sound sleep, was almost too drowsy to speak. I was sorry because she had done the best job in the family in keeping me informed of things at home by letters. Certainly the call gave my morale an enormous boost.

The next day, the ham radio performed still another highly important function. On the 28th, the P2V was expected and Slats, Woody, Nolen, Powell, McCormick, Wagner, McCrillis and Patton stood by for evacuation. When the plane had failed to arrive at five P.M., we tried to reach McMurdo by regular radio, only to find that weather conditions had blacked out Hut Point for us. Since we wanted to allay our fears, we took another tack. We called Jules Madey, the sixteen-year-old ham operator in Clark, New Jersey, and told him our dilemma. Fortunately, McMurdo was not blocked for him and he was able to relay our questions, so it was from New Jersey that we learned shortly afterward that McMurdo reported its P2V would arrive the following afternoon at three. This was certainly a round-about method, but its importance was that it worked.

The 29th of December arrived. I noted as soon as I rose that this was my twentieth wedding anniversary and I regretted that I was not with Ruth. All day this sadness pervaded me, until after three when the local problem interceded. The P2V failed to show up on schedule. Captain Cordiner had reported at 3:15 that his plane would be over us in five minutes. But it was almost six P.M. before the Neptune skied to a halt on our snow strip. By this time we were certain that the worst had occurred. As on the occasion of his previous late arrival, Cordiner again blamed our homing beam, but whatever the difficulty our feeling of relief was almost tangible.

Again there were sad farewells as eight more Seabees whom I had come to know so well in only a month made their departure. But there was little time to dwell on their leaving. For here was Jack Tuck, seven other members of the permanent wintering party, 600 pounds of IGY equipment and almost 50 pounds of yelping five-month-old Husky— Bravo.

Chapter 17

INTERIM WITH THE NAVY

THE arrival of Jack Tuck and all of his crew except his builder heralded the beginning of the permanent occupation of the South Pole Station. I noted:

We are now rapidly moving forward in preparation for the International Geophysical Year. The *impossible* has been accomplished. Who could have guessed that the IGY dream of a station at the exact bottom of the earth would become a reality. That it had was due to the combined efforts of many men in many different fields. Especially there was the magnificent effort the Navy had made to gather the necessary materials and concentrate them at McMurdo and the miracle the Air Force had performed in delivering the tons of equipment and supplies to the Pole itself. Who would have conceded at the outset that a young Yale graduate and a crew of Seabees would within a month master the cold, the altitude, the deep snow, the winds and the ever-present sun and erect a half-dozen buildings at the Pole? My hat is off to Bowers and his intrepid lot for withstanding the rigors and removing the first veil of mystery from this unknown land.

I hope and pray that our wintering-over party will reveal similar qualities in removing the rest of the veils, both in the fields of science and in withstanding the unknown winter ahead. For we shall see the effect of six months of darkness on man: temperatures below −100° F., raging and withering winds; and, of course, the isolation and its effect on the minds of men. A grand experiment indeed! Would that it all proves worth while and a benefit to mankind.

Jack Tuck's men were all eyes as they at first kept close to their twenty-four-year-old leader.

This feeling of unity even included Bravo, our new mascot. I was happy to see him again but Bravo, even more than before, had become Jack Tuck's dog. Now he exhibited an aloofness rare in a Husky, almost as if he sensed that I was a "foreigner."

"These are the members of the Navy support team," Tuck introduced his crew on the short hike back to camp from the runway. I took a long and hard look at each man. We will know each other better than our closest friends we have left behind, I thought to myself as I acknowledged their response to Jack's roll call.

The first was bearded and mustached Lieutenant Howard C. Taylor III, who was to be the South Pole Station's medical officer. Taylor, who outranked Tuck yet fell under him since medical officers do not command, was an intelligent-faced young doctor in his late twenties whom I had met previously in Washington. In fact, outside of Jack,

Taylor was the only member of Jack's crew whom I had met before. "Hello, again, Doctor," I said by way of welcome.

The next man was our radioman, William C. McPherson from Rhode Island. McPherson looked very Irish and I hoped he would have the delightful humor and lack the proverbial belligerent temperament.

Whereas McPherson looked older than his late twenties, our new electrician, Kenneth L. Waldron, a twenty-one-year-old, looked like a teen-ager and answered to the name of "Junior." Like McPherson, Junior was also clean-shaven, making them the only members of Tuck's crew who had not already begun to try their luck at growing a beard. These were sea-grown beards however, begun on the ship en route to Antarctica, for save for two, none of the men had had any previous Antarctic experience beyond the five days they had spent at McMurdo before coming to the Pole. Tuck had had a whole year in Antarctica and young Waldron had visited Antarctica as a member of the Deepfreeze I crew and had helped in the construction of Little America V the year before.

Then there was Martin L. Brown, the new mechanic, a husky muscular young man who looked as though he would be a brute for heavy work. I had the same impression of Earl F. Johnson, who informed me shortly after we met that he had led a troop of Boy Scouts from Cleveland as Senior Patrol Leader to the Second National Boy Scout Jamboree at Valley Forge, Pennsylvania.

Slighter in build than these two, Clifford R. Dickey was our new electronics man. Despite a slight stammer, there was a strong look of healthy leadership about Dickey that I liked from the start. The last of Jack Tuck's crew was Chester W. Segers, our new cook, who had by far the most luxuriant beard among the new arrivals except for Jack's year-old one. At thirty, Segers was also the oldest member of the incoming Navy party, and had already spent twelve years in the Navy.

Dick Bowers, who was still in naval charge of camp until his own departure, lost no time putting Tuck's crew to work. Their first tasks, carrying avgas and JATO bottles to the airstrip, however, brought on the usual altitude afflictions of headaches and shortness of breath. And that sun-filled evening after supper, Dick called a meeting in the mess hall to advise the new men of the routine they would be expected to follow until he left.

"First off I've kept the key men of my crew here to check you out on the details so that you can take over as soon as we leave a day or so from now. We haven't done any of the interiors of the buildings," he told them. "Instead, we figured that you men would prefer putting them in to suit yourselves because you'll be living here."

"The amount of construction work you've done here during December is prodigious," Tuck cut in. "Damned amazing."

"Thanks," Dick said. "Anyway," he turned to McPherson, "some of the radio gear is set up, but the radio shack hasn't been enclosed. You can do that. And the galley utilities have been connected," he told Segers, "but the general arrangement of the galley setup and the shelves is up to you.

"I know you won't be happy to learn that we have little more than some gauze and iodine," Dick went on, turning to Taylor. "I hope you brought your black bag with you. But you can expect to get all your supplies soon. And I hope luck holds out, because we haven't had any real accidents so far."

"I hope so," Taylor said, "because this would be a terrible place for an operation, even when we get all the supplies."

Immediately after the meeting ended, Bowers and Tuck went into a huddle as Dick proceeded to suggest to Tuck how he might proceed to complete various construction tasks after he left.

The next day, the 30th of December, the new men dug right into their briefings and check-out tasks. Dickey and McPherson began to set up the radio shack, checked the homing signal unit and went over the spare-parts list with Montgomery of Bowers' crew. Segers had his galley 90 per cent operational that first day, and with Bevilacqua's help he installed the first partitions, and a few shelves and counters. It developed, however, that Segers was a butcher and had not cooked for two and a half years. Still he was so intent on doing a good job that I was certain we would eat well that winter.

Earl Johnson spent most of the day with Chief Hubel, who showed him how to check utility installations and make certain kinds of repairs. Johnson was a plump, smiling-faced youngster and I liked his good-humored air of friendliness. While Earl went about with Hubel, some of us concentrated on salvage and cleanup. Brown and Randall, who was in charge of vehicles for Bowers, cleared off a salvage area for me on the Grid South side of the science building. Then Brown

Robert F. Benson
Seismology
Minnesota

Edwin C. Flowers
Meteorology
Maryland

Paul A. Siple
Scientific Leader
Virginia

Herbert L. Hansen
Meteorology
Nebraska

South Pole

Edward W. Remington
Glaciology
Maryland

William F. Johnson
Meteorology
Oklahoma

John F. Guerrero
Meteorology
California

William S. Hough
Ionosphere
Colorado

Arlo U. Landolt
Aurora
Illinois

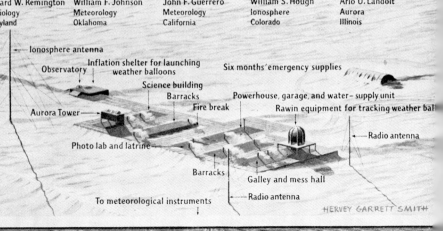

Ionosphere antenna
Observatory
Inflation shelter for launching
weather balloons
Science building
Barracks
Fire break
Aurora Tower
Photo lab and latrine
Six months' emergency supplies
Powerhouse, garage, and water-supply unit
Rawin equipment for tracking weather bal
Radio antenna
Barracks
Galley and mess hall
Radio antenna
To meteorological instruments

HERVEY GARRETT SMITH

Weather balloon
Astron
Observa
Snow-filled
fire break
Recreation room
and quarters
for six men
Tunnel
Science building,
Dr. Siple's office
Tunnel
Inflation shelter

Clifford R. Dickey, Jr.
Electronics, ET1
California

Wm. C. McPherson, Jr.
Radioman, RM1
Rhode Island

Kenneth L. Waldron
Electrician, CE2
Iowa

Thomas M. Osborne
Builder, BU1
Pennsylvania

Earl F. Johnson
Utilities Man, UT1
Ohio

Pit for seismographic research

Burlap-covered snow tunnel

Pit for geomagnetic research

John Tuck, Jr.
Military Leader, Lt. (jg.)
Massachusetts

Howard C. Taylor III
Medical Officer, Lt.
New York

Melvin C. Havener
Mechanic, CM2
Iowa

Chester W. Segers
Cook, CS1
Rhode Island

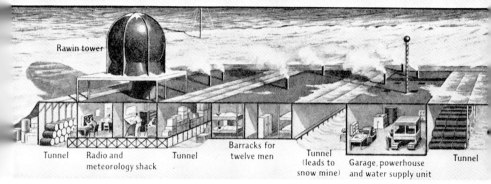

Rawin tower

Tunnel Radio and   Tunnel   Barracks for   Tunnel   Garage, powerhouse   Tunnel
        meteorology shack   twelve men   (leads to   and water supply unit
                                                   snow mine)

The 18 men who conquered the winter night at the South Pole. Nine Navy men and nine civilian scientists, they came from 14 states. Drawings show their midwinter camp lit by the full moon.
© NATIONAL GEOGRAPHIC SOCIETY

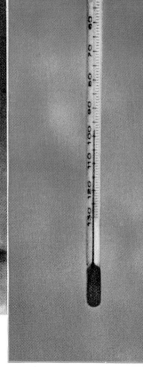

Top left: *Bob Benson, John Guerrero and Arlo Landolt attempt to hold a wiener roast outdoors at 70 below zero. It was so cold the flames did not melt the ice.*

Above: *98 degrees below zero. The author took this striking photograph a month before the sun rose.*

Bottom left: *Bravo romps with Doc Taylor. Salvaged parachutes brighten this Jamesway hut.*
© NATIONAL GEOGRAPHIC SOCIETY

Right: *By the light of a lantern Bob Benson inspects the seismometer in its pit 1,000 feet from camp. Aluminum foil was used to protect the delicate instrument from radio interference from the camp's transmitters.*

Below: *Meteorologists Herb Hansen* (left) *and Ed Flowers plot data from weather balloons in their equipment-crowded workshop.*

© National Geographic Society

Building the seismic tunnel. A trench five feet deep was excavated and, with the aid of improvised forms, a bordering two-foot-high wall was raised. The top of the tunnel was formed by boards and layers of burlap.

With the temperature hovering in the minus 60's the barracks building is erected. The walls, roof and floors were formed of four-inch-thick aluminum and plywood sandwiches filled with insulation and designed so they had only to be clipped together.

The heavy winds of the winter night carved the sastrugi in fantastic shapes. These samples ranged from one to two feet in height.

The shadows on typical sastrugi show the way the winter winds undercut them.

PHOTOGRAPH BY ED FLOWERS

and I proceeded to clean up some of the front part of camp. Husky though he was, Brown worked too energetically and I had to caution him to accustom himself gradually to the work.

Before I had gone to bed the previous night, I had taken Dr. Taylor about the camp and told him of my desire to salvage as much scrap material as we could for future construction jobs as well as for winter use. Early the next day, having finished partitioning off his sick bay in the mess hall (we would shortly decide to move it to the quieter science building), he felt that as a doctor without medical supplies he could make himself most useful doing salvage work. He walked to our drop zone which extended over a three-mile-square area and retrieved quantities of plywood, parachute bags, parachutes and boards. I was pleased to find I had a "string-saving" ally at last.

That day I also acquired a new temporary job. Bowers had retained only those Seabees who could train the winter party in essential matters, such as utilities, mechanical equipment and radio installation and repair. McMurdo had therefore sent a blistering message criticizing Dick for having sent Nolen, his meteorologist, back to Hut Point. Thus as a professional climatologist but not a meteorologist I offered to take weather readings until the IGY Met men came, though I didn't realize what I had promised. For though I had once taught meteorology and reading instruments was second nature to me, the polar readings had to be put into an international code, with which I was unfamiliar.

While I struggled over the complex code, Dick went out to calk the cracks on every roof in camp with a special calking gun. Unfortunately, the mastic material for the roof cracks was a tarlike substance that had to be kept warm to flow. It was a maddening job in a sub-zero wind. When he returned to the Jamesway in the evening, Dick's clothes were ruined and the black substance clung to his skin despite vigorous scrubbing.

I noted in my diary for that day: *I have had to have patience today. I still feel like an outsider. This new crowd is "too Navy." But the Antarctic and time are on my side.*

During the first day I had already had a regretful clash with one of Tuck's men. Jack had agreed to my proposal to try to work the Navy and the soon-to-arrive civilian scientists into a single team, though he wanted to retain exclusive authority to give instructions to the Navy

———

a festive mood, the polar shut-ins celebrate Midwinter Day, June 22, with od and fun. © National Geographic Society men. "Tell me what you want or need and I'll tell my men to do it," he told me.

"Okay," I agreed, "and I assume in return that you will leave any instructions necessary for civilians up to me."

"Sure," he replied.

Then came an incident with McPherson. It occurred when he told me bluntly that he was making it clear that he was running his radio shack Navy style and that no civilians could enter it without his permission. There was no excuse for this strong view, I told him, since this was an IGY Station and we expected no classified traffic. "We just don't erect 'Keep Out' signs at small isolated bases," I said. "Well, it's my place and no one else's," he insisted.

Jack was upset because he knew that McPherson was both discourteous and wrong, yet he did not want the resolution of such a matter to be argued between me and one of his men. However I, on my part, realized full well the importance of correcting errors at the outset lest they become permanent.

There thus stood between Jack and me the possibility of a rivalry between civilians and Navy personnel. Between Jack and his men lay the inevitable problems of command, that of officer and enlisted men. These were serious problems for Tuck, and they would still have existed had he been older and more experienced. There was only one answer, and that was the experience, the mutual understanding and confidence that the passage of time would bring.

Fortunately, the solution to our first major problem brought the first lessening of tension. I still hoped to get a barracks building delivered to the Pole so we could house our men properly. In fact, I had enlisted Admiral Byrd's aid by radio to urge the Task Force to co-operate in the matter. "But if that falls through," I told Tuck, "I'd like to move the little Jamesway into the hole left for the barracks building and sleep six of our men there and the rest in the big Jamesway."

Jack opposed this, holding to the Task Force's plan to house all eighteen of the men in either the mess hall or science building.

I pointed out that if possible we should not have men sleeping where they worked and ate. And if we had men living in the science building, this would cut down on actual work space. But despite my arguments for using the Jamesways for living quarters, Jack insisted that I draw up a plan for dividing the science building into living and work space while he made a plan for housing some in the mess hall. Since there was no point in pursuing the subject further, I dropped my arguments and went along with his ideas for making plans for the science building as a sleeping quarters.

Later when I completed my drawing, I handed it to him with the comment that his idea had been good. He studied the design for a long time. "You've got everything in," he said finally, his heavy brows furrowed. "But what about yourself? You haven't got any work space left." He shook his head and smiled. "Let's forget about both the mess hall and the science building and try the Jamesways instead if we don't get the barracks building."

This decision was the break-through in our relations. In only a few instances after that did we have any disagreement. Our troubles were over and as Jack began to relax, there began a friendship and co-operation that grew steadily. "During the four weeks I was back at McMurdo," Jack later admitted, "several prophets of doom forecast a bitter Navy-IGY war. But this is a battle in which the first shot will never be fired."

On New Year's Eve we celebrated with a party in the galley. That day the men had completed the garage portico just outside the garage which I had suggested to Bowers be built to store the Weasel and the D-2 tractor during the winter so we would have more work space in the garage. Bravo was the belle of the ball, having been permitted to enter the building for the first time. So in a small city that had not existed a month before, sixteen men toasted the New Year at midnight. For eight of these men, it would be the strangest year of their lives. "To the success of your venture." Bowers raised his glass and nodded to me and Tuck. But soon the men were in small huddles planning details of their work and the celebration remained but a symbol.

My diary for the first day of 1957 opened with these words: *The wind was down some—and so were the men.* Bowers' men had heard that they were now on stand-by for evacuation and I could read in their faces their desire to leave. Bowers had a hard time getting them steamed up for work, though I was glad he succeeded because some heavy tasks still remained to be done.

After supper we added officially to the Station's status by burying a time capsule contributed by the citizens of Peoria, Illinois. Inside a cylinder of a D-8 tractor, built in their city, Peorians had inserted a newspaper and other material for us to bury, with the notation that the capsule was "to be opened in the year 2000 A. D." Some of the men wanted to dig into the snow and deposit the capsule, but I pointed out that if they did it would never be found again. Instead, I suggested that we put it in Bowers' South Pole marker, the 4 x 4 x 8 plywood shack 1,200 feet away from my garage-top Pole. Bowers and Tuck acted upon this and we held the ceremony.

By the 2nd, the remaining Seabees were more eager than ever to leave. Their anxiety showed in their faces, voices and actions. But a white-out condition prevailed and with the horizon lost, there would be no arriving planes, so Dick put his men to work again. Original plans called for installing 12-foot-high garage doors that would swing open overhead. But it would have required so great an expenditure of effort to pull open such doors that Dick had Bevilacqua change the direction of the doors so they would open accordion fashion to one side. These were heavy doors, but the crew succeeded in hanging them although they were never destined to fly open easily. The crew also framed another tunnel section in front of the garage in the evening.

There was other activity, too. Junior Waldron, our permanent electrician, grounded the walls of the inflation shelter to prevent sparks by using electrical wire to connect the layers of aluminum sheathing of the panels together and tying the entire building into the ground of its electrical system. This was highly important for safety reasons since our weather balloons would be inflated with always dangerous hydrogen.

That day also brought a pleasant surprise for me. *Time* magazine had featured me in a cover story the previous week and I received a cordial message from Wilbur M. Brucker, the Secretary of the Army. His message read:

> Congratulations on your significant scientific and military achievements which make happy reading in December 31 *Time* magazine. It is a pleasure to see you receive national news coverage for your splendid leadership in the organization and research of the best integrated expedition in Antarctic history. Your work with Naval Task Force 43 is a praiseworthy example of how effective co-operation among all branches of our armed forces strengthens our knowledge as well as our defenses. Accept my personal commendation for your years of outstanding performance in behalf of the United States Army.

Now that I was famous I spent part of the day cleaning up salvage material on the Grid North or 0° side of camp and hours hauling in among other things ten rolls of chicken wire. The chicken-wire rolls were bent by streaming in and were full of snow, making them doubly heavy and hard to carry. I also helped Earl Johnson drag in fifteen parachute bags filled with at least 150 pounds of snow each. The Weasel dragged the bags on sleds to the front of the garage, but from there we had to drag them by hand the full length of the garage to where we dumped the snow into the snow melter. Even this last step was a strain, since the melter was four feet high. But this task was of utmost importance because this was our only means for getting water. For in a strict sense, the Antarctic is a desert and a man lost on it could die of thirst. The snow in the melter was melted by running the exhaust pipe from our diesel generators through it.

"No planes today," Dick told his crew on the 3rd as the white-out persisted, "so let's get to work." One of the nasty heavy jobs still uncompleted was to raise the sections of the Rawin Dome in place, and the men set to work on this in the afternoon.

The Rawin Dome was indeed large, resting on a spindly-legged platform six feet above the roof of the mess hall. In its high setting and with its size, it was the most dominating object in the Pole Station. Almost black in color, the Dome with its odd shape gave off the aura of the mysterious future. Actually, the Rawin Dome was constructed of banana-skin-shaped pieces of Fiberglas, and the radio set could thus be kept within the warmth of the Dome and "look out" through the plastic; to follow a balloon when it was released to float up miles above the earth with a little radio transmitter fastened to its bottom.

Bevilacqua gave abundant evidence of his skill in handling and putting the Dome together. But the Rawin Dome produced the first serious accidents of the entire construction period. In his zeal, Bowers strained his back lifting while his cook, Spiers, who came to lend a hand, almost left it behind when he caught one of his hands between the panels. He suffered great pain, but fortunately Dr. Taylor found no broken bones. And later when we went to the mess hall we found Brown, Jack's brawny mechanic, almost unable to stand upright, with an injured sacroiliac from lifting too many heavy objects.

Nor were these all of our troubles with the Rawin Dome. Some days later Junior Waldron tried to do the outside bolting of its panels by lowering himself in a bosun's chair from an opening at the top of the tower. Coming down from the Dome, he banged his head on a low sharp-cornered truss under the platform. When he reached the mess hall he called for a doctor. We thought he was joking, as he usually was. But when he removed his cap, blood streamed down his face. Fortunately it was not as bad as it looked, for though he suffered a gash in his scalp, he required no stitches.

At last on January 4 the white-out dissolved and we notified Mc-Murdo that its planes could land with safety at the Pole. I had hoped that the R4D's and the P2V would bring some of the IGY scientists. However, Dufek ruled that no further Pole personnel would be sent to us until enough food was delivered to maintain us for a year.

I walked the quarter mile to the airstrip when the planes were expected, to see them come in with a large supply of frozen food, non-drop IGY equipment and mail.

Bowers and his men came out carrying little gear since they had decided from the start to leave their extra clothing, sleeping gear and equipment for us. I said good-by to each man: Ed Hubel, Spiers, Bevilacqua, Randall, Bristol, Montgomery and finally Dick Bowers himself. "We'll always remember you," I said to Hubel. He had made a deep pit behind the camp to burn our trash and garbage. "Your pit will always be known as the Hubel Hole."

With the Seabees, I had never become much more than an accepted outsider. Yet it could not have been otherwise, for they were a closely knit group, having spent far more than a year together. Their little jokes and wisecracks were endemic, and without knowing the history of their development I had not been able to interpret or anticipate the raucous humor that followed a seemingly innocuous retort. Now suddenly I felt the loss of these friends.

It was especially hard to see Bowers leave. I would genuinely miss him for many reasons. Not only was he the source of knowledge about the Navy-packed Station supplies and construction details, but he was in every way a splendid young officer destined to do well at any assignment that required ingenuity, daring and conscientiousness.

I think Dick was genuinely sorry to leave, too, from the firmness of his handshake and his long sweeping last look at the Pole Station. "Well, I guess that's done with," he said as we awkwardly stretched out the final moment. "See you some time."

I stood with Tuck and his men as Bowers and his party took off for McMurdo. And as the planes disappeared in the clouds, leaving the inevitable heavy vapor trails behind, I looked about me at the new Navy personnel. My friends were gone and these were strangers, though I knew that soon I would know them far more intimately than I had those who had just departed. Suddenly, too, I was the old-timer of the party. It was to me the new men turned to seek knowledge of where things were stored, where the tools were, what had happened to Box 32 that was supposed to be here, and so on ad infinitum.

Chapter 18

AIRSTRIP TROUBLES AT McMURDO

WHENEVER Doug Cordiner landed his P2V at the Pole he came to camp for coffee and a chat before returning to McMurdo. "What's the good word, Doug?" I had asked him when he flew in to get Bowers and the remaining six Seabees. "Have the ships arrived with the aviation gasoline so that we can get some more C-124 drops?"

"That's only part of the trouble," he said. "Dufek pulled three of your boys off my plane so we could bring in more food. And you still don't have all you need for those here right now in the event we have to abandon the rest of the flights this season."

"But our IGY equipment," I said. "We only have part of the stuff we have to have to carry on the program."

"What's the minimum number of IGY men you can get along with?" Cordiner asked.

"We'll need all eight, if we are going to run the IGY program," I said. "Why?"

"Because several things have come up," Doug explained. "As you know, we're running short of aviation gas at McMurdo and until tankers arrive our air activity will be severely curtailed. Besides, most of our operable planes are being assigned to deliver food to the Byrd Station. They've only got food there for a month. And the Weddell Sea group is having heavy going. Progress there's almost at a standstill. The sea ice over there sure was a rough place to pick for an IGY Station, wasn't it? But the Cape Hallett and Knox Coast stations aren't much better off. They've had trouble with the unloadings there too. The *Arneb*'s hull was punctured in several places and the *Northwind* wrecked her starboard propeller pushing a 700-foot-long iceberg out of the way so it wouldn't completely wreck the *Arneb*."

Doug frowned. "I haven't told you the worst yet," he went on.

"What's that?" I asked dismally.

"The runway at McMurdo is beginning to deteriorate. The ice is breaking up to within a few miles of Hut Point, so we're really on a spot. There's a lot of mud and water already on the runways and you should see some of the melt holes. They're three feet deep."

"I sure hope they didn't try filling holes by flooding sea water on the ice as someone on the Task Force suggested. Your midsummer temperature at McMurdo is well above the freezing point of salt water."

"Actually," said Cordiner, "that's neither here nor there. What can you do here at the Pole if we don't bring you any of your eight scientists?"

This prospect was appalling. "Well, if you leave us at this point and don't bring us further supplies and men, it won't be a very enlightening enterprise," I said. "First of all, we'd probably have to abandon part of the camp because our fuel supply is inadequate to heat all the camp. And if you leave us at this point, there'll be virtually only Jack Tuck, Dr. Taylor and myself to handle the science projects. We'd have to give up the IGY program and spend the winter trying to stay alive."

"So what's your minimum number of IGY scientists?" he asked again.

I munched this over. "Willi Hough, Ed Flowers and John Guerrero are all at McMurdo," I told Cordiner. "And Arlo Landolt is with the five other IGY scientists in New Zealand. If you could get me these four, I might have the nucleus for some stripped-down scientific accomplishment if worst came to worst. At least we could carry out a token IGY program." I explained what could be done. Willi Hough could make the ionosphere, seismology and magnetism observations; Landolt would make aurora studies; Ed Flowers and Guerrero would handle some meteorology, and I could handle part of the glaciology aspects. However, all of it wouldn't add up to more than half the program because of the missing gear.

"I'll see what I can do to get you at least that skeleton crew," Cordiner said. "After we've gone this far, that's the least we can do. . . . But don't count on anything."

When Cordiner left with Bowers and the last of the Seabees, we were now down to nine men: Lieutenant Tuck, Dr. Taylor, the six Navy enlisted men and myself. Perhaps we'll get our IGY scientists after all, I thought. If we did not, it would be a bleak year indeed. In any case, there was no time for depressing thoughts. We would have to go about our work as though Tuck's builder and my group of eight would be arriving any day.

But it was not a simple matter to get a work party together when we rose the following day. The radiomen and the cook could not leave their work. Tuck's big mechanic, Martin Brown, lay on his bed in pain from his injured sacroiliac, and Earl Johnson was swamped attempting to handle Brown's duties as well as his own utility work, which included dragging the runway to smooth out the ruts in case more planes came. I had found him up at two A. M. the previous night fueling stoves.

So the heavy field-work party on the 5th would have caused raised eyebrows at the class-conscious IGY and Task Force 43 headquarters. Free drop lumber had been dragged into camp during the construction period. Tossed into a jumble and filled in with drifting snow, the wood mess lay in our back yard not far from the buildings on the Grid South or the 180th degree side of the Station. "This is wood that we'll need to complete our tunnel system and interiors," I told Jack. So from ten in the morning until six P.M., he, Dr. Taylor and I worked ceaselessly, digging out the wood by shovel, sorting and stacking it.

That night, exhausted and pondering a grim future filled with similar tasks, I fell into bed thankful for these hours of rest. I was now the sole occupant of the little Jamesway since Jack and Doc were living in the science building. I turned up the heat for the hut seemed cool and my chilled bones ached. But hardly had I dozed off than I was wide awake again. The stove top was cold and my bedside thermometer already read 32° F. The yellow marker on the fuel gauge measured three quarters filled, but no matter how I tinkered with the stove the room grew progressively colder. Finally I beat a shivering retreat to my bunk, threw Bowers' abandoned sleeping bag over my own light one and slept fitfully the rest of the night. When I crept from my covers the next morning the room temperature hovered near zero. It was an unpleasant reminder of the old Antarctic days of my youth. With freezing hands I checked the stove again, and to my chagrin I found that the marker on the fuel gauge was only a careless splash of yellow paint. The stove was out of fuel.

I finally got warmed up when I went out with Tuck and Taylor to continue cleaning up trash around the camp.

The 7th of January arrived with overcast skies, light snow and a semiwhite-out. Nevertheless, word came at nine-thirty that two P2V's had left McMurdo for the Pole, and were bringing three IGY men. They were the Weather Bureau meteorologist, Ed Flowers, his electronic maintenance specialist John Guerrero, and Willi Hough, the Bureau of Standards ionosphere specialist. Certainly I wanted IGY personnel but I was concerned, for I wanted them alive, not dead. From our end it was disturbing not to have received departure reports, for we could have warned them of the conditions prevailing.

Out on the runway Jack and I sweated out the planes' approach, fearing the worst if they attempted to land. But as we stood there a blue patch suddenly opened in the sky and sunshine streamed over the runway. And just at this moment the first plane appeared overhead and came in for its landing. Flowers and Guerrero were aboard along with 5,000 pounds of food and 500 pounds of highly important non-drop IGY equipment.

"Welcome to the South Pole," I greeted the two new arrivals enthusiastically, for to me that day marked the beginning of the IGY operation at the South Pole. However, I must admit I was taken aback by Guerrero, who arrived bareheaded, in an oversized badger fur parka on top of an aloha shirt!

Nevertheless, I was pleased with his eager interest in everything, despite the high altitude headaches from which he and Flowers were suffering. I spent several hours with the two men, showing them the camp and discussing the facilities for the scientific program. Flowers was not tall or particularly husky and I am afraid I discounted the physical contribution he would make to the manual labor facing us. (My impression, I am glad to say, was later to prove completely erroneous.) As our senior meteorologist, Ed would be in charge of the four-man Met group which at present included only Guerrero of the aloha shirt. Flowers was only a week away from his thirtieth birthday and Guerrero was but twenty-two. Flowers was a regular staff member of the U.S. Weather Bureau in Washington, while Guerrero had just previously been a student at the University of Alaska at Fairbanks and had had only limited experience as a weatherman.

The second plane with Willi Hough never did arrive that day for it had run into prop trouble at Beardmore and turned back. Squadron Commander Doug Cordiner, who had again been a passenger aboard the landing P2V, promised that Willi would come the next day.

"When you get Hough," Doug told me, "it will be the last flight for some time. You may not get more of your men in for the winter unless things change at McMurdo."

Sure enough, the next day Willi Hough arrived, wearing tennis shoes and brandishing a camera as he emerged from the plane. I hardly saw him for the next fifteen minutes as he dashed about feverishly snapping pictures. "Willi," I said finally when I had caught his attention, "you are going to be here a while, you know."

I had met Flowers and Guerrero in Washington before I left, although our total previous acquaintance amounted to one or two short chats. Willi Hough, however, I knew better, for after I had left Washington on Deep Freeze II, I had entrusted him to handle some of our states-side problems. Everyone who met Willi liked him. A veritable dynamo of energy, with a strong healthy ego and ability to match, Willi was perhaps the first person who volunteered for South Pole duty. He had come bursting into IGY headquarters immediately after plans for the Pole Station were made public. And to the startled receptionist he had announced in a loud voice: "I'm Hough here in a puff and I'm going to the South Pole." Verily he had.

Flowers and Guerrero moved into the large Jamesway with Jack Tuck's crew, since there at the Grid South end of this building they would be only twenty feet from the radio and Met shack. Willi, however, moved into the small Jamesway with me because his ionosphere work would eventually center on the far side of camp from the Met boys. "If we four constitute the sum total of the IGY personnel," I told the new arrivals, "we'll have to work double time to get even a small part of our program underway. But we'll keep our fingers crossed and hope we get our other five men here eventually."

That night as I lay in bed I pondered the arrival of Guerrero and Willi Hough. What would Amundsen and Scott have thought had they seen John and Willi in their polar attire? But this was a different era and perhaps they would have considered it amusing, too. Outside, Bravo alternately barked and whined from loneliness and the cold. Our other eleven huskies had gone back to McMurdo on the P2V and he was the only dog left. He would have no further companions and neither would we twelve men at the Pole unless the McMurdo runway became safe again.

Chapter 19

TWELVE AGAINST THE ELEMENTS

THE temperature was dropping steadily now and the winds were rising. Blizzards hit us more frequently and drifts began piling, for we were now over the hump of the summer and every day brought us closer to the third week of March when the sun would set to remain out of sight for six months. So far, in little more than a month, the outside world had already become a vague, shadowy world with which we could maintain contact solely by a sputtering, often blacked-out radio.

There were many things to be done, and Jack and I devised a work program which we hoped would begin to prepare us for the coming winter. There was need for work unity among our forces because of our limited number, yet each group also needed time for its own specialized duties. Obviously there was need for a strict daily schedule. Early we set reveille at 8:15; breakfast between 8:30 and 9 A.M.; lunch from 1:30 until 2; and dinner at 7. But we were never allowed to forget that we were a satellite of McMurdo and Little America—and, as the moon to the earth, had to conform with the larger body. Thus later in January when radio McMurdo required different radio schedules as well as weather reports at 6 A.M., and 3 and 9 P.M., we readjusted our day to the less inviting rising hour of 6:45 and spaced our eating times accordingly. Even so the two Met men had to rise still earlier than the others in order to complete observations and code their weather radiogram.

The shortage of work hands necessitated a compromise between Jack and me regarding daily activities. The IGY personnel of most of the Antarctic stations were responsible for carrying out the science program and were not required to perform manual labor essential to the running of the stations. At the South Pole Station, however, the separation of functions was less sharply defined. We first had to make certain that we could survive and then carry out our science program.

Therefore the Pole IGY men knew that all hands would often be needed to complete the camp and maintain it through the winter night. Consequently the IGY men readily agreed to pitch in on community projects. Thus the IGY personnel were to work on jobs relating to their IGY disciplines until lunch, then devote the hours from 2 P.M. until seven to community projects, such as salvaging, hauling, digging, stowage, fuel barrel handling, or whatever daily tasks confronted the Station. Jack and those of his Navy crew who could be spared from specific camp service or maintenance jobs worked all day on community projects. Dr. Taylor, free to choose, usually oriented his day toward my group both on science and community projects. In addition, all men including Jack and myself would take daily turns serving as "housemouse" and cook's helper as well as take part in the snow-gathering crews which would keep the Station supplied with water. Housemouse duty consisted of filling the stoves, sweeping the buildings and carrying out refuse to the Hubel Hole. "Evenings" were by and large left as the individual concern of the men, while Sundays beginning on January 13 were theoretically rest days. Nevertheless, the men found that though they awakened late on Sunday, they generally worked as hard as on regular workdays. The men could use these hours to make their bleak bunking spots more livable or as was generally the case, they could catch up on opening boxes and inventorying supplies relating to their own specific Pole Station duties. So in effect we had a twelve- to eighteen-hour day, and a seven-day week, an arrangement poles apart from the short and sedentary work schedule some of the men knew back in civilization.

Yet there was never a complaint from any of the men about this rigorous schedule. Furthermore, I was justly proud when the IGY men offered no complaints against the half-day inroad into their scientific specialties. They were eager to get to their work and were being called on for more manual work than they bargained for. However, they realized that Tuck's number was decimated by injury and ailments, and they must of necessity take on a disproportionate share of the heavy chores. The fact that some of Jack's crew were under the weather already appeared to be in part at least the result of inadequate physical examinations of the men. Muscular Brown, the mechanic, a hard and skillful worker when he first arrived, still lay stretched out on his bunk, with little appetite and in continual pain from what Dr. Taylor now diagnosed as a possible ruptured disc. It turned out that he had worn a back brace for a long while before coming to the Pole and his trouble was no new ailment. If the planes started flying again from McMurdo,

Brown would have to be replaced, even though he was a diesel engine expert and a willing worker with an even temperament.

But Brown was not the only casualty. McPherson, our sometimes fiery radio operator, had come to the Pole after several operations on chronic hemorrhoids. Now Mac was suffering again. Earl Johnson, who had once had an operation for hernia, had begun to develop nose-bleeds while overexerting in the cold, rarefied air; and Junior Waldron, our youthful Station electrician, had a game leg that was to send him to bed for a day or two at a time every week or so. Many other days he limped about in pain. He, too, had come to the Pole with a history of this trouble, but like the rest he was doing his level best to keep up with his work. The trouble was of course that these ailing men were unable to join general work parties that went beyond the scope of their basic assignment.

With our mornings crowded with IGY preparations, the afternoons with scavenging, making stock-pile caches, fixing interiors, arranging supplies and building tunnels, and the evenings spent on pressing immediate duties, life was a continual cold −25° F. to −40° F. windy rush from one heavy task to another.

Our morning tasks were varied. Ed Flowers located our standard instrument shelter in one of our big IGY crates and we quickly replaced the makeshift thermal screen with the dark door on one side that had given us faulty temperature readings. At once, by checking temperature readings in the new thermal screen against the makeshift thermometer, Ed Flowers found that true temperatures averaged about ten degrees colder than the Navy construction weather observer had at times reported. As near as we could tell, the temperature even on the calmest days when the sun was at its maximum elevation had not risen much if any above 0° F.*

Flowers also made a graph of temperature and altitude corrections for the anemometer, or wind speed indicator, which the senior Task Force meteorologist had stoutly claimed required no corrections for altitude. Later he and Guerrero assembled and set up one of the aerovane anemometers to permanently replace the Navy type hand-held wind velocity indicator.

Another morning task with which I was occupied was to open our IGY general boxes, a delight in itself because we were so short of necessary items. *It's like Christmas,* I noted in my diary, *finding these little odds and ends of office supplies, tools, books, etc.* Still another

---

* During the 1957–58 summer season there were seven hours of official temperature above 0° F. The absolute maximum on one hour reached +7° F.

morning job was the planning and constructing of our darkroom, which was to occupy part of the head, or toilet building, situated midway along Main Street in front of the garage. Willi Hough, who would be concerned with the daily development of ionogram films exposed every fifteen minutes, wanted as much space as possible and was requesting two-fifths of the 16 x 20-foot building for the darkroom. On the other hand, Jack Tuck wanted to move an oil tank into the head which was large enough to seriously curtail room for getting dressed at the shower as well as block the path to the principal conveniences. As it was, we already had toilets, a washer, dryer, shower, washstands, a stove, drain tanks and water tanks in the head. I finally drew up a compact plan that not only included a small but adequate photo lab with the fuel tank tucked out of the way and individual toilet kits and towel bins on the outside of the darkroom wall, but also a small hobby photo lab championed by Doctor Taylor and radioman McPherson for the amateur photographers among the Station's personnel.

With the Met observations taking on a steady rhythm, Jack and I began taking an interested look around us. The snow surface was not flat, as it had seemed from the air. Instead, the Pole area was actually a series of widely spaced low rolling hills and the Station itself sat slightly on one of the hillsides. The polar hills were low gentle rises which reached crests 50 to 100 feet high every five or ten miles. These long, low swells were aligned with the prevailing wind direction and were apparently large-scale migrating snow dunes. The snow was hard and rough at the top of the hills and soft and smooth at the bottom. Apparently they moved like sand dunes, although much slower, for it would take hundreds of years for the wind to move them any distance by wearing away the summits and filling in the valleys. The South Pole itself was located in the ice slope of one of these dunes.

Looking off from our Station toward Bowers' South Pole shack a quarter of a mile away, we could see on downhill for a great distance. At a distance of 17 miles, we later found that we could still see our Station. In the opposite direction, we were looking up a hill and the horizon was little more than a mile or so away.

To help Ed Flowers judge distances for his Met work, Jack and I went out one day toward the short-horizon side of the Station with the Weasel. Calculating the equation of time, we lined up the Met Rawin Dome and the sun at precisely noon and set up a ten-foot bamboo pole four inches in diameter and draped with a dark green parachute as a marker. We had noticed at this point that our camp was partially below the horizon. Only the dark Met Dome and the orange boxlike Aurora Tower stood out clearly, which meant that we had topped a gentle rise and descended slightly. We were on virgin snow and as I walked about while Jack drove the Weasel closer to the marker the surface suddenly readjusted downward an inch or so and the "row of dominoes earthquake" that we called Antarctic Hush rumbled over the terrain.

Before we returned to camp, we also set up a snow marker at the one-mile point and two snow cairns a half-mile from the Station. In a crude fashion, these three markers served for visual observations. Now when the Met men looked in that direction and saw only the half-mile marker through ice fog they could report: "Visibility is down to a half-mile."

For we were faced with several unique problems at the Pole, two of the greatest of which were how to determine time and direction. Because we were at the Pole, all time differences around the globe converged on us. As a result, we could have arbitrarily selected any twenty-four-hour basis we desired. It was my original intention to adopt Greenwich, England, time as our standard because all scientific observation time was to be based on it. Instead, for convenience of the radio operators reporting in schedule to McMurdo or Little America, we adopted their local 180th Meridian time. This was seventeen hours ahead of Washington, D.C.

One humorous aspect regarding time at the South Pole was that making a circle around the Pole, even one of a few feet, theoretically put you into the day ahead or following the one on which you began this short trek depending on whether one crossed the date line to the right or left. This could have been a handy implement for our four Catholic Station crewmen, since they could have walked around the Pole and skipped Fridays in this fashion. However, the Vatican had ruled that since the Friday food rules could not be observed at the Pole, the men could forego them, thus removing temptation.

As to geography, every direction from our polar Station was, of course, north. We had no east, west or south. To avoid confusion we used the "Polar Grid" system, or one of artificial directions, with our own man-made compass points. Grid North, as we referred to it, faced toward Greenwich, England, on Longitude 0°. Grid South was generally toward McMurdo and Little America, along the 180th Meridian, the International Date Line. Grid West, or 90° West, pointed toward Chicago, and Grid East, or 90° East, toward India. The "front" of our Station with the mess building on the left and the

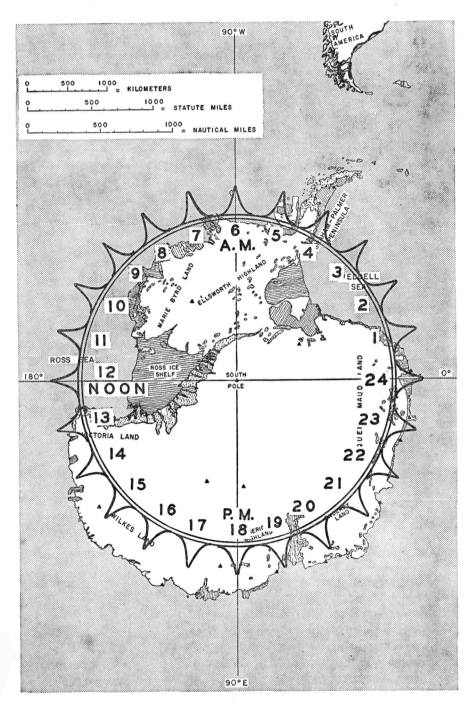

*South Pole sundial follows counterclockwise direction of the sun at the Pole.
Noon was arbitrarily set as the time the sun crossed the 180th meridian.*

science building on the right lay facing Greenwich while our "rear" lay toward Little America and McMurdo. On the polar navigator's map, the Grid System divides the Pole area into squares by straight lines like a street layout in a city, a system that made directions simple in case of emergency.

In reality the navigators set up the system to eliminate the confusion of direction and convergence of meridians by arbitrarily superimposing a standard Mercator projection over the top of the polar map. The line along Meridians 90° E and 90° W becomes a new base line equivalent to the 0° Latitude line of the equator. When forced to report their actual positions they can translate grid headings and locations by reading the regular polar map down through the superimposed artificial grid lines.

Our community projects, which occupied Jack's men all day and took up the afternoons of the four-man IGY group and Dr. Taylor, were as onerous as they were varied. One major task was to dismantle the smaller Jamesway that sat on the Grid South or 180th degree side of the mess hall and move it between our mid-station firebreak and the science building storage cache.

For three days Jack, Doc Taylor and I concentrated on dismantling and rebuilding the Jamesway, a task complicated by the fact that we had to raise the snow level at the prospective site by three feet in order to make the Jamesway roof come up even with those of the other buildings. With Bowers gone, this leveling task fell to me. The Jamesway floor panels were made of twin layers of plywood, with a spongy composition between the plies that gave the floor an unpleasant springy feel. To eliminate this, Willi Hough joined Jack, Doc and me and we set large wooden blocks beneath the center of each panel, filled in the empty six-inch space with excelsior for further insulation and tacked on burlap to hold the excelsior in place when we turned over the sections. When this floor was nailed down to the sills it had none of the rock and roll characteristic of Jamesways. And on top of this floor we laid and tacked a felt and canvas covered "rug" salvaged from A-22 paradrop containers. We used gravity-flow oil space heaters and prevented cold floors and hot overhead by use of an electric fan installed above and blowing down on the stove.

Once the Jamesway was up, we connected its self-contained wiring into the camp electrical system, erected room partitions and began making the individual rooms livable. This smaller Jamesway, measuring 32 feet in length, was big enough for six men. Since the Met men should most conveniently live toward the other end of camp

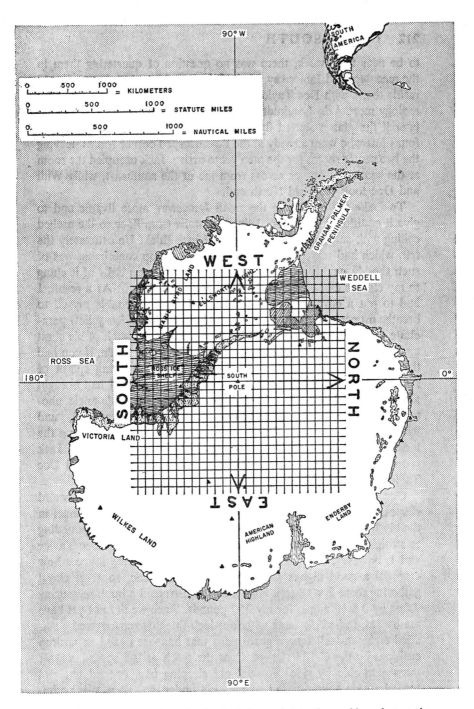

Grid directions adopted at the South Pole to obviate the problem that at the Pole all directions are north.

to be near their work, there was no question of quartering them in the reconstructed Jamesway. Instead, Jack and I agreed that we would reside there, with Doc Taylor and Willi Hough. Our aurora and seismology men, Arlo Landoldt and Robert Benson, would join us here later if the planes started flying again from McMurdo. For now the four of us who were already at the Pole usurped corner rooms, leaving the two center rooms for the men yet to arrive. Jack occupied the room at the southwest corner across from me at the southeast, while Willi and Doc took the Grid North end.

To make my cubicle in the small Jamesway more livable and to give it additional insulation, I lined its walls from floor to the arched ceiling with salvage felt about one-half inch thick. Unfortunately the felt, which had served as padding in the paradrop containers, was of such shoddy quality that it shed miserably and soon balls of it clung to my clothes and cluttered the floor and filled the air. As a result, I had to put a cover over this insulation if only to enable myself to breathe properly. I selected a sunny-looking bright golden-yellow parachute as my "wallpaper," a choice that made Jack clutch at his chest and exclaim, "It's horrendous. It would make a fine harem if you had the women." Willi Hough's reaction to this eye-opening splash of silk-canopylike room lining was just as unenthusiastic. I had brought along a large internally mirrored glass sphere for wide-angle photography. "Put the crystal ball in your room," Willi suggested, "and with another chute for a Gypsy-style headdress, you can become the local fortuneteller!" Seeking to counterbalance my wild wall, Jack soon lined his with a somber green parachute while Willi and Doc Taylor employed white ones.

Our metal beds had streamed in and four were bent in weird shapes. We gave the good frames to the Navy and IGY personnel in the big Jamesway, while Jack and Willi managed after much pounding to straighten out two of the damaged steel bunk frames. Doc Taylor and I, however, had no success. From past experience I knew how essential a good night's sleep was in the Antarctic, so I set about gathering some 2 x 10-foot lumber and constructed a bunk measuring 7 feet by 3 feet, ample for my 250 pounds. Since we did not yet have mattresses, I filled the bunk with four-inch-thick canvas-covered wool-filled eighteen-inch-square crash pads that had been used as airdrop cushions by the C-124 riggers. Over the crash pads I spread two air mattresses side by side. Bowers' old sleeping bag, opened out and turned upside down, served as one quilt under me. Then, using additional salvage-box lumber, I made a series of shelves, handsome in a modernistic way, at the head and foot of my bunk. Finally, with this work completed, I had my own private sanctuary at the South Pole. Unfortunately after the bunk and shelves were in there was only about two feet left for dressing room.

The afternoon community jobs seemed without end. Three receiving antennas were erected but our radios still caused us continual concern. Our two main Navy 350-watt transmitters oscillated even when they weren't keyed. With nothing being sent, they nevertheless transmitted a whistle. It was Dickey's job to get and keep our sets in operation so that McPherson could transmit and receive messages other than by means of the construction crew's less powerful field radio. One night I stayed up until two A.M. with Dickey, going over what progress he had made, more to encourage him than from belief that I could possibly spot his trouble. The sets had been stored outdoors over the preceding winter at McMurdo and in the spring the boxes had filled part way with melt water and ice. Later they had been airdropped to us. Thus it was little short of a miracle that after two weeks of careful and deliberate work, Dickey put one radio into operating condition.

A large part of our community effort was devoted to completing our tunnel system around the Station buildings. Bowers' crew had erected frames and some chicken wire and burlap covering over sections of the alleyways, but had left most of the job for our permanent crew. But even in those sections that we considered completed, snow drifted through the chicken wire and burlap during a blizzard and we ultimately had to double and even triple the layers of burlap. The quantity of burlap airdropped to us had become a community joke, for we had enough to bag the annual snowfall for miles around—not to mention the hundreds of square yards of nylon parachute cloth.

The elaborate tunnel system was to include the continuous tunnel circumscribing the camp plus six transverse tunnels which were to run from Grid South to Grid North at the east and west ends of camp as well as between the mess building, big Jamesway, garage, small Jamesway and science building. Most of the work on the covering of transverse as well as exterior tunnels was done by Jack Tuck, Earl Johnson, our utility man, and Junior Waldron, our electrician. Nor was this easy work, since the tunnel corridors had to be wide enough to provide large-scale storage of boxes and full drums as well as for the passage of large hauling sleds. The task of securing the burlap was no small one. The construction crew had used a heavy staple gun but now that we took over the task, we discovered that there were no staples left to fit it. With the temperature hovering about −30° and the wind at 15 knots, there were frequent curses at the regular fence-post-style individual staples which had to be held with bare fingers to be driven.

Wisely or unwisely, I had rejected Bowers' offer to erect the 2 x 4 tunnel framework outside the science building, on the 90° east side of camp. My reasoning was first of all that I hoped that airdrops would bring us more suitable framing lumber than we had left, and, second, that Willi Hough's ionosphere contraptions were so large and heavy that it would be best to get them indoors before starting this tunnel. One of Willi's transformers did not look like much because it was a one-foot cube. However, within that small cubic volume, 400 pounds of materials were packed. Willi, Jack and I carried it up the four-foot stairs into the science building amid considerable panting and groaning and wailing and cursing. Willi's Automatic Ionosphere Recorder, which he called "The Monster," weighed over a thousand pounds and had been placed on the science building floor by the construction crew before the walls were erected. The Automatic Ionosphere Recorder required 120 vacuum tubes and countless relays, switches, lamps and other electronic mysteries. Once the Monster was connected, it would send electronic impulses vertically to the ionosphere and photographically record any direct reflection of the radio energy impulse, a principle rather similar to radar. The purpose of the Monster was to record electrical manifestations in the ionosphere and from them to learn about the ionosphere's general behavior. "Well, Willi," I gasped after our ordeal, "how much bigger a monster would you need to check outer space?"

The building of the tunnel outside the science building offered its own problems. We had hoped to use ten-foot two-by-fours, but not enough had been dropped. Since we had only eight-foot lengths, we had to improvise a construction technique. In its cold dry state it was impossible to make a snowball out of the snow at the South Pole. However, if you mixed cold undersurface snow with warmer surface snow and tramped it down, even though both types were loose like granulated sugar, they would cement together within a few hours into a substance of amazing hardness. This process is called "compaction," and is one in which an exchange of heat and vapor between snow particles even far below zero unites them solidly. So hard did the mixed snow become that if you tried to pound a 20-pound crowbar into it with a 20-pound sledge, the crowbar would peen without sinking deeper into the hard snow.

Utilizing this principle of compaction, I worked with Willi, Ed Flowers, John Guerrero and Doc Taylor to build a footing for a ten-foot-high tunnel wall with eight-foot timbers. Crudely mixing cold and warm snow, we built a compacted two-foot snow wall against a movable packing box form. And on top of that wall we erected the eight-foot timbers, bringing the tunnel to the height of all other Station buildings. Then after three afternoons of work, this tunnel was completed with chicken wire and double layers of burlap.

Still another community project was to improve our snow-delivery system to the melter. Most of this work was done by Earl Johnson, whose vigor during this period was gratifying, though his puzzling nosebleeds continued to be a source of concern to Dr. Taylor. Since the men were divided into groups of four, every four days I went out with my group with the Weasel dragging two large sleds with plywood sides to the north side of camp. Here in the area on the windward side reserved for clean snow, we filled the sleds with snow. Then we pulled the sleds to the garage entrance on the south side of camp with the Weasel. At first we had to gather the snow into bags made from parachutes and drag the bags the length of the garage to dump into the melter. Soon, however, Earl cleverly built a hatch and snow chute in the garage wall, which connected with the snow melter inside. Thus we were able to eliminate filling bags and just fill the sleds with snow. Because Johnson had effected such a labor-saving device, we rewarded him by adding the job of hand-shoveling the snow into the chute to his other burdens.

Scavenging and salvaging were also vital community tasks. For instance, the drop zone was still studded with useful plywood, planks, parachute bags, crash pads and parachutes. We were able to stack two cords of the 18 x 10 x 2-inch wood blocks we found there, and we assembled giant piles of the rest. Another dismal job was that of trying to salvage the enormous nylon parachutes which had become heavy with drifted snow. We first had to prop the chute "heads" on sticks and clear them before dragging them in by Weasel.

Now we set up a "classified" salvage cache on the Grid South side of the tunnel near the science building, where we sorted and stacked all sorts of remnants. We spent one entire day breaking up a construction crew junk pile the size of a house. With the temperature at −23° F. and the wind at 12 knots, we laboriously moved it into our salvage cache. I remember this day particularly because the air still seemed so perceptibly thin that it made our heavy labor breath-taking, and caused our hearts to pound rapidly.

Another day we tore down the huge pile of 8 x 8-inch wooden timbers that Doc Taylor, Tuck and I had dug out a few weeks earlier, and moved them into our salvage cache. It was here that I learned a lot about Ed Flowers. I had seen him first back in Washington in a business suit and he had impressed me as a quiet person of no extraordinary stamina or strength. If I had had to judge him then, I should have put him in the strictly white-collar category and I wondered what use he would be to us on physical tasks.

Some of the timbers we moved that day were extremely heavy and twelve feet long, so that it normally required four men to carry them conveniently over the uneven snow surface. As I glanced up at one point, I suddenly froze. There walking over the snow, as if he carried a fence post over a shoulder, came Ed Flowers by himself with a heavy timber! I had misjudged him completely. Certainly he was the strongest man in camp. I found out later he had been an amateur wrestler in college.

Doc Taylor was so disappointed when we had to move the neat pile he had helped to erect to the salvage cache that he refused to join in the operation. A newcomer to the wiles of snow drifting, he failed to see any reason for moving the stack from out on the open snow surface back under shelter. But from my own sad experience on other expeditions, I knew that even larger objects than Taylor's isolated stack of wood could fall prey to drifts in storms and get lost. On one occasion at Little America III in 1940 we had actually lost a large pool table. During the time we were constructing that base on the Bay of Whales we had needed no such diversion. However, later someone suggested bringing in the pool table and erecting it in our garage. Since everyone remembered the big crate that stood not more than thirty feet from the main entrance to the camp, we went out to bring it in. But it was nowhere in sight, and prod and dig as much as we could we failed to locate it. Thirty men dug systematically into the entire area and created a huge man-made pit far below the surface without any luck. The snow has a habit of swallowing things up.

Doc Taylor, however, was unmoved by this and other stories of equipment lost forever in snowdrifts, thinking only of his labor in creating his original pile. However, he did not permit his emotional attachment to this one pile to keep him from moving other salvage material. This was fortunate because Taylor was a hard and excellent worker and did not consider such menial work beneath his dignity as a physician.

Nor did he complain when the weather sharpened and nipped our noses with frostbite and split our fingers near the nails. By January 20 my nose was running almost continually outdoors, an affliction also common to some of the other men. Fortunately we had facial tissue, for frozen handkerchiefs become like sandpaper in the polar cold, and without facial tissue we would have been forced to rely on what was called the "Antarctic Noseblow," a method frowned on in polite society. Doc Taylor early covered his face with a face mask, unmindful of the rugged pride and dislike of masks exhibited by the others. He pinned the oversized nose part together with a safety pin—which gave him an eerie appearance on salvage work, since the pin seemed to pass right through his nose.

Certainly the punishing weather slowed our work. For instance, there was one cold and blustery day when the IGY group, Tuck and Taylor went scavenging out on the drop zone. Suddenly while we worked an ice fog enveloped us. Greatly concerned that any delay might completely obliterate our view, we turned back to the safety of the Station. Looking back into the sky just before going indoors, I saw a strange polar rainbow in the sky opposite the sun. It was a rare fogbow, similar in shape to a rainbow but all white.

Still another community job was the cleanup. Under none of society's compelling demands, isolated men can easily lose direction and purpose. I knew from experience that without the presence of women the men might quickly lapse into slovenliness and indifference. Yet camp and personal cleanliness were ingrained in me as necessities for morale and health. In our normal daily life we had our housemouse duties to perform. But there was a great deal of ugly litter both inside and outside the buildings that had to be cleared away before we could achieve a photogenic camp. Other camps I had lived in, including McMurdo, had been so poorly attended to that I had resolved not to let the same conditions prevail at the Pole.

For a week we accelerated our efforts to clear away the litter left by the construction crew. We packed the large quantities of clothing they had left behind into duffel bags and stored them in a cache near the science building to serve as our emergency haberdashery. But the big cleanup took place on the Grid West side of camp, which had been the "other side of the tracks" to Bowers' Seabees. This was the area known as "Dog Town," since the eleven dogs had been tethered there. There lay an unsightly trash pile, as well as the toilet tent, and strewn odds and ends of gear including sleds and ice axes. Ed Flowers, Guerrero, Doc Taylor and I now plunged into the task of cleaning up Dog Town and in four days had the area spotless.

Another important community task fell to Jack Tuck and Earl Johnson. This was the job of bulldozing tons of snow into an artificial snowdrift against the Grid North wall of our village, or on the outside of Main Street Tunnel. Jack was quite worried about doing this work because although he had driven farm tractors since childhood he had never done much bulldozing and this was a delicate operation. A few inches too far in bulldozing and our two-by-four tunnel frames would collapse. But he realized that his other men were also inexperienced as tractor drivers and it was best that he learn to handle the dozer and assume the responsibility.

Fortunately, his work was nearly professional, as was everything he undertook. Slowly he bulldozed the snow against the north village wall and at the precise moment when another foot would have ruined our tunnel he backed away. Our objective was to bank the snow along the entire northern wall to the windward, so that winter winds would flow over the rooftops rather than penetrate the thin burlap wall. The bank of snow would speed the normal drifting and it would also provide good insulation, since prevailing winds would not strike the camp directly. I knew this last from my experience at Little America III where after snow walls were up our fuel consumption dropped 50 per cent.

There was also a considerable amount of work to be done on interior building problems, which offered a welcome relief from the outdoor tempest. With the continued absence of Tuck's builder, Tom Osborne, we all had to pitch in, and a flurry of activity produced chairs, tables, desks, shelves and stands, with Dr. Taylor revealing a skill for gadgeteering superior to the rest of us. We also constructed room partitions and furniture in the various buildings. Within several days, for instance, the interior shell of the science building blossomed forth into eleven rooms lining both sides of a lengthwise corridor. My office occupied half of one end, with Dr. Taylor's sick bay, moved from the mess hall, across the aisle. At the opposite end were Willi Hough's ionosphere laboratory and the glaciology office. Other offices included a medical lab, aurora room, instruments room, Jack Tuck's office, work space, emergency radio storage space and a technical library.

It was with considerable regret that I observed the installation of field telephones throughout the Station. Perhaps this was the price we had to pay for no longer living on pemmican. But I questioned whether it was worth it because it signified further end of the traditional Antarctic quiet. The phones were hooked up country-style with a different number of rings for each building, which meant that all phones rang when any building was called.

There were minor troubles as well. One morning the camp awoke to the fact that we were running short of tobacco and no more would reach us unless the planes began flying. Having once been a heavy smoker myself but now for the past year or so a nonsmoker, I was unaffected by this crisis, though the gloomy faces of the half-dozen heaviest smokers gave cause for alarm regarding morale. I had brought along a few pipes and two cans of tobacco, thinking that I might feel the desire for an occasional pipeful during the winter night. But when I realized that Chet Segers, who was seldom without a pipe between his teeth, was becoming almost morose, I gladly gave him my small tobacco supply. With loud thanks, he accepted the gift but within a few days his face turned sad again, for the small supply was soon gone. He even tried filling his pipe with coffee grounds and tea, only to become ill after a few puffs. After this he joined the other tobacco-less bloodhounds searching for cigarette butts to stuff into their pipes.

But soon even butts became a luxury. Men searched carefully through wastebaskets, in the snow and in corners. The time soon arrived when Dickey went around holding tiny butts to his lips with a long-nose pliers, while Doc Taylor employed long toothpicks for the same purpose. Jack had trouble with either system because of his year-old fleecy beard. After a few days not even a butt could be found, but only Dr. Taylor was brave enough to announce that he was giving up smoking. However, a few days later he let it be known that he had "given up giving up smoking."

Then, just when it seemed the smokers would not survive their ordeal, I chanced upon a bonanza of fifty butts in an overlooked trash basket. As a joke I colored the tips of two with red penciling to resemble lipstick before laying them out for the men, although I doubt the joke was appreciated. Once these butts were gone the men prayed more than ever that the runway at McMurdo would be fixed soon.

Actually, there were no real evidences of the variety of tension known as "cabin fever," the result of living for considerable periods in isolation with limited companionship. There was, however, one small incident that gave promise of future trouble. Met man John Guerrero was an amateur radio operator, and our regular radioman, Bill McPherson, had made it clear that he didn't want anyone, especially a civilian, operating the ham set. This, of course, was his own idea and it was contrary to Navy and IGY agreements. However, it was Tuck's responsibility to set this point straight and not mine.

A few days after John and Mac exchanged words, Guerrero was using an electric drill which apparently interfered with McPherson's radio. Mac came storming out of the radio shack and expressed his opinion of such sabotage with considerable vehemence. He searched around camp for the source of interference and ultimately found Guerrero to be the culprit. The abusive language Mac used on John naturally ruffled his feelings, but since he had only one more hole to drill, he proceeded to do so on the grounds that he would be finished before Mac could walk back to his radio shack. The result was that Mac stormed off to Jack Tuck demanding justice.

Jack was very much upset when he came to me to adjudicate this personnel problem. "Mac was right in doing what he did," Jack told me. "John had no business drilling when he did."

Perhaps naturally I favored my IGY man Guerrero and said that Mac should at least have shown more courtesy. Jack could not see this and for a moment there was danger of open friction between us, a bad situation in a camp so small. Finally Jack and I agreed that we had personality problems that bore watching and that it would be fatal in the future if either he or I should defend our men on emotional grounds. "Good personalities," I told Jack, "tend to become better under hardship. But the reverse is often true, too. Personalities don't remain long in a gray state in Antarctic isolation. They either tend to turn white or black." It was too early yet to tell about the feud between John and Mac. We would have to watch and act together to control it. Above all we must not take sides.

I had no desire to exert authority over Jack's Navy men. But I could show him by being friendly and impartial that he had no need to remain on guard. For example, all radiograms went to Jack for checking out before being sent, including my IGY scientific radiograms. In addition, he saw all the messages I received by radio, whereas I did not see any of his. Many of these dealt with Navy personnel problems and regulations of no concern to me, but I was interested in ones that gave news of events involving the Task Force operations. But I controlled my curiosity and it was not long before he realized that I might be interested in some of the messages. Soon he was asking me, "Wouldn't you like to see this one and this one?"

After a while, he showed me all the radiograms, even those pertaining to internal Navy business. And he admitted afterward that he had been put into this position by the Task Force, always sensitive to allowing civilians access to what they felt to be military matters.

But by the end of January with telephones jangling, nerves taut from a growing tobacco shortage, isolation and worry about the condition of the McMurdo runway and rapidly worsening weather, we could nevertheless look back on a month of useful and satisfactory employment. Nor had all our time been spent at the grindstone.

To avoid boredom, we occasionally broke our routine with extraneous activities. One midnight Johnson came around in his underwear to invite us to his birthday party. It turned out that the next day was also Ed Flowers' birth date. We held the celebration in the big Jamesway where the sleepy Navy men and the two members of the Met crew toasted each other and ate Dickey's fruitcake at a "Long Underwear" birthday party.

On those occasions when the wind was stiff but steady, some of the men stood on skis and sleds and let the wind propel them by means of billowing attached parachutes. For a few days parachute riding ranked as our No. 1 sport though falls were frequent on the rough surface. Steadily dropping temperatures soon brought this pastime to an untimely end.

But certainly eating was a more popular sport. Even though he had come without recent cooking experience, Chet Segers was proving to be a pillar of polar society with his work in the galley. If he had a serious early failure, it was not of his own doing. In his first attempts to bake, his cakes fell flat. But he and Mac sent a message to Arthur Godfrey for aid, since one of his sponsors was the company whose cake mixes Segers relied upon. The cake-mix people responded by baking cakes in an airplane at an altitude of 9,000 feet, almost the same as the Pole altitude. And we soon received a long hamgram informing Chet to add flour, which would cut down on the baking powder that controlled the cakes' rising. Some stir resulted from this private exchange, for the station received a stern Navy query on alleged "unsatisfactory baking mixes." Later we heard that national magazines had played with the joke in cartoons. The blunt truth was that the baking mix was not unsatisfactory. The Navy had simply failed to instruct Segers in the fine art of high-altitude cooking.

Armed with his new instructions, Chet gingerly put a new cake in the oven while we hovered about as official testers. His finished product was a mountainous four-layer affair that was a meal in itself. After that he prepared bread and pastries with the assuredness of a Waldorf baker.

Another welcome break in our hard existence were our phone patches to our families and friends back in the states. Because we could get no mail, our hamset was our sole contact with the outside world. In 1940–1941, when I was at Little America III, the phone companies back in the United States had frowned on ham patches. By 1957 the telephone company, by and large, no longer took such a dim view of being hooked into ham radio communications.

Jules Madey, a sixteen-year-old ham who operated Station K2KGJ in Clark, New Jersey, was our first contact with the outside world from the South Pole. It was he who connected me with Ruth and my mother on separate occasions on their birthdays in January, 1957. My mother was celebrating her eightieth year. When Jules returned home from school, he went to bed and then rose to be with us the entire New Jersey night. All of us owed him an immense debt, and I cannot speak too highly of the comfort he brought us.

Our ham system was simple. In making a ham patch, we got in touch with Jules, and later with other operators, by radio. Jules took down the name and telephone number of the person to be contacted. Then he rang up the number and plugged the telephone line with a device known as a "patch" into his radio connection with our South Pole ham radio. If the receiving person accepted the call, Jules monitored the conversation and at its completion, he disconnected his patch. The person receiving the call paid the phone company only for the regular telephone call between his home and the ham operator's house.

We chuckled for months about Willi Hough's wrong number. Once when he wanted to talk to his wife, Willi gave the ham operator his wife's phone number, but somehow it became garbled in transmission. The man who answered the phone at the number which was rung inexplicably agreed to accept the reversed charges. Perhaps it was the hour, which was 1:30 A.M. at the recipient's home.

"Hello!" yelled Willi. "May I speak to my wife?"

"Who?" the angry voice shouted back.

"To my wife," Willi repeated.

"Who is this calling?" the strange voice snarled.

"This is Willi calling from the South Pole."

Crash went the receiver and Willi stood openmouthed, wondering what strange man was in his home. But imagine the state of mind of the gentleman to whom Willi spoke when the next morning he tried to make his friends believe that he had been awakened at 1:30 A.M. by a wrong number from the South Pole!

February was now upon us, and we were still building and cleaning up. The winds were stronger and more penetrating; the temperature was falling at a rate of roughly three degrees per day; the skies were more often overcast; and blowing snow paid us more frequent visits.

We had trouble tying down parachute covers over our caches. There was an edge of danger now in the lack of tobacco.

But in addition to all our continuing tasks, a new job faced us. We required a geomagnetic-seismology tunnel, and though this was a job sufficiently onerous to require the attentions of the full complement of IGY personnel, I could not wait for the arrival of our five scientists who were still at McMurdo. "We'll have to do it ourselves," I told Flowers, Guerrero and Hough. Doc Taylor agreed to pitch in with us to my great relief.

This new tunnel, to be a seven-foot-deep affair, would run east from the science building to a point a fifth of a mile away. At a distance of 500 feet out we planned a shelter, or pit, for geomagnetic recording instruments; and at 1,000 feet another pit for the seismometer. The geomagnetic instruments would thus be far enough from camp to be unaffected by any local magnetism, while the seismograph would be sufficiently distant to be unaffected by man-made vibrations and record only nature's earthquakes. As for the long tunnel itself, it was needed so that our scientists would be able to reach these instruments without having to go outdoors into the dark and the extremely low winter temperatures.

To save ourselves from having to excavate a seven-foot-deep tunnel, Ed Flowers and I first built a plywood form consisting of two four-by-eight sheets and set them up vertically three feet apart. Then we dug a trench to a depth of five feet, banking the freshly dug and variably temperatured snow against the outside of the form, stamping it down to about two feet high. Thus we had a tunnel seven feet deep as soon as the banked snow set solidly against the form. Then we pushed and pulled the plywood form along another eight feet and repeated the digging-and-banking operation. We finished 25 feet of tunnel that first afternoon, while Willi and John, seeking even easier methods of construction, cut snow blocks and set them in place on the surface as walls for a tunnel to connect ours into the camp system. They did not get as much accomplished actually as we did, and we were certain we could complete 50 feet a day, especially with Doc Taylor's proffered assistance.

And we did so day after day with the three of us digging and John and Willi building up the sides with the plywood form and covering the tunnel with scrap boards and burlap.

There was news from McMurdo early in February. The runway was still in wretched condition and unsafe for heavy planes. Ice was continuing to go out to sea at points only a few miles from Hut Point.

In fact, the thaw had resulted in the tragic death of a tractor driver named Bartlett, who was killed when his Weasel broke through the ice near Vince's Cross at Hut Point.

Admiral Dufek was finally reaching the conclusion that McMurdo's airstrips could not be repaired. However, as a last resort, I heard with relief he had turned to the Snow, Ice and Permafrost Research Establishment of the Army (SIPRE) for aid. SIPRE's expert, Dr. Andrew Assur, had flown to New Zealand and was now at McMurdo, and with the news of his arrival my hopes rose. He had previously gained an excellent reputation for maintaining safe sea-ice landing fields in the Far North during the Dew Line construction.

We continued to work steadily at our tasks at the Pole while we kept in touch with Assur's activities at McMurdo. But our goal of 50 feet a day on the seven-foot-deep, three-feet-wide 1,000-foot geomagnetic-seismology tunnel proved more fatiguing with each passing day. Some nights the five of us were too tired to eat and my back, hands, elbows and shoulders ached constantly. Splits in my thumb and fingers due to dryness added to the pain of cold hands and my nose kept peeling from endless refreezings.

Assur's plan at McMurdo was to bore holes in the airstrip, suck out all the salt water he could, fill the holes with salt-free ice and fresh water from the snow melts, then let it refreeze. Since fresh water froze at higher temperatures, this was his only hope for strengthening the runway, the surface of which was full of pits, some reaching three and four feet into the subsurface. These he was also cleaning out and filling laboriously. After this he proposed to regrade the runways.

With news of Assur's activities at McMurdo, the Pole Station took on new life. "Now they'll bring cigarettes and I'll get some pipe tobacco," said Chet Segers, a dreamy expression on his face as he prepared my morning pancakes. "Maybe now we'll get the rest of our IGY Met equipment," Ed Flowers piped up. "And our other five men," I added.

Jack had been busy putting in escape hatches in the tunnel overhead at both ends of the mess hall. He had also pushed Bravo (who whimpered like a baby) out into the snow on February 2 as a substitute groundhog and reported that Bravo had seen his shadow, a sure indication of a cold winter. Now with the news of Assur's work at McMurdo, Tuck and his crew set to work to improve our own runway, too.

Earl Johnson, pinchhitting as tractor driver for the ailing Brown, began dragging the long runway with the D-2 tractor on February 4.

Earl barely reached the runway when his tractor went dead. "What a a time for this to happen," he reported to us in a highly emotional state. In Brown's absence no one had checked the oil in the final drives and the bearings on the left tractor track had burned out. "What are we to do?" wailed Earl.

Brown, who had been confined in bed with his bad back, painfully crawled out now and went out to this strip. By the time the rest of us got there, he could inform us that the tractor would have to be brought back to camp and dismantled. "But how are we going to move the tractor?" Brown asked Jack.

Jack had a plan and it worked. We forced a metal skid under the immobile left track. Then we hitched the Weasel to the skid to pull the left track along while the right track proceeded under its own power. Weaving and wobbling, the tractor finally negotiated the mile from the airstrip to camp. Getting the tractor into the garage proved a major effort by all hands, but the job was completed in three hours to the surprise and relief of all. Then with Brown's "from the bunk" instructions, Jack and Willi disassembled the tractor housing to get at the bearing. Cliff and Earl joined in the operation which went on far into the night.

Word came on the 7th that the condition of the McMurdo runway was rapidly improving and that the Air Force might be able to fly in its C-124's by the 10th. Johnson immediately went back to dragging the long runway using a pipe-drag behind the Weasel. Then Jack dragged the short runway in case both runways would be needed. Afterward, he and Earl relocated the fluorescent red cloth markers and the fuel drums marking the approach end of the long runway, placing twelve drums 200 feet apart from each other. We were ready for the planes.

February 10 arrived with a partly cloudy sky and a temperature of −32° F. Had the Globemasters returned to McMurdo? I pondered.

Indeed they had—and more. Word came in the morning that the first airdrop since December 15 would take place within a few hours! Our five IGY men, Jack's builder and a replacement for Brown were to be delivered in a few days.

Prior to the arrival of the first plane, I was called to the radio. Aboard the plane were Larry Gould, chairman of the Antarctic Committee of the U. S. National Committee for the IGY; Harry Wexler, chief scientist of the IGY Antarctic Program who was making his first trip to the Antarctic; Paul-Émile Victor, the noted French polar explorer and an old friend of mine; and Colonel Crosswell, in charge of the Globemaster planes and crews.

I conversed briefly with each and had the strange feeling that I had been away from civilization for years instead of four months. Then I hurried out to the drop zone, for Crosswell reported that he had three drop loads. What a welcome sight, I thought as I watched the plane come into view, for I had forgotten the heartaches of former stream-ins.

Of the first two chutes, one ripped and its packages landed hard a quarter of a mile off. The second run over the drop zone missed us by half a mile, and when nine packages were tipped out at once, two streamed in and set off a surface tremor of large magnitude. We could hear this Antarctic Hush approaching us like a loud surf and when it reached us the surface seemed to drop, a frightening experience for those among us who had not heard it before.

But the real heartache came on the last drop as Crosswell brought his plane in low to drop the mailbag. Unfortunately a heavy package of film at the bottom of the sack tore the mailbag apart and we watched with horror as our precious mail scattered over an area of half a mile. For two hours Dickey, Guerrero and I wandered about retrieving letters. One was a Valentine from Ruth, which made the effort worth while.

Among the stream-ins was a replacement pendulum for Willi Hough's IBM clock. The original had been bent in transit, though Willi had been able to straighten and use it. Now he would have to continue using the original because the replacement was bent into a near perfect U. A Japanese reporter named Tsubokawa had sent me two flags to fly at the Pole, one of which the Japanese Antarctic explorer, Lieutenant Choku Shirase, had used in his 1911 expedition to the Bay of Whales. I recovered these flags, flew them as requested, and ultimately they were returned to Shirase's family through the American State Department.

The men's interest in this first drop was extraordinary. They quickly stowed away the bulk of the four boxes of food, which included 1,300 pounds of coffee, none of which we needed unless we planned on doubling our heavy coffee drinking during the coming year. Then came cases of peas, corn, beans, oatmeal and most-welcome cranberry sauce. Enthusiasm reached a high point with the discovery of a box of ships store stock. And there among the soap and candy lay the prize . . . cigarettes and pipe tobacco.

Chapter 20

ALL OUR MEN ARRIVE

EARLY on the morning of Tuesday, February 12th, word came from McMurdo that an R4D was departing for the Pole and would land at our Station. Thus we could at last expect the rest of our personnel.

Jack hurried to drag the runway once again with the Weasel. For two hours he drove back and forth putting a smooth surface on the strip, while I tended to last-minute chores. But the first plane over the Pole was a C-124 and soon we were engulfed in drops, parachutes and stream-ins. Fifty-five-gallon oil drums thumped heavily into the snow. Then came a second C-124 and while it was in the act of making its drops, the R4D approached.

I walked to the airstrip after the plane had landed in time to see a small clutch of immigrants emerge from it. There were seven men to be exact, two of whom were sailors and five IGY personnel. The first thing that caught my attention was that there was little gaiety among the arrivals. In fact quite the reverse. But there was no time to find the reason for their anger now, for other trouble was developing. The R4D's Navy pilot was loudly objecting to waiting even a few minutes for Brown and the outgoing mail, which were our last letters to civilization.

"You will wait!" I told him, and he agreed gracelessly, glancing at his watch as if he had an important appointment elsewhere. In contrast, poor Brown, who had always been enthusiastic and agreeable despite his injured back, stood noiselessly crying at the thought of leaving the Pole. I was genuinely sorry to see him go. Then when Brown and the mail were finally aboard, the pilot refused to wait for us to clear the area. Instead, he fired his JATO bottles in our faces and took off in a cloud of snow.

"What got into the pilot—he acts frightened?" I asked the new arrivals. "Did any of you have trouble with him coming here?" They all grimaced, groaned and shook their heads. During the flight he had arrogantly forced them to remain standing in the narrow passageway alongside the fuselage gas tanks for hours. And when the men had grown cramped, cold and hungry, he had refused to let them move forward or aft to don warm clothing or get food, even one at a time. Nor would he permit them to sit down or strap themselves during the landing. Had he been forced to make an emergency landing en route, the men would have frozen. In fact, many of them were frostbitten as soon as they were hit by the prop blast from the pilot's rude take-off.

"Let's get you indoors," I told them, and we soon had them in the warmth of our buildings. Forgetting about the Navy pilot after a while, we moved on to other subjects. The first tales were of the scientific cutting and filling of the McMurdo runway under the direction of Dr. Assur of the Army's SIPRE. It was clear that without Assur, none of the arrivals would now be nursing grudges against the pilot.

The new arrivals' second piece of news was a bit more difficult to take. Some of the incoming men had participated in a dedication ceremony for the South Pole Station held at McMurdo on January 23. Pomp and ceremony had been the order for that day, with Marines in full dress and speeches by Dufek, Gould, Wexler, plus messages from President Eisenhower, the King of Norway, the British and New Zealand prime ministers, and others. "You may not know it," one of the new arrivals said, "but this is now officially the Amundsen-Scott IGY South Pole Station."

This was more than somewhat surprising to Jack and me, for eighteen days had already passed since the dedication and we had not even been notified by radio. And what of Gould and Wexler, who had conversed with me from a Globemaster only two days ago and never mentioned the dedication?

The news was disconcerting to all who had been living at the Pole the past month. Not only was there the ignominy of not having been notified of the ceremony beforehand and of receiving no report of it since—but we who had built the base and would man it over man's first long winter night had been offered no opportunity to participate in its dedication, even by radio. We had been left out of the entire affair as if we did not exist. And though we venerated as few others could the memory of Amundsen and Scott, for the rest of our stay the base to us was the U.S. IGY South Pole Station instead of the Amundsen-Scott IGY Station.

However, we had little time for gripes, for the winter night was only a month away. "Our main task during the next few weeks," Jack and I told the new men, "will be to retrieve airdrops and bring the material into camp and button up for winter. After that we'll have time to get going on the science programs."

I liked what I saw of the new men from the outset. To replace Brown, we now had twenty-year-old Melvin Havener as our mechanic. My first glimpse of him was seeing him hurtle past me without a greeting as he headed from the plane. He was in thin dungarees and deck shoes and was obviously chilled to the bone, but under his arm he clutched his guitar. I couldn't help smiling to myself at the incongruous sight. Thomas M. Osborne, the shortest man in camp, who stood a foot shorter than Jack Tuck's six-foot-three, was the builder we had regretted not having with us from the start.

Of our five new IGY men, I had especially looked forward to meeting Benson, for I had been erroneously informed that Carl Benson was coming and Carl had a fine reputation as a polar glaciologist. Instead our arriving Benson turned out to be Robert F. Benson, Carl's twenty-one-year-old brother, who would be our seismologist. Ed Flowers and John Guerrero had two more Met men to work with them, William Floyd Johnson, called Floyd, and Herbert L. Hansen. Edward W. Remington, our glaciologist, was a husky World War II pilot. And last but not least was small, studious Arlo U. Landolt, our twenty-year-old aurora and airglow specialist. Floyd and Arlo were the only ones I had met previously.

The Station was fully manned now: nine Navy men and nine IGY specialists. Now when the IGY officially began on July 1, we could maintain our full program embracing ionosphere physics, meteorology, aurora and airglow, glaciology, seismology, geomagnetism and special individual studies. This took a considerable load off my mind.

As soon as they were settled I took the new men on an enthusiastic tour of our village and got them oriented. Benson and Landolt, who would be using the science building constantly, were berthed in the center rooms of the small Jamesway, Benson in the space left between Tuck and Taylor, and Landolt between Willi and myself. The others moved into the larger Jamesway.

The first essential order of business was retrieving the airdrops, which we had been informed would continue for approximately two more weeks before halting for eight months. So the next day, despite a temperature of $-38°$ and the fierce high altitude headaches that had overtaken the new arrivals, Jack and I routed our men out for drop zone duty. How they stood up under it I don't know, but as for me it was both rough riding and cold standing on the Weasel side while we went after drops.

Because of the importance of the Globemaster flights, we altered our daily schedules until the drop period would end, setting reveille at eleven A. M., an hour before the first plane would arrive, and working almost around the clock. And as during the earlier period, it seemed as if half the drops streamed in. This was even more unfortunate than before because now there was no time to get replacements. It was young Mel Havener's job to dig out the streamers with the D-2 tractor and we dreaded discovering the condition of the equipment he uncovered. Sausages popped out of cans, juices colored the undersurface snow, and metal equipment lost its original shape entirely. But at least the salvaged equipment was sometimes still useful to some extent, whereas that which we could not dig out was lost forever.

In addition to the danger of being out long hours in the penetrating cold, there was again, as during the earlier drop period, always the lurking danger of flying loose boards, containers and platforms.

By and large the Navy men hauled in the airdrops while the IGY crew spent its time opening boxes as they were brought in and sorting and storing the contents. Our drop zone was marked by red fluorescent cloth strips shaped like a big T, but few pilots managed to hit the T with their drops. In fact, during drops we quipped "The T is the safest spot in camp," for the drops were scattered over so wide an area that we had to establish a veritable bloodhound system for locating equipment. And, of course, our problem was complicated by reason of our not knowing what we were getting. We were supplied no manifests to check against the McMurdo lists of drop items, for no one at McMurdo seemed seriously concerned about the Pole supplies and labeling seemed to have become a joke. Medical supplies turned out to be sweet potatoes. Other items clearly marked NOT TO BE AIRDROPPED were dropped with abandon. An electric automatic calculator which we sorely needed and had carefully labeled thus was located completely smashed.

On the 17th, the C-124 overhead contained Sir Edmund Hillary and Admiral Jerauld Wright, to whom Dufek reported, far away from his post as Commander in Chief of the Atlantic Fleet. Ed chatted with me by radio and told me that Fuchs was having difficulty establishing a base on the Weddell Coast and might be delayed in starting his traverse next summer. Admiral Wright made a most welcome gesture by dropping us a box of excellent Havana cigars for use on some special occasion.

In addition to the cigars, there were two special items among the Air Force drops that day. The first was a crate of four dozen eggs which came floating down under an Easter-egg-colored chute with a white petticoat. We hurriedly opened the crate, expecting to find a mess of shattered shells and running yokes and whites. But only one egg was cracked and when Chet removed it, he found the following message scrawled on it: *This egg was cracked before we dropped it. (Signed)* U.S. Air Force.

The second item was a life-sized female mannequin in an ill-fitting sunsuit. "It's amusing," Jack observed coldly, "but there are a lot of things we need worse." Someone else quipped, "With a little more effort they could have sent us a live one."

Doc Taylor's long-awaited medical supplies finally came in with a large amount of ships stores. We who dragged them into the combined cache near the garage entrance estimated the total at 20 tons. Doc quickly found the metal band for his head mirror in all this chop, but it took him two weeks to find the mirror. Our mattresses also came as well as hundreds of movies, a tape recorder, hi-fi set and stacks of records. But Arlo Landolt, Chet Segers, Junior Waldron, Mel Havener and Oz, who constituted our hillbilly enthusiasts, expressed loud disgust on learning that we had received only two or three cowboy records.

On February 20, two boxes of fresh vegetables floated down with an accompanying card:

> Stolen, rigged and dropped by four of the most competent thieves of the First Aerial Port Sqdn, SGTS Smith, Combs, Landrum and Howard.

The final drops were nearing, we knew. The many things we still hoped to receive were vainly sought from one drop to the next. There was no clear assurance of what we would or would not receive. However, suddenly our gloom lifted when the pilots informed us that the long-sought barracks building was on its way to the Pole. The C-124 with the first platform of house parts arrived at the Pole at a difficult moment.

We had been unable to get the Weasel started, for the battery had run down. The day was windy and visibility was so poor because of ice fog that we could see little more than a mile. Jack tried to get the C-124's pilot to circle a bit longer until we could get the Weasel started or scatter men downwind across the drop zone with knives to cut the parachute risers. Jack finally gave in to the impatient pilot and let him drop his load of girders at once. The parachutes failed to collapse on landing and dragged the heavy load off out of sight in the fog. Later, after the drops were over and visibility improved a bit, Jack and Willi started off in the now-working Weasel to follow the furrow plowed in the snow by the dragging platform. Only after a chase of 25.1 miles from camp did they locate the platform! These were men indeed.

Far away as they were, Jack and Willi calmly hooked the two-ton platform and trusses to the Weasel and started back. All the while we maintained contact with them by radio. In fact, the tower way off at McMurdo overheard our dialogue and broke in to ask what was going on. They managed to haul their load to within sixteen miles of camp when it became obvious they did not have sufficient fuel to make it back to camp with their load. Unhitching the platform they made a prayerful run in without it.

It was not until two days later that Jack and Willi went out again with the Weasel and hauled the trusses the remaining distance into camp. They reported that they could see our Rawin Dome and Aurora Tower from seventeen miles out. And on their route in they came across the flags Jack, Bowers, Bristol and Powell had planted in the course of their historic eight-mile dog team trip to the Pole last November 22. The trip took ten hours and they returned just as the Weasel's gas gave out.

At 7:30 in the evening of February 21, the last Globemaster came in for a drop which would be our final physical contact with the world until the following October. It was a typical drop session full of regrets. Unwanted floor trusses streamed in; then came heavy steel pipe, 6 to 8 inches in diameter, the purpose of which we never did learn; then a box of dishes streamed in. Many highly essential items did not arrive at all, a particular sore point to Jack and myself since we knew they and the lumber we needed for finishing the camp had been stored near the McMurdo runway as far back as Deep Freeze I. But there was nothing to do now except to substitute and improvise wherever we could and somehow live through the winter. I was already happy about the salvage materials we had hoarded. They would serve their purpose.

With the departure of the last C-124 we were on our own. Our camp had to be buttoned up securely before the winter night set in on March 23. And already the temperature had dropped below −50°.

Chapter 21

BUTTONING UP THE POLE STATION

Wɪᴛʜ the ending of the drops, we reverted to our old reveille time of 6:30 ᴀ.ᴍ. However, now I reversed the daily routine by placing the IGY complement on community projects mornings and reserving afternoons and evenings for IGY disciplines and personal concerns.

The most important thing to me was that the new men had come through the airdrop grind in excellent spirits. They had begun to acclimatize to both low temperature and high altitude. On the day following the last drop, waves of laughter and handclapping greeted a broadcast by Lowell Thomas monitored by the Voice of America. According to Lowell, "Eighteen men stood at the South Pole and sadly watched the last airplane fly away, leaving them to face six months of darkness."

There was little laughter, however, when the men had to leave the warmth of the buildings for the cold outdoors. The sun which was still circling us continually was gradually dropping lower in the sky. From its midsummer height of nearly twenty-three degrees above the horizon, it had already dropped to nine degrees by February 23 and would touch the horizon by March 22. At that time it would begin to rise over the North Pole, heralding summer there while our six months of darkness would begin. Long shadows of the late "polar afternoon" added an eeriness to the hazy ice-fog horizon.

By the 26th, the temperature was down to −61.5° F., a new experience for most of the men. Those with beards discovered that their breaths turned them into masses of ice, and a few were dismayed occasionally, after becoming winded, to cough up blood, though I assured them this was routine and not serious. In order to hammer outdoors while building caches, the men had to remove their heavy outer mittens, and the cold now quickly numbed their fingers. We had long ago passed the point where we dared remove mitts entirely and touch metal with our bare hands. For if we did so, the skin would immediately turn white, a blister would form, and the pain would be severe for several minutes. In fact, skin might actually tear away and cling to the metal. From my own experience a bad metal freeze was nearly as bad as a real burn in the long run.

Once, during the second Byrd expedition in 1934, I had fallen asleep despite the cold while taking a breather for five minutes while constructing our blubber house. I stretched out on a board beneath our plumb bob, which consisted of a string hanging from the ceiling with a big steel nut at the end. I awoke, suddenly imagining I felt an angry insect on my lip and instinctively slapped at it. But the insect turned out to be the nut and a piece of lip tore off with the slap.

Our first big job after the airdrops ended was the construction of our barracks building. Now some of the men were sorry that I had won the battle to get the building and that Jack and Willi had retrieved the essential roof trusses without which the barracks could not be erected. Nevertheless all hands turned out in the biting cold for this task, which actually consisted of four separate operations. First, the large Jamesway had to be dismantled since the barracks building was to occupy its site. Then we had to erect the barracks building. Following this my plan was to split the big Jamesway to serve as a sitting room for Bravo and the six of us who lived in it. With spare ends we would erect the rest of the Jamesway 200 feet away from the Station on the Grid South side to serve as our emergency refuge in case the rest of the Station should be destroyed by fire.

I could not help but notice that we sounded like consumptives as we tore down the big Jamesway piece by piece. Outdoor breathing in −60° F. cold now made one moan and groan audibly, although we did not suffer actual pain. But before our two-hour stint was over, we were coughing continually, a matter which focused Doc Taylor's discerning attention on this strange new phenomenon which was to end mysteriously after a few days, but the consumptive breathing was to continue off and on throughout most of our remaining stay at the Pole.

After we removed the Jamesway, Mel Havener drove in the D-2 tractor to bulldoze the site and bring it up to grade. The laying of the foundation proved to be a time-consuming task because we had no snow sills and had to use four-foot 2 x 10's as pads under the ends of the timber. Then after a big steak dinner, we egged one another on to go out again to finish laying the floor panels.

We were determined to complete the shell of the barracks building the next day, and we succeeded, even though reveille was accompanied by the announcement that the outside temperature was "sixty below." The barracks was supposed to measure 20 x 48 feet, but we found extra panels and lengthened the building to 56 feet. Not only did the longer building tie in better with the rest of the base but it also provided us with additional welcome space. A demon for work, Oz, our carpenter, enclosed the barracks on all four sides within our tunnel network. Then he built two skylights into the ceiling, and joined Earl Johnson and Mel Havener in installing two stoves and sealing cracks, while Junior Waldron ran electrical power into the barracks.

Partitions dividing the barracks into six double rooms went up some days later but promptly the twelve men who were sleeping here and there about the camp moved into the barracks building. It was with considerable pride that I saw this job completed, for our alternative might have been to sleep some of the men in the mess hall and science building. The twelve men were given their choice of having single rooms or pairing up. All chose double room arrangements, with three rooms on either side of a lengthwise hall. On one side, Mel Havener and Oz shared a room, as well as Mac and Chet, our radio operator and cook, and John Guerrero and Herb Hansen. Across from Mel and Oz were Earl Johnson and Cliff Dickey, our electronics man, then Junior and Moose Remington and finally Ed Flowers and Floyd Johnson. Each man had his own six-foot locker in his room, though outside of the lockers and bunks the setting was quite austere.

While the interior work proceeded in the barracks building, six of the men joined me in erecting the 36-foot emergency Jamesway 200 feet from camp and installing bags of clothing, emergency food and sleeping bags in it as well as fuel drums outside. "Just in case," as Willi Hough put it.

At the same time Tuck, Doc Taylor and three other of the men attached the 20-foot addition to our small Jamesway within the station. It was while this work was in progress that we got a radio call from Little America giving us the smug information that they were lolling in the tropical temperature of zero as compared with our more than sixty degrees below. We had broken out some extra clothing that day and some of the men had put on trousers made of down. "Tell those fellows back in the banana belt we can't be cold," someone shouted to Jack, "because our pants are down!"

The 20-foot addition to our six-man Jamesway did not, of course, add to the dimensions of our individual sleeping cubicles, since we had planned it solely as our lounge. Besides, it was possibly better for morale, Jack and I agreed, that our own sleeping space be smaller, rather than larger, than the individual space in the barracks building.

There were other outdoor buttoning-up jobs awaiting us besides the barracks and Jamesway tasks. In keeping with my theory, Mel Havener bulldozed a 10-foot-high snow wall in a wide arc 200 feet from the north side of camp, previously banked with snow. This ridge was to act as a "spoiler" that would force snow to drift on the 0° Grid North side of camp instead of all of it drifting over the buildings onto the 180th° lee side of camp.

Every IGY discipline now had its own construction problems. For instance, the Met group had to complete the setting-up of their instruments, most of which would lie beyond Mel's windbreak, and then lay cables to the recorders in the Met shack to the rear of the mess building. The Met group also had to build an access shaft and a ladder from the roof of the mess building to the Rawin Dome standing high on stilts above it. This was a cold and nasty job, but no worse than digging the 10-foot-deep pit at the other end of camp adjacent to and south of the inflation shelter which was necessary to catch the runoff slush from the hydrogen generator. But the Met boys had a difficult time rubber-cementing thick Fiberglas insulation to the inside surface of the Rawin Dome. In fact, at one point Guerrero found his hands stuck together and had to have them cut loose. As for Flowers and Floyd Johnson, they were gassed with carbon-monoxide fumes one day from the small Herman-Nelson heater they set into the Dome while they worked on insulation, but fortunately they escaped before being felled.

Others had their problems, too. Originally, no plans had been made by the Navy or IGY for gaining access to the Aurora Tower from the science building except by going out into the cold. Now I joined Arlo Landolt in building a 4 x 4-foot connecting shaft into which we set a 2 x 4 ladder and then built access hatches from both ends. An important feature of Arlo's aurora and airglow program was the three plastic domes at the top of the Tower in which his instruments were mounted. One of these instruments was the auroral spectograph, which recorded the spectrum on film. Another was his all-sky camera which, by means of its optical structure, was able to record auroral forms from nearly the entire visible part of the celestial sphere. The third dome served for making visual observations.

But now it developed that we were not able to clear the frost from inside his plastic domes. Unless this was accomplished he could, of course, do no recording. Jack, Oz and I held long conversations on how to aid Arlo, who was daily growing more morose. Yet even when we installed a jet heater and ducts the frost remained thick. Finally, after Earl and Junior inserted several jet heaters and fans and this still failed to solve our vexing problem, we grew as worried as Arlo. Thankfully a last-resort solution worked, though this came two months later. This was to use two space heaters and several turbine fans equipped with ¼- and ½-horsepower motors which kept the air within the domes in a turbulent condition and prevented frost from forming. The small towers required more fuel than the much larger science building protected from the wind by its surrounding snow tunnels.

But perhaps our most difficult single IGY installation job involved Willi Hough. The Navy had agreed to supply the mast for Willi's ionosphere antenna. But when it was discovered that what Willi had in mind was a 75-foot telephone pole, the Navy backed out. Instead they promised a sectional plywood mast. Twenty-five feet of the mast was delivered to the Pole during Bowers' era and the construction crew set up the base of Willi's antenna mast. However, after the last airdrop, it developed that the last 50 feet had not arrived.

We procrastinated as long as we dared despite Willi's rightful insistence that we quickly erect a makeshift mast before it got too cold to wire the antenna. Finally Jack agreed to take down 25 feet from each of two of the 50-foot radio communications masts and join them to the top of the 25-foot mast already in place.

Unfortunately, the day on which we promised to do the work was the worst we had experienced so far weatherwise. This was on Thursday, February 28, when the thermometer read within a fraction off −70° and a brisk biting wind was blowing. It was so cold that we dared not risk taking our vehicles out to pull the radio mast up into position. Instead we did it by hand and then raised the mast with a 25-foot jack boom and block and tackle.

All this while the IGY crew each day put in hours on the tedious and heavy task of stowing the 400-pound fuel drums, cleaning up the outside of the Station and burning rubbish in a new Hubel Hole we dug, finishing off caches and making the interiors more livable. And each evening the hamset crackled away, even though Mac tried unsuccessfully to limit each man to two hamgrams a week and a phone patch every other week. Chet Segers even got into a National Gin Rummy Tournament over the ham radio set. We also had several other contacts with the outside world via the phone patches. One of these was with Art Linkletter, the television master-of-ceremonies,

who called us one night, as he said, just "to bat the breeze around."
The men learned from him which movie actors and actresses were still
married and which had divorced. I assumed that he wondered if we,
living at the Pole, were also funny people. There was also a contact
with a somewhat gay Dean Martin, the singer who was in Las Vegas.
The men related that he sang a line from a song, then said he wished
he could talk longer but "I have to go back to the bar."

Then there was still another radio report. Moose Remington came
to me about three P.M. on March 12. His face was clouded and his
eyes avoided mine. "What is it?" I asked him.

"I just heard the news over the Armed Forces Radio," he said
softly, "that Admiral Byrd died today in Boston."

A wave of sorrow swept over me though I tried to remain composed. "Of all the people in the United States," I told Moose, "Admiral Byrd was undoubtedly the most interested in what we were doing
here at the Pole." I felt numb.

Remington offered to lower the flag to half-mast on the barber-pole
South Pole atop the garage, but I wanted to do this myself. When he
left I wrote a message for Mrs. Byrd, Marie, Dick's loving helpmate:

> My grief is as one of the family. I am here at the Pole largely
> because Dick wished it so. I will do my best to continue my job
> as he would want it to be done. Please accept my deepest sym-
> pathy for the loss of a loving husband, father, loyal comrade and
> one of our greatest American citizens.
> Affectionately,
>
> PAUL

The men one and all came around when they heard the news. But
outside of a press on my shoulder and a "We understand how you
feel," I was left to my own thoughts.

I finally went out and put the flag at half-mast. We would keep it
flying thus until the sunset on March 22. And as the cold struck me
and the wind rattled the flag, the full meaning of Dick's death slowly
overtook me. This day I had lost my best friend.

I recalled the day I last spent with him and how he had given me
the watch I was wearing. He had seemed to realize more than I that
this was our last meeting. His eyes and voice on that occasion had
revealed more sentiment than I had ever before witnessed. My mind
flitted to Mrs. Byrd. How sad for Marie. She had spent many difficult
hours worrying about him during his many flirtations with death, but

she had been his strength—and he had known it and had never forgotten it.

A kaleidoscope of random episodes in our experiences together flashed before my eye: how he had wanted to take one last look at the Antarctic sky before leaving the continent during Operation Highjump; his fiery temper, which he rarely displayed; his graceful mastery of the art of living which was distinguishable even in the confines of Little America; his remarkable leadership abilities and his optimism; his willingness to withstand insults when he believed that the honor of the nation or the Navy was at stake; and his many kindnesses.

Nor was my sorrow alleviated the following day when I was handed a message Byrd had sent me shortly before his death.

> Delighted to learn all men safely at Pole and nearly all supplies in. Please convey my wholehearted congratulations to all hands at Station on their part in this splendid achievement. Am sending separate messages to Seabees and USAF. Confident that under your leadership scientific achievements will be significant contribution to over-all IGY Program. Regret I cannot be with your history-making sojourn. But at least the U.S. Antarctic Program will be represented in the person of my deputy. My best wishes to you and all the men. Please continue to keep me informed. Warmest regards.

Hard work was the best way to keep from thinking about Byrd and I plunged back into our multitudinous physical activities. Before the new personnel had arrived, our small IGY contingent and Doc Taylor had completed 400 feet of the 1,000-foot geomagnetic and seismology tunnel. Now with a ten-man working party we went ahead at the rate of 100 feet a day. But even so this was not as swift as I had hoped, for I had not taken into consideration the fact that the air and snow temperatures were now almost identical, and compaction of the mixture of undersurface and surface snow did not result as easily as before when the temperatures had varied considerably.

By the close of Saturday, March 16, with the temperature at −76°, our tunnel diggers were within 150 feet of the tunnel end. Some of the men welcomed the opportunity to dig in the trench instead of standing in the raw wind to put up the abovesurface two feet of snow wall and then cover the three-foot-wide tunnel top with wood rafters and burlap.

On March 19 we finally completed the tunnel, but when I tried to take pictures to record this happy event I found my camera was frozen.

We also dug two necessary pits, one about 20 feet off the tunnel at the 500-foot mark for the geogmagnetic instrument, an oscillation-deflection type magnetometer which measured the changes in the declination and intensity of the magnetic field in all directions. This geomagnetic pit was ten feet deep, four feet wide and six feet long and was aligned along the magnetic meridian. The seismic pit at the end of the 1,000-foot tunnel was also ten feet deep, but was six feet wide and six feet long. Here we would later install a Benioff Vertical Seismometer to record seismic vibrations, or earthquake waves. About 25 feet from the seismic pit, we dug access stairs up and out to the south. As a last step Mel Havener drove the D-2 out and pushed a 1,200-pound platform to the top of the snow mound circling the seismic pit. Then with cable and winch, we gingerly moved the platform over the ten-foot pit to form a roof. It was a tricky operation and I sighed thankfully when it was over. Then Mel bulldozed eight feet of snow over the lid and we congratulated each other.

March 22 arrived, the day for the sun to set. The temperature reached a minimum of $-81°$ and the wind hit 18 miles an hour. All morning my crew worked hard covering the cache in front of the mess hall with parachutes. Then in the afternoon we covered the tunnel along the east side of the science building, and hauled nearly all the loose material remaining in the "front yard" under cover.

True to schedule the sun was actually below the horizon this day, but because of refraction and an ice-crystal phenomenon a column of light shone directly up into the sky above the sun. I could see in the faces of some of the men growing concern about what life would be like in a dark world.

We held our official sunset ceremony at five P.M. Dickey and Moose took pictures of the ceremony as Dr. Taylor and John Guerrero first raised the flag, which had remained at half-mast in honor of Admiral Byrd, and then they lowered it for the winter night.

I took a last close look at the Pole area that day. Here, where Amundsen and Scott had once stood for a few fleeting moments, the IGY and the American Navy and Air Force had accomplished a miracle. And we who had finished the construction job Dick Bowers and his remarkable Seabees had begun would work and live here through the winter night. I glanced out toward our South Pole marker, then I looked at our Station village—above the snow now but in time to be brought level with the surface by the heavy cold katabatic winds blowing snowdrifts downhill against our shelter. Then I thought of my family and my departed friend Dick Byrd, and walked indoors.

Chapter 22

DARKNESS AT NOON

W ILL it be pitch dark?" one of Tuck's Navy men had asked me when he first arrived at the Pole.

"Not very often," I had assured him, though he was far from convinced.

All my previous experience in Antarctica's winter night had been centered at Little America off the Bay of Whales on the Ross Ice Shelf. What would happen at the geographic South Pole some 800 miles inland was something we would experience for the first time in man's long history on earth.

Three times I had spent winter nights at Little America. There the sun disappeared for four months beginning in late April, and during the first and last months of the winter night there was enough light to permit work outdoors several hours a day. During May, even though the sun dropped deeper below the horizon each day, we had a twilight around noon. And even during the two real months of total darkness at Little America there was a flush of pale reddish light to the north over the Ross Sea, for at most the noon sun lay only about 12° below the horizon.

The dark we faced at the South Pole, however, would be deeper and would last far longer. For our night would last six months instead of the four at Little America, and the sun at its farthest point from us on June 22 would lie a full 23½° below our horizon instead of 12°.

Our neighboring Antarctic IGY stations would fare better than we with respect to the amount of light they would have. The British, Argentine and Chilean stations on the Graham-Palmer Peninsula north of the Antarctic Circle would, of course, have sunrises and sunsets every day in the year. The sun would not rise very high nor would their day be very long on midwinter day (June 22), but nevertheless they would have several hours of light each day. The U. S. Wilkes Station, France's D'Urville Station, Russia's Mirny and

Oasis stations, Australia's Mawson and Davis stations, Japan's Showa Station, Belgium's Baudoin Station and Norway's Maudheim Station were all so close to the Antarctic Circle that they would celebrate midwinter season with gaudy brilliant sunsets with the sun barely, if at all, below the horizon at noon.

Other stations, like Little America, McMurdo, Ellsworth, Byrd, Hallett, New Zealand's Scott Station, Argentina's Belgrano Station, and British Halley Bay, Shackleton and South Ice would have respectable polar nights but they would be nowhere near as long or dark as ours would be at the Pole Station.

Inside the polar areas the four seasons of the year take on a meaning of their own. Summer and winter are of course the periods of 24-hour sun and sunlessness respectively. Fall and spring apply to the periods when there are true sunrises and sunsets. How long these periods last depends on one's latitude. At Little America halfway between the Antarctic Circle and the Pole fall and spring last for two months each. The length of the sunup and sundown periods during these two months ranges from one minute to 23 hours and 59 minutes.

The twilight season at the South Pole lingers from sunset on March 22 until May 4 when the sun's angle, from its position below our horizon, was 18°. This latter date represented the real beginning of the dark period. Just how dark it is when the sun is 18° below the horizon can be garnered from the fact that a smaller 6° to 8° angle represents twilight back in civilization, or the time for turning on streetlights. Twilight lasts much longer in the polar regions than anywhere else because of the relatively flat trajectory of the sun's rays. It is longest at the Poles themselves, where twilight lasts for a whole month.

During this prolonged twilight from March 22 until May 4, when we walked outdoors we could distinguish an ominous and ever-increasing gray arc rising farther from the horizon opposite the sun each day. It was the earth shadow, a phenomenon rarely noticed in temperate latitudes where the sun sets in a matter of minutes rather than weeks as at the Pole. This earth shadow is actually the portion of the atmosphere completely shaded from the setting sun by the earth, and here at the Pole was separated from the sunlit portion of the atmosphere by a distinct gray line which rose higher in the sky each day. As it advanced across the sky, the oranges, yellows and pinks of the sunset seemed actually to increase in brilliance and intensity. It was my observation on such days that the beauty of the sunset at

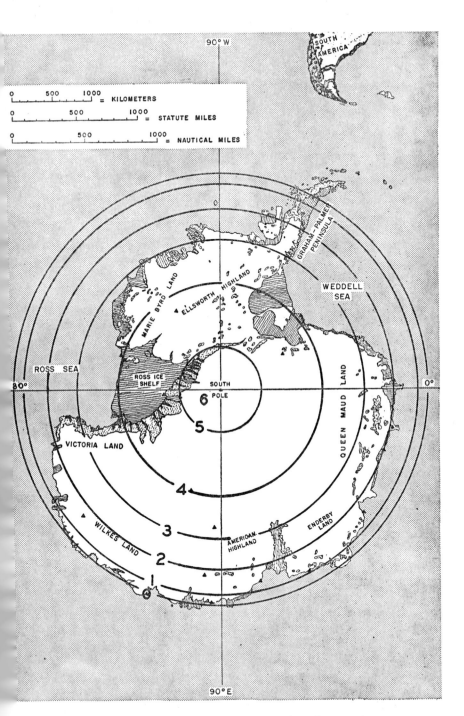

The number of months of continuous sunshine and sunlessness decrease as shown by the above circles as one moves outward from the South Pole.

the Pole surpassed that at any other point on the globe. For with the occasional red of the sky and the white surface, we were living in a pink world. And then before my eyes, our pink world would turn green or purple or a host of other pastel shades.

The ending of the astronomical twilight was another matter, however. Now not even the faintest glimmer of twilight loomed over our horizon. Yet oddly, only 300 miles above our cone of darkness the sun shone brightly into space all the while. But this offered little compensation to us on the ground, for there is no side emanation from a beam of light, and there were not enough atmospheric particles of moisture or dust that high up to reflect back any light to us. The sun's rays went by us invisibly, as they do in the sky until the moon or a planet reflects them to let us know they are there. Sunlight, or even the indirect light the sun sheds, is one of the accepted blessings of life. Without it, apprehension crept into the hearts of the uninitiated.

This was so even though the South Pole winter night frequently has periods of light from other sources. For two winter weeks each month, the black sky would be punctured by the light of the moon as it swung around the sky from right to left. During the first week the moon would spiral its way upward and ride higher in the sky each day. The second week it would creep down toward the horizon and then disappear. In addition the Pole sky, except on cloudy days, would be dotted with starlight and occasional auroral light. It would only be on these cloudy days that the blackness would be all-encompassing.

The men's reaction to the winter night varied from individual to individual. A few of the men expressed their apprehension about the unknown perils ahead in blustering aggressiveness or in elaborate practical jokes as some men do when depressed. Others turned to the hamset for reassurance that there still was an outside world. Oz, our builder, sawed wood and pounded nails as nonchalantly as if he were back home in Pennsylvania. Some of the other men grew quieter while others grew noisier.

I realized what was running through most minds. We were like men who had been fired off in rockets to take up life on another planet. We were in a lifeless, and almost featureless, world. However snug and comfortable we might make ourselves, we could not escape from our isolation. We were now face to face with raw nature so grim and stark that our lives could be snuffed out in a matter of minutes. Every day would bring us new problems to solve and our ingenuity would be taxed over and over again. And all this to carry out a somewhat difficult fragment of the world-wide scientific program of the International Geophysical Year.

An occasional overheard conversation gave me good evidence of the concern the men felt at living in a dark, womanless wasteland. The blink of an eye revealed the wonder that crossed a mind. There was no escape now from the truly lethal wall that separated us from the rest of mankind.

The perils of polar life were many. A fire could toss us to the bitter mercies of a savage, unknown land. If a man were lost outdoors he could not hope to survive more than a few hours. After that he would run out of energy and his body would cool down to the danger point. There was danger also from the restricted vision possible in the darkness, cold and wind-drifting snow. A man wandering only a hundred yards from camp under such conditions might lose his way and never be found. Vapor from a man's breath could freeze his eyelashes shut in an instant and make him believe he had gone blind. His breath would come in gasps and his joints would ache. The intense pain of the cold on fingers and toes could easily distract him, and even destroy his ability to reason clearly.

The dark presented its own danger, for there were no landmarks to help a man find his way. It was like walking out on the ocean where every wave was like every other. If the stars were out, it was possible to fathom your direction—if you knew your stars. But even then it was possible to walk right past the station. Jack and I found this out one time when we walked out 200 yards to collect snow samples. We thought we were walking parallel to the thousand-foot seismic tunnel when suddenly we crossed it and almost fell in. Had this fortuitous accident not occurred and given us our bearings, we might have gotten well lost.

The wind also presented a danger. If it was strong (and it often blew in excess of 30 miles an hour), it was natural to turn your face away when traveling downwind. But returning to camp a man would also tend to avert his face and might easily wander off course. With the surface rough, walking was often a matter of stumbling along and this, too, would tend to turn a man off his path. Then again, the winds blew up snow and drift and made the horizon indistinct. Herb Hansen, one of our Met men, got religion polarwise as the result of a wind on one occasion. Out to check meteorological observations, he became befuddled due to the wind and drifts. For safety we had placed flags along the route to the meteorological station, but Herb could not find them. He changed his direction several times when he saw he was lost, though he managed to keep himself from growing panicky. Then by sheer accident he found himself at camp. "Guess where I've been?" he whispered when he got indoors.

There was danger also in the very temperature outdoors. My early observations led me to believe that the winter night temperature might easily reach a low of $-120°$ F. If such cold was combined with even a modest wind, a man had little chance for lengthy survival, for almost any wind would triple the body's rate of cooling. I had spent years developing tables to show the effect of wind chill on humans, and the prospects of outdoor movement at this temperature were nil.

The wind-chill factor is an index expressing the relative loss of heat from a heated body. It is determined from the formula which I developed: $K_0 = (\sqrt{V \times 100 + 10.45 - V}) \times (33 - Ta)$. Here K_0 equals the total cooling power of the atmosphere in complete shade without regard to evaporation expressed in terms of kilogram calories per square meter per hour; V the wind velocity in meters per second, and Ta the temperature of ambient air in degrees Centigrade. With a temperature of $-40°$ (the point at which the Fahrenheit and Centigrade temperature scales coincide) and a wind of 2 mph ($1°$ meter per second) or more, the wind-chill factor is 1,400, at which exposed flesh freezes! There was every indication now that on the coldest and windiest days of the winter night, the wind-chill factor would surpass 3,000!

Still another danger to be faced was the possibility that an ice fog would roll over you outdoors. An ice fog is a mass of crystals of ice that float and form a fog. An ice fog could render the camp invisible from a very short way off. Our camp formed its own ice fogs as a result of the clouds of steam which poured from exhaust pipes and condensed on contact with the frigid air, erasing most ouside markers from sight.

So in a physical sense we at the Pole were 18 men in a box. Only with the aid of our "box" could we survive, yet it bound us in. There was no way we could make our way to the outside world. Nor was there any possibility that we could be rescued should tragedy strike. We would have to remain put until the next summer—in October or November—come what might.

There was also the very large problem of how the men would stand each other's company in the daily rub and grind that would be their steady routine for months without respite. Friction was bound to arise from a variety of minor details, from the way a man chewed

WIND CHILL INDEX

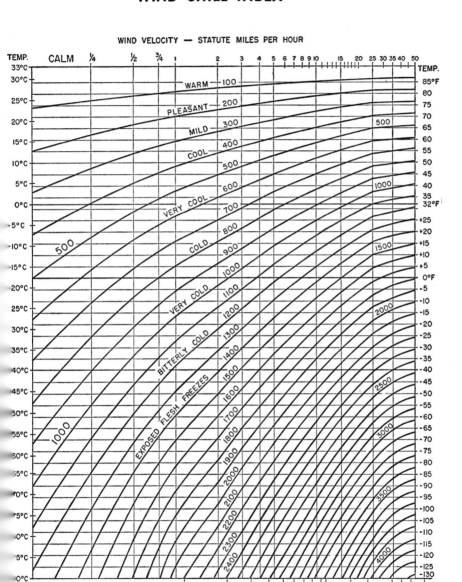

to how he closed a door or talked. There would be the monotony of constantly seeing the same faces when one rose, ate, worked and relaxed. Whatever a man was inherently would be intensified during the close-quarters winter night. A mean man would grow meaner; a kind man would grow kinder.

Men in a box; that was what we were.

Chapter 23

BATTLE OF WINTER BEGINS

THE official sunset ceremony did not herald the beginning of a quiet period of hibernation for the eighteen of us at the South Pole. A bear might crawl into his cave, yawn a few times, then pass into a world of suspended animation until spring.

We were not so blessed, for winter signified our busiest season. This was a condition unlike those on some previous expeditions I could recall nostalgically where winter was a time for making plans and preparations for activities to be pursued once the sun reappeared above the frosty horizon. Winter then was a time when men planned traverses and dog sled journeys into the unknown, studied maps in preparation for aerial assaults and prepared gear and equipment with great expectations that carried them through the darkness. But at the Pole this was a relic of the past.

For us now winter signified the beginning of a period of continuous scientific investigation. There would be no rest, no hibernation, no planning for some arbitrary period ahead.

I thought of this when Admiral Arleigh Burke sent us an eerie message Admiral Byrd had asked him to pass on to us at the beginning of the winter night. The message read:

> With the 21st of March the long winter night commences. For most of you it will be the first winter in the Antarctic, but for some probably not the last. For all of you the annals of

history and the pages of science will *bear* record of your service. Perhaps this will compensate insofar as this is possible for the inevitable loneliness and long separation from your loved ones at home. Your work together with that of the men at six other bases may well mark the beginning of permanent occupancy of the Antarctic Continent. We are on the threshold of a new era and you are the pioneers. Good luck and my affectionate greetings.

Admiral Richard E. Byrd

Doc Taylor dropped into my office in the science building shortly after this message arrived. "The covered-wagon pioneers had it a lot easier than we," he commented. "I'm concerned about our physical condition at the threshold of this new era. Buttoning up the Station with all that work, wind and cold has taken a pretty heavy toll. And there's no rest ahead for the weary.

"Look at this." He dropped a chart on my desk. "Our weight loss would make Elizabeth Arden happy. But I'm worried."

My eye ran down the chart and what I saw was startling. Man for man the weight loss since arriving at the Pole was enough to make one apprehensive. It ran as follows:

Name	Original Weight	Wt. At Present	Loss
Benson	162	154	− 8
Dickey	160	150	−10
Flowers	186	161	−25
Guerrero	185	170	−15
Hansen	165	156	− 9
Havener	165	154	−11
Hough	185	155	−30
E. Johnson	195	185	−10
F. Johnson	180	160	−20
Landoldt	140	134	− 6
McPherson	187	155	−32
Osborne	162	132	−30
Segers	163	150	−13
Remington	213	179	−34
Taylor	165	136	−29
Tuck	180	167	−13
Siple	250	211	−39
Waldron	160	138	−22
Bravo	45	84	+39

"These pounds may be a great deal to give to science and national honor," I told Doc Taylor. "But we're finished with the worst of our buttoning up and we will start gaining some of it back."

"I hope so," he said, unconvinced. "Too bad we can't all be like Bravo."

He left me more concerned than I cared to show, for if we lost more weight, men would lay themselves open to a number of difficulties. And a situation like that was fraught with dangers since we were entirely cut off from the outside world until the sun returned.

Fortunately, we had indeed completed most of our major outside work, though several smaller outdoor jobs remained. Of course, a crisis might develop which would necessitate large-scale outside activity. But we would pray doubly hard against such happenstance.

As the late March cold began to deepen and the wind raged, we plunged into our remaining outdoor tasks. The men went after all tunnel leaks, for it was now evident that there was too little difference in the temperature inside our tunnel network and that outdoors. Some of the caches between buildings had to be redone because their parachute covers sagged under the pressure of snowdrifts and winds and tore loose. Oz was busy sawing and pounding escape hatches in the tunnels. Junior completed the tunnel wiring and Willi Hough, a man with tremendous mechanical talent, helped Earl Johnson on our heating problems, which bade fair to overwhelm us because so many of our heaters had suffered in transit or had been stream-in victims.

In the course of these buttoning-up activities Moose Remington came into my office one day in a state of acute excitement. "Doc," he said, "there's something funny going on outside I don't understand. Either there's some kind of St. Elmo's fire or someone is playing tricks on me with a flashlight."

I went outside with him to see the phenomenon. The sky was overcast, but the combination of dying twilight and a bright full moon back of the clouds gave the world a weird grayness. It was, I realized, a nocturnal white-out. In the grayness dark objects were visible, but barely so. The sky and the snow were a uniform gray which threatened to swallow up all visibility.

Moose explained that he had been digging on the Grid North side of camp in an effort to improve the entrance to the snow pit he called the Siple Pit, an experimental pit I had dug early in December to explore subsurface temperatures. Remington planned to put some electrical thermometers into the pit to measure the temperature of the snow layers as they yielded their heat to the winter deep-freeze.

Moose said that as he looked up from digging he saw flashes of light that resembled the beams of flashlights coming up out of the snow at the base of the ionosphere antenna. We went out the south exit of camp, which was closer at hand, but search as we might we saw no sign of any strange flashes of light.

Moose went back to his work perplexed and unsatisfied. A half hour later he was back. "Doc," he said, "I hate to bother you, but I'm seeing those lights again. Come out where I'm digging and assure me that I'm not crazy."

By this time others had been attracted by the story of Moose's mysterious lights and half the men in camp had gathered by the pit where Moose was working.

This time many of us saw the flashes. The beams seemed to flash upward from the base of the antenna pole and Ed Flowers noted that a number of spots on the snow surface around the camp seemed to light up with a soft glow of light.

Amazement ran through the assembled group. Then while we were at the height of our excitement at this strange new phenomenon, Floyd Johnson let out a horse laugh. "We're all nuts—it's just after-images."

Sure enough, the "light flashes" were merely our eyes differentiating the dark objects from the gray background. As our eyes moved across the grayness and almost unconsciously spotted a dark object a luminous afterimage flashed against the gray snow and sky. The beams of light were merely the afterimage of the antenna pole itself and Flowers' luminous spots were caused by trash and various dark objects lying on the snow about the camp.

We dubbed these "Remington's Ghosts" from then on.

Men were beginning to relish the indoors and it grew noticeable that fewer volunteered for outside jobs. With the loss of weight, several felt a concomitant loss of strength, especially in their ability to grip and lift. For some, long outdoor exposure brought on severe headaches and coughing jags. Still others suffered from an arthritic-like aching and stiffness in the shoulders, elbows, knuckles and knees. Doc Taylor and I came to the conclusion that this last tendency was due to anoxia, or lack of oxygen, as a result of the altitude and to a reduced rate of blood circulation.

We no longer could go outdoors without donning some 25 pounds of clothing and many of the men, particularly those who had grown beards, now felt the need for face masks. Of course, there were some among us who could take the cold better than others. Ed Flowers' face for instance, was particularly susceptible to the cold. Shortly after he went outdoors freeze marks would dot his face. Yet Ed's hands could still function nimbly when others' hands succumbed to numbness. About the time the sun went down, Ed was working on his 30-foot anemometer pole in a 20-knot wind and a temperature of −75° F. While he worked atop the pole two of my cameras and my thermal boots froze solidly. Even beneath their thick mitts my hands ached with cold. Yet when I watched Ed, he was unemotionally working in light gloves.

Another outdoor task was that of finishing and supplying the emergency Jamesway 200 feet Grid South from camp. We hauled food and clothing there by sled and stored them under the parachute covering the building and the caches on either side. Deep down I felt that should our eighteen men be reduced to living in this small building, our chances of surviving the winter were not bright. However, the emergency Jamesway provided a necessary psychological lift for the Station and thus served an important purpose. Our best bet was, of course, to prevent fire, and with this in mind we maintained a day-and-night fire watch and held a fire drill, with Jack and Earl Johnson serving as fire chiefs and I as deputy. Obedient to the Navy's instructions, Junior had installed an elaborate fire-alarm system which had been supplied us with thermostats in each building. But while it went off several times by itself without provocation, it did not go off on another occasion even when a burning match was held close to the triggering apparatus. Obviously it had not been checked out for cold-weather operation.

Besides our very noticeable drop in weight as a result of our outdoor activity, Doc Taylor also noted a distinct drop in the body temperature of men who had been working outside. For instance, an hour or two stint in the cold would drop a man's temperature a degree or two.

So it was with considerable pleasure that the Station personnel turned their attention to indoor activities designed to make our camp livable in the long months ahead. We had been bothered by a number of gaps in the floor where the clips were attached, but though we had asked for cement none had been sent us. Nevertheless, we had plaster of Paris, and a bit of experimentation showed us how to use this as a suitable substitute mixed with silica gel. Then we worked on beautifying the galley and mess by laying down tar paper and covering it with green linoleum; after Doc Taylor did his sick bay, he undertook a similar mission in the head. Remington then moved in and painted the head a striking orange and gray.

Dickey, who kept our radios in operation, developed a surprising talent for painting in his spare time, and was commissioned to begin a decorative mural featuring the female form on the food counter of the mess hall. He acquired a number of enthusiastic kibitzers in the course of his task, and perhaps because of this ended in equipping one of the damsel's legs with two knees. When his "fluff" was called to his attention, however, he ascribed it to the fact that he had been too long in the Antarctic, and pleading the absence of a model and an insufficiency of memory, abandoned the project.

Another indoor job I took on during the first weeks after official sundown was that of fixing up the sitting room of the Jamesway that Tuck, Taylor, Willi, Landolt, Benson and I occupied. I covered the interior with red, white and blue parachutes, establishing a striking patriotic theme which Jack could not in good conscience label "horrendous," as he had the yellow-orange parachute-covered walls of my bunk room.

All this while, our IGY men were devoting their afternoons and evenings getting their instruments into place and testing them. Much of this activity required outside work, double exposure for those who had already spent part of their mornings outdoors on general camp projects. One task that had the men gasping for breath and rubbing frostbitten yellow-white marks on cheeks involved a race against time to drag full length a half-inch rubber-covered cable through the tunnel to the seismic pit a thousand feet away. The insulation froze stiff within a moment or two in the tunnel, so the heavy reel was thawed out and mounted in my office, which lay in line with the tunnel. A hole was bored through the wall and the men, working in relays, seized the cable and ran it down the tunnel before it could freeze. Then, before the cable could be attached to the seismometer, its end had to be heated over a primus stove.

Ed Flowers and his three Met men had their hands full installing their various meteorological equipment. They manufactured their hydrogen from aluminum chips, caustic soda and gallons of water in a tank-shaped iron monster. On March 26 they released their first hydrogen-filled test balloon, but the wind was so wild that it battered the radio transmitter attached by a long string to the bottom of the balloon. Nevertheless, I was delighted that Ed's fears were not fully justified regarding the top release doors of the inflation shelter. Certainly they were large enough to pass his inflated balloons through.

Later Ed and his crew erected an eight-foot windshield on the north and east sides of the inflation shelter to prevent the delicate radio transmitters from being battered about by the winds at time of release. This was a real benefit, though it never compensated for another flaw that revealed itself. This was the poor quality of many of the balloons, for they contained pinholes and thin spots which bulged alarmingly when inflated. Even the good balloons did not rise as high as desired. But the Met gang solved this problem by soaking them in diesel oil, a trick that enabled some of the radiosonde balloons to rise above 90,000 feet over the Pole.

By April first, as we moved deeper into our month of twilight, the continued cold of −75° to −80° had produced an entirely new problem I had not foreseen. Jack and I had organized the men into four-men teams which alternated as our "Snowflake Brigade," with the duty to gather clean snow for our snow melter.

However, by the end of March it was no longer possible to take the vehicles outdoors. Antifreeze froze and motors died in the low temperatures and high winds. Even more serious, the vapors created by the machines in the intense cold made them look as if they were on fire and, since we were forced by darkness to proceed slowly, clung about the machines and often reduced visibility to practically zero. Moreover, the climate was debilitating to the men, a matter of even greater concern to me.

"We can't go out and get our snow," I told Jack Tuck, "so we'll have to gather it from within the camp."

"What do you propose?" he asked. "We need enough clean snow to produce about twelve gallons of water a day for each man."

My plan was simple in design. We would dig a deep sloping pit with a ramp beginning by the west side of the head about twelve feet from the snow-melter chute and then run the snow mine down in a due Grid North direction. "This will serve a dual purpose," I told Jack. "In addition to water, we'll also get a deep pit for glacial study. The temperature in the snow mine should remain at a fairly steady 60° below zero and we won't have the wind."

"About how much digging do you foresee until next spring when we can go outdoors again?" Jack asked.

"If we maintain about a 15 to 20 degree slope," I said as I drew a diagram, "in the months ahead we should end up with a tunnel about 300 feet long, 100 feet deep, 6 to 10 feet wide and 7 to 10 feet high."

Jack whistled. "That sounds like a Siberian salt mine."

On April first my section of the Snowflake Brigade began digging the snow mine ramp. The compacted surface snow proved miserably difficult to cut. But after two hours of steady work we managed to dig down five feet. Then suddenly we could go no farther. I had believed our shaft would clear the buildings. However, now we had hit the foundation of the head which completely blocked our five-foot-wide initial tunnel. Nor was there a suitable way to bypass the timbers. We were exhausted, cold and completely frustrated.

"This is a darn poor April Fool joke," Willi snorted and our spirits rose at the humor of our misadventure.

"We'll call it the 'April Fool Mine,' " I said.

The following day Oz joined us and with a chain saw we cut through the troublesome foundation timbers. "Clean snow at last," shouted Arlo, who immediately began digging out huge cakes for the melter. Jack built a sturdy bridge over the intersection of the ramp and North Main Street, while Moose Remington carved a stairway along the downward slope of the ramp. We were in business.

At first we considered chain-sawing our snow from the April Fool Mine. But this did not work because the saw produced heavy vapors that filled the mine. Instead we turned to using a pick and mattock and then, as the deeper snow got harder, we used two basic tools: a spoon-bladed Swiss ice ax and a coal scoop. We would scoop the chipped ice into salvage parachute bags, then hand-haul the bags to the surface on plastic sleds.

This method was all right at first, but as we drove deeper into the mine hand-hauling grew too difficult. Finally Mel Havener our mechanic, Earl Johnson our utility man, and Junior Waldron our electrician constructed an elaborate winch from bits and parts of other equipment which hauled our sleds to the head of the mine by heavy nylon cord. This was an excellent improvisation, though occasionally we had trouble when the cable caught in the teeth of the mechanical crank. When this happened the men in the mine had to find a hole quickly, for hurtling downward toward them would come two sleds filled with 400 to 600 pounds of snow. Fortunately, all our miners proved agile at these treacherous moments.

The snow mine required electrical wiring both for our hauling device and to provide lights for the working men. Junior Waldron, who had this wiring assignment, was faced with two problems. First, we had run out of insulated wire, and second, plastic insulation popped off his wire in the cold. Thus Junior finally had to use ordinary bailing wire in the snow mine. But first he came to me and expressed some fears because this bare wire would have to carry 110 volts. "Don't worry about it," I told him. "The men who work in the snow mine are so bundled up that they carry their own insulation."

Par for one man picking, shoveling and lifting the filled parachute bags onto the sled was approximately 600 pounds in an hour, and about twice this in an average work session. Jack and I as pace setters often did twice this amount, though we probably suffered twice as much cold and backache as a result. Working two hours or more at a stretch could be painful. Even at −60°, if a man worked without pause he would sweat for the first hour. After that as he slowed down, a growing chill crept in and toes grew cold and his nose frosted. And as we dug deeper into the snow mine, the snow grew steadily harder. When we hit it, the snow gave forth a glassy sound and when we pried it loose it was solid as rock. After a man finished his stint in the snow mine, it required several hours after he returned "upstairs" to the heated buildings for him to recover the warmth his body had lost. And one and all agreed that, as the pit grew deeper, the hardest job was climbing those stairs to the head of the mine.

Chapter 24

ROUTINE IN THE WINTER

APRIL passed and astronomical twilight ended on May 4. We were into the heart of the winter right now. All-pervading darkness settled over the featureless landscape except for cloudless periods when we could see the moon in its two-week cycle about us as well as the stars and auroral displays. The stars especially presented an interesting display, though there was no South Pole star. As twilight had settled, the first stars to appear were the brightest of all stars—Sirius and Canopus. As for the winter clouds, they were essentially filmy, unlike the summer clouds which had been more dense and possessed individual character.

But the beauties of nature held little interest for us at the moment. For the temperature was sliding down and down until it had sunk past the world's record low temperature of −89.7° F., experienced in 1933 at Oimyakon, Siberia. On May 9 we hit −96.3°. I was up in the astronomy loft taking star shots and it was literally breath-taking when the wind hit me through the open slot of the pibal dome.

On May 10, the temperature dropped to −98.7° and with a northwest wind of 21 mph blowing, the wind-chill index reached a new high of 3290. A change came over the men now. Before, many had shown concern about the dropping temperature, but now all were rooting for it to hit −100°.

I had stayed up until two A.M. on May 12 working on star sights. At three A.M. I had just tumbled into my bunk when suddenly my lights went on and John Guerrero was shouting, "It's minus one hundred point four degrees Fahrenheit!" All of us leaped excitedly from our beds, and relatively lightly clad so as to feel what a hundred below was like, filed outdoors.

By the time we finished our day's work the temperature had shot up into the minus sixties and the wind fell off to practically nothing. After the movie that evening, Jack, Bob Benson and I went out to see what the weather was like. None of us put on hats, coats or mitts. In fact, Bob went out with only light underwear under his light clothes, light socks and shoes. We walked out to the emergency Jamesway some 200 feet away and then on to our ceiling light which sent a beam of light up to determine the height of the clouds and was another 500 feet distant. "This reminds me of the time on Byrd's first expedition," I related, "when our doctor went out for a hundred-yard walk at forty below with nothing on but a pith helmet and boots, and suffered no ill effects." Actually I was stretching a point here for the truth was, the cold had nipped an extremely tender and vulnerable portion of the good doctor's anatomy. We however were more fortunate, for while our ears were cold and we were a bit chilly, by the time we returned we actually enjoyed our crazy hike.

After that the temperature remained in the minus sixties and seventies for a long while, to the keen disappointment of some. But the wind made up for this rise in temperature. It grew so tempestuous that we could hear its roar even inside our insulated buildings. By May 26 snowdrifts had risen to roof level on the Grid South side of camp. Some of the outside doors were now completely sealed by the snow and we had to get outdoors with our shovels. That day, too, the Aurora Tower began shaking crazily above the science building. After the evening meal Jack went out with Earl Johnson, Oz and Junior and they strapped the tower to the science building with guy wires while Arlo stood alongside audibly expressing his concern about the future of his aurora program.

In the calmer cold of our tunnels we could actually hear our breath as well as see it, for as our breath emerged, it made a noise like escaping steam. In addition, minute ice crystals formed and popped with a delicate crackling sound as they trailed past our ears.

With the winter night routine now established, our days took on a more settled procedure. "Failure to observe a routine," Admiral Byrd had cautioned me decades before, "is the cause of much of the unhappiness that overtakes a wintering expedition. Without it the days and nights lose their line of divisions, and the months prolong themselves into a monotonous, unending period."

Actually, since our winter night period was a busy work period, we did not have the same problem Byrd had. Nevertheless, we lived by certain time breaks during each twenty-four hours. In a fashion then, all of us maintained regular hours, although some of the men were on day shift and others on night shift. For instance, the Met group operated on a twenty-four-hour basis and rotated night and day responsibilities among themselves. Occasionally a man who did his work by day suddenly shifted to night operation. For in truth, each of the twenty-four hours of every winter day was similar to all others. Sometimes a man changed his time schedule simply to avoid another man who irritated him. Other times a man did so because he found that he preferred the luxury, found only at night, of not being disturbed from his concentration on his work.

Those of us who were victims of civilization's dictum generally rose at 6:45 A.M. Some relied on alarm clocks, a few of which had faulty ringers; others waited for a call from Chet, our inspired cook. Still others could not be brought to consciousness except by the Met man coming off duty who would come in, heckle the sleeper and engage him in silly conversation that on occasion evoked even sillier responses from the muddleheaded sleeper.

There was no problem in getting out of bed such as there had been at Little America, where rooms had cooled off below freezing every night. We set our stoves to maintain a constant temperature of between 55 and 65 degrees day and night, which was sufficient for us because of our heavy underwear and woolen clothes. Both the barracks building where twelve slept and the Jamesway where the remaining six lived contained two stoves and were excellently insulated. Yet although our space heaters had fans on top to circulate air and disperse heat, we did not get all the circulation we needed, and Doc Taylor, who had a window on his end of the Jamesway, kept it partly open all winter. He even found curtains that had been included in our waste rag bag and dressed up his window.

Individual room space was the largest of any of my expeditions. On the first Byrd expedition, eight of us had slept in a room ten feet square. Now each of the men in the barracks building enjoyed almost this much individual space, and by doubling up with a roommate, and in some cases arranging their beds vertically in double bunk-bed style, had sufficient space remaining for sitting rooms. Over in the little Jamesway, we six had less space, confining ourselves in individual cubicles measuring 6 x 9 feet. The Jamesway was only 16 feet wide at the floor and 10 feet at shoulder height, at which level there was only a three-foot passageway between the east and west sides. The barracks building came equipped with partitions and doors for each of the six double rooms, whereas the Jamesway had neither but relied on improvised nylon parachute curtains. Only Bob Benson and Arlo in the center rooms had space for lockers, while we other four had to make do with shelves attached over our bunks. Our space was so closely rationed in the Jamesway as compared with the barracks building that Jack and I could converse in normal tones while sitting on our bunks and looking at each other through two doorways and across the little passageway. Bravo, who slept in Jack's room, was always ready to participate in these conversations by growling a willingness to romp with either of us who could spare the time for him.

The mess hall was open between six-thirty and seven A.M., which meant that those who wanted breakfast had to scramble out the door and down Main Street Tunnel to the mess hall before closing time. There, no matter how cold it was outdoors, we would find Chet Segers, our cook, in his undershirt and hot from his session in the galley. Along one side of the mess hall were four tables, each with room for four eaters, but since some of the eighteen men were always on duty elsewhere, there was seldom a question of playing musical chairs. The men coming into the mess hall picked up silverware, while Chet and an assistant mess man set the food out on the counter.

Breakfast consisted of the usual fare one ate back in the States, except for fresh eggs, fruit and milk, though after a while the men began to crave greater variety, and some badgered Chet for more exotic items. Always co-operative, Chet threw the issue back on the men. I recall that I was one who offered suggestions and found myself confronted with the task of planning a menu one week. Among my breakfast suggestions were such items as corned-beef hash, omelets made with cheese and green peppers, corn fritters, blueberry biscuits and minced beef and tomatoes on toast. Chet received many even stranger requests for special dishes and cheerfully filled them all. For example, though he scratched his long beard in surprise, he nevertheless prepared ginger-flavored steaks for breakfast on occasion because some of the men had told him of their fondness for them. He also brewed large quantities of iced tea, oddly enough a favorite beverage at the South Pole.

Without question Segers was the best cook and one of the best all-around expedition men I had known in the Antarctic. Considering that all he had to cook with was an ancient iron stove, his productions were all the more amazing. The stove was so small that we had to set it atop high blocks in order to keep Chet from developing a curvature of the spine. From a telltale stamp mark, we discovered the stove was made in 1890 and had only recently been converted from coal to oil. It had a defective fuel injection system that made it vibrate, and produced a racket which would build up almost to a scream at times and then subside to a hoarse roar. The noise filled the mess hall though in time we accepted it and learned to converse above it. On one occasion, our mechanics managed to eliminate the noise and the men whooped with joy. But a few hours later the din returned to last throughout our stay at the Pole.

From past experience, I was well aware that the camp cook was one of the most important personages in camp. The men who were scattered about the station at their various tasks were together chiefly at mealtime. This gave the cook the opportunity to play a dominant role in camp life, for the mess was his kingdom. If he wanted to—and most did—the cook could determine the character of the camp's conversation. Whatever he wanted to discuss became the subject material of the eaters.

As a rule, men on day duty went directly from breakfast to their specific tasks. Mornings were now reserved for tasks that *had* to be done either in the scientific disciplines or Navy support activities. Outside of a coffee break, I usually spent my mornings in my office in the science building where Jack piled messages McPherson had received during the night which required answer. From the flood of inquiries about supplies for the coming year it became obvious that our foothold on the Pole was considered sufficiently secure back in Washington for plans to be laid for a relief party to replace us the following summer. Jack was kept busy preparing estimates for the logistics requirements for the next year and I had to work with the IGY team to determine the essential replacements and new items the Station would require.

My mornings were not all involved in such activity. There were also the various scientific projects I was pursuing as well as reports to be written and other paper work to be cleared away. In addition someone usually had a problem either related to his work or to personal matters that he felt required consultation and some mornings a steady stream of callers came through my door. As necessary I went out to get a firsthand look at the problem and offered suggestions on the spot.

All about me the men were pursuing their tasks. Moose in the 8 by 12 foot "cold" shack scabbed outside the science building was deep in his glaciology work. Down in the garage Mel Havener was periodically going over our tractor and Weasel, seeking to preserve them against the ravages of the cold. He and some of the other Navy support crew members also worked steadily on our vital generators, keeping them greased and fueled. At either end of the Station the Met men were busy in the Met shack writing reports and in the inflation shelter preparing their balloons for ascension. From my office I could hear Willi Hough struggling to keep his massive ionosphere equipment in good repair. His Monster, or C-3 Automatic Ionosphere Recorder, with its 120 vacuum tubes and other assorted complex equipment was still proving to be a constant headache. One morning after having gone sleepless the previous night when his Monster died, Willi let out a loud oath. "It was only a socket that had burned out," he told me red-eyed.

One of Willi's problems was a bright spot that appeared unwanted at the close of an ionosphere record. Some of the neophytes in camp claimed that this was the most spectacular part of his record, for it exploded like a skyrocket. Willi studied the Monster's diagrams with an intensity worthy of an Einstein and at last discovered that a single wire among his miles of wires had been hooked up wrong at the factory. By correcting this error, he eliminated the bright spot, to the disappointment of some of the other men.

At noon a long ring on the phone called us back to Chet Segers' domain to lunch and to kid Bob Benson, our seismologist, as he ate. Bob was our uncrowned eating king and his prodigious capacity was a wonder to all of us. "What's the matter? Losing your appetite, Bob?" the men often teased him when he finally left the table. Bob could take anybody's razzing and was our camp favorite. "I don't eat much," he called back. "It's just that I eat slowly."

Bob's eating habits were highly amusing indeed. He could make a breakfast or lunch of Jello, mixing almost anything Chet had in the galley into the huge colored mounds. He would do the same with peanut butter, dumping it on whatever food sat on his plate. He had a similar penchant for ice cream, one of the few dishes Chet disliked preparing. On one occasion, I recall, Bob prevailed upon Chet to let him prepare a special ice cream. He came up with an almond-lemon-flavored ice cream with side touches of all other flavorings in Chet's storehouse. Though Bob beamed with pride, the rest of us found his concoction sickening. I remember Ed Flowers showing his contempt and putting an end to the mess by emptying a bottle of green ink over the top of Bob's specialty.

All the men still shared community duties which as a rule were performed during the afternoon. At another IGY Station in the Antarctic, the IGY scientists had rebelled against doing anything other than their scientific work, a situation that had divided the Station into two angry camps. At the Pole this question never arose, because the IGY personnel realized that the Station could not be maintained without their help. As leaders, Jack and I shared equally with all the other men in menial tasks.

For example, every six weeks I spent a portion of each day for seven days taking rubbish out to the Hubel Hole, cleaning up the floors of both the Jamesway and the science building, chopping ice that formed at our doors and checking our fuel supply. As a rule, I tried to do such a thorough job that the man following me would have little to do. Rolling in fuel barrels was a particularly difficult task because each barrel weighed more than 400 pounds. Bringing the drums into some of the buildings which had entrance steps was an exhausting job. More than one man was needed at such times.

Jack's Navy crew took on the task of tunnel maintenance, though the IGY men helped out when necessary. Snow dust, or fine powdery particles, continually accumulated in the tunnel network and made walking treacherous. Earl Johnson made a rake for leveling the snow and also a sprinkling can that he used to make the fine dust solidify into a hard surface again.

Each man also had mess duties on a weekly rotation. In addition to helping Chet at mealtime, this meant cleaning the head and the galley, and carrying out the garbage. We had been burning the debris frequently in the Hubel Hole, but as winter wore on drifts filled it, so that before long we were throwing our garbage upward into the hole instead of downward. Later in the year Ed Flowers took it upon himself to dig a new garbage pit which we named the "Flower Pot" in his honor.

Providing normal mess duty assistance for Chet occupied about an hour for each meal. Tables had to be set and food put out. Clean scoops of snow had to be put into pans to mix with the dehydrated juices. Afterward there were the dishes to wash, though more than half the time Chet took over this chore himself. "I've got nowhere to go anyhow," he would say as he excused his mess helper to go back to his own scientific or technical chores.

In an effort to make the job of mess assistants less onerous, each man on mess duty was given the privilege of selecting the music to be played at meals during his week of duty. Unfortunately some of the men had such raucous taste in music that food sometimes stuck in my throat. A few like McPherson were strong on classical and light operatic scores. In general, the younger members of the Station were addicted to rock-and-roll and hillbilly records, though a few developed some appreciation for better music as the winter night wore on. At one point a few members of the younger set protested bitterly when someone hid three of their most offensive records. For a moment an amusing mutiny seemed imminent. I recall especially that one man's "Joe College" pieces occasioned so many protests that he finally discarded them for less "hot" selections.

The minimum two-hour-a-week duty in the snow mine was accepted as a matter of course by some and regarded as drudgery by others. It provided a setting for many stories. On one occasion Arlo and I were digging in the snow mine when my saw struck into some fabric. "We may have hit Amundsen's tent," I said jubilantly. But as I hurriedly dug around the prize I discovered that some wit had dressed the mannequin model dummy the Air Force had dropped us in a parka and buried it in the floor of the mine. Arlo and I left our find covered with snow for the next digger to re-find.

Our snow mine and outdoor attire differed greatly from what we wore indoors, for part of the art of living in the Antarctic is to learn to stay warm. The most common indoor dress was long-handled underwear, wool trousers and shirt, cushion-soled socks and fleece-lined boots. John Guerrero, however, who had a mild mania to prove that he required little clothing, would stand around shivering in a short-sleeved summer shirt indoors and on one occasion when it was almost one hundred below zero John actually went outside barefoot for a few seconds. To keep the fleece lining of my boots dry, I put bags of silica gel on top of the stove where they warmed and desiccated all day. Then at night I pulled out the insole from my boots and put the bags inside. As a result, my boots were always dry the next morning. Some of the men also wore silk scarves about their necks both for cleanliness and for protection against the abrasion of rough wool shirts.

Outside clothing was another matter. For example, my normal attire for working in the snow mine consisted of a suit of Navy waffle-type underwear, a pair of Army heavy wool ski socks, a pair of Army rubber-insulated boots, Army trousers with cotton shell and frieze lining, heavy wool shirt, silk neck scarf, Air Force detachable parka hood, unlined parka windproof, a pair of wristlets (fingerless gloves) and wool mitt liners. This ensemble weighed over 18 pounds. In two and a half hours of work, I normally lost a pound of weight. Ice always formed inside my boots and on my socks from the $-60°$ temperature in the mine. The vapor from one's breath obscured vision in the mine all the way back to the surface a hundred feet away. For such heavy labor I could not have donned more clothing. Yet, several hours after I was back upstairs the skin over my solar plexus and kidneys was cold to the touch.

Our big meal was supper, which came at six and was the occasion for gabfests as well as heavy eating. Chet's main cooking problem was the fact that he had to cook to the average taste. This meant that to please the average man he had to overcook his meat and put us on a basically meat and potato diet, which was fine for the men with a farm background but offered a distinct hardship for the few gourmets in camp. Chet had a good supply of frozen and canned vegetables. Our canned tomato juice had streamed in, though we had sufficient tomato paste for Chet's excellent pizzas.

In the meat line, someone in the Navy's commissary area had obviously worked on certain mistaken assumptions about meat in the Antarctic. The most unfortunate of these was that pork, veal and ham would not keep, so that very little of any of these was sent us. Actually we had kept hams for long periods of time at Little America wrapped only in tar paper. As for other meats, we had plenty of chicken and more than enough beef, though perhaps too many roasts and not enough steaks for our liking.

In general, then, our food supply was excellent and we had no real cause for complaint. There were, of course, certain items that we lacked for obvious reasons. One was fresh milk, although we had canned and powdered milk as substitutes. We also lacked green items, such as lettuce and celery, during the winter night, though we'd had some earlier. Most of the men had assumed they would miss fresh fruit most at the Pole; however, our powdered orange juice was of excellent quality and the fresh oranges began to spoil before they were all consumed. As for the oranges I had so carefully frozen earlier, when I exhumed them they looked beautiful and seemed perfectly preserved. But when I parceled them out and we tried to eat them, they tasted as bitter as persimmons. The main reason, however, that oranges were not popular was that in the Antarctic, peeling an orange was a messy job and washing after eating one was a laborious job.

"Let's just thank our lucky stars we're not at that Station," Jack said to me one evening. The leaders at a neighboring Station had not examined their supplies in advance and fought to make up for shortages as had Jack and I. As a result their meat supply was all beef with no pork, and the few canned goods which came in disappeared after a few weeks while no seasoning whatsoever arrived. "That isn't the worst of it," I told Jack. "I was talking to the leader on the hamset and he told me that they never got sheets, blankets or toilet paper and they won't until next summer."

"What are they going to use?" Jack asked.

"Sleeping bags and parachutes, they said," I replied.

After the supper dishes had been carted away, some of the men remained in the mess hall for talk or an occasional game of cards or chess. Most of the men, however, returned to their work or to their rooms. Our office and room furnishings were field grade in general, and the legs were none too sturdy. We also had metal folding chairs, but these had streamed in and were still bent despite all efforts to straighten them. But in Oz, our builder, we had a master craftsman and in time he ingeniously produced desks, cabinets and other needed furniture from broken bits of wood from our lumber cache.

During the first part of the winter night Jack and I had a task that occupied most evenings. By July first we were requested to report the pinpointed location of our Station in relation to the true South Pole. Dick Bowers had made his preliminary calculations by taking sun shots, checked against faulty tables; now we were to try our luck on star shots.

So as winter came upon us, Jack and I put in a great deal of time in the small astronomy shack, peering into the skies. Sometimes one or the other would be up all night taking reading after reading and making calculations. There were many problems involved. First, our theodolite, which was a precision instrument, was not meant to

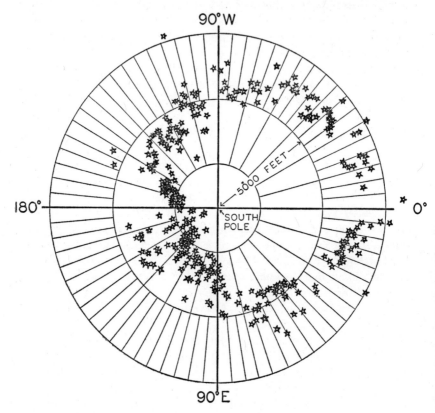

Step 1 in determining the location of the geographic South Pole during the winter night was as follows:

The height above a horizontal horizon of the bright star Canopus (with an average southern declination 52° 40′ 31″) was measured some 300 times during May and June, 1957. The uncorrected difference between the actual and observed height (largely due to refraction through an atmosphere which varied due to wind and temperature inversions as well as the difficulty of keeping the theodolite leveled at extremely low temperatures) was plotted in the direction observed at various times of the day from a presumed position at the Pole. Theoretically, the resultant pattern should have formed a circle concentrically about the Pole. It is obvious that stars did form a crude wreath centered over a ground point displaced toward the upper right of the diagram. Normally refraction corrections would have been applied to each star reading, however the values were too uncertain to be trustworthy and, therefore, were obviated by the simple procedure used in step 2.

be used in cold weather and it became hard to move as its lubricants hardened, so that we had difficulty adjusting it into position. We were able to maintain the temperature inside the shack at approximately zero, but at this temperature when the instrument cooled it "warped" and the bubbles which we relied upon for our vertical accuracy often expanded into the housing of the theodolite.

There was only cramped standing space in the astronomy loft and this made it doubly difficult for us to step softly as we had to so as

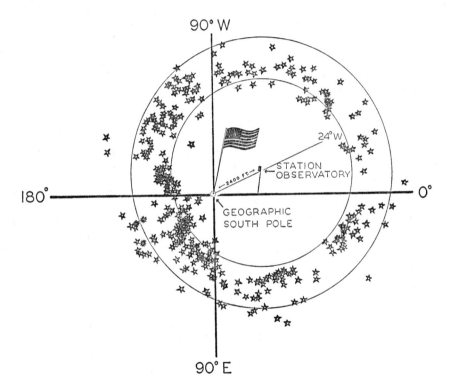

Step 2. In order to find the relative position between the observatory location at the South Pole Station and the actual Geographic Pole, a circular grid shown here by two circles was fitted over the wreath of stars plots of step 1. The center point of this circle was found to be 2,400 feet on the map scale away from our presumed pole approximately along Meridian 24° W. Thus, by measuring the distance (0.4 nautical miles) "south" along the indicated meridian (Grid East direction of 156° E) we located the position of the Geographic South Pole on the ground. Since the Pole is known to be wandering about somewhat (see Chapter 25) and since also our accuracy, because of the severe weather conditions, was not too precise, we chose to assume that the Pole's actual position lay within plus or minus 100 feet of our calculation. The Geographic Pole was marked by 157 fuel barrels, set in a 200-foot-diameter circle around a flagpole.

not to upset the instrument's delicate balance. We had to stoop over and reach around to open the slot in the metal dome (not an enjoyable task in a temperature of —95° with a strong wind blowing), recheck the bubbles in the theodolite, line up the star, read the time, read the instrument, write down the angles and colunation, close the dome, plunge and reverse the instrument, relevel it, then open the dome again . . . and then repeat the entire ten-minute operation about eight to ten times.

The star I selected to observe was Canopus, the brightest high star. Jack used Al Na'ir, a smaller star that was not given to flaming quite so much as Canopus but could not be seen quite so often as Canopus. But we had our troubles because the midwinter sky was not as clear as we had expected. Thin veils of moisture often dimmed the heavens, and at times some aberration between the lenses of our instruments and the outer atmosphere made the stars appear to flame and lose their sharpness. Because of our uncertainties, we made four hundred plots of star movement that covered a table like a large tablecloth. In this way we were able at last to pinpoint the Pole at a point 2,400 feet from our camp, in the direction of the east coast of Australia. This was the geographic South Pole, where the southern end of the earth's axis theoretically emerges. To be safe, we said the Pole was situated either plus or minus a hundred feet from this point outside the backside of our Station.

As respite from such trying work by all hands, we had frequent movies which were shown in the mess hall on Wednesday, Saturday and Sunday evenings after the Met men finished their pilot balloon run and theodolite checking. The men were given turns selecting the movies to be shown and we had a wide enough selection to please most of the Station. As a rule many recent movies sent us were lower grade than old-time favorites and there was greater attendance at these older movies. On earlier expeditions we had also had movies, though the number of films was few. On my third expedition to the Antarctic, for instance, one movie perforce was played more than a dozen times. The last time it ran we cut off the sound and the men chanted the dialogue without error.

The men at the Station came to rely on movies as their chief entertainment and they did indeed serve a useful purpose in relaxing the men and bringing out their natural good humor. Several unexpected events also occurred at the movies that furnished additional entertainment. On one occasion the hero, Errol Flynn, was robustly kissing Olivia de Havilland when suddenly the table at which Jack

Tuck and Oz were sitting collapsed, dumping both men on the floor amid a debris of sugar, powdered cream and butter. Bravo immediately plunged on top to play and the resultant tangle provoked the loudest and most prolonged Station laugh of the year.

At another movie, when the same two actors approached each other Oz jumped up from his seat at a table and announced, "Oh, no, I'm not going to let them do that to me again." I think this was the same night Bravo swallowed a sound bulb which Junior Waldron, our projectionist, inadvertently dropped.

Our other opportunities for recreation were limited. Of course there were gabfests at which the chief topics of conversation were usually women and food, in that order. However, there were also third-layer subjects involving history, authorship and quotations. Unfortunately, with our Encyclopaedia gone, Jack, Doc and I found ourselves hard put at times to settle arguments. Often a solemn tone added authority to an unsure response.

Actually, we had been supplied with a large mass of recreation gear. However, I am quite certain it was picked out by those inexperienced in the ways of the Antarctic. For instance, when I opened the recreation boxes, one of the first packages contained baseballs and bats. The men had also been asked in advance to select the magazines they wanted shipped to the Station. These ran the gamut of the popular magazines as well as some of special interest to young men. What arrived were a few sporting magazines and some Western pulps.

The difference between what we got in the way of recreational gear and what should have been sent us was the difference between myth and reality. But perhaps it was best, because it made the men rely on themselves to find ways to pass extra time.

Two evenings a week we held lectures. Doc Taylor presented one series for an hour and a half on Thursday evenings and they were well received by the men. His talks covered such subjects as embryology, the brain, the heart, the digestive system, the kidney, the male reproductive system, the female reproductive system, pregnancy, childbirth and alcohol.

We didn't see completely eye to eye on the question of bringing alcohol to the Antarctic, though Doc presented a well-reasoned argument in favor of it. "The advantages of having alcohol in a small isolated base are numerous," he argued. "First of all, the personnel of the small base are deprived of the many comforts normally found in even the most distant parts of the world. There is no contact with women for a year, no liberty, no chance for a change of friends or environment, no sports, and only scattered fragmentary news from the outside world. These things combine to make the men feel restricted as well as isolated so that as many privileges must be used to offset this as possible. Although the use of alcohol may not be condoned in regular duty, in isolated duty it actually is small compensation for the freedom lost in other departments."

I questioned whether this still overshadowed the dangers. "Well," Doc said, "then alcohol is most important in adding variety to the weekly routine. It may be hard to express just how vital 'variety' is to the maintenance of good morale, but when men are confined to five buildings for a year, six months of which are darkness, morale is dependent to a large extent on varying the monotony. And alcohol serves this purpose well. Besides, alcohol fills a significant function in maintaining a harmonious, well-knit group."

Despite my opposition we did, of course, hold occasional "Happy Hours" when the few men who wished to were permitted to drink. I came to dread the effect of these sessions on certain of the men.

Doc Taylor was also concerned with camp hygiene and sanitation. Our head contained two sinks with hot and cold running water, a shower stall, a washing machine and a dryer. Hot water was always available, though for some reason the Station had not been supplied with free-issue soap. Early in the year we had all chipped in and bought from the ship's store service two cartons of soap which Doc tended and put in the head for everyone's use.

The men showered and washed clothes on an average of once a week. When our dryer failed, we hung our clothes in the garage on lines in front of the big fans of the generators. We had no system of pipes or conduits for sewage disposal at the Pole, but sewage once outside the buildings was frozen permanently. And even if left unventilated, frozen sewage was relatively odorless and unoffensive. As for the galley waste, much of it could be dropped down the galley drain, which was below the galley sinks, and with hot water draining down the pit below was self-perpetuating.

However, there was one problem that caused every man in camp great and direct concern at the outset. This was the fact that our toilet seats had a temperature of −40°. A man had to steel himself to use the facilities and Doc considered this a serious hygiene problem. After two years the Task Force "scientists" at McMurdo had failed to offer a solution and there appeared to be none.

Then one day Doc Taylor came in with a wild gleam in his eye.

"I've got the answer," he exulted, "and it's so simple that I'm amazed." What he had done was to raise both the seat and the lid and cover the hole with a third hinged lid of plywood which opened to the side. This system raised the seats to room temperature, though nothing could be done about the roaring wind that blew upward from the pit. The grateful crew was willing at that point to award Taylor a medal as "Number One Humanitarian of the Antarctic."

For a while small groups held Spanish, German or French language classes utilizing phonographic records. We also played bingo occasionally with Doc Taylor as caller, and I recall that on one occasion I won a prize of aftershave lotion, a very slow-moving item on the ship store shelves. We also had a dues-free chapter of the Izaak Walton League with Moose Remington, who had a deep interest in conservation, as our president. At one of these meetings I talked about seals and Earl Johnson about penguins. Certainly we could swear to protect all the wild animals and plants of our lifeless Pole where bacteria and molds were the largest life before we arrived.

Bedtime was generally late. A few of the men, like Bob Benson and Arlo Landolt, averaged only five hours of sleep at night because after their work was done they stayed in their offices or lay in their beds and read—usually classics or technical books in their scientific fields. We suspected they slipped in a Western or pulp story now and then from the chuckles that came from them.

Usually before Jack and I turned in, we roughhoused with Bravo. He was, by now, a brute of a dog weighing nearly 100 pounds. When he jumped up, he could knock over a man who was the least bit off balance. He ate anything and turned up mysteriously whenever a can of beer or peanuts was opened. At a single meal he sometimes devoured as much as five pounds of meat and no one dared touch his food dish except Chet or Jack. He knew that the men would drop scraps in his dish for him, but if we had a meal without scraps he grew agitated. He would bark with a startling loudness at each one who failed to make a contribution. He also had a fit whenever the vacuum cleaner was turned on. He was definitely Jack's dog, stayed close to him, and when separated from Jack, grew morose. I taught him to shake hands, but his favorite game was mouthing the men's hands or playing roughly with a mitted hand. He could move fast and only our thick clothing prevented accidental slashes from his fangs or claws. One of Bravo's pet joys was to chew on my slippers with my feet in them, a somewhat disquieting experience. He also loved a tug of war on shirt or underwear sleeve. Doc Taylor had a special sweater he put on to play with Bravo. Doc would wear gloves to protect his hands. He would tickle Bravo's nose to make him growl as the big Malemute held onto the sweater and backed away. When Doc got tired of the game he would say, "That's all." Bravo would look disappointed but walk off to look for someone else to play with. The tussles would go on for an hour at a time.

Bravo had an even greater dislike of the dark and the cold than the men. However, he would usually follow Jack out and we wondered what kept his paws from freezing. Once Jack hitched him to a sled to carry out an empty fuel drum to our "empties" cache, and despite his size and strength, Bravo whimpered melodramatically. "He's so much like us," said Jack, "that he doesn't even know he's a dog."

On one holiday some of the men decided to hold a wiener roast outdoors. Though the temperature had warmed to —75°, the day was dark and the wind blew at nearly 30 miles per hour. No inducement could make Bravo join the group of "six idiots," as Bob Benson referred to himself, Doc Taylor, Arlo, Moose, Hansen and John Guerrero as they took hot dogs, ice cream on sticks and some Benson Jello out to the Hubel Hole. One match at a time could not ignite the rubbish there and the fire was started only when six matches were struck at once. The men had warmed firewood in Moose's office and now they tossed these pieces on the blaze. The hot dogs charred slightly on one end but remained frozen solid in all other parts. In fact the six had to keep putting their ice cream sticks right into the fire in order to warm them up sufficiently so that they could get their teeth into them. Doc Taylor brought out a ukulele to entertain the group but the cold strings changed tone every time the wind blew away from the Hubel Hole fire. "Say, you should hear our electric guitar," Bob said to us stay-at-homes afterward.

This desire to seek a release from the hard work most of the men performed was a natural one. It would have been inhuman to expect them to repeat the same grind day after day without respite. A change of pace was as essential as orderly routine, so Jack and I decreed Sunday a free day except for necessary emergency duties and scientific observations. On Sundays, supper was the only formal meal. Many of the men slept late and ate brunch any time up to two P.M. Chet generally brought in some steaks on Saturday night so they could thaw out by mid-Sunday for the men to cook for themselves. Oz, our builder, usually continued his usual work pace every day, however. "I've got nothing better to do," he would say.

On Sunday afternoons, and for that matter for several hours every evening throughout the week, one or two men at a time used the hamset to reach American ham operators and talk to their families and friends by phone patch. Our first routine contact each time was with Paul Blum W2KCR North Syracuse, New York. He and his RAGS (Radio Amateurs of Greater Syracuse) companions were a godsend to all Americans in Antarctica. Through the American Red Cross they would receive and transmit to us written messages from our families and friends. Often when patches couldn't be made due to radio conditions we could still get coded radio messages in and out through Paul. He and his friends who operated the set when he was at work or catching a bit of sleep were almost daily "visitors" to our camp. From them we got all sorts of bits of world news as well as highlight stories from other stations.

Of course we could get some news broadcasts as well as entertainment programs and occasional baseball or football games over the Armed Services broadcasts, as well as an occasional program from BBC, New Zealand, and Australia. Russian English-language programs stuffed with subtle propaganda from Moscow also came booming in. But at least their music was of good quality.

However, of all our radio contacts those that gave the men the greatest personal pleasure were the two-way voice contacts with friends and loved ones. We had by now developed contact with quite a few other ham operators throughout the United States in addition to our reliable standby, Jules Madey. Since the person receiving the call had to pay the phone charges between his home and the ham operator's station, it was economically sound to find a ham operator as close as possible to the town you were calling. I am afraid though that a few of the men were so anxious to make contact with the outside world that if they could not contact a ham operator near the target town, they thought nothing of using a ham operator in New Jersey to contact a friend in Minnesota and then talking for half an hour or more, running up a large long-distance phone bill. Another problem involving our ham radio operations was that while our calls were made in midafternoon our time, it was seventeen hours later on the East Coast of the United States. Placing a collect phone patch more than once at such hours could chill a close friendship.

Fortunately for me, I was able to make frequent contacts with Byron Roudabush W4AHG near Washington, so I didn't have to make as many long-distance calls as some of the fellows who couldn't find an amateur in their home town. At times we felt these friends were regular members of the Pole Station.

I had several radio conversations with other IGY leaders in the Antarctic. For instance, one day I had a long talk with Bunny Fuchs, at the Shackleton Base. We exchanged descriptions of our camps. Bunny's main building was 70 feet long and he had 13 men living in it. His planes were stationed one quarter of a mile away. He also had three men at his advance plateau Station at 81° 55′ S. "We lost two men for a while," Bunny told me, "but thank God we found them before they were done in. It's rough, old man," he said. "We've got our food and material boxes outdoors and our sea ice is continually moving west." On later contacts he told us of his plans to cross the continent.

On Sunday evenings two important events took place: the church service and the third movie of the week. Our religious service was held after supper with Cliff Dickey taking an active role both in planning each week's service and in carrying it out. The formal part of the service consisted of a reading from the Bible and the singing of hymns. We had been led to expect an electric piano to be air-dropped to us, but when it failed to arrive we relied on records, though unfortunately the recorded hymns were not generally familiar to us and with the absence of hymnbooks we did not prove to be very articulate singers.

The formal part of church service lasted about twenty minutes and was nondenominational. After this came a weekly discussion period, many of which Doc or I led off. Discussions were sometimes heated among the dozen of our eighteen who normally showed up for church services. It was amusing that one man who at first loudly professed to be agnostic or atheist took to dropping in on church services after a while. At times we took on topics that taxed our combined scientific and philosophic ingenuity such as Time, Space, Energy, Love, and Marriage.

As we moved ahead into our winter night, our biggest celebration came on June 22, or "Midnight," after which date the winter night was half over so that we could begin to look forward hopefully to eventual sunlight.

The men exhibited great enthusiasm in planning this gala celebration. Earl Johnson made candelabra from pipe fittings. Doc Taylor and Junior Waldron turned out the paper decorations; a red flag cloth was thrown over the four joined mess tables as a tablecloth; balloons and streamers hung from the rafters. Willi and McPherson even made firecrackers, although they proved largely a fizzle. I helped

Segers with the turkey dressing as he outdid himself in preparing a superb meal.

Dinner began at four P.M. with grace said by Doc Taylor. Then Jack and I proposed four champagne toasts with a bottle Moose Remington produced. "To the forty-eight states, our country and the President," said Jack. "To the IGY as it begins on July first," I offered. "To our families, wives and sweethearts." Jack raised his glass again.

I raised mine again: "To Byrd," I said, "and to Scott, Amundsen and all those who made our presence here possible— To Antarctica."

Chapter 25

POLE DANCE

ALTHOUGH the individual members of the station complement at the Pole Station had been motivated by the worthiest of considerations in their willingness to devote a year of their personal and career lives to the IGY effort at the Pole, it early became evident that many of the scientific observers, as well as most of the Navy personnel, had arrived at the Station with little real knowledge of the Antarctic or the Poles from the point of view of their historical or scientific significance. Also while each man had been trained to perform his own job, a number were uncertain as to how his particular piece fitted into the over-all scheme of things and was specifically related to his neighbor's job. In the case of the scientific personnel, this was accentuated by the fact that at the Pole Station, as with the American stations throughout the Antarctic, the majority of the individual scientists, while academically qualified in their discipline, had had a minimum of field experience in it. This was in sharp contrast to some foreign Antarctic stations which tended by and large to employ maturer scientists with considerable field experience in their disciplines.

The relative inexperience of our scientists caused difficulties in the beginning, but as the winter night progressed it tended increasingly to have its positive aspects. Certainly these younger men possessed the vigor of youth and the intense scientific curiosity of the scientific newcomer. And as they learned to adapt themselves to both new and changing situations, they performed at least as well as a more experienced man might have.

It was because of the curiosity the men exhibited that Jack and I organized a program designed to broaden our collective Antarctic and polar education. Jack had read more about Antarctic history than most polar neophytes take time to do on their first winter night. He had lived his first winter at historic McMurdo and he knew the Shackleton and Scott stories well. He related these in one or two lecture sessions and I filled in with the early history of the discovery and exploration of the continent: Amundsen's trip to the Pole; the Byrd expeditions; Highjump and other modern expeditions. I also discussed the development of IGY, and Jack and I together briefed the men on the highlights of Deep Freeze I and the construction of the Pole Station. I was amused at times to find myself telling what to me were old stories of the IGY and construction days here at the Pole to wide-eyed men who had arrived a month or two after me, fresh from their problems at home, school or Navy station. True, they were young, and the rapid sequence of events had never permitted them time to read up on their new polar world. But here they were right at the cherished goal of so many gallant men of the past who had either never reached the spot or had made it the hard way— on foot. It was not essential that they know the history of Antarctica or even what it was like to carry out their assignment. Still they realized as I did that when they returned home their friends and colleagues would expect them to know all about the Antarctic and the South Pole.

The lecture program was so popular that the men supported it with enthusiasm on a two-a-week basis. So with Doc Taylor's weekly medical lecture and three movies a week, all our evenings except one were filled. Tuesday was a blissful time when one could plan his own aftersupper activities.

Our lectures gradually branched out into various scientific and technical subjects. Some of the Navy men not only explained their specialties but volunteered to be assigned polar books from our limited library, and read up on certain subjects which they later reported on for the benefit of the rest. The science staff provided the *pièce de résistance* as they told how their instruments functioned as well as why and how they were taking their observations. Bob Benson, our seismologist, proved to be a most popular speaker; he kept everyone laughing uproariously at his witty asides.

On several subjects, such as glacial deformation of the Bay of Whales, cold weather, cold weather protection, the navigational fix of the poles, as well as one on the various south poles, I gave several talks, one of which I think it fitting to paraphrase here. It concerned a concept of the behavior of the earth's axis, a subject which has been of primary interest to me throughout my scientific career.

The Queen Maud Mountains, 200 to 300 miles from the South Pole and Spitzbergen in the far north, afford ample fossil evidence in their coal beds that the polar regions had once supported far more abundant life than at present. What had changed them to a cold dead world could have been a change of climate due to greatly fluctuating climate cycles all over the earth; or the moving of the earth's crust as Wegener, the author of the Continental Drift Hypothesis, had postulated; or thirdly, the change could have been the result of the poles wandering from their present positions during the course of millions of years.

The IGY glacial program may in time provide one of the clues to changes in climate, for by determining the nature and thickness of past annual snow layers from a study of the walls of our snow mine and those of the pits and drill holes being dug at each station, we may collectively detect slow systematic trends of weather changes which cause greater or lesser amounts of snowfall. The quantity of such snow would tell a great deal, for to the analyst it would suggest the weather patterns and temperatures as well as corollary events that went on elsewhere on the globe each year.

Naturally, to understand long-range changes of climate and link them to changes in the sun's output of energy, it is essential to study the present happenings in the atmosphere and oceans. Thus the IGY's intensive efforts in Oceanography and Meteorology were necessary to fill in gaps in our knowledge in these areas. One couldn't very well explain the variations in the snow layers we might find without first finding how our present weather worked. The meteorology program Ed, Floyd, Herb and John were slaving over was thus not so much concerned with forecasting future weather as it was with establishing a link with our understanding of the mechanics of past weather. Once we found how past changes came about and whether they followed sequences of solar disturbances, we could predict far better what would happen in the future. However, I found it difficult to accept the fact that climatic changes alone could possibly have been great enough to account for the luxuriant vegetation which had once flourished close to the Pole. Nor could I conceive that big trees could ever have grown in an area which had no sunlight for five or six months out of a year. Nor had I ever felt happy about adhering to the theory of cold periods in the earth's past history which caused great glaciers to grow in areas which were now tropical in climate. I pre-

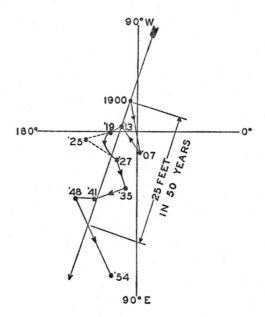

Actual drift of the spin pole from 1900 to 1954.

ferred to look for further causes that might account for "polar coal" and "tropical ice."

The mechanism of how the poles could shift is interesting. Actually there are three poles beneath us—the balance pole, a fixed line through the earth around which the earth is in perfect balance and around which the earth turns once in approximately 14 months; the spin pole on which the earth rotates every 24 hours but which is not fixed in the earth; and the geographic or map pole, an arbitrary surface point to which the meridians all converge.

Everything that takes place on or around the earth's surface affects the balance of our whirling planet and thus the balance pole. A heavy snowfall in the Dakotas, atmospheric pressures flowing over the earth, tides ebbing and flowing, millions of tons of silt carried down the Amazon or the Mississippi, as well as possible internal movements deep in the earth—all disturb that delicate balance of the whirling earth. Even heavy automobile traffic out of New York City on a summer weekend minutely unbalances the earth as it rotates.

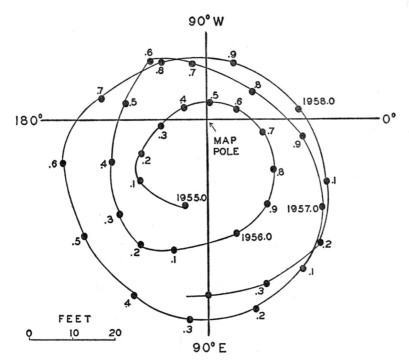

Actual motion of the earth's spin pole from 1955 to 1958 by tenths of a year.

Rotation is the continuing turning about an axis. As the earth turns, it tries desperately to spin on its north and south balance and spin axes together, but it cannot compensate rapidly enough for all the changes in its balance taking place on or in the earth to accomplish this. So it also rotates through its spin poles. Thus the earth is trying to turn on both these axes at once. If we imagine for the moment that the axis of the balance pole passed through the plane of the equator instead of very close to the spin pole as the earth's elliptical shape tends to locate it, we would find that once every 14 months the entire earth would rotate completely around this fixed balance pole once.

This would have the effect of bringing the South Map Pole surface to the equator, then on up to the North Spin Pole, and then on back through the equator to its original position—all within 14 months. Of course all this time the earth would continue its normal once-a-day rotation on its spin axis. As it is, with the balance pole being normally not more than 10 to 40 feet from the spin pole, the spin pole merely traces a small circle around the balance pole every 14 months (as it remains, so to speak, on the same latitude line relative to the balance pole).

During the course of every six or seven years the balance poles and spin poles separate a short distance and then draw closer together. This causes the Chandler Circles, as they are called, formed by the path traced by the spin pole as it grows first larger and then smaller. I have noted considerable evidence to suggest that the greatest earthquake activity takes place during the period when the Chandler Circle is getting smaller and the spin and balance poles are coming closer together. This implies that the earth is subject to a great strain when the poles move apart, and that the earthquakes represent periods of isostatic adjustment or rebalancing.

Actually, after each periodic rebalancing, the position to which the spin and balance poles seem to come to acceptable equilibrium sufficient to greatly slow down the frequency of the earthquakes is a slightly different one in relation to the map pole on the earth's surface. This new series of positions has proceeded in one general direction so that in the first half of this century the poles have wandered about 25 feet or an average of 6 inches a year. The South Pole seems to be moving imperceptibly in the general direction of the west coast of Australia. Should this continue for a million years, it would result in a 2° change in the position of the Pole on the earth's surface! And since the spin pole remains constant in its relationship to the sun, the territory now covered by polar ice could, in the course of millions of years, shift to a place that is temperate.

But evidence suggests that large-scale events, such as glaciation changes, could unbalance the earth from time to time much more than it is being unbalanced today. However, the unbalance would never cause a sudden topple, a popular science-fiction concept.

But as the Pole moved slowly, the equator with its 27-mile-greater diameter created by centrifugal force would also migrate, and this change in the earth's shape would account for some of the mighty forces which in the past built great mountain ranges.

One day, perhaps, we will have telescopes and other instruments at the South Pole that will enable us to locate the spin pole exactly and even to follow its path, actually marking out the circles on the polar snow. But now, strange as it may seem, we must rely on astronomers in temperate latitudes to tell us where the spin pole is at any given time, and thus fix the position of the geographic or map pole. The International Latitude Service receives data on star observations made by five or more groups of astronomers near the 38th

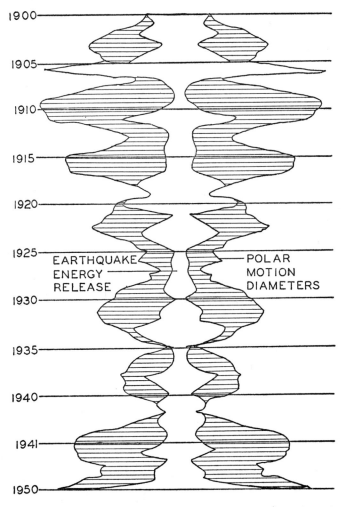

Dynamic adjustments of the spin pole, apparently due to the action of earthquakes, 1900–1950.

Parallel—one in Japan, one in Russia, two in the United States and one in Italy.

But it was not for us here at the Pole that the astronomers performed their work. It was for the timekeepers, surveyors and mapmakers of the world. An important IGY effort to pinpoint these small motions of the earth was a part of the Latitude and Longitude Program, but was carried on in temperate and tropic latitudes rather than here in Antarctica. A moon camera which took precisely timed photographs of the moon and its starry background could determine the exact position of the camera on earth by one exposure far more accurately than we had been able to do at the Pole with 400 star shots. It was hoped that not only would scientists get better data on polar movements from such a program, but that we might also get ideas as to the structure of the inside of the earth. Scientists were looking to sudden minute changes in the speed of the earth's rotation as proof that the earth possessed a liquid core.

However, unless you know exactly where something is on the planet—and the somethings we start with are the poles—it is impossible to determine where anything else is. In an age of aerial navigation and, even more important, of satellite and guided missiles, locating points on the earth's surface with respect to the spin poles becomes a matter of prime interest. What must be taken into account is that as the spin pole moves, the astronomical latitudes and longitudes of Moscow, London, Washington, and every other point on the earth's surface change accordingly. Even on a day-to-day living level, if one relied on celestial fixes, what is your back yard today might be your neighbor's property a few years from now as the earth shifts its spin axis.

Certainly we cannot discount the fact that the sun's output of energy fluctuates and the earth's atmosphere responds climatically in a cyclic fashion—enough perhaps to account for the comparatively recent ice ages. But I feel certain that the coal found in high latitudes near both Poles and the evidences of ancient glaciation of relatively similar age found in the tropics is more probably due to polar wandering. Of course, some bodily movement of the crust equatorwards over the more molten subcrust as a result of centrifugal thrust on the land masses in the temperate latitudes could also be responsible for our finding coal at the Poles and glacial evidences in warm regions of India, Africa and South America. Such shifting—if it occurred of course—would have forced the earth to readjust its balance which in turn would have brought the centrifugal thrust onto the drifted land mass from a new quarter. Unlike Wegener's simplified continental drift concept, I hypothecate that due to polar wandering the continents may have been nudged now this way and now that—wrinkling, buckling and breaking up at the edges and in the weaker internal zones. At one time in the geologic past, forests and swamps thus may have existed in the Antarctic only to be replaced by the present inhospitable environment. Then in time as the earth grew older its crust grew thicker and continents found it harder to move around.

"But what of the magnetic poles all this time?" one may ask.

We have ample proof through geological evidence that iron particles laid down in sediments and volcanic outflows orient themselves to the earth's North and South Magnetic Poles. Some beds laid down over periods of thousands of years suggest from the orientation of the particles that the Magnetic Poles not only have moved a great deal but in some instances have migrated completely around the site of the sediments as though the Magnetic Poles had changed their polarity. I have long had a hunch that the Magnetic Poles were struggling to readjust and catch up to the changing position of the spin and balance poles. The Geomagnetic Pole, which is the focal site of the earth's total magnetic field, is about 12 degrees away from the geographic poles, but the more actively moving magnetic poles are nearly twice as far off and not even diametrically opposite to one another. They seem to be a compromise between the earth's magnetic field and the variously locally magnetized ore bodies in the earth's crust. I suspect that if the earth always rotated with fidelity to the axis on which it turns today, the Magnetic Poles would be closer to the spin axis.

Of course the matter of the magnetism of the earth is by no means a closed book, which is why we were studying it so intensively during IGY. We were studying its daily abrupt fluctuations which cause compass needles to fluctuate in both horizontal and vertical planes. Willi and Arlo noted that their magnetic instruments kicked up every time there was or was about to be an auroral display. At the same time Willi found his C-3 recorded ionospheric irregularities and the ionosphere did not bounce back radio signals as it normally did. Naturally there had to be a reason for these disturbances. So IGY was looking to the sun and sunspots. In fact, as mentioned before, the IGY had been scheduled at this particular time because maximum sunspot activity had been forecast.

The IGY stations responsible for observing solar flares and sunspots in truth never took their camera eyes off the sun's disc for a moment. Whenever they saw something happening, they sent out a warning—a call for an alert! That was when Willi, Bob and Arlo went on continuous duty for days at a time. The events that happen during and after a flare would give us much information and with thousands of stations around the earth taking down measurements at the same exact moments we couldn't help but learn a lot even if it would take years to sift and analyze the accumulated mass of data.

In respect to the magnetic field itself, there are many theories. Some think the earth is one big magnet or set of magnetic dipoles, and the earth's lines of magnetic flux are similar to those that can be seen when iron filings orient themselves to a magnet held close by. The interior of the earth, however, is probably too hot for such magnetism to exist. Its temperature is well above the Curie point for iron or nickel, at which metals lose their magnetic properties.

This reasoning leads another group of science philosophers to theorize that the earth's interior may be so liquid that great convection currents exist inside it as the hotter magna seeks to rise to the surface (which on a spinning sphere could be in any direction). These movements of matter, they suggest, create a dynamo effect which generates an electromagnetic field around the earth.

As long as it is still anyone's guess, I offer my own concept. We know we are in the sun's electromagnetic field and are influenced by solar flares and cosmic radiation. I suggest that our own spinning earth may modify this field into its own magnetic field. To illustrate simply, if you move a loop of wire through a magnetic field, you set up a current in the wire and a field around it. The shell of the earth with its metallic components, conductive sea water and ionized atmosphere could function as a cluster of spherical loops. If they then rotate in the earth's magnetic field and are trajected through it on the earth's trip around the sun, such a crust could well set up a magnetic field not unlike the one we have. Of course if this is true there should be evidence of annual variation in the earth's total magnetic field as it ranges closer or farther from the sun on its annual trip around the sun.

Questions poured fast and thick on me after this talk. "Has Antarctica not always been at the South Pole? Could it once have been somewhere in the tropics where the sun rose and set on it every day? Has this land not always been on the bottom of the world?" These were questions that whirled around in the minds of the men as they sat in our mess hall on the very axis of the earth—the South Pole.

Chapter 26

SCIENCE PROGRAM IN ACTION

THE International Geophysical Year began with a bang on July first, ushered in by perhaps the most severe magnetic and sunspot storms of the year. Coincident with this we had our most spectacular red aurora. A large portion of the sky to the Grid North was a foggy glowing red, while a still fainter red appeared to the southwest. The red aurora resembled the light reflections cast by an invisible city beyond the horizon, and occasionally some yellowish-green corona rays built up toward the zenith.

So with the horizon blood red in the enveloping darkness and the electrical storms raging above us, we were well begun on the IGY program. For the International Geophysical Year had been set up to coincide with the period of maximum sunspots and these were occurring, as we learned by radio, at the very outset.

We were not alone in our work, for men from eleven countries were wintering over in the Antarctic at more than 40 IGY stations. Scientists from France, Great Britain, Belgium, Chile, Argentina, Australia, New Zealand, Japan, Norway, Russia and the Union of South Africa were also manning IGY posts. And we at the Pole had American companions at McMurdo, Little America, Byrd, Ellsworth, Wilkes and Hallett stations. In our IGY work there was complete co-operation between stations of all nations, a decided contrast to animosities elsewhere in the political arena. An American meteorologist lived with the Russians at Mirny on the coast of Wilkes Land near 90° East; a Russian and Argentine scientist were stationed at Little America; and we shared Hallett Station with the New Zealanders.

Although there were clusters of IGY stations on the Graham-Palmer Peninsula, some almost at each other's back door, at the Pole we were far distant from other stations. Our closest neighbors were three men living at South Ice, some 560 miles away, the British sub-station of Bunny Fuchs's Shackleton Base. Byrd Station with its 23 men some 700 miles from us in Marie Byrd Land, was our closest American neighbor. Other IGY accredited Antarctic stations lay as far as 3,700 miles from us at Latitude 37° South!

The South Pole's scientific enterprises constituted just one small link in the chain of simultaneous observations being made around the globe on weather, ionosphere, aurora and airglow, geomagnetism, seismology and glaciology. Our role then was not much more than the small spot we made in the center of the snowy continent. Yet in a sense it was a vital dot, for we provided an anchor point for the three world chains of longitudinal science stations, and the Pole Station provided the vital midpoint in an otherwise 2,000-mile gap in the chain of IGY stations. Moreover, we had something unique to contribute because we had the longest period of darkness in the Antarctic.

The uniqueness of the Pole Station's six-month winter night was especially significant to the ionospheric program because the sun has a pronounced influence on the ionization of the rarefied gaseous elements of the upper atmosphere. Would six months of darkness so deteriorate the ionization that communication would prove impossible? Our central location was significant also because so many phenomena appear to have a concentric pattern about the earth's axis.

In truth, the location of most of the American IGY stations in the Antarctic had been chosen so they would have something special to contribute. Our South Pole Station provided the best spot for studying inland weather and the ionosphere. At Little America the IGY had one of its better opportunities to study the Auroral Australis phenomena. Also, Little America was developed as a radio communication center in order to act as the IGY's Antarctic weather central to collect, analyze and report on simultaneous, or synoptic, weather reports from all other meteorological observatories in the Antarctic. At inaccessible Byrd Station, deep drill operations were going on to probe 1,000 feet down into the snow and bring up cores of ice that had fallen as snow a thousand years ago. Byrd Station, also under the wreathlike zone of greatest auroral activity, was significantly located for analyzing the inland weather of West Antarctica. Then too, since the Pacific Coast has continued to defy access from the sea, the Byrd Station enclave would serve as the crossroads of West Antarctica traverse operations aimed at geological reconnaissance as to the age, thickness, movement and rate of accumulation of the snow and ice as well as gravity and other general geographic relationships of the entire region.

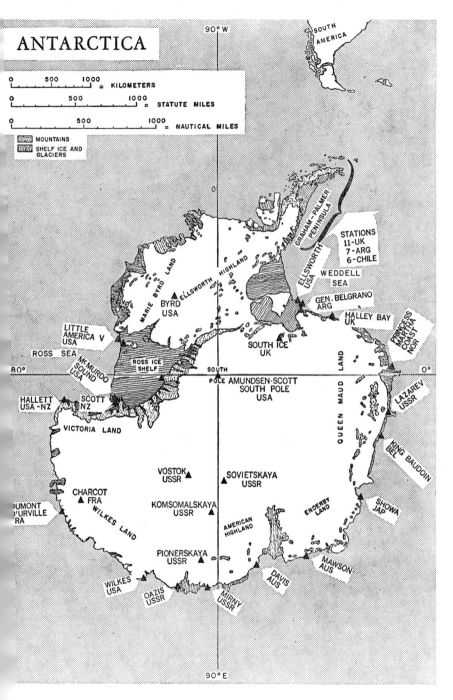

IGY stations in Antarctica 1956–1959.

At other stations scientists were studying the movement of glaciers, taking measurements, determining the age of the ice, its rate of flow and its growth and shrinkage. My own investigation of the Ross Ice Shelf on earlier expeditions had revealed that it grew at the rate of a third of a mile each year. When ten miles broke off the Barrier into the Ross Sea sometime between 1948 and 1955, this represented thirty years of ice build-up. Still other stations were planning traverses that would be as long or longer in distance traveled as the dash Bunny Fuchs planned for the summer season in late 1957 from the Shackleton Station across the South Pole to McMurdo Sound.

Wilkes Station, set on the coast of East Antarctica among Russian, Australian and French stations, was also under the circular belt of greatest auroral intensity, and lay in a complementary position on the opposite side of the magnetic and geomagnetic poles from Little America and Byrd Stations. This would aid in studies involving magnetism, the aurora, the ionosphere and cosmic radiation. The region was well located for study of the notoriously windy Wilkes Coast, and its warmer temperatures favored Antarctic animal life. My old friend Carl Eklund, scientific leader of this Station, was an ornithologist, and he expected to spend much of his time studying the life of penguins and skua gulls.

Ellsworth Station over on the Weddell Coast, with Captain Finn Ronne as its leader, lay close to British and Argentine stations. It fell in line with the chain of IGY stations coming down through South America from North America and the Western Arctic ice island stations so that it would provide an important link in that chain of stations. Study of meteorology and radio propagation phenomena were of particular importance here. It was hoped too that the over-snow glaciological traverses from this station could eventually link up with those from Byrd Station. The Ellsworth Station was also well situated to study whistling atmospherics, or "whistlers," to determine how they were generated and transmitted. Whistlers are "wolf call" sounding radio noises heard randomly at the audio-frequency end of the radio wave spectrum. They come in a variety of sounds often repeating their notes in an echoing fashion. The results of the "whistler" program were expected to contribute a great deal to the understanding of phenomena relating to radio wave propagation and geomagnetism. One theory about whistlers is that they are short bursts of radio waves, generated by lightning bolts, which travel far outside the maximum ion-density region of the ionosphere along the magnetic meridian and come back down to earth at the conjugate geomagnetic location to be found at similar latitudes in the opposite hemisphere. Then after striking the earth, the energy is reflected back along the same path to the point of origin. During its travels the energy is dispersed in frequency and can be recorded through radio as an audible whistle.

The inauguration of the South Pole Station's IGY program on July first, shortly after "Midnight" of the winter night, brought on our busiest period since the initial construction of the Station itself. Besides the various scientific disciplines carried out routinely, there were special World Days and Intervals called by the IGY when the giant storms on the sun that caused sunspots increased in intensity and required a stepping up of scientific observation. Such days ran our limited number of scientists ragged. For instead of sending up a balloon every twelve hours, the four-man Met group had at times to send one into the sky every six hours; instead of climbing the ladder to his Aurora Tower to make hourly observations, Arlo Landolt had to race up every fifteen minutes around the clock. Willi Hough had to send radio pulses into the ionosphere every five minutes instead of his usual fifteen minutes.

Our four meteorologists, with Ed Flowers in charge, worked in pairs around the clock whether there was a World Day or not. And like all other personnel, in addition to their scientific work they had to find time for their other camp duties, such as serving as housemouse, mess assistant to Chet Segers, and digging at least two hours a week in the snow mine.

Ed Flowers, Floyd Johnson, John Guerrero and Herb Hansen kept continuous weather records by remote telemetering from a wide variety of instruments exposed about 200 feet behind the Station. Because of possible malfunction due to low temperature and drift snow it was necessary, however, to check these instruments regularly. This meant that every three hours one of the four had to don an additional 15 or 20 pounds of clothes and stumble out over the drifts, lighting his path with a flashlight. It was on one such trip that Herb Hansen lost his way and found the camp by sheer accident.

At the instrument exposure site, which housed the regular thermometers, thermograph and resistance thermometers, the Met man had to work fast because of the cold. He also had to hold his breath while he read the thermometers, so that the exhaled vapor did not blur its fine gradations or warm its toluene fluid even a tenth of a degree. Then he had to check the anemometers which registered wind velocity and direction, and then the radiometers that determined the amount of heat being exchanged between the snow and the sky.

There were also four other thermometers: two on the 30-foot wind mast—one at five meters above the surface and the other at the top of the mast; and two other resistance thermometers—one on the snow surface and one 30 feet below the surface.

While outdoors, the Met men also looked for precipitation—ice crystals which might fall from an almost clear sky—and for clouds or changes in the snow surface due to wind or precipitation. In the winter when you turned your flashlight upward, you saw ice crystals falling continually, like dust beams in the attic when the sun pours through small peepholes. Some days the Met men saw "snow down," wispy balls of frost one to two inches in diameter, but so delicate that the slightest touch caused them to collapse into nothing. Under a 10-20 power glass, Remington and Taylor found that the feather-weight snow down looks like the assembly wires of an umbrella without the cover. The fine, dainty spicules are quite long. Snow down appears mysteriously when the air warms faster than the snow surface—i.e., goes up to −60° F. after being down to −90° F. for a few days.

The summer snow surface that had been relatively soft (although a man walking on it barely left a footprint) became increasingly glazed, while the sastrugi etching grew deeper, their forward edges undercut by the wind. Blizzards broke upon us frequently, piling the surface snow into drifts. Nevertheless, the annual snowfall at the South Pole was only about six inches, which would melt down perhaps to a half inch of water. And none of its particles were the fat snowflakes seen back home. Truly, we were on one of the great deserts of the world as far as the amount of precipitation was concerned. One snowfall in New York City produced far more snow than would be produced in several years at the South Pole.

To supplement our precipitation gauges atop the wind mast, Moose Remington and Cliff Dickey set out snow-measuring stakes in a three-mile-long straight line. Months later we checked the stakes and despite the hummocks and ripples of the sastrugi, the snow accumulation was at most six inches. Yet through the ages our snow had piled up until it was almost one and a half miles deep. Some rime precipitates like frost onto the snow surface but it may well be counterbalanced by direct ablation or evaporation into the air. Certainly the snow that falls or blows onto the surface at the Pole Station never melts. Lateral flow of the plateau which falls imperceptibly off to the coasts may carry some of the snow away. If the rate of accumulation is no greater than at present, and allowing for compression, the snow lying on the land itself must be two or three thousand years old.

In moonlit periods during the winter night, which occurred for two weeks each month except when clouds covered the sky, the Met men often recorded observing a halo around the moon. But it was a pale and fanciful halo compared with the rainbow-hued circles so often visible around the polar sun in the summer. Both these beautiful polar spectacles resulted from the minute ice crystals in the air.

But if the Met man took time to admire the moon, he was quickly brought back to earth by the brisk and biting breeze. His returning step quickened and a sheltering hand went up to protect his nose. The only Met man to sport a beard was Herb Hansen, and when he returned to the Station he soaked his beard in a basin of water to help it thaw out rapidly and melt the icicles, as did all of us who wore beards. John Guerrero had attempted to raise a beard, but after winning the Station's prize for the grubbiest beard he cut it off. Flowers, too, had tried to raise a beard, but it proved rather disappointing and he got rid of it. Floyd, an Arctic veteran, had tired of beards and stayed clean-shaven all year.

The Met men also studied the atmosphere high overhead by sending their large hydrogen balloons aloft with miniature radio transmitters suspended beneath. A maneuverable radio antenna housed in the plastic Rawin Dome above the mess hall tracked the balloon, and with an array of telemetering recorders registered its transmitted data on the temperature, humidity and pressure of the upper air plus wind direction and speed. Sometimes the Met men attached a tiny battery-powered light beneath the balloon to make it visible against the black sky and aid them in following its initial flight in the winter winds, which often blew in different directions at different altitudes.

Generally, Ed Flowers paced his day so that he would be present at the launching of the two balloons normally sent aloft each day. Since these were released twelve hours apart, Ed had a long day. Not only did he and the other Met men track the balloons as they soared upward to 90,000 feet, but they also had to prepare their hydrogen for their balloons in the iron monster from aluminum chips, caustic soda, and water. Their invention of soaking their balloons in warm diesel oil so the rubber remained pliable longer in the bitter cold aloft enabled them to get more height and they also developed a steam condenser between the hydrogen generator and the inflating balloon

to prevent water formed in the hydrogen-making process from getting
into the balloon. Floyd Johnson was responsible for inventing the
steam condenser. The Met men also sent up pilot balloons which they
could follow with a theodolite to record wind direction. Two of these
pibals went up, one at six A.M. and the other at six P.M. Considering
that the inflation shelter from which they released their balloons was
at the opposite end of camp from their Met shack, our weathermen
had a rugged time.

Nor was their job finished when the balloons were finally aloft.
For an hour or so after a balloon disappeared the meteorologists
plotted and interpreted the results. Summaries of their data were then
radioed to the central Antarctic weather station at Little America.
These were in addition to the measuring and recording on punch
cards of visibility, pressure, wind and temperature at four levels close
to and below the surface.

We at the South Pole Station had, in effect, the first true inland
weather station in the Antarctic. There was a theory that the intense
Antarctic cold prevented storms from breaking into the continent, that
all winds flowed out from its center and that the air was replenished
by air from the tropics which flowed in above the outgoing cold air.
Our findings did not support this theory, for we experienced storms
which apparently cut right across West Antarctica from the Weddell
Sea on the Atlantic side to the Ross Sea on the western Pacific side of
the continent.

I had anticipated, perhaps under the influence of this theory, that
we would have possibly the calmest weather and the clearest skies in
the world during winter, but actually a thin film of cloud covered the
sky much of the time although only occasionally was it heavy enough
to blot out the moon and stars.

Our weather balloons also confirmed the presence of an "inversion" zone about 1,000 to 1,500 feet above the surface where the
temperature of the air was warmer than at the surface. Strangely the
temperature at this zone generally remained within 5 degrees of
−40°. The constant dribble of ice crystals we experienced plus the
presence of this inversion zone suggests that supercooled moisture
brought in from the sea exists at that level, since −40° is the lowest
temperature to which water vapor may be cooled before crystallizing.

One of the most puzzling things about our winter was that we did
not hit the −120° F. temperature I had earlier predicted. Our average
temperature curve, which I had expected to round normally at the
bottom as it did elsewhere on the globe, instead flattened out in the

—90s F., save for a brief dip below this level at the beginning and end of our winter night. We could only hypothecate that the normal curve was flattened by the mixing action of the winds, which were considerably stronger than we had anticipated, and that without the winds the temperature curve would have dropped as predicted.

Our meteorologists also collected air samples to determine the carbon dioxide content of our air. There was widespread belief that the Antarctic did not have as great an amount of CO_2 in its atmosphere as did other places in the world, where industrial contamination from burning tremendous quantities of fossil fuel poured millions of tons of carbon dioxide into the atmosphere each year. Most of the carbon dioxide produced in this manner was known to be absorbed by the oceans and plant life, though there was the possibility that the carbon dioxide content of the atmosphere would rise sufficiently to affect the world's climate. It was already suspected that increased CO_2 was helping to make Greenland warmer. Studies made by our meteorologists as well as others in the Antarctic showed that the air of our continent contained just about as much CO_2 contamination as did that of the civilized world. It may be that the ocean plants of the lush polar waters are as effective in rebalancing oxygen and CO_2 as tropical vegetation on land.

All four men of the Met crew were competent, and it was seldom that they had to come to me for assistance on a problem or advice about their work. Ed Flowers had come to us from the U.S. Weather Bureau and had a strong sense of duty which permeated everything he did at the Pole, and forbade his asking for favors or help. I realized this when he arrived at the Pole with only the regulation 60 pounds of gear stipulated by Navy and Air Force regulations. No one else paid any attention to this regulation and our men had arrived with approximately 150 pounds of personal gear each. The result was that we had to scrounge about to provide Ed with adequate clothing to protect him from the cold.

As I noted earlier, Ed had not impressed me physically when I first met him but had soon revealed an amazing strength. When he and I went down in the snow mine he made the ice fly, even when we reached the lower levels where the ice was so solid it had to be extracted coal-mine fashion. A quiet sort who talked little and had an ingrained modesty, Ed had all-around capabilities and my admiration for him grew daily. Ed was always willing to take on any additional work which we felt would be of benefit to the Met program, which was certainly one reason why I valued him so highly.

Two of Ed's colleagues already had experience with polar climate before coming to the Antarctic. Thirty-five-year-old Floyd Johnson, a lean six-footer, had spent more than a year as a weather observer at Isachsen, Canada, only 770 miles from the North Pole. John Guerrero, our meteorological electronics expert, had attended the University of Alaska and worked for a few months as a technician on the DEW line, the Distant Early Warning system that spans Arctic North America.

Floyd was a good and conscientious worker with few idiosyncracies. When he had first heard there would be a South Pole Station he had sat at a ham radio set at Isachsen for three days before he was able to make contact with Washington and apply for a Met post there. In many ways Floyd was a lone wolf who nonetheless had many sage suggestions to make as a result of his previous experience in the Arctic. About the only problem I had with him was that he normally spoke so softly that it was difficult to hear him.

John Guerrero was another type altogether. John of the aloha shirt was a nonconformist both at work and at play. For instance, John was always cold when he went outdoors to check Met instruments because he refused to wear long-handled underwear. Many a time I would watch him return with his teeth shaking and his body shivering. John's father was Spanish and his Czech mother had once been cook to Thomas Masaryk, the first President and founder of Czechoslovakia. John was on the pudgy side, unlike Ed Flowers or Floyd Johnson. Fresh out of college at twenty-three, he did not come as well prepared in weather work in terms of actual experience as did the other Met men, but toward the end of our stay he came up with several excellent ideas and proved himself capable. Truly he came to the Pole a boy and left a man.

Herb Hansen, the only bearded Met man, was the most enthusiastic of the four Met men about being in the Antarctic. He lacked the physical strength of Ed Flowers, but Herb had the observant, critical mind so vital to a scientist. Whenever a strange phenomenon of nature was encountered, Herb seemed almost invariably to be the first to probe for its cause. This was the case, for instance, when the men first saw "snow down." While others stared at it in wonder, Herb came up with the cause of its formation. Herb was basically a teacher type who took his work as seriously as Ed Flowers. The chief difference in their approach was that Herb enjoyed explaining to others the discoveries he had made whereas Ed was more apt to refrain from volunteering an explanation until asked. And of the four Met men, Herb's analysis was often the most penetrating.

The tallest structure at the South Pole was the 75-foot makeshift antenna designed to send radio signals straight upward into the rarefied and ionized layers of upper air known as the ionosphere. Every 15 minutes of every day Willi Hough's automatic ionosphere sounder—the C-3 Monster—hurled radio pulses into the sky at successively higher frequencies, like a pianist running up the musical scale. A recorder listened for the echoes bouncing back and reproduced them on movie-film graphs called "ionograms."

The ionosphere is the electrically charged upper region of the atmosphere some 50 to 250 miles above the earth's surface. It acts as a giant mirror for long-range radio communications, reflecting radio waves back downward and thus enabling messages to be sent far beyond the horizon. By reflecting radio waves, the ionosphere thus makes possible radio telephony and navigation and long-range radio communication.

Scientists have long been aware of the fact that it is the sun's radiation which energizes the ionosphere. One question that Willi hoped to answer was whether or not the ionosphere thinned out almost to the point of disappearing at the South Pole where there is no direct solar radiation for six months of the year. For over the Pole, where sunlight never reaches the lower levels of the ionosphere in winter, the boundary between constant darkness and constant sunlight lay 330 miles above us. Here one could readily determine whether or not the sun was the sole energizer of the ionosphere.

To our surprise, Willi found that ionization remained high all winter despite the darkness. Moreover, small daily fluctuations occurred in the ionosphere. These variations gave evidence of a secondary ionizing agent other than direct radiation from the sun, perhaps something related to the earth's magnetic field. Willi's findings may contribute appreciably to achieving new standard concepts of the ionization and recombination processes in the earth's atmosphere.

The lowest reflecting E layer of the ionosphere was prominent in summer, but it became a sporadic or ghostlike layer in winter and often disappeared entirely. Above this were F_1 and F_2 layers in summer which combined into a single layer in winter and furnished the main reflecting region for transpolar radio communication.

Although we were at the Geographic Pole, the behavior of the ionosphere was eccentric above us. Each day when the sun lined up

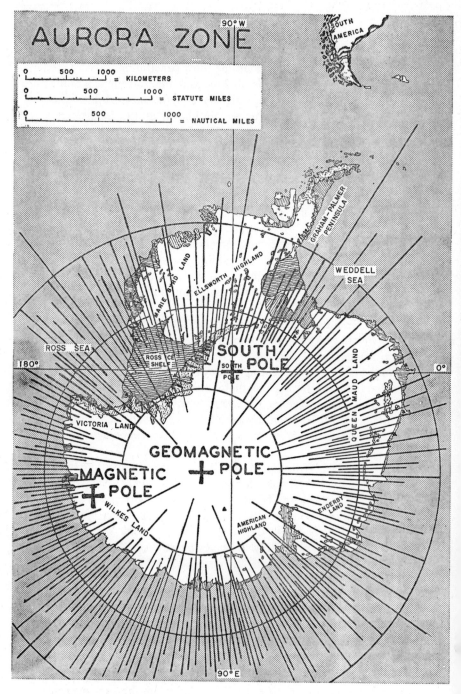

Maximum aurora intensity forms a wreath centered around the Geomagnetic Pole as shown by the rays.

with the geomagnetic and magnetic poles which lay in the direction of Australia, the reflecting layer of the ionosphere was noticeably higher than at other times and, conversely, when the sun was opposite the magnetic and geomagnetic poles, the reflective layer was noticeably lower. In addition some unexplained fluctuations in the ionosphere also appeared day after day near the same hours, the causes of which we in the field could not explain.

Willi's work on the ionosphere, combined with his studies of earth magnetism, kept him busy. In addition to keeping his Monster healthily firing every fifteen minutes, he and his assistant, Bob, also had to develop and interpret his ionogram films each day.

Willi was in the upper third in age among the Station's personnel. Wiry and second tallest to Jack Tuck, he was physically strong and probably possessed the best mechanical ability at the Pole. Not only did he run his own programs but he also helped on the aurora program, repaired our radio equipment and heaters and advised on tractor and other mechanical repairs. Willi had a level head, and a great enthusiasm for a variety of subjects. One often found him, a green parachute cord holding his camera from his neck, taking pictures of any unusual event or scientific phenomenon.

Equally as busy as Willi was Bob Benson, who, in addition to helping when he could with the ionosphere and aurora research, also ran our seismology, or earthquake, program.

To keep his delicate seismometer from detecting camp vibrations as well as earthquakes, we had earlier built the thousand-foot tunnel ending in a pit for his seismometer. In working to set his seismometer in place properly, Bob was able to point to thick frost-produced calluses on his knees from long hours spent kneeling on cold snow to adjust his delicate equipment in the pit. Aluminum-foil shielding was installed over the whole chest covering his instrument to keep out stray electric currents emitted from the C-3 ionosphere and the camp radio transmitter. Bob often scurried through the tunnel to check both the insulation and the seismometer by lantern light. After a while, his attitude toward the tunnel grew so possessive that he expressed a hurt which may or may not have been feigned whenever anyone stumbled over the tunnel top by accident. "Who's been messing up my tunnel again?" he would say as he came stumbling into the Station. Moose, our lumbering glaciologist, out examining the snow surface was often the culprit.

Bob had never worked in seismology before coming to the Pole, and he had actually come down to assist Willi. His undergraduate work had been in math and astronomy, but his mind was so keen that he was soon doing a lion's share of the work. No one who worked with him failed to come away sensing that one day he would make his mark in the world as a top scientist.

Bob's seismology program here at the Pole was unique among the 16 IGY seismic stations. Not only were we sitting on top of a mile or so of ice and snow,* but Bob's program was the first one to be run in the dead center of the polar regions. There was some speculation as to whether distant earthquakes would be recorded by a seismology station here at the Pole, due to the cushioning effect of the great depth of snow beneath the surface. And we expected few quakes close to the Pole since the stresses at work on the earth, as mentioned earlier, are more apt to make themselves felt in the temperate and equatorial latitudes where adjustments to compensate for changes in the earth's balance are most likely accomplished.

Yet Bob's instruments recorded an average of three disturbances every two days. Almost one-half of these were subsequently confirmed to us from Washington as having been recorded also at other stations. The most distant of these was in the Kamchatka Peninsula off eastern Siberia some 9,900 miles away. Many of the disturbances not verified were undoubtedly caused by snow tremors, snow slides and other continental phenomena, although a true answer to all of their causes is still being sought in study of the records.

Bob was a man of enormous appetite and energy although he seldom managed to get more than five consecutive hours of sleep each night, what with his work, his study and his dozens of side interests. Tall and slim, he was a fine-looking lad with a congenial smile that spread above his light-colored chin whiskers.

Bob was never ruffled by the problems he faced in keeping his delicate equipment working. I remember marveling at his patience as I watched him work a full week repairing a galvanometer. One of the broken parts was a frail gold strip less than 1/1000 of an inch thick! I'm told that there were perhaps only a very few persons in the entire United States technically qualified to make such repairs. In the first place, he had to use strong magnifying glasses even to see the gold strip; and second, the patience and steadiness of hand required were almost inhuman.

When Bob left the University of Minnesota to come south, his major professor sagely advised him to dream up some experiments all

---

* 8,300 feet of snow and 900 feet of land above sea level, as determined by Linehan in December, 1957.

his own. "It doesn't matter too much what they are, so long as they are your own and you follow them through," the professor added. Bob had many projects, but fun loving as he was he carried out one just to take back to the Prof. Meticulously every night before his bedtime Bob would go down to the head and ceremoniously place a long laboratory thermometer beneath the false toilet seat lid. After 155 days of observation he compiled the results: *The seat temperature averages −21.8° F. The maximum temperature was −7° and the minimum −39° F.* Then he made his conclusion in the best scientific manner. *I believe my observations point the reason why our library there in the head has met with a cool reception.*

Benson's more serious experiments included his elaborate photography. The most sensational of his many photographs was a five-day shot of the setting moon as it passed in broad band sweeps past his homemade pinhole camera. Each streak was nearly horizontal and separated by the three degrees or so of the rate the moon sank each day.

Throughout the dark winter night we observed frequent displays of the Aurora Australis, or southern lights, which was the Antarctic equivalent of the Aurora Borealis. Besides the red aurora that ushered in the IGY, numerous other of our auroras were beautiful but less breath-takingly so than those I remembered at Little America. The typical display was a series of undulating curtains of varied colors across the heavens, usually radium watch dial colored with an orchid tone at the bottom.

It was the job of Arlo Landolt, our aurora specialist, to keep a continuous record of these displays with a spectograph and an all-sky camera. Normally, Arlo made hourly visual observations, though on World Days he did so at fifteen-minute intervals. Arlo's observations were made in the dark boxlike Aurora Tower atop the science building, and when the aurora was especially active, setting the sky ablaze with light, he virtually lived up there, often getting no more than two or three hours of sleep a night. Like the irregularities in the ionosphere, geomagnetism and cosmic rays, the aurora is directly related to solar activities and radio blackouts.

As mentioned before, there is a circular band of maximum auroral intensity about 18° from the Geomagnetic Pole. Since we at the Geographic Pole were some 12° from the Geomagnetic Pole, we had not expected to encounter as much auroral activity as at Little America, Byrd, Wilkes and Ellsworth stations, which lay almost directly under the band of greatest intensity. Actually we saw auroral displays almost daily and they were of greater intensity than anticipated, although not as intense as those witnessed under the auroral ring. I had never, however, seen a red aurora like the one I witnessed there at the Pole, although I had seen considerably more lavish displays in the course of my three winters at Little America. The red aurora was also witnessed at other IGY Antarctic stations, and occurred during one of the most violent magnetic storms and severe radio blackouts experienced for years.

Arlo, the shortest man in camp and the lightest, looked older than his twenty-one years because of his dark thick beard. He was seldom without a cigar or his pipe. Arlo was another whose future as a scientist looked assured from the abilities he displayed at the Pole. Despite his small stature, Arlo was extremely dependable in work parties. Casting aside his scientific ability and his physical labor, Arlo would still have been a welcome addition at the Pole. For he was a man of eternal good spirits possessed of an infectious laugh which broke many a tense period at the Station.

While Arlo worked above the camp, Moose Remington worked below it. As our glaciologist, his was the coldest job of all. It seemed that when Moose was not digging in the snow and ice outside, he was digging in the snow mine. Of course when he had removed a block of ice for study, he could retire to his laboratory. But even here, to keep his specimens from melting, he maintained a temperature of about −25°.

Basically, Moose's job was to discover as much as possible about climate in years gone by through the study of snow. This work required him to spend time sawing blocks out of our snow mine wall. Each of his blocks was three feet long, one foot wide and one foot thick and weighed about 75 pounds, and Moose had to be meticulous, since the blocks could contain no cracks or breaks. It took an hour or two to cut the block without breaking it and then he had to struggle to the top of the snow mine with it. Remington was hard pressed to process a block or two a day under this system.

At other IGY stations where the temperatures were considerably higher, Weasels used to help dig out glaciology pits. These were dug almost straight down and a man could ride in a box to the depth at which he was working. Then when he cut his block, he placed it in the box and the Weasel pulled it up. Remington had none of these advantages; however, he had had the physical aid of every man in camp to dig the mine.

Once he had a block in his cold room, Moose sliced it into sections about one inch thick, three feet long and a foot wide. Next he laid these long thin slabs on top of his table, noted the layers and determined their density. After this he took a picture of each in order to photograph the striations.

These photographs, together with melt-water samples, were sent home later for analysis and study, which indicated that it is possible to read yearly layers in much the way tree rings are read. A study of this sort should eventually show precisely how much the polar icecap grows in an average year, and how much it has actually grown, layer by layer, over past centuries. But the greatest accomplishment of our glaciology program was the digging of the 90-foot-deep pit in −60° temperature. Its gradual incline would make it easier for glaciologists who would follow us the next year to proceed with an inch-by-inch analysis of the snow from the surface down as far as possible. Who knew, they might even dig the pit deeper!

The snow at the Pole was perhaps as chemically pure as can be imagined. Yet when we melted down samples of it as part of the glaciology program and poured it over a small plastic trough with magnets beneath, we captured small, almost invisible, particles which appeared under a magnifying glass to be spheres, some solid and some hollow. Later we also found considerable quantities of these in the bottom of the snow melter. They proved to be very similar to ones recovered from the snow of the Greenland Icecap. There is still considerable discussion as to whether these are dust from the earth or actual micro-meteorites.

As scientific leader of the Station, my function was, of course, to keep our scientific programs running smoothly. When the men had problems in their disciplines, I helped them to the best of my ability, but in most cases the men needed little supervision. My personal field of interest was glaciology and climatology and I undertook a number of short-term glacial technique projects which I turned over to Moose Remington after a while on the principle that the various disciplines should handle matters within their bailiwick. One of these was the concept of the light table, which made it possible to photograph the striations of the glaciological samples. Another was a method of measuring the size and shape of ice crystals by direct shadow exposure on a piece of unexposed photograph film without benefit of a camera.

Among my own projects was the long series of star shots Jack and I made to determine the true location of the Geographic South Pole. Another was a static counter that Cliff Dickey of Jack's crew and I constructed to record the static electricity accumulating on the antenna devices protruding above the science building. By means of this counter we were able to show during one or two severe blizzards that there was a reasonable correlation between the static electricity our detector recorded and the concurrent fluctuations in the wind as recorded by the Station anemometer.

I had been supplied some ancient but serviceable cameras by the Army for various experiments on which Arlo and I worked together. One of the more successful was a series of star shots running for as long as twenty-four hours. Delicate changes in filmy cloud covers were detectable. I also spent many hours analyzing and summarizing the hourly changes in temperature and wind speed recorded by our instruments. I made these into tables showing the per cent of hours a month that each temperature or wind speed occurred.

Dickey, whose field was electronics, was of great help to the IGY men in our various disciplines as well as keeping our radios going. This latter task was often difficult because he lacked essential repair parts and had to work under conditions where the sunspots produced frequent radio blackouts. One of his problems in caring for our radios was that soot from the galley accumulated on these vital parts. This was a problem that the Met men faced too, since the Met shack and radio headquarters were in the same building as the galley. Both Dickey and the Met group spent a great deal of time taking their instruments apart and washing them with soap and water until Oz finally erected a partition sealing off the galley from the instrument rooms.

"Skinny," as some of the men called Dickey, had a passion for gardening and he helped Doc Taylor and me grow the first hydroponic garden at the South Pole. The first plant to survive a whole year at the Pole was a potted philodendron which we nursed with artificial light. A neighbor in Arlington had given it to me and it had had a rough trip to the Pole and started with no leaves at all.

My hydroponic garden was an interesting affair. Dickey and I constructed it in a large baking pan of heavy-gauge aluminum which stood about eight inches high and twenty-one inches long. I painted the inside with varnish to keep the water and chemicals off the metal and inserted it into a pasteboard box. A thin plastic-clear window lid went over the top, and I covered the entire box with aluminum foil as a vapor barrier and insulator. Then, after varnishing three breadbasket trays, I set them inside the aluminum pan. The first tray contained sweet potatoes and my philodendron. The other two had

South Pole Temperature Distribution by Percentages

°F.	1958 Jan.	1958 Feb.	1957 Mar.	1957 Apr.	1957 May	1957 June	1957 July	1957 Aug.	1957 Sept.	1957 Oct.	1957 Nov.	1957 Dec.	Year
+20													
+10	1.0												1.0
0	21.5	2.2									6.2	17.9	4.0
−10	72.8	12.7									21.4	80.5	15.6
−20	4.7	28.6		2.4							6.8	1.6	3.7
−30		31.8	0.5	3.0	5.7						22.1		5.2
−40		21.3	6.3	2.1	7.1	1.0	3.6	1.2		1.6	28.1		6.0
−50		3.4	19.9	12.1	12.1	5.7	10.1	10.6	2.1	39.1	15.4		10.9
−60			41.9	19.0	27.4	51.0	13.7	32.8	16.9	34.4			19.8
−70			26.9	36.2	21.5	29.9	20.7	28.4	27.4	18.3			17.4
−80			4.5	25.2	15.7	8.7	25.3	16.3	33.8	6.6			11.3
−90					10.4	3.7	26.6	10.6	19.0				5.9
−100						0.1		0.1	0.8				0.1
−110													

South Pole Wind Speed Distribution by Percentages

Knots †	1957 Jan.	1957 Feb.	1957 Mar.	1957 Apr.	1957 May	1957 June	1957 July	1957 Aug.	1957 Sept.	1957 Oct.	1956 * Nov.	1956 * Dec.	* Year
Calm	1.2	1.3	1.1	0.1	1.7	0.0	0.5	0.0	1.1	0.1	6.9	9.7	2.0
	16.1	12.4	6.6	0.6	3.2	0.0	2.1	0.5	2.6	1.2	27.8	29.8	8.6
5	45.2	35.5	29.7	10.3	16.3	2.3	17.7	9.2	16.1	18.5	41.7	52.0	24.5
10	26.2	33.9	41.4	40.6	34.3	33.5	29.7	30.9	54.2	39.6	22.2	7.7	32.8
15	8.9	16.2	15.6	29.4	20.4	37.8	24.2	41.0	19.5	29.8	1.4	0.0	20.3
20	2.4	0.7	5.6	16.5	15.6	24.6	14.9	16.4	3.9	9.4	0.0	0.8	9.3
25	0.0	0.0	0.0	2.5	4.7	1.8	10.3	2.0	2.5	1.4	0.0	0.0	2.1
30	0.0	0.0	0.0	0.0	3.8	0.0	0.6	0.0	0.1	0.0	0.0	0.0	0.4
over 30													

Note: low winds in Nov., through Feb. during summer season.
Note: high winds in Mar. through October during winter season.
* Includes non-standard observations.
† 6 knots equal approximately 7 miles per hour.

burlap strips at their bottom, on and under which I planted water cress seeds, radishes and clover.

The water cress sprang into leaf in 48 hours. And in general, success attended our efforts at gardening except for one major difficulty. Molds and other fungi reared their ugly heads and put up a strong rear-guard fight to destroy what we had so lovingly nurtured.

Doc Taylor's scientific curiosity was equally as keen as that found among our regular IGY crew. With a mind as sharp as a razor and an inquisitiveness that reached in all directions, he had numerous scientific sidelines from his medical practice. It is to Doc Taylor that I must attribute what was perhaps one of the most sensational discoveries made at the South Pole. It was made in carrying out a project Doc and I had planned with a group of mycologists before coming to the Pole.

Taking a sample of uncontaminated snow from the bottom of the snow mine and melting it down in a sterile container, he found it contained spores and pollen grains. He made an ingenious device which permitted all of the snow to melt inside a sterile system so that each drop dripped through a small filter. Next, without exposing the filter to possible contamination, he inserted some sterile nutrient on the filter and then set the entire container in an incubator. Using great pains to nurture the invisible particles, he managed to cultivate fungi into visible colonies that resembled the typical green and white molds that grow on stale bread. We could only conclude that the molds had grown from spores that had somehow been carried to the Pole by high-altitude winds and deposited there to be preserved, perhaps for centuries, in the polar deep freeze.

Taylor also invented some astonishing gadgets. On one occasion he dreamed up a scheme to melt a hole in the snow surface and continue downward right through the entire icecap. His plan was to heat a large piece of metal and drop it on the snow. I argued with him that his idea would not succeed because he did not take into consideration the thermal capacity of his metal as compared to that of the ice. His industry and enthusiasm outweighed his respect for my judgment, and he found a big chunk of metal, attached a chain to it and heated it on Chet's stove until it was red-hot.

All the men gathered at Doc's testing point to watch his plan in action. Guesses had been made that the metal would penetrate anywhere from 10 to 15 feet into the ice, heralding the beginning of the eventual disclosure of what lay at the bottom of the South Pole. Doc emerged grim-faced for the countdown and dropped the hot metal.

Instead of going down, it merely lay sizzling on the surface and cooled almost immediately. "Well, another good idea shot," Doc said, shrugged and walked away.

Taylor also dreamed up a monorail system to carry things through our tunnels. This was an excellent idea but we lacked the materials to construct one. Lacking a clinical incubator at one stage, he built one from scratch. The strap steel spring thermostat was so sensitive the light bulb went on and off like a movie projector.

Perhaps his most fantastic invention was his "insomniometer"—a device for recording movements men made while they slept. Built principally of tin cans and powered by dripping water, it marked with a stylus on smoked paper wrapped on a drum the motions of strings running to a sleeper's mattress and bed springs. The drum was rotated by the dripping-water drive. Doc also set up a watch with a pointer to scratch time marks on the smoked paper.

Doc worked on his insomniometer for weeks. Then he put it to use, though a test graph showed only a monotonous straight line. His subject, Bob Benson, who generally stayed up nineteen hours each day, slept five hours without moving a muscle! After the second modification of his third revision in electrical contact form exploded in a blinding flash of blue light, Doc Taylor finally gave up in disgust.

There were others in Jack's support crew besides Dickey and Doc Taylor who helped out our scientists. For instance, Earl Johnson, our plump utility man, helped Arlo take his aurora observations at times, and Herb Hansen and Floyd Johnson went out of their way to teach our youngest man in camp, Mel Havener, our mechanic and barber, the rudiments of meteorology so that he could help make observations.

When I had first considered going to the Pole, I had questioned how much scientific work would actually be accomplished. I had felt it would require almost all the combined efforts of the Station's personnel merely to stay alive. So it was gratifying that as things turned out, the results of our scientific endeavors were of a reasonably high order.

One must never underestimate mankind—not even at the ends of the earth.

Chapter 27

LIVING IN ISOLATION

T HIS is a poorly devised arrangement for running a small isolated camp," I had said to Jack Tuck even before the winter night set in. "A split command for eighteen men can lead to all sorts of troubles unless we can consciously work together as a team. It's the kind of thing that always happens when men plan an expedition they know they won't be on themselves. They always let their theories run rampant at the expense of what they know is practical."

Fortunately Jack readily agreed to eliminate any local distinction between the scientific staff and the naval support group. To have the camp divided nine and nine into "sheep and goats" was asking for serious trouble.

I told our eighteen men frankly that though they were strangers to each other when they came to the Pole, by the time they left they would know each other better than they knew their own families. For there would be no real escape from one another, no possibility of getting away, and no other men to see and listen to for almost a year. "We are all in the same dark pickle barrel," I told them.

Leadership in a small and isolated community has to be planned and carried out with precision, yet it must also appear matter-of-fact or it will be offensive. One of Admiral Byrd's chief tenets regarding leadership in Antarctic was that a leader had to remain aloof to keep group morale high. This, he felt, gave a sense of security to the men by causing them to believe their leader was different from and somehow superior to them, whether he really was or not. In addition, where a leader had to make arbitrary decisions it was important that he not get too close to the men under his command. At the same time, therapeutic leadership was also essential, so that a man would be willing first of all to come to you with his personal problems, and second, that he would feel you were interested in his welfare.

There are other important ingredients in successful Antarctic leadership. One is to avoid a caste system. All men must be put on an equal basis and no favoritism must be shown any individual. Each troublesome person has to be treated on the basis of his own character. For instance, some individuals must be handled with sympathy; others with a firm hand. Another, and perhaps the key, factor in maintaining group discipline is to place great reliance on the "group-pressure system." Because there can be no strong-arm leadership in isolated living, the wise leader lets the group "ride" a man who is shirking his duty or becoming obnoxious. But the leader's sense of timing must be right. When the riding is overdone or when it is unfair, he must step in to get things back on an even keel. At the same time, when he does step in he must handle the problem in such a manner as to make clear that no one can get away with shirking or obnoxious behavior.

Sometimes men would come to me and complain that certain individuals were egging them on to an eventual fight. Others complained that they were irritated by persons they disliked. "So you don't like him," I would say. "Then live *around* him. And remember that you don't have to live with him after you leave here."

On minor infractions, a man will not be offended by group discipline. On one occasion, for instance, Junior Waldron and Mel Havener played a tape recorder until 2:30 A.M. and kept most of the barracks building awake. Early the next morning while Junior was still asleep, the men entered his room, turned on his lights, beat on the walls and clanged pot covers together. Junior got the point and later went around and apologized for his thoughtlessness.

Our men at the South Pole Station had undergone extensive psychological testing before being finally selected. This was important in weeding out men who suffered from claustrophobia or mental disorders. The men were also tested for manly interests and qualities.

As a matter of fact, one striking characteristic of the men on all six of the Antarctic expeditions I have gone on is that almost all were of the type popularly known as "he-men." Expeditions may have brought men together in a womanless world, yet paradoxically the men who went on such adventures had a great regard for women. They might get along without them during a stay in the Antarctic but they did not like it one bit.

Only a single instance stands out in my mind where this was apparently not so. We had the misfortune on an earlier expedition to have a man who had hidden his tendency toward homosexuality. But the strain of keeping his feelings pent up within him proved too great a burden during the winter night and he attempted suicide rather than reveal them. Later when we returned to civilization he succeeded in doing away with himself.

The true penalties then for living in the isolation of the Antarctic were the absence of women and families, exotic foods, knowledge of what was going on in the outside world and a general lack of privacy. Away from the influence of women, men have a tendency to become unkempt and sometimes surly as they suppress their heartfelt emotions behind a hardened exterior of sham gruffness. Even though Chet's food was excellent, men drooled over the thought of a special meal they had enjoyed back in civilization. As for news of the outside world, I knew from previous experiences that it would be years after I returned before I would catch up with news events and deaths that had occurred during my absence. I often missed the entire birth, life and burial of a popular piece of music without ever having heard of it.

Privacy was not possible in a camp the size of the South Pole Station. Yet even in a crowded base such as ours, men somehow found opportunity for solitude. At the Pole, for instance, when I went to bed I could almost draw a blind on my life at the Pole and enter into another world mentally in which I would read and think about matters away from the Pole. In fact, I resented it a bit when someone invaded the privacy of my secret life and thoughts, so that in a true sense this forced solitude was isolation within isolation.

Whenever Admiral Byrd was asked what men missed most on Antarctic expeditions, he would reply with the single word "temptation." This was a splendid summation. Whatever a man cannot have, he wants. Things taken for granted become priceless in their absence. Perhaps one of our Pole men (just which one I do not recall) put it well when I asked him what he missed most. "Tomatoes," he blurted. "Both kinds."

This year, only the Russians brought women along to the Antarctic: women scientists and stewardesses served aboard Soviet IGY ships. From all reports they were capable and were no problem. The only American women to get to the Antarctic in 1957 were two Pan-American stewardesses who stayed at McMurdo for just a few hours.

Another thing the men missed at the Pole were pets. I had suggested bringing in birds and fish, but this suggestion had been rejected. On earlier expeditions we had had many dogs and the men had lavished attention on them. Jack Tuck's Bravo was the only pet at the South Pole, but he was by and large a one-man dog. When Jack was ill on one occasion, Bravo lay at the foot of his bunk and would not take his eyes off Jack. And when Jack went off to the snow mine for his hours of exhausting digging, Bravo fretted continuously, looking all about the camp for Jack until he returned. (A Bravo fence kept him out of the snow mine.) I wrestled occasionally with Bravo, and Doc Taylor let him tug ferociously on his sweater sleeve in a make-believe tug of war, but no man cared to expose a hand when he dropped leftovers into Bravo's dish in the mess hall.

The pressures of close-quarters living were numerous but never serious at the Pole Station. Nevertheless, in the course of our year there, every man had at least a minor personality problem involving someone else. Doc Taylor made his own investigation of daily attitudes with a unique chart that he devised.

He distributed a clip board, paper and pencil to each man. They were to record their state of mind for the entire day and whether they had had a good night's sleep. Doc Taylor devised a scale from a low of 1 to a high of 5, and instructed the men to insert the proper number in the DAY and NIGHT columns. When a man was a bit sad and his self-determined rating was low, others would nod and say, "Gee, let's get him a radio contact with his family." Generally this worked wonders and produced a 5 for that day.

The men all recognized that a bad night was invariably followed by a bad day. But a bad day was not always followed by a bad night. Once during the winter night, I had worked late for several consecutive days and felt myself keyed up. Two nights in a row I gave myself a 2. Then I had a hamgram from Ruth, and the poor pattern changed abruptly.

When Doc Taylor summarized his 1–5 Day and Night Study, he said to me, "Paul, you are going to be surprised at my astounding discovery that the average is 3, or normal."

At one time Doc considered moving from our Jamesway to the barracks building where ratings were lower and some of the men were having petty arguments with one another. But Jack and I dissuaded him and it was for the best.

Well-meaning psychologists back in the States hoped to make use of our experience living in isolation during the six-month winter night by using us as guinea pigs to supply them with data. Of course there was nothing wrong with this proposal, for we were a unique breed on the face of the earth and the scientific value of a study of our small isolated group could have borne fruitful results. However, some of the tests they sent us to take from their far-off position proved injurious to Station morale.

Each man was to take one of these tests at the outset of the winter night and again at its middle and end. Each test consisted of true-and-false questions, paragraphs to be completed, pictures to explain, and questions regarding opinions of others in camp. This last test was dangerous because it forced each man to examine himself and the camp clinically and to take apart his buddies. Other tests seemed condescending in attitude to our hard-working crew.

Certainly there was nothing wrong in asking a man several times in the course of a period of months to complete a paragraph beginning: "A woman is a . . ." Where a man might initially write a dull paragraph, by the time winter ended he would often reach new heights of lyrical description. But the pictures he was asked to explain and the buddy test were another matter.

The first time the men took the picture-explanation test they explained the scenes as they saw them. However, when the same five pictures came up again in the second testing, most of the men were smart enough to realize that their interpretation of the pictures was intended to reveal any deterioration they had suffered in the interim. As a result, none explained them seriously. Some deliberately wrote lewd explanations that would have singed the eyes of most readers. Others made up the most preposterous tales their minds could devise.

For instance, one of the pictures depicted a man standing on a piece of floe ice with one arm raised, the shore in the background and a ship to one side. It obviously was intended to raise a melodramatic concept of a man adrift on an ice floe. "If those psychologists are looking for something screwy," one of the men said with a laugh, "then I'll give them something."

His explanation ran as follows:

A bunch of guys on the ship got tight. Looking over the rail, they saw that the bay ice had broken up. "What do you say we fit it all back together again like a jigsaw puzzle?" one of them shouted.

They managed to fit all the pieces together again with the exception of one piece that they could not find. One man had continued the search, and just before he was ready to give up he found the piece of ice. So here he stood standing on that last piece and yelling back to the boat, "Guys, I found it!"

The Buddy Test, however, was the test that almost caused serious trouble. It revealed poor psychological thinking on the part of the psychologists, for the questions asked were of a nature disruptive to our continued peace in camp. The Buddy Test required each man to list his best friends among the Pole personnel, as well as those he disliked most. Then he had to explain why he liked and disliked the persons in question.

The men, who had never given consideration to such matters, now found themselves forced to choose sides. "Those psychologists are trying to split us up," one man charged. "I'm not going to do it."

The entire Station was soon up in arms at the Buddy Test. Wisely, Doc Taylor destroyed the papers. Then he got in touch with the psychologists by radio and persuaded them to call off further Buddy Tests at the Pole or other such isolated small communities.

In general, the men were too busy to get into serious trouble. The IGY men especially had to run from morning to night to complete their observations, and in between times often had to straighten out serious problems involving maintenance of their instruments. The cold slowed down cameras, made emulsions alter chemical composition, cracked vital parts of instruments—and sapped human energy. Then there were the community tasks that always seemed to pop up just as they felt like relaxing. Jack's crew, too, had their work problems. The question of maintaining radio contact with the outside world plagued us continually; new electrical and heating difficulties cropped up unexpectedly; tractor and Weasel repairs for the coming summer were hampered by the absence of spare parts and the necessity to devise adequate substitutes.

The threat of fire was always on our minds. Once Mel Havener and Floyd Johnson were working on a gasoline-powered Herman-Nelson heater in the warming room of the inflation shelter when the stove caught fire. Luckily their fire extinguisher was next to them and they managed to extinguish the blaze before the gasoline fire spread. Another time one of our jet heaters backfired and started a fire in the science building. But here again it was quickly put out, though the stove was ruined by the powdered extinguishing matter.

Boredom and too much leisure time had caused trouble on some of the earlier expeditions I went on. But these were not our problem at the Pole. Nevertheless, we did have some. For instance, at the outset there was some resentment on the part of various individuals in Jack's Navy support crew against the IGY men. These tensions were based primarily on the fact that the scientists were better paid and were doing professional work. Some of the Navy men groused and referred to the IGY personnel as "sand crabs." However, this early ceased to be a problem when the IGY men took on some of the heaviest manual labor connected with buttoning up the camp for winter and carried the load in supplying the camp with fresh snow for the melter, as well as sharing housemouse and mess duties. In addition, five of the IGY men lived in the barracks building and were not standoffish in any respect.

There were special built-in tensions, however, involving the entire IGY group. Contributing chiefly to these was the men's feeling that they were being forgotten by the IGY national group back in Washington. Added to this was a concern that the ground rules laid down for their scientific observations were at times needlessly bureaucratic and tended to impede the men's efforts. Actually, they were right on both counts, though it was my business to persuade them to ignore these irksome matters. As a new organization, the IGY had quickly become even more bureaucratic than the government at times and far too impersonal. Of course, they had a multitude of problems and insufficient time or help. Seldom however did the national staff take time to get in touch with our Station by radio, and when they did, all too often it was to register some petty complaint. Also, our science staff was being made to understand that they were simply employees who could be ordered to carry out certain tasks while conclusions would be drawn by the desk sitters in Washington.

There were also minor arbitrary rulings that momentarily took the heart out of our hard-working and capable men. One of these was a shortsighted regulation that they were not to discuss their work on the ham radio set with other IGY scientists at other Antarctic stations. The men were shocked by this order and morale suffered until we were able to get this dictum removed. Another odd display occurred on the winter night "Midnight," June 22, when we were ordered not to reply to congratulatory messages from foreign IGY stations in the Antarctic, since this would tend to tie up the radio sets. However, we boldly ignored this, for not to have exchanged messages would have been taken as a show of rudeness by the leaders of other stations in the Antarctic, some of whom I knew well.

I was not greatly upset by these frictions, however, for I had often observed on earlier expeditions, as well as during the war, that field groups and headquarters often tend to feel the other is performing below par, particularly when communications are poor. Perhaps the old saying that distance makes the heart grow fonder is not all that correct.

It was not enough for Jack and me to sit and wait until problems arose. Nor was it wise to make decisions without consulting some of the other men: especially when we knew a decision would be unpopular.

The result was that we set up a council of five which met infrequently but at critical times. Besides Jack and I, other members of the council were Doc Taylor, Ed Flowers and Willi Hough. From time to time this council recommended men for outstanding work not in their field. It was of interest to me how proud the recipients were to receive our typewritten notations: ON BEHALF OF ALL MEMBERS OF THE STATION WE WISH TO EXPRESS OUR APPRECIATION FOR THE EXCELLENT JOB YOU HAVE VOLUNTARILY DONE FOR THE BENEFIT OF ALL HANDS.

In addition to this camp council there was another council, a streamlined affair consisting of Jack, Doc and myself which met informally almost daily to take up immediate problems. A young man of humor, kindness and the highest integrity and ability, Doc Taylor's basic thought on the subject of morale maintenance was a call for strict discipline. But in a camp such as ours, this would only have caused morale to deteriorate. In the first place, strict discipline cannot be maintained without the threat of punishment and there were no facilities for a court-martial at the Pole Station. And secondly, we were a mixed group of military and civilians, and it is not easy to order civilians around under the best of circumstances. Therefore, Jack and I saw to it that disciplining was done indirectly, slowly and without any onus of punishment.

Morale is a word of many meanings, as I so well learned on other expeditions. Admiral Byrd, on his first expedition, brought along a morale officer whose job it was to keep our spirits high. This man was remarkable in a sense because he equated good morale with an ability to play the ukulele. He had brought along boxes of ukuleles and was prepared to teach us how to strum the strings to keep us from growing morose or homesick. Unfortunately, the men considered it a morale booster not to have him or his ukuleles around.

One of the surprising things about any major expedition is the way in which leadership qualities will arise from unsuspected quarters. On one expedition I appointed a man as my executive officer who had had excellent leadership training. He had been an officer in the armed forces and was obviously accustomed to exercising authority. Or so I thought. For I found he was unable to handle men. He lacked the ability to give simple instructions with the necessary finesse.

Fortunately I had a noncommissioned officer who rose to the occasion and I let him take over. He had the knack of jollying men into distasteful tasks and using enough force when necessary to show them he meant business. He instinctively said the right thing at the right time, and spoke in a voice that commanded respectful co-operation.

Cliff Dickey, who was Jack Tuck's electronics specialist, was one who showed such latent leadership qualities. Almost from the outset he proved to be a strong and stabilizing influence among Jack's enlisted men. The men recognized that he was always cheerful, reliable and sympathetic. If Chet Segers was being snowed under with galley work, Dickey was always the first to offer to help out as well as to talk other men into lending Chet a hand.

Jack often came to rely on Cliff to straighten out many matters affecting morale. For instance, one of our radio operators let personal messages go untyped and frequently failed to meet schedules when there were messages or patches. The result was that a crisis brewed. Quickly Jack turned over basic responsibility to Dickey and soon everyone was pleased with the ham service and the personal attention Cliff gave them.

I knew from previous expeditions how important word from home was to morale. On the negative side, I was concerned about the effects of illness and poor health on camp morale. One thing I worried about repeatedly was what would happen to our teeth at the South Pole. Doc Taylor had taken a short course in dentistry before coming to the Pole, for we considered it essential on the basis of previous expeditions to have a man with dental training available.

My previous sojourns at Little America had found our camps repeatedly weakened by recurring attacks of mouth trouble. Hardly a man got by without losing fillings or even a tooth and sometimes spending long nights of misery nursing aching molars. For reasons never properly determined, the Third Expedition of 1939–41 had had tooth trouble of almost epidemic proportions. Dr. Russell Frazier, physician on that expedition, discovered something strange when he tried to treat teeth. The smallest injection of adrenalin with novocaine resulted in sending a man into adrenalin shock. Frazier reported that an abnormal amount of adrenalin was secreted in glands during the long, dark winter night. This he suggested was the reason for much of the cabin fever that overtakes explorers and prospectors.

Doc Taylor had an almost completely opposite experience with teeth at the South Pole. Only John Guerrero needed a filling. Why we were so free of mouth trouble is still a happy mystery. Was it our high elevation? Our better mouth hygiene and care? I suspected that even though the air we breathed was colder than at McMurdo, for instance, it had less thermal capacity than the somewhat warmer sea-level air because of our altitude. This could mean there was less differential expansion between the fillings and the teeth. There may be something to my theory, for McMurdo kept a dentist busy almost full-time.

An important factor in maintaining morale in the Antarctic was to make certain that the routine did not become onerous. If a man could not be assured of a change from time to time, both his work and attitude suffered. But how was this possible when a tight schedule must be maintained?

The answer lay in declaring holidays and holding celebrations that were somehow sandwiched into the routine. For instance, we declared a holiday with the appearance of the full moon each month. This meant a special meal and a special effort at camaraderie. Chet never let us down on such occasions. In addition, those with no urgent morning duties could rise late, and at the end of the day we enjoyed a movie.

Holidays were also declared when the sun went down, at the mid-winter point, at eclipses of the moon, on birthdays—even Bravo's—and at such times as Jack and I thought the men deserved a holiday even without a special occasion. My idea was to hold them frequently and at irregular intervals. Bravo's first birthday came in August and we all celebrated it. Chet baked a special cake for Bravo with one lonely candle on top. Jack lighted the candle and Bravo wandered over to the cake as if he knew something was expected of him. With one loud sniff he blew out the candle, to the surprise of all except Jack.

These special occasions gave the men a chance to "let their hair down." This was especially true when the meal was unusual. There was one occasion when Doc Taylor and I spent almost an entire day preparing a unique *smörgåsbord* dinner of twenty-five separate dishes, including one of vitamin pills.

Ours was not a singing crowd, though a few were proud of "talents" who were woefully lacking in talent. One small group, labeling itself the "Three Lonesome Polecats," actually went so far as to make a tape recording of several songs. Someone suggested that when the sun returned and the planes landed, the recording should be sent to some individual deserving major punishment. On earlier expeditions when movie shows were few, the men had put on local talent shows that were always amusing and well done, though of a sort for a stag audience only. At the South Pole, a show such as this would not have been possible. There, talents were of a different sort, with Doc Taylor devoting a well-attended lecture to future fathers on "How to Deliver a Baby," and Bob Benson putting the group into hysterics with a seemingly serious talk on "How to Locate an Earthquake."

Another chance for a change of pace was offered by the physical phenomena surrounding us. Whenever one appeared, the men reacted excitedly and afterwards exhibited renewed enthusiasm for their regular activities.

Actually, when the men first came to the Pole what most impressed each in turn was the "nothingness" of this southernmost spot. There was no other place in the world where there was less to look at. The eye could not feast on a distant mountain, the ocean, birds, foliage— or even a crevasse. The nearest mountain peak lay 300 miles away and the ocean was 800 miles off. But as they began looking closer, they saw new things each time. There was beauty in the snow surface that was not apparent at the outset. The snow had different shapes and forms, from massive drifts to sastrugi-carved fields and on down to exquisite tiny crystals. Optical phenomena were all about us and some of them were awesome. We may have been people in solitary confinement, but the beauty of what lay about us was awe-inspiring.

Certain types of men have a hard time in the Antarctic. Those who come without good motivation are generally unhappy. And those who come because of romanticism are quickly disillusioned. For the cold and the dark and the hard work necessary to stay alive hit them like a tidal wave. On one expedition one of our men had come simply to take pictures with the hope of returning to the United States and making his fortune on the lecture platform. The unexpected work demanded of him brought on a sullenness that led to group razzing and he was happy only when he embarked for home. Even his picture collection was a sad one!

It is easy for a man to lose face in the Antarctic and when he does it is difficult to regain it. The code of the Antarctic is cruel in many ways. A man who walks away from a task, no matter how justified he is, soon finds himself without friends. For the code is that when a man shows a weakness, he is letting the group down.

On one expedition when I was off on a trail trip, one of the dog drivers twisted his knee. He had the opportunity of suffering his way along and perhaps injuring his knee further or returning to camp in a tractor. The decision was left to him and he chose to come back by the tractor. To the other men his action implied a quitting attitude and he was all but ostracized when his trail companions returned. The next spring when Admiral Byrd asked me to lead a trail party, I, like the other party leaders, took untried men with me and ignored the man with the "trick knee." I was fearful that he might let the others down on the trail. And yet, there was no logic to what I did. Robert Scott had taken the same attitude toward Shackleton when he fell ill on the trail early in the century. But Shackleton had gone on to become a great explorer in his own right. And the man I helped ostracize later became a leader on other expeditions to the Antarctic.

Perhaps the reason for such unusual group behavior stems from the belief that only "he-men" are worthy companions on an expedition. Thus those whose physical abilities fall off through illness or state of mind are for the moment no longer "he-men." Oddly, on one expedition a man who was physically weak used counterpsychology to win group acceptance. He made sport of his own inabilities and the other men accepted him wholeheartedly, perhaps because they could look at him and feel more like "he-men" themselves.

This code of the Antarctic was employed at our South Pole Station, though I worked strenuously to see that it did not get out of hand. Earl Johnson and Junior Waldron had been among our hardest workers during the frightful interim when the McMurdo runways gave out. At that time there were only twelve of us at the Pole, and Junior and Earl worked almost around the clock at necessary tasks. For this they both paid heavily: Earl developed high-altitude nosebleeds as well as a hernia; Junior's leg went bad and sent him to bed for days at a time. Doc Taylor put both men on light duty and the others in our small group accepted his decision.

However, when the rest of our crew arrived and settled down to life at the Pole, trouble broke out. Two of the enlisted men who had not been present to witness the period when Earl and Junior worked so hard took to riding them as slackers, a charge that had no basis whatsoever. One of the men, who had a latent mean streak, took to writing nasty notes in the maintenance logbook that Earl kept. One of them read: *Why don't you cut snow, slob?*

This same individual also challenged Earl and Junior to fight him. "Don't rise to the bait," I cautioned them. "Jack and I have our eyes on him and if the time comes, Jack will handle the situation."

They followed my advice and in time the riding stopped, though the complications that ensued were many. For example, Moose Remington, our glaciologist, lived in the barracks building, along with the Navy men and our Met crew. Moose, who was an outgoing and friendly sort, became the champion of anyone being ridden by others.

As a result, he soon found himself being ridden along with Earl, Junior and John Guerrero.

Moose was another who became ill at the Pole. A flyer in the South Pacific during World War II, he had contracted malaria there and at the Pole he came down with the tropical disease known as amebiasis. In his usual generous enthusiasm, Moose had offered to cut all the snow for the camp in the snow mine when that operation began. He had even erected a sign: REMINGTON MINES, INC. *Visitors Welcome, Hours* 0001.5–2400, 7 *Days a Week*. However, when he became ill he could not work in the snow mine for a while, and the code of the Antarctic was applied to him by some of the men.

Living at close quarters, the men often found some things in the manners of others to be highly irritating. Sometimes they allowed their imaginations to run away with them in a search for reasons why a man who had been friendly yesterday was standoffish today. On one occasion Doc Taylor was baffled by one of the men who was down in the dumps. Doc sent him to me, expressing concern that he could do nothing for him. After a talk with this man, he left me smiling and happy, and his face had resumed its normal color.

"What happened?" Doc asked me. "What was your cure?"

"Nothing much," I told him. "He had an idea I was down on him and had stopped considering him as a friend."

In calling attention to shortcomings, it was necessary to consider the personality of the individual involved. In the case of a man who was the ringleader of a small group riding one of the men, I called him in one day and brought up the problem. But I didn't challenge him directly. Instead I said, "Some of the men have been picking on —— ——. Would you see what you can do to get them to stop this nonsense?" The riding toned down considerably after that.

When Willi Hough fell behind in the required hours of digging in the snow mine, I knew he was exceedingly busy in his ionosphere work. Yet camp morale demanded that each man somehow find time to do his digging stint. Willi had a sense of humor and I relied on it to straighten out the problem. One night, when all the men were together, I said to the wall, "I wonder if there's any truth to that rumor that Willi Hough has been released from his responsibilities in the snow mine." The men roared and Willi's mouth fell open. Then he smiled. And the next day I found him in the snow mine working hard.

Occasionally one of the men did things unwittingly that hurt the feelings of the others. Arlo Landolt was a delight to have at the Pole.

Hard-working and brilliant, he had to spend a great deal of time developing film in the science darkroom. He and Willi were fearful someone might mess up the chemicals or dirty up film and thus possibly destroy valuable scientific records. They put a padlock on the door. I was besieged almost immediately by irate Station members who considered a locked door in such a small closed community to be a personal insult. A feud was in the making and I had to call Arlo and Willi in. "Hang a key on the hook beside the door," I told them, "and issue an invitation for visitors to come by appointment. But don't make it appear as if you have staked out the darkroom as your private kingdom." They were both quick to get the point.

It is difficult to judge a person on short acquaintance. Bob Benson was a case in point. When Bob first got to the Pole, some of the men resented his immaturity. He talked about his home state of Minnesota as if he were a paid employee of the Minnesota Chamber of Commerce, and also spoke of his most excellent professors at the University of Minnesota as if they were superhuman. In addition, he was an overzealous camera bug. In the midst of the early work jobs he would rush away to get his camera, and return to announce, "I'm going to take a picture of the moon!" Some of the others kidded him a great deal about his moon pictures. "That's the same moon that's over Minnesota," they would tell him. But Bob stuck to his moon shots and eventually got pictures that could not be duplicated away from the Pole.

Every expedition I have gone on has included the same general types of men. Each had one man who was the strongest and most dependable man in camp. In ours it was Ed Flowers. There also was always the heaviest eater and camp wit. Bob Benson was both at the Pole. And then there was the camp practical joker. Ours was Moose Remington.

I recall that on my first expedition, when I was "Byrd's Boy Scout," we had a man who pulled the most outlandish of stunts. Once in the dead of night he got the night watchman to come running into the barracks screaming, "The Barrier's broken!" The men hurriedly gathered their gear in an effort to save what they could before Little America was swept out to sea. Of course, it was a false alarm, and the men were ready to commit mayhem when they found out.

On another occasion, he put flash powder in the toilet and triggered it to go off with a roar when the seat was lowered. One of the men, who was not aware of the surprise awaiting him, went to the head while the men gathered outside in suspense. A moment later they were rewarded by an explosion that shook the building. They waited for the victim to come running out, but he did not appear. The men who had laughed until they almost cried now grew worried. They banged on the door and called out his name. Finally they broke the door loose. The man inside stared at them blank-faced and said, "What's the matter, gentlemen?"

Some of Moose Remington's jokes backfired too. One World Day especially, Arlo could not physically keep up with the demand that he take observations every fifteen minutes around the clock in his Aurora Tower. As a consequence he made them for eighteen hours and Moose and Bob Benson spelled him for the remaining six. To get to the Tower from his office in the science building, Arlo had to go through two trap doors while climbing a ladder. The men had asked Arlo to put a rope on the trap doors so they could open them easily, but Arlo had procrastinated. He was smaller than they and could manage more easily to maneuver the doors in the narrow shaft.

Moose decided to teach Arlo a lesson. When Arlo woke up from a short sleep and came to resume his observations, Moose told him that Bob had fallen down the hatch and broken a leg. Arlo suffered immediate remorse, but when his eye caught the open record book and saw that Bob had initialed observations several hours after the alleged hour of the accident, he suspected a trick and refused to act alarmed. Moose responded by accusing him of being calloused and unconcerned about his friend.

All this happened at six A.M. and Arlo cornered me shortly after that to ask if Bob was really hurt. Nothing about this so-called joke was funny to me. Even worse, Arlo and Moose were peeved at each other, and I had to spend the better part of a day straightening out both their perspectives so they would resume their friendship.

Sometimes in the Antarctic a man will get in wrong with his companions and only by an unusual exploit on his part can he alter his reputation. We had one such man who underwent considerable riding from some of the men because he did not work as hard as they, nor was his approach as serious. Although he exhibited as much enthusiasm as the other men, it was mostly vocal. Some of the men complained that he would show up exceedingly late for assigned tasks and then find some reason to quit early.

Interior of the snow mine which burrowed 90 feet deep into the snow
© National Geographic Soci

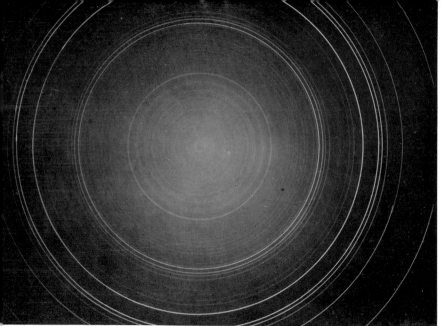

At the South Pole the stars appear to move in concentric rings. To record this phenomenon a camera was set in the Aurora Tower aimed directly overhead. The length of the exposure was 24 hours and 3 minutes.

Jack Tuck and Paul Siple taking star fixes at the theodolite in the station observatory.

Members of the wintering-over party on their way across the flat polar landscape to erect the flagpole at the South Pole after the winter night. Note the way sastrugi have marched across the trail left by the tractor eight months before, indicating how little snow falls at the Pole.

The U. S. flag flies at the Geographic South Pole 2,400 feet from camp. Ring of barrels surround the Pole at a distance of 100 feet to allow for possible error in fixing the Pole's actual site.

Green-haloed suns glow above the Pole in this photograph made with the aid of a filter which minimized the sun's glare and lent a greenish cast to the scene. Visiting photographer Tom Abercrombie took six exposures over a three-hour period in November as the wintering-over party made ready to depart from the Pole. The sixth

sun is off picture to the left while the first exposure (upper right) was made without the filter. The crownlike Rawin Dome and the box-shaped Aurora Tower stand atop pilings which let the wind-driven snow sweep through and thus prevented the structures from being buried by drifts.

With the long winter night ended the 18 men and dog of the Pole Station pose for a group picture by the light of the new-risen sun.

Preparing for his return to civilization Bob Benson pauses in the middle of shaving his beard to survey his image, half bearded, half shorn.

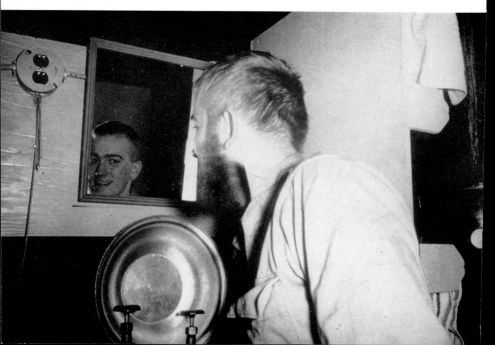

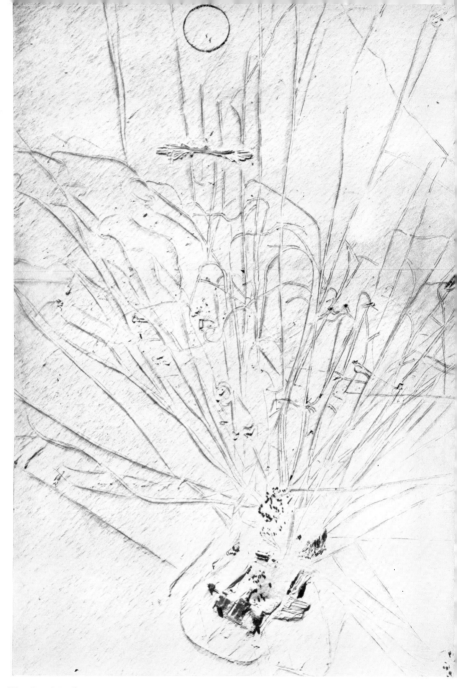

The South Pole is marked off by a circle of oil drums at the top of this U. S. Navy photograph. Below, just 800 yards from the Pole stands the South Pole Station. The heavy horizontal markings just below the polar circle are the result of efforts to retrieve the tractor which plunged 30 feet into the snow when its parachute was severed during an airdrop.

Gradually the group brought pressure to bear on him. Several men began to comment openly about his bragging, poor work habits and general lack of co-operation. I watched this situation develop, but without too much concern since the man in question obviously possessed a thick skin and was accustomed to being the butt of jokes. However, the group-pressure system in time made inroads on his morale, though it did not cause him to step-up his work. At a crucial point I spoke to a few of the men who were riding him the hardest. But even this did not alter the group's harsh opinion.

And then came a disaster which proved to be a fortuitous event. The ham radio set, one of our leading morale boosters, went out of order. The original set had had a weak power-amplifier "final" and the power had gradually dwindled with use. Cliff Dickey, our electronics man, had worked frantically to keep the set in operation, though he had no repair parts. But gradually, continued operation of the hamset caused it to deteriorate beyond Cliff's ability to repair it, and finally the set gave out.

"What are we going to do now?" Jack Tuck asked me.

There was nothing I could suggest. We both recognized that the hamset was actually our mail system. It was simple to predict a quick drop in the men's spirits with the loss of opportunity to remain in touch with loved ones back in civilization.

It was at this point that the man toward whom the group had shown little kindliness or good will asked for permission to work on the hamset. There were the usual silent sneers because of his previous performance on other tasks.

Several weeks had already passed by now, however, and there was nothing to lose by granting him permission. "How can you do anything?" I asked. "We don't have any repair parts."

"I can make them from bits and pieces of other unserviceable equipment," he said.

With a perseverance he had never before revealed, he set to work. Wires and tubes gradually fell into place and then one day we were on the air again! His achievement had a profound effect on the way men regarded him. Instead of a person who had been reviled, he now emerged a hero. The men recognized that he was far smarter than

←

Wrecked tractor lying at bottom of 30-foot-deep hole it plowed when it severed shroud lines of its parachutes and plunged to earth.

most of them had realized. As for the man himself, after his electronics achievement he began straightening out. He took his work more seriously, came up with several excellent ideas and became in every way a worthy member of our camp.

On one of our holidays, while we were lingering at the mess table after a meal, one of the men asked, "Tell us, Doc, now that we're well past the middle of the winter night, how are we doing in comparison to other men you've wintered over with?"

I told them I thought they were doing well. "Better in fact than any of the other camps."

Each group I had lived with had gotten along well together, but here at the Pole we had been even more like a big family, with far less bickering and squabbling than one would find in most families. The men were pleased and asked for more evidence of their success as compared to other expeditions.

"Well, maybe I can actually let you judge for yourselves."

I brought in my tape recorder and a small tape some of the construction crew Seabees had made for one of our wintering-over men. Admittedly the tape had been recorded on our less than sober Christmas Eve, but still in my judgment it illustrated the uninhibited degeneration which language could undergo. I explained as I put on the tape that this recording showed how we might all be acting and talking if we devoted no attention to our manner of speech.

It was a short tape and lasted no more than five or ten minutes. The man to whom it was addressed, who was able on occasion to give vent to colorful language himself, blushed. No one wanted to hear the second side of the tape.

Intentionally I have told here the actual nature of the minor frictions that arose among the men. Actually our small isolated station was blessed with a minimum of personality problems. Yet certainly they were real when they occurred and could have been serious had the men not exercised their own self-control. Each man in our group had his virtues and his weaknesses. We were an average cross section of Americans descended from a wide variety of European stock.

Close *esprit de corps* prevents many writers from presenting a full account of their difficulties. I have dared to, for any less frankness might hold us suspect. Humans just don't live without impinging on one another, even in civilization.

All things considered, our group-pressure control system worked well. Other stations which tried to rely on court-martial or arbitration of disputes by long-distance appeal to higher authority outside their

Station found that they were stymied. Neither the Navy or IGY wanted the disgrace of a public hearing.

We had to solve our own problems. No one else could help.

Chapter 28

RETURN OF THE SUN

So THE winter night moved along with the men busily working at their assigned tasks. On July first the IGY had officially gotten underway, but well before then, we were already attacking the various geophysical problems as well as others of our own formulation. There were special World Intervals which forced us to step up our scientific observations: digging in the snow mine for the clean snow necessary for our water; housekeeping routines; repairs of tunnels and equipment; ham calls home; a few apprehensive experiences in the cold darkness that ended without mishap; and the continual watch over the men's behavior toward each other to prevent cabin-fever animosities from developing into cause for serious concern.

It was important to retain as many ties with customs back home as we possibly could. One such occasion was the celebrating of the Fourth of July. At home, a day of high temperature and rain (if one planned a picnic)—at the Pole that day the temperature was almost —60° and it was dark and windy. What was the Fourth without fireworks? some of the men asked. So Moose made a home-fashioned bomb by taking shells apart and pouring the powder into a film can. But this proved a dud when his fuse did not work. Willi and Bob Benson fared no better when they tried to fire off an almost empty gas drum; nor did Cliff Dickey succeed when he tried to set off a drum filled with all types of liquid fuels. Finally, as disappointment mounted, Jack fired off a few flares from his Very pistol.

In May the temperature had fallen to —100.4°, the coldest outdoor temperature withstood by any man in the earth's history. Despite the searing effect of this temperature, the men looked forward to even colder days. But the days had grown warmer, and several faces evidenced clear disappointment. "Do you think we're going to break our own record?" a number of the men asked me.

"It depends on the wind," I told them. "We may not, with winds always at 10 to 20 miles an hour."

By July 9 we were once more below —90°, but while the temperature fluctuated up and down a few degrees, it did not drop below our record. On July 29, with the temperature at —98.8°, Mac, our radioman, and Herb Hansen, of the Met crew, pounced on me excitedly before breakfast. "We want to go out and make a cold-endurance test," Mac insisted.

"But you two have been up all night," I said. "Perhaps you should wait until you're fresher."

Herb commented, "But the temperature is near minus 100° Fahrenheit and it might go up."

Mac looked disappointed. "All right," I told them. But I was not especially happy about letting the two go outdoors and determine how long they could endure the cold without seeking shelter, especially since I was not certain that the motivation for the venture was entirely scientific. I was also concerned since only a few years back a close associate had lost his life testing cold-weather clothing he and I had helped devise.

Both men went outdoors at 8:30 A.M. Herb wore 26 pounds of clothing and Mac, 27 pounds. Herb's attire included Army-type underwear which was 50 per cent wool and 50 per cent cotton, wool-nylon socks, one pair of heavy wool Army ski socks, Army felt boots with two pairs of felt insoles, a coat-type Army wool shirt, Army Arctic cotton trousers with a frieze lining, down-filled vest, a wool stocking cap with face opening, Army-type parka coat of wool pile lining and fur-trimmed hood, Army Arctic mitts with wool mitt liners. McPherson wore waffle-weave Navy cotton underwear, Army cushion-sole socks, Army white insulated rubber boots whose design was based on one of my inventions, cotton fatigue trousers, cotton shell trousers with wool lining, Army Arctic mitts, detachable fur-trimmed parka hood and Army pile cap with ear flaps. Each man looked almost like a monster from outer space as he went out the door carrying a headlight with wires leading to batteries around his waist, where they would not freeze. They needed the lights in order to see in the dark outdoors.

I had estimated that they would return in two hours or so. Mac reported that his white insulated rubber boots had frozen hard in five minutes and that his wrists were cold after fifteen minutes. Not long afterward, he had to get rid of his leather gloves to keep his wrists from freezing. Herb informed us that his shoulders and arms cooled in thirty minutes and that the big toe on his right foot was cold after fifty-five minutes. Fifteen minutes later he reported that his torso was growing cold, and his feet started freezing whenever he stopped walking. By 11:15, Herb found the bridge of his nose freezing, and at 11:30 he gave up and came indoors. "My wrists were too cold," he said, "and so were the toes and heel of my right foot."

Mac gave up after four hours because of a great feeling of exhaustion that came over him. Each man had lost a pound in weight and had suffered a one-degree loss in temperature. Both immediately went to bed and later that day, I spoke with the two after they rose at ten P.M.

"How do you feel?" I asked Herb, who did not look well.

"I slept poorly," he said, almost in a whisper. "That stretch outdoors left me with a headache and I'm a little dizzy."

Mac also complained of feeling dizzy. This symptom suggested that their oxygen consumption had gone below the bodily requirements during their stay outdoors.

There is a strange urge to heroic martyrdom in men who frequently face danger. They want to see how far they can go and get away with it. Not long afterward several of the men suggested tests to determine the freezing time of exposed flesh. And one night when the temperature was again almost −100° this test was made on exposed noses, cheeks and ears. My nose froze almost immediately on exposure; my right ear in 54 seconds with an audible snap; and my cheek in two minutes and 55 seconds. Bob Benson's right ear froze in 40 seconds and his nose two seconds later. Of hardier stock, it took Jack Tuck's nose two minutes to freeze. Certainly the wildest of experimenters on that occasion was John Guerrero, who surprised me by dashing barefoot on the wretchedly cold snow for 26 seconds before he scurried back indoors. But his feet pained him for a long time afterward.

Besides the desire to watch us break our cold-temperature record, a new interest appeared among the men with the beginning of August. They were all tired of living in darkness and anxiously inquired about the return of the sun. "Astronomical twilight should begin on the third," Arlo confirmed my calculations, "when the sun will be about eighteen degrees below the horizon. Then should come nautical twilight on the twenty-first with the sun's angle at twelve degrees, observational twilight on the twenty-seventh with a ten-degree angle; and civil twilight on September sixth with the angle at six degrees."

"But when will we get real sunlight?" Earl Johnson asked.

"On September twenty-third—or thereabouts," I said.

To men who were starved for a glimpse of the sun, this six or seven weeks seemed an interminable time away. August 3 was officially the beginning of the Twilight Day, but the sky was overcast and not even the stars were visible. On the 13th, Bob Benson came running into the Jamesway, his eyes flashing with excitement. He had climbed into the Aurora Tower to take an observation when he had seen what he claimed was a "headlight beam of a locomotive or a tractor going sideways to me and shooting across the horizon." He looked at me eagerly. "Someone is out there with a vehicle!"

I went up to the Aurora Tower to check, and after nearly falling through the thin floor I finally had to chuckle with amusement. Certainly there was a mysterious beam of light that resembled a vehicular headlight. But the explanation was that it was a mirage of sorts. "It's just a streak of twilight on the horizon beneath a layer of clouds, Bob. We aren't getting any company," I said.

"Too bad," he agreed. "But if it's sunlight, it's just as welcome."

Twilight had returned so gradually that no one could tell the exact moment of its reappearance. But once it was back, the men accepted it and hungered for more light. Bob and Ed Flowers came in on August 23 to tell about another mysterious bright light on the horizon. "Let's go out and see what it is," I said. It turned out to be Venus, which was returning to view after a long absence and lay now only one degree above the horizon. By the following day, dawn light had already grown surprisingly bright and one could begin walking about outdoors with no flashlight without stumbling too much. The only member of our scientific group not too happy with this increasing twilight was poor Arlo, whose aurora program would have to end with the return of light.

By September 6 the dull grays of the sky were interlarded with other colors. Most of the color lay in the quadrant Grid Southeast to Northwest, which suggested that it was due primarily to multiple reflection of the snow from the bulk of the continent lying in that direction. After Civil Twilight arrived and the sun was only five degrees below the horizon, its rays reached the mountain peaks of the Queen Maud Range and a crepuscular fan of blue and pink reflections spread over our skies, reminiscent of the sunburst rays of the Japanese flag.

By now the men of the Pole Station were hoping that the temperature would drop before the sun truly appeared to warm the area. On September 11, the temperature fell to $-99.7°$ and the Met men "sweated out" the day, hoping it would go below $-100°$. But this did not happen; the temperature rose instead.

Then on the 14th, at eleven P.M., the temperature dropped to $-90°$ again. All through the 15th the temperature did not rise. Nor did it during the 16th or 17th. We were in our coldest period now and the men sensed that we might break our cold record.

The 18th of September found us firmly anticipating a new world's record. We were already nearing ninety consecutive straight hours with the temperature below $-90°$, and the barometric conditions were right. But the wind was blowing between 14 and 19 miles an hour toward Grid South from the east—and this wind might prove a villain, for we needed calm conditions for the temperature to drop further.

"This is the day," the Met men assured us at breakfast, and excitement raced through the mess hall.

"It had better be," shouted Willi, "because spring is only five days off."

"Personally, I'd rather live in the tropics," one man called out, "if there weren't so many bugs."

At nine A.M. Ed Flowers poked his round, beaming, unbearded face into the mess hall, looked from one set of eyes to another with feigned casualness and said softly, "It's at minus one hundred."

Jack and I joined Ed and we headed for the Met shack. A parade formed right behind us and there was hardly room in the shack for all the men as we clustered about the thermograph, the remote recording electrothermometer machine. Ed's crew had several thermometers set to give readings at various levels between 30 feet below the surface and 30 feet above. Each thermometer reading was recorded by the thermograph in a different color. The one we were interested in recorded in red the temperature reading in the thermoscreen shelter about five feet off the ground.

About every minute the cycle returned for another red mark, printing another number automatically on a moving roll of paper like a stockbroker's ticker tape but much wider. Tension grew as the wind speed dropped. One of the men broke the heavy silence. "Pipe down," several others warned him, as though he might break the magic spell.

Finally I left and got hold of Moose Remington and asked him to load his motion-picture camera. Then we went outdoors and set up a spare thermometer, which promptly confirmed the −100° cold. The horizon was looming and flaming with bright orange, the wind causing it to shimmer. A group of clouds aligned with upper winds came down to sharp points just above the flaming. I warmed the thermometer up to zero with my bare fingers and we filmed progress back down to −100°. And while we were outside it happened. At 9:30 on the morning of September 18, the temperature on the Met thermograph dropped to −102.1°, establishing a new world record low temperature.* My thermometer registered −103.5°, but this was unofficial. If only the incessant wind would die for a few hours, I said to myself. Even now, a light breeze of four to five knots held the temperature from sinking perhaps another 10 or 20 degrees.

The noon radiosonde balloon run told us an interesting story. There were strong winds aloft from the eastward. 1,400 feet up the temperature was 74 degrees warmer than on the surface, but much higher above this inversion layer the temperature was below −130° F. Oddest of all was that at the cold point on the snow surface the temperature was −104°, but atop the 30-foot anemometer pole the temperature was 27 degrees warmer.

The men wandered in and out all morning, intent on feeling and remembering what life was like at that temperature. It would be something to tell one's grandchildren. But no one remained outside for long. After lunch, Jack and I started down to the snow mine to do our stint when we found that Floyd Johnson and Chet Segers had beat us to the job. "Let's go out for a hike," I told Jack, "and enjoy the minus one hundred temperature."

He agreed. "But only a leisurely walk," I added. "Not like the time we took out the empty oil drums." That had been an experience. At −85°, we had pulled two empty barrels on a sled to our barrel cache about a hundred yards away. Since Jack would not stop to rest along the way, I made no such request even though I should have. The result was that we were both completely exhausted at the end of the short haul. The high-altitude cold had literally taken our breaths away and we coughed almost without stopping for several hours afterward. Bob Benson alternated with us on the hauling and he suffered the same way.

* A year later, on August 25, 1958, Russian IGY Station Vostok at the Geomagnetic Pole, 78° 27′ S, 106° 52′ E at an elevation of 11,220 feet, reportedly recorded a temperature of −125.3 F. The conditions of this station were calm with snow soft. The greater height and calmness accounted for the difference at the Pole Station. The average wind chill at the Pole Station was probably more severe.

Now at $-100°$, I tugged at the wolf-fur ruff of my parka hood to give my face more protection, and stepped out of the tunnel exit where Jack and Bravo were waiting. The cold seemed even more searing than it had been when I had gone out briefly with Moose Remington that morning. The breeze blew the vapor of my breath back at my face, and it condensed instantly on the gray tangle of my ten-month-old beard. My hands shot instinctively to my nose and cheeks, which felt as though they were being consumed by shooting flames. I waited for the telltale needle-pointed sharp prick, or "ping," as polar men call the freezing moment for the nose.

After a short sortie forward, two things happened: my white plastic-rubber insulated boots designed for $-65°$ froze as hard as cast iron; and I grew conscious of the sound of my freezing breath. My ankles ached where the unyielding frozen rubber cut, even though I had left my shoelaces loose in order to give my feet more play. As for hearing my breath, that, of course, I had heard at warmer temperatures, too. But at $-100°$, the jet was stronger and the sudden expansion and fracturing of the almost subvisible ice crystals produced louder musical crackles and pops.

We proposed to walk to the Geographic South Pole, some 2,400 feet from camp in the direction of the east coast of Australia. This was the spot Jack and I had determined from our star computations in the months before July. Willi Hough had paced off the distance the day before, and our task was easier because he had planted a straight row of red flags at 100-yard intervals. I pointed a hand toward the Pole and the brilliant orange dawn colors in the sky beyond it.

Immediately Bravo hurled his 106 pounds of muscle at me full speed. I warded off his inch-long teeth as he snatched at my mitt. Then he turned, made a quick lunge at Jack, wheeled, and dashed off in a bluish cloud of flying snow, his breath leaving a white vapor trail for at least a hundred yards behind him. I pointed toward him and Jack nodded as we turned to follow, for he had run off following Willi's trail in the direction of the Pole.

So we went along, grunting and pointing at unusually graceful sastrugi or colorful changes in the sky. All winter long the winds had blown constantly, on one gusty day reaching fifty-two miles an hour. The result was that the featureless plateau now possessed a new sculptured surface of fantastic shapes. The sastrugi waves of snow were etched into graceful, swanlike curves, high and low furrows, undercut anvils, all spotless white but reflecting the pastel shades of the rising dawn. We stumbled along, our eyes feasting upon the wind's handi-work.

We were making our way over the drop zone now, and here and there lay pieces of parachutes and other reminders of those days of airdrops and stream-ins. Despite the wind, the sastrugi erosion and the moving of the snow dunes, tractor tread marks and debris from the drops were still visible. Bravo pulled out corners of snow-covered parachutes with his teeth and danced about on the fabric to relieve his unprotected paws from the cold. Here was the spot where we had searched diligently for our streamed-in Encyclopaedias; there was the tomato-juice stain—reminder of our famine on that score all winter; and there the spot the steel girders for the hard-fought-for barracks buildings had landed before dragging 25 miles away.

We were at the last flag now, and I remembered the hundreds of star shots we had taken to determine the Pole's position. Above us the stars were now drowned out by light, though technically it was still nighttime. Just outside the range of the brightest dawn light I could still see the planet Venus shining alone like an old friend. But Canopus and Sirius, the brightest of all stars in the Southern Constellations, were gone from polar sight until the next winter night.

Bravo was first to reach the red trail flag that denoted the Pole and he made three trips around the world before we arrived. Not to be outdone, Jack and I circled the globe at a 100-foot radius from the flag. "It's Thursday for us because we crossed the international date line," I commented. "We're a day ahead of the men in camp." To avoid this hypothetical confusion, we strolled again around the world, "unwinding" in the opposite direction. "Well, we are back in Wednesday," I heard Jack's muffled words.

We stood facing the bright orange core of light where the sun lay just below the horizon. We unharnessed our cameras, kept warm inside our parkas, and pulled off our heavy outer mitts to take pictures. There was no question that the temperature was still formidable, because after a half-dozen quick shots my fingers grew unbearably cold. Thin cotton contact gloves and wristlets offered scant protection against (as the Briton would say) 132° of frost. Woodenly I managed to thrust my throbbing fingers back into the wool liners and then into the warm pile-backed Army Arctic mitts. When I glanced over, Jack was pounding his hands together as he tried to increase circulation. We looked at each other reassuringly, as though we were having a gay time.

But even Bravo had reached the limit of his endurance. He had unearthed a crash pad, and like a circus lion balancing on a shiny ball, he was attempting to get all four feet onto the pad. His legs were constantly in motion for he would not permit a paw to remain at rest, because this would bring on freezing. "What's the matter, boy?" Jack asked him. Bravo's reply was to turn toward the camp a half-mile away, leaving us to our own uncomfortable devices as he hurried back with animal sense toward warmth and survival.

Watching him scurry, I could see the snowbound village that had harbored us through the coldest winter man had ever known. There was the blackish Rawin Dome that had caused us so much trouble to erect, but had later served the Met crew so well in tracking weather balloons. Above the science building sat the Aurora Tower, its scientific work completed for the year, but soon to be important as our air-control tower when the planes returned. In addition to the radio masts, windbreaks and piles of metal drums, the rest of the camp was ice fog and vapor shrouded. I sensed more than ever a consuming feeling of isolation on being at such a remote point from civilization. The gentle, rolling white plateau led to the horizon, and then continued on for hundreds of miles beyond.

We glanced toward Shackleton Base, some 800 plus miles away, where Bunny Fuchs, one of our nearer neighbors, was preparing for his November traverse across the continent. Off in the other direction were the Russians, with whom we had conducted but one direct radio talk. Scattered elsewhere in the great white beyond were the other American IGY villages at Little America V, McMurdo, Ellsworth, Wilkes, Byrd and Hallett. And all around us were our foreign colleagues: New Zealanders, French, Russians, Japanese, Australians, Norwegians, British, Argentines and Chileans. We were all on a vast and hostile continent of frozen wastes and penetrating cold blasts. And yet I loved it, even though at that moment, compared to our own body temperature, Jack and I were exposed to air close to one third of the way from comfortable room temperatures down to absolute zero, where molecular motion is presumed to cease entirely.

We blew warm breath into the fur of our hoods, held snugly against our noses. My whiskers were by now almost solidly iced over and my ankles inside my heavy frozen boots felt raw. I burrowed a little deeper into the parka and wished that the distance back to camp and a piece of Chet Segers' cherry pie were less. But my attention was drawn to the horizon behind the camp, away from the sun, where I noted a shallow, slate-blue arc of sky, darker than the rest. I knew it as the last remnant of the earth shadow that had been retreating slowly from the circling dawn like a dark canopy during the past few weeks. To my right streaked a long wedge of pink from the unrisen sun behind me. And superimposed on the pink and gray backdrops, as delicate and tenuous as though they had been applied by the brush of an expert Japanese water-color artist, were series of long wisps of white clouds. These were so magnificent that once again Jack and I disregarded the cold to take more pictures.

Then, as we snapped photos, we turned again toward that bright orange area nearest the submerged sun. It was no longer a patch of cold brilliance, I noticed. Instead, it had grown notably brighter during our walk and it rolled, heaved and surged like a distant forest fire or like a restless, flaming tidal wave. Framing it rose a great fan of cloud streaks, streamers of alto-cumulus clouds that ran parallel to the course of the upper winds. And then we saw strange flashes of light.

"Paul, did you see what I saw?" Jack asked in a muffled voice.

"You mean those flashes of light above where the sun is closest to the horizon?"

"Yes! Do you suppose it could be a mirage of the sun?"

"Maybe so, but it's the strangest one I've ever seen," I said.

While I watched, the flashes increased. "Sparklers," we called them spontaneously. They were tiny, jewel-like points of light that flashed for an instant and then disappeared. Their brilliance was almost blinding. Some were bright green, blue or blood-red, but most were a blazing orange. These sparklers were in continual motion and clustered about what appeared to be a wind in the clouds, a lateral space only a little wider than the sun itself might be.

We used a polar test for mirages. We stepped up on snow mounds and then found a depression and squatted low. If what we were witnessing was a mirage, it would loom higher or disappear at different eye levels. But we discovered that while any change in eye level made a temporary difference in the number of sparklers visible, they remained at the same brilliance. We both ran out of film trying to take pictures of this phenomenon.

We had been out for nearly two hours and we hurried back to camp. Bravo, who got "cold feet" regarding our prolonged outdoor stay, greeted us warmly. Immediately I spread a general announcement over our telephone system. "The sun is coming up." Sunrise was officially five days off, but something was happening.

Within minutes the men were all outside to see for themselves. The snowdrifts banking up to the flat top of our camp became a metal forest of camera tripods.

The sparklers we had told everyone about were no longer in view, but an even grander sight began to appear. Though the sun was still two degrees below the horizon, there loomed up a distinct arc of its upper limb.

At first, unlike the real sun, it refused to stay up, but seemed to be pulsating up and down—struggling to rise, and then losing out and subsiding again. The pulses came minutes apart and the men danced about, trying to keep warm between "shows."

However, during the next hour or so the entire sun seemed to come up and remain above the horizon. By squinting or using a colored filter, we saw that the disk was wondrously strange. For it was composed of an irregular series of horizontal lines, like a stack of progressively shorter orange neon tubes.

What had caused this mirage which brought us the sun several days before it was due? The warm layer of air high above our heads acted as a mirror to reflect the sun's rays around the curvature of the earth. That evening the temperature rose rapidly. There was a dense ice fog followed by a snowfall and a blizzard.

It was now the end of winter, and after the poor weather during the next few days we saw the sun's reflected image much of the time. Surprisingly, it rose in the Eastern Hemisphere sector and set in the Western. At the Pole the rising sun ought to skim in an even circle around the horizon and make an ever higher circle until midsummer. A plausible explanation for this false sunrise and sunset is that the unknown territory of the interior of Antarctica toward Asia lies considerably higher than the South Pole. Thus its higher "sky mirror" would reflect an image of the sun from farther away, causing a mirage to "rise" in that direction.

The sunrise came five days later, September 23, when the sun crossed the celestial equator into the Southern Hemisphere. Of course, this called for a holiday and we celebrated with a banquet: onion soup and shrimp cocktail, two turkeys, dressing, peas, corn, white potatoes, candied sweet potatoes (especially good), gravy, rolls, olives, cranberry sauce, nuts, gumdrops, potent camp-concocted wine and fruit punch. The men were so gorged that a rest was in order before our flag-raising ceremonies. It was 186 days now since the sun had set, and as the men stood at attention I glanced at the precious sun. Certainly it was desirable, yet it looked so comical with a flat bottom and stacked layers of bright lines rising to a narrow top, looking like an old-fashioned beehive.

"It will have to do better than that before it counts," one of the men turned away from the sun and said.

Chapter 29

HARBINGERS

THE sun was above the horizon now and each day it rose higher by almost the width of its diameter as it circled about us. Soon the katabatic winds would subside, the character of the snow surface would change and the usually filmy winter clouds would give way to the swift-moving denser summer clouds that hugged the horizon.

On some days there would be crystal shimmer, as there was on one occasion after a fog bow when John Guerrero and I were outdoors. Fresh deposits of snow crystals lay on the surface and the wind was rather quiescent as we walked along. "We're walking on a field of diamonds," exclaimed John, who had never seen crystal shimmer before. And in truth we were, for the refractions from the faces of the ice crystals lent credence to the optical illusion of a field of iridescent rainbow-colored diamonds. There were about ten of them per square foot: one would be a brilliant green, another shiny blue, bright red or flashing yellow. Every move we made brought changes in the colors. But the diamonds did not seem to be on the surface. Our eyes apparently lost their normal ability to perceive depth, so the diamonds seemed to be suspended in space a few inches above the snow.*

On other days we lived in a more prosaic world, one characterized by the continued grind of housemouse duties, snow mine labor and scientific observations. However, something new had crept into our daily existence. Home.

---

* The depth perception anomaly was apparently due to the fact that our eyes were trying to make crystals of like color match, whereas a pair of 3-D stereo pictures showed that the same crystal seen in both camera lenses was a different color in each. This was caused by a minute difference in the refraction angle.

"It won't be long before the planes will be back and dropping mail," I heard one of the men say as he gazed into the sky. "And then they'll bring our replacements and we can get out of this place."

"You'll miss it," I said, and I knew each one would.

"When I get back," Chet Segers said with a chuckle, "I'm going to finish twenty years in the Navy and then retire. Then I'll put the old lady to work while I sit under a shade tree and drink beer all day."

"Just think of poor Bravo." Floyd Johnson smiled. "He's never seen a woman or a tree."

For all their humorous banter, the men had begun to think of leaving. I myself wished to remain long enough to see our scientific program through to a successful conclusion. In addition, I wanted to be on hand to greet Bunny Fuchs, my acquaintance of many years, when he arrived at the South Pole on his 1,200-mile traverse of the continent. He planned to arrive at the Pole, he told me by radio, between Christmas and New Year's. "See you then, Paul," he said.

There were to be equally long if not longer American cross-country treks during the summer's operation. But these would be triangular traverses of some 1,400 miles out of Little America, Byrd and Ellsworth stations, not journeys from one side of the continent to the other, and thus would lack the glamour attached to a continental traverse across the Pole.

"Good luck, and keep out of crevasses," I told Bunny.

The returning sun had long since put an end to Arlo's auroral observations, but he kept busy processing his observations onto standard punch cards so that back home the data could be machine-correlated with the findings from all the other IGY stations. The meteorologists were also busy transferring their observations onto punch cards. The mass of data from thousands of co-operating stations over the world would swamp any processing system short of high-speed mechanized business machines.

One of the early fears of the national committees had been that the data would pile up so hopelessly that it might take years before analyses could be completed. To meet this approaching avalanche, the International Committee CASAGI (Comité Spécial de l'Année Geophysique Internationale) had approved special data centers as depositories and analysis centers. The sticky question as to whether the United States and Russia, who were making lion's share contributions, would surrender certain unprocessed data to one another or to some "neutral" smaller country was neatly side-stepped. There would be three major data centers: Data Center "A" the U.S.A., Data Center

"B" the USSR and Data Center "C" Europe, with various countries of the latter area responsible for certain specialties. The U.S. Data Center "A" in turn was to be a decentralized organization with subjects distributed among many universities and research institutions.

We took advantage of our weekly Thursday evening science meetings in the mess hall to summarize the accomplishments of the various disciplines for the exchange of information. These meetings often turned into real bull sessions. One evening Herb asked, "Except for science, will Antarctica ever be worth anything?"

"Yes," I replied, "I'm certain it will. Possibly not through conventional mining methods, however. So far we haven't even found much of the metallic minerals. There have been a few finds of copper, lead, zinc, tin, molybdenum, antimony and uranium, but the quality and quantity don't indicate any bonanzas. Of course, there's been little geological reconnaissance and prospecting on the continent as a whole and probably there'll be some valuable discoveries. And even though the coal reserves are believed to be extensive, they are reportedly of low quality. The chances are if it's ever mined it will be for production of chemical by-products rather than for its thermal assets.

"But if one becomes imaginative, the future of Antarctica is almost unlimited. Antarctica's richest resources may be the very things which appear most useless, namely her ice, cold and emptiness.

"It is conceivable that Antarctica's average mile-deep mantle of almost chemically pure ice and snow could prove a boon to industries which need large quantities of water and coolants. In a rapidly growing world, industry must compete with domestic and agricultural needs for water. Then, too, surface and lower atmosphere space requirements of modern science and industry are growing so rapidly that even in desolate wastelands competition is keen over mineral claims, traffic routes, water rights, recreation and wildlife reserves, testing grounds and the like.

"The processing of atomic energy concentrates is a good example of an industry with ever-increasing space requirements. Certainly, atomic energy is such a potential boon to mankind that it is here to stay. Nevertheless, the product is lethal to life in all forms and requires plenty of elbow room. Pressure will soon be brought to bear to bring about the removal of processing plants from populated and agricultural areas of the world. What better made-to-order place could one find than here in Antarctica, with its minimal human population and paucity of plants and animals? An internally drained basin beneath the ice might be a safe depository for hot atomic waste products that could be stored safely for hundreds of years."

"But how about food production?" asked Bob, looking up from a heaped bowl of ice cream.

"You would think of food," I said with a laugh, and went to the big pan which was brought in for the occasion and scooped out some for myself.

Bob continued as though to defend his pet subject of food. "I read somewhere that Admiral Byrd once suggested storing surplus food here in the Antarctic, using the place like a deep freezer and extracting the food as needed when there might be a famine in some part of the world. But I was wondering if you visualize Antarctica as a food-producing region?"

"Of course," I answered. "It would be possible, during the summer sunshine, to grow hydroponic vegetables in a heated greenhouse. A permanent colony would certainly devise such a system."

Dickey broke in with a chuckle. "I hope they have better luck than you and I did with ours."

"Well, we did grow some fine molds," I said, recalling the futile little desk-top gardens we had started under artificial light, each of which had ended with a plague of mold that killed off the seedlings.

I recalled for them that the whaling industry had been extracting oils and fertilizers from Antarctica. Japanese whalers even took the meat of the whales home for human consumption.

The cold seas surrounding the Antarctica, although ice laden and storm tossed, offer a strong contrast to the nearly sterile snow-covered continent. The seas virtually teem with life of all sorts. The basis of this life lies in the fundamental process of photosynthesis. Cold water can hold larger concentrations of carbon dioxide and the long hours of summer sunshine provide the energy required for microscopic plants to thrive luxuriantly. Old sea ice is often stained by the concentration of these minute forms of life. This food source provides a cycle of life that extends on up to include the largest animals in the world—the blue whales, which attain lengths of over 100 feet and weights in excess of 100 tons. Seals and bird including the most publicized Antarctic inhabitant, the penguin, abound. When the time comes for serious international efforts to find a solution to world food problems, the Antarctic seas may conceivably become a "farming" area for basic proteins and carbohydrates.

"But the sixty-four thousand dollar question is, could Antarctica ever become self-sufficient?" asked Arlo.

"Why not?" I said with my tongue figuratively in my cheek. "I think it could eventually."

This impetuous reply was not based solely upon the concept of plastic-dome-covered mining communities with greenhouse farms, even though these may be a step on the way. The future of Antarctica, I implied, lies in chemical manipulations. Man is still in the kindergarten stages of organic chemistry despite the wonders he has wrought. For example, four elements are basic for life. Carbon, oxygen, hydrogen, and nitrogen—COHN, I call them for short. These elements form the basis of our food, fuels, power, and much of our clothing and construction materials. Remembering Antarctica's coal and inexhaustible fresh water, I asserted that these four basic elements are as abundant in Antarctica as anywhere else in the world—more so than in some other desert or barren regions. With the aid of such energy sources as sunshine, deep earth heat, or atomic power, the chemicals will some day be converted directly from the basic atomic building blocks to fill man's daily requirements. But you say those four elements are not enough by themselves. And, of course, you are right. However, the world's oceans offer bountiful sources of almost all the other chemical requirements, and also Antarctic rocks will undoubtedly be found to contain some valuable mineral concentration.

Indeed, if we could but live long enough, we might see thriving industrial communities on the periphery of Antarctica manufacturing their own foods, producing their own fuel, clothing, and construction products; extracting their minerals from the sea water—producing atomic products for world needs. Meanwhile, their inhabitants can travel to other parts of the world in a matter of hours or even minutes by rocket transportation.

Fantastic? Yes, but so America would seem to Columbus if he were able to rediscover it today.

Our bull session continued late into the evening. It touched on many topics. We agreed that what the Antarctic lacked most were women. We also concluded that the continent will never be without a human population again and that it would be only a short time before the continent would be open for tourist trade. Then would come small villages in which whole families could reside for years at a time. Weather stations and other scientific observing points could be conveniently manned by married couples. With women and children, we agreed, there would come still better self-contained housing. I related to the men how the U.S. Army scientists had already developed, on the Greenland icecap, the technical capability of placing whole villages under the snow. Snowplows like ditching machines can cut artificial crevasses with wide, flat bottoms and narrow surface openings, as well as side-jutting caverns in which houses and living requirements can be ensconced. Snow, conventional materials, or even clear plastic roofs render the tunnels impervious to the vagaries of wind and extremes of temperature. Army research and development teams have also devised thermonuclear power plants which could free a future Pole Station from the heavy logistics of 250 tons of fuel. These same Army polar research engineers have also developed and tested simple snow-compacted runways for fully loaded planes like the C-124 at elevations comparable to the Pole Station.

The fact that these innovations were not incorporated into our IGY Pole Station was due to four primary factors. The first was the lack of advanced engineering knowledge about the terrain and the uncertainty of whether any airlifted station at the Pole was possible. Secondly, the fact that the IGY was scheduled for only a two-year period made it debatable whether a more elaborate subterranean village, compacted runway, and thermonuclear power plant were worth the expense. The next plausible excuse was that such projects would require an increased number of construction personnel which, with such a short work season the first year, might be too much of a gamble. Finally, despite the fact that the Department of Defense had the responsibility for the logistics, it does not necessarily follow that the agency given primary responsibility must request help from another service with greater technical skill as long as funds are available to try to do the task their own way with their own personnel.

Nevertheless, man has found it possible to live at the South Pole Station. If, after the IGY, the U.S. were to abandon the site, it would likely be occupied by others. The uniqueness of the stable platform at the South Pole (as compared to the drifting of the sea ice at the North Pole) makes it a choice observation point in the satellite age for orbiting research instruments sent on a north-south course. On each pass they will transit the Pole and, therefore, make possible transfer of data by high-frequency line of sight radio during each circuit to the same ground station. For example, it is possible that the South Pole Station could become the primary global weather forecast center. A television camera and other auxiliary sensing instruments in an earth satellite could view cloud patterns and weather fronts twice daily over the whole surface of the world. At each pass it could transfer its 90 minutes of data of that orbit at the Pole Station which in turn could dispense it to the rest of the world.

Our pioneer year at the South Pole proved that it is possible to inhabit the most remote spots on earth. Man can safely and productively live in a spot as cold as nature can produce on earth. Thus, we proved there is no technical limitation to habitation required for scientific or commercial enterprises.

For the near future scientific knowledge will continue to be the most valuable product extracted from Antarctica.

From the way they talked and by their actions, the men were now revealing a growing restlessness. It was recognizable first from the rash of long walks the men took. I insisted on the buddy system in order to know who was outdoors and to prevent a man from wandering off alone. But despite the low temperatures the number of men outside at a given time often exceeded the number indoors. Yet save for the short hike to the site of the Geographic Pole or to artifacts on the drop zone and runway, the only thing to do was to amble about appreciating the beauty of the sastrugi in its myriad fantastic wind-sculptured forms. The men did, however, invent one game that got some of them as much as a mile or two from camp.

This was to try to find Amundsen's tent at Poleheim. Of course, the tent had been pitched and abandoned back in late 1911. If it had not blown away during the 45 treacherous winters between that year and our stay at the Pole, it no doubt lay far below the surface. Nevertheless, I did not oppose this romantic endeavor and several of the men persisted in their quest. It was with amusement that I watched Willi, Herb, Moose and others break out primus stoves, sleds, snow saws, shovels and trail food and set off in vain search. Actually, from Amundsen's book *The South Pole,* I calculated that his tent probably lay within a one-mile-square area, the farthest edge of which lay about 1½ miles from camp in Grid North. But if the men wanted to explore elsewhere, there was no harm done. In fact, only good resulted because the search afforded quick relief from the pent-up feeling that had developed during the dark, cold winter.

Jack, Moose, and I envied the stations equipped to carry out traverses. We had often talked of journeys we would like to make out from the Pole Station. We hadn't been furnished seismic equipment of the type used for measuring deep ice thickness, for the seismic sounding device originally purchased by IGY for use at the Pole had been diverted elsewhere. I was certain that radiating journeys of 50 or 100 miles in a spokelike pattern out from the Pole would add much to our knowledge. We wanted to know the gradient of the surface especially toward the unexplored Grid Northeast. What sort of slopes were those winter surface winds rolling down? How high were the long low ridges that seemed to swell up on the surface five or more miles apart? Were these ridges really parallel to the prevailing winds? Did the snow surface differ to any extent even a few miles away from the Pole?

We pondered long and hard whether we could make a few short journeys. I agreed with Jack that until the supplies for the incoming parties were in or we had a new tractor and Weasel, we wouldn't dare risk a trip of even a few miles from the Station for fear of losing our only means of dragging in supplies. Of course, even now it would be too cold to chance taking our Weasel out for anything but essential tasks. If only the Task Force weren't so impatient to remove us early, we might spend the warmer summer months making some of these short trips. But from the radio messages we were scheduled to depart by the numbers as rapidly as planes could come in to take us out.

Jack and I often pondered cross-country journeys of a grander scale after the IGY. He wanted to continue a polar career after taking time out for graduate training in geography and to do a thesis perhaps on polar transportation, then return to the Antarctic. I told him of some of my ideas for post-IGY Antarctic activity.

"I hope," I told him, "that either Congress or some of Admiral Byrd's old friends and supporters will originate a Byrd Polar Research Institute in the United States like the Scott Polar Research Institute associated with Cambridge University in England. We need a permanent polar organization in the U.S. that will give continuity to our polar effort. The trouble with locating it in a government department is that if we do, Antarctic interests will be of necessity a minor function. It will have to compete for funds and prestige among all the other functions carried out by that department. Furthermore, if the director is a political appointee, the leadership will change frequently. Although such men might be well-meaning and interested in their assignment, their background in Antarctic matters might be nil."

"How have Antarctic matters been handled by the government in the past?" Jack asked.

"As piecemeal jobs by whoever happened to be at the desk of the division to whom it was sent," I answered. "In fact nine out of ten times a repeat action would be handled by a different man if not even a different division. For example, the State Department handled Antarctic matters in the division of Northern European affairs back in U.S. Antarctic Service days. I presume because the Scandinavian countries are in the Arctic. Recently, the State Department transferred the job to the desk concerned with Latin American affairs. At least it was closer to Antarctica, but they catered to Chilean and Argentine feelings to the consternation of our other Antarctic foreign friends. What's more, they keep replacing their pro tem Antarctic man. It's only a job to him and he's happy to go on to other, more familiar, spots.

"The situation is even less stable within the Defense Department. Officers come and go so rapidly that there's seldom more than a year or two in a row that one can even locate the man who last spoke for his agency.

"The Interior Department which would normally have had responsibility for Antarctic affairs if it were a formally claimed American territory has generally closed its eyes to the area over the years as though they wished it would go away like a bad dream.

"Unfortunately, the Arctic Institute of North America showed little interest in the Antarctic. Canada's strong interest in the Arctic kept it looking north although it has taken some part in Antarctic matters during IGY.

"Such organizations as the American Geographic, National Geographic, and American Philosophical Societies have kept up scientific interest through their publications, maps, and support of exploration. However, attention to Antarctic matters was only one phase of their broad world interests.

"Oddly enough, from a historical standpoint, the American Polar Society providing its members with news service of both Arctic and Antarctic matters may have been the nearest to a continuing public society promoting U.S. Antarctic interests from 1934 until IGY came along. Its continued existence was, however, due largely to the indefatigable efforts of its secretary, August Howard, who edits and publishes the *Polar Times*.

"Basically, however, in the past quarter century it was the private and personal drive of Dick Byrd and his associates that kept American interest alive in Antarctic matters. Our polar tradition through Wilkes, Greeley, Peary, Ellsworth and others has been an honorable one and a symbol of inspiration."

Jack and I agreed that there was a need for an organization, perhaps quasi-governmental, like the Smithsonian Institution to foster our Antarctic future. It should provide a means by which anyone with an interest, scientific or technical, in Antarctica could find association with kindred souls.

As to future field work, geology and mapping neglected during IGY require post-IGY emphasis. I picture mobile tractor-drawn air bases from which scientists can work during the summer season. As an area is well studied, the mobile base moves forward a hundred miles and the small aircraft and helicopters haul the scientists off to neighboring mountain peaks and areas of scientific interest. Larger aircraft operating from coastal stations, like McMurdo and Little America, can bring the scientists in and out as well as handle supply requirements. At the end of a summer season, the mobile base could be left in position and the personnel flown back home to work on their data until the next Antarctic summer.

I have long been a proponent of what I call a "package base concept." This system envisages the placement of tiny unmanned shelters stocked with a small quantity of food, fuel, and emergency supplies and situated at intervals of 50 to 100 miles throughout the coastal and hinterland mountain belts. If such a system of little stations were laid down with the idea that the supplies would be usable as needed over the next 25 years, they would provide a safe and convenient means for small summer parties of scientists to move about with a minimum of costly support. That is, the scientists could be landed by air on one of the landmark sites. They could then move from one "packaged base" site to another while performing their field work. Later they would rendezvous with a pickup flight at the end of the field season.

This system would be like a normal expedition in reverse. The logistics are planned first and then the scientific field work is fitted to it. The systematic scatter of small stations would provide safety for Antarctic air operations in the future as well as work centers. Each small packaged base would be anchored firmly to a rock outcrop and each visitor would be required to keep a careful inventory of the supplies he used or removed so that a future traveler would not find the cupboard bare.

Such discussions as these were frequent during the winter night, but now, with the sun back, we were eager to get outside to work. If only the temperature would rise a bit. One could walk around all right, but it was difficult to do jobs that required much dexterity at −70° and −80° F.

On September 30, word came by radio that on the morrow the first planes would fly in from Christchurch to McMurdo. This was official word that the Task Force recognized that winter was over. Once the planes were back on the ice strip at McMurdo, it would not be long before they would be on their way to the Pole. With this in mind, we hurried to dig out the snow-covered entrance of the garage so we could take the Weasel into the open for heavy duties. Our tractor lay broken and in need of repair parts, but these could come in airdrops. With a big grin on his face, Earl Johnson, our postmaster, brought out the gaudily painted mailbox for letter deposits. From every room men appeared almost immediately to stuff Earl's box with the letters they had written all winter. Moose showed up with 26!

It was a sleepless night in general. In the morning, Mac tuned the radio to the McMurdo frequency, and off and on all that day we could hear the conversations between the pilots and McMurdo as three Navy planes flew in from New Zealand. Jack talked to one of the pilots. "When are you coming on here?" he asked.

"You should have some mail in a few days," came the reply. "Byrd Station has to be serviced first and then you guys."

"Be sure to bring us a ham and some radio tubes and spare parts for the tractor when you come," Jack requested.

"Roger, you sun lovers."

The sun was still too low on our horizon for reliable navigation and the McMurdo early October sunless nights were too light to see stars, so that I knew that the prospect of a plane flying mail in so early in the season was highly unlikely. We'd be lucky to get it before mid-October.

Nevertheless, reaction in camp was like a lightning bolt. And excitement increased the following day when the Task Force joined the radio traffic with questions. "What temperatures can you work under to make recoveries of airdrops? What are the cold limits for a Weasel?"

"For mail and light items, you can airdrop at any temperature," we told McMurdo. "But for protracted use of the Weasel, minus fifty degrees Fahrenheit is about the safe limit."

The men scanned the skies for planes bringing precious mail. "Perhaps tomorrow . . ." McMurdo radio reported. "Perhaps tomorrow . . ."

The promise was repeated again and again to the disappointed men, but no planes came. The men reacted as though they had been cheated of their birthright. "This indefinite promise is worse than no promise," I told Jack. "They should never have made such a promise when the navigators are stalling for the sun to get higher." Men are content and happy with definite assurance. But a promise that is offered for almost immediate fulfillment and then not completed brings on frustration and anger.

We tried to keep the men more than busy on camp activities to take their minds off McMurdo's daily promise. On October 5 when the first Soviet satellite was launched, I organized an around-the-clock observation team of Arlo, Bob, Willi, and myself to tape-record and to count its pulse rate, audible periods and signal intensity. We, too, shared the excitement the world felt concerning this event. Previous to joining the IGY Antarctic activity, I had been associated with discussions concerning our own satellite program and wondered why ours wasn't up also. We were able to hear the Sputnik for some 30 consecutive passes as it approached circularly around about the horizon. But it seemed peculiar to us that the longest and clearest signals were not when the satellite was closest, but rather when it was in its dark path circuit returning to its northernmost turning point.

Earl made us our own 20-foot flagpole out of pipe and on October 9 Jack and I raised Old Glory in a breezy −85° F. but impressive ceremony at the "exact" South Pole. Another special job ahead was to ring the Geographic Pole with empty oil drums at a 100-foot radius.

But these and other tasks plus regular assignments were not sufficient to distract the men. Old grievances that had died with the rising sun suddenly began to reappear.

Thus it was with good reason that I was disturbed as the days passed without the coming of the planes. On the 12th, word came that an Air Force plane would soon be over us. But our hopes were dashed again when the flight was canceled. Fortunately, when a devastating blizzard blew up, the men found good reason why no plane was coming.

Partly to work off our own feeling of restlessness Jack and I went out to the Geographic Pole to set up and align empty fuel barrels around it on Sunday, October 9, when the wind had receded a bit and the temperature had warmed up to −65°. Oz and Mel made quick sorties with the Weasel to haul empty barrels to circle about the Pole, and Jack and I spaced them at eight-foot intervals. It grew into an impressive fortress. Oz brought out some coffee but my beard was so iced that I could not get the cup to my lips. Back indoors I discovered after our three-hour stint, my stomach turned bright red and hurt with the cold. My thought was that it would do me good as well as the others if the mail plane came soon.

It was not until October 17 that we had our first aerial visitors. "You sure look nice and big and beautiful," Jack shouted over the radio as a glint of sunlight hit the wings of the Globemaster. My diary for that day read:

> Today was the great day we have awaited! The C-124 was about an hour off schedule and didn't arrive until about 1315. Everyone was cheerful and hustled about getting ready. The load consisted of two drops. The first was a rain of 40 barrels of diesel fuel on ribbon chutes, falling in a string of 10 bundles of four each. Only one barrel split open. The second drop was a container with our precious mail along with 600 pounds of pork and chicken, some galley gear, and a few minor repair parts for the Weasel. (The vital Cat parts for our broken-down tractor were not available to drop, the pilot informed us.)
>
> The American Ambassador to New Zealand, Francis Russell, was aboard the plane, also Bob Miller, Ed Hillary's second in command, Mr. McAlpine, the New Zealand Minister of Transport, and some news correspondents. An hour before arrival the pilot asked Jack if he wanted to make a statement. Because radio reception at that distance was poor, Jack suggested that they wait until the plane approached closer to the Pole. However, for some unexplained reason these first visitors in so many months didn't even pass the time of day with us. This apparent lack of friendliness by our benefactors was a disappointment indeed to several of our men.

But this disappointment was short-lived and vanished once Earl sorted the five bags of mail at the counter in the galley and distributed the letters to the men. "First mail in eight months and it's good to have friends," Arlo exclaimed.

The men retreated into their bunks with faraway looks in their eyes to read the mail from home, from wives, children, parents, sweethearts, and friends. There were few up for breakfast next morning because reading continued far into the night. Earl got a letter from his fiancée that proved a prize package. Her letter was on a roll 37 feet long and a foot wide. One man got an eight-month-old Valentine from his girl plus a more recent "Dear John" letter from her with news that she had tired of waiting and had married someone else.

My mail amounted to a fourth of a sack, of which about one-tenth was from family and friends. Ruth was my top correspondent with 12 letters, though our three daughters, Ann, Jane, and Mary, wrote in detail of their activities during our separation. I thought of how much I had missed family life in this year of absence.

Saddest correspondence to me were the letters from Dick Black, and Murray Wiener, my old exploring companions, who wrote me about Dick Byrd's last days. What would it be like to return to civilization and not find the Admiral there? The world would not be the same.

My IGY mail consisted of mimeographed instructions for scientific procedures, but not a single personal note from IGY headquarters to indicate that they were pleased that we had survived. However, there were several from scientists, ministers, newsmen, political figures and children. The camp was fairly inundated with old magazines, and it was significant that news magazines were generally ignored though the magazines showing pretty girls and new automobiles were highly popular.

With the arrival of the mail, the tone of our camp changed. The jolly laughter of older days reverberated again. The gloom of the preceding week or two was gone and high good spirits prevailed. Word came a few days later regarding scheduled departures. Navy P2V's were to land bringing in the new crew to replace our eighteen and take out our men. This would be done over a period of a week or two of overlap so our present crew could teach the ropes to the new men. In addition, it was my belief that our experienced men should be on hand during the Air Force C-124 resupply airdrops. This would be particularly important if the drops came before the weather warmed up.

In most areas of the world that experience low temperatures, activity out of doors, requiring long exposure or a considerable amount of dexterity, tends to cease when temperatures drop below $-40°$, especially if it is the least bit windy.

Since the date of our last airdrop on the 21st of February (just nine days after the last six of our wintering crew arrived at the Pole) we had had only seven days on which the maximum temperature had risen above −40°. A further tally showed that the average temperature for these same seven unseasonably warm days had not exceeded −40°.

Chapter 30

GONE WITH THE WIND

ALMOST everyone in camp is busy packing to go home," I wrote in my diary on October 21. "Jack and I told our respective groups to get the bulk of their belongings ready to go out when a plane lands here. We suggested being ready from this weekend outward." Soon the barracks, Jamesway and science building were full of half-packed boxes, and the camp began to take on the appearance of a riot's aftermath.

But if planes were to land, our airstrip had to be improved, for high drifted winter sastrugi made the runway hazardous. Jack and Mel were up most of the night of the twenty-third dragging the runway with a piece of pipe and chain behind the Weasel, followed by Bravo prancing and barking. It was maddening not to have the D-2 tractor in operation for this job. When word reached us the next day that a P2V was on its way with several of the replacement crew, I anxiously went out with Jack to examine the runway. It was a sorry sight. The first 4,000 feet on the Grid South end were full of holes and bumps. The next 4,000 feet were better, though also hazardous. Obviously there was far too much risk involved and we recommended against a landing until we could drag the strip properly with a D-2 tractor or until a storm had filled in the holes with drift snow. Fortunately, the flight was canceled.

This gave us a further opportunity to smooth the runway and

all the next day Mel, Oz, Jack and Bravo ranged the runway with the Weasel dragging a large timber and a steel truss as a scraper. "Take a look at it now," Jack said to me at nine that evening. I trudged out in the sunlight expecting little and was more than pleasantly surprised at the improvement made in such a short time with almost primitive equipment. The base of the runway was hard with furrows of loose snow running longitudinally. There were also foothigh undulations some 20 to 30 feet long running crosswise about every 50 to 200 feet. "It will be rough," I commented to Jack, "but it's undoubtedly safe."

On Saturday, October 26, McMurdo notified us that a P2V with sixteen men aboard, including five replacements for the South Pole Station, had left at 1100 and was due at the Pole at 1500. Moose and I prepared the manifests for the 2,265 pounds of outgoing gear for the return flight, and the men turned out en masse for the first plane landing at our station since February 12. But at 1500 no plane was in sight. Though it was −60° outdoors, the men continued to stand scanning the skies.

"I wonder where they are?" Doc Taylor asked worriedly. I thought of his efforts a few days earlier to dig a hole in the snow off the runway for use as a temporary shelter in case any planes crashed.

"They're coming," Jack finally notified us an hour and a half later from his radio control and lookout perch in the Aurora Tower.

"We were lost," the pilot, Commander Coley, said in chagrin after he landed. "But we finally picked you up on radar and came in on your description of the cloud cover above you."

Our visitors were to remain on the ground for only an hour or so. So, we took them on a short guided tour while JATO bottles were attached to the plane and our gear was stowed aboard. Only five of the sixteen were to remain, including Navy Lieutenant Dr. Houk, who was Jack Tuck's replacement as the new Navy C.O. as well as the medical officer replacement for Dr. Taylor. The other new Station members included De Witt, the new cook, Du Bois, a mechanic, White, a utility man, and Berg, the new radio operator. The other sightseers in addition to the plane crew members were Commander Witherell, the new Seabee Commander at McMurdo, reporters Tom Abercrombie of the *National Geographic* and Bud Crick of the *Oregon Journal* of Portland, and Warrant Officer Conger, Navy photographer.

Tom and Bud had won by lot the right to be the first pressmen to visit the Pole. They were representing the losers as well and you never saw such busy fellows as they dashed about the camp trying to take more pictures and reach more conclusions than we eighteen had managed in ten months. Only shortness of breath slowed them down as they rushed out to the South Pole—down into the mine—out into the seismic tunnel, and in and out of buildings.

As time drew near for departure, Tom Abercrombie came to me and asked that I permit him to stay. Although I'd like to have agreed, the decision belonged back in McMurdo where he had won the right to come in the first place. As way of persuasion Tom pleaded, "Dr. Siple, I'll work twelve hours a day down in the snow mine if you'll let me stay."

Since Ed Flowers, Jack, and I, who were known as "the first team," couldn't stick it out for more than three or four hours without respite, Tom's offer made our hearers guffaw.

Commander Coley finally managed to coax Tom and Bud aboard and we moved out of the prop wash to wave a farewell. Then the port engine let out a cloud of smoke and oil splattered to the snow as it came to a stop.

The plane crew made a quick inspection and it was soon apparent that it would take a while to fix the oil leak.

"Well, we'll be able to put you up overnight if it takes that long to replace the gasket," I told Coley.

While the plane crew worked on the P2V, our station crew placed cots in the emergency Jamesway 200 feet outside the regular camp, heated the building, and strung wires for electrical power.

"At least you'll be able to say that you spent a night at the Pole," John Guerrero told some of our sixteen guests. There was supposed to be food, fuel, and clothing in the emergency Jamesway to last eighteen men for six months, though we hardly expected anyone to test the accuracy of this computation.

"As for you," I said jocularly to Tom Abercrombie, handing him an ice ax, "there is a job you promised to do." Twenty minutes was his limit in the snow mine that first time, but he got "A" for effort.

We saw the plane crew and visitors off again the following day at 5:45 P.M. This time the engine on the port side that had caused so much trouble the previous day started easily and there was no sign of oil leaks. Then the engine on the starboard side was started. The cylinder head temperature rose quickly, but not the oil pressure. Then the engine stopped with a definiteness that suggested a mechanical freeze. Soon the crew and passengers were piling out again. This time the inspection took much longer and there was no optimism on their faces as the tired crew later came back into the mess hall.

"It looks like we'll have to have an engine change before that Neptune will fly again," Coley said grimly.

A field change of an engine is no easy matter on a tropical isle, but up here nearly two miles high in the center of the Antarctic it was another matter. It could take weeks for the job to be completed.

"You're welcome to stay," I offered though they scarcely had an alternative until the weather warmed and another plane could come in. "I'm certain you understand that our hospitality is warm, but we'll need some help in return. With thirty-four in camp, everyone will have to put in his share of time in the snow mine to supply enough water, and help with other communal chores."

There were few groans as our guests made their adjustments to South Pole living. And in one sense our old hands were pleased that the P2V had come. For the Neptune had brought us our first fresh foods: New Zealand lettuce, radishes, onions, hams, eggs, and fresh milk.

"This is some place," Commander Witherell said to me. "I never realized it was this cold."

"This is warm now," I told him. "At minus sixty-two degrees it feels like spring." For it is one of the illusions of the Antarctic that when the spring temperature rises ten or twenty degrees above the winter norm, the "heat" is almost stifling. "You should have been here when we enjoyed ninety-three consecutive hours with the temperature at minus ninety degrees Fahrenheit or colder." He looked at me askance.

Our schedule also called for C-124 drops of supplies for the coming year for the new crew, as well as repair parts for our Weasel and tractor. For our sturdy Weasel had suddenly gone bad. Mel Havener and Du Bois of the new crew went to work on it but the starter assembly was broken. Until a new starter assembly was airdropped we would have to man-haul equipment to camp from the drop zone. But this would not be too difficult as a temporary measure with thirty-four men in camp.

It was almost midnight on the 29th when the second postwinter Globemaster flew over. About fifteen of us had gone out to the drop zone armed with knives to intercept and cut off parachutes when the drops came down. Sickness had overtaken several of the newcomers at camp, and now the task of retrieving the airdrops proved too much for the unacclimatized strength and endurance of several other green hands. Perhaps, had the drops been nearer to target, our job would have been simplified. In any case hauling a Herman-Nelson heater even a half-mile haul by hand was a grind. Tom Abercrombie of the *National Geographic* hauled only a short distance before he fell. Then, to add to his discomfort, we ran over him with the sled and he could utter no outcry to tell us what we were doing to him. In fact, he was so exhausted he couldn't speak for several minutes.

"What happened to you?" I asked him in concern, when he had recovered a bit.

"My lungs didn't seem able to draw enough air into my chilled body, and my legs folded under me," he gasped. "And plodding along head down into the wind you fellows pulled the sled over me before I could protest."

Our visitors and replacements brought on a complete change in the atmosphere of the camp. During their isolation the men had looked forward impatiently to the time when there would be others to talk to besides those imprisoned with them. Now suddenly there were strangers in our midst.

During that first week our men were eager to talk with the newcomers. But by the end of the first week, the novelty began to wear thin. In addition, the "old-timers" found it particularly difficult, I saw, to fight off a feeling of annoyance when the "foreigners" did not show proper respect for some cherished scientific study or for some piece of improvised apparatus or other laboriously achieved features of the camp. Within a relatively short time a new *esprit de corps* had developed among the original crew and formed a growing barrier between the veterans and the newcomers. As an attempt at humor some of our boys went diligently through our movies to select one we had enjoyed a few months earlier for reshowing now —the hilarious, if unsubtle, *The Man Who Came to Dinner*.

To complicate matters, the newcomers brought along with them a variety of colds and related ailments. By the close of their first week with us most of them lay in bed wracked with coughs and fever. Most of those who did not take to their bunks due to such troubles were hit with customary high altitude headaches, causing one of our old crew members to say unsympathetically, "I'm glad that some of them have seen how hard we've had it, now that they've had a taste of it."

This uncharitable attitude was not shared by many of the others, even though they had to do the work of the sick—including the man-hauling of airdrops. For instance, on October 31 there was a 15-mile spread in the drops, ranging from 13 miles off one side of camp to two miles off the other. Fortunately, repair parts for the Weasel were in the first pallet dropped, thus ending the need for further man-hauling assignments.

"Some of you men don't look well," Doc Taylor told the old crew. "That new gang has dirtied up the Pole with imported disease and I'm afraid you'll catch it from them."

He urged all of us to take Asian flu shots sent in by the Navy to counter an epidemic sweeping the country back home. He told me, however, he feared our visitors had brought other bugs with them. "We'll just have to hope for the best," he said.

But the best was not for us. Doc Taylor himself was one of the first to go down; then came Moose and Mac and soon it spread to the rest of us. Eventually, all eighteen came down with the ailments to some degree. The Korean hack, a dry persistent cough I had witnessed during the Korean War, had been a minor affliction compared with what hit us at the Pole. In fact, the colds we caught were worse by far than any I had seen on five previous expeditions to the Antarctic.

Doc Taylor developed a high fever that made me worry for his safety. John Guerrero suffered pains throughout his body; Moose Remington required antibiotics and found it difficult to breathe; and I lost my voice for almost three weeks. One of the worst sufferers was Jack Tuck. He coughed one entire night without respite. Another morning at five he began coughing and coughed steadily for three hours while I tried from time to time to give him what aid I could.

Despite our coughs, fevers, sore throats, and pains, several of the men attempted to keep up with their duties. Work in the snow mine continued, though at a slower pace; the runway was dragged some more and our men worked on their reports and personal pieces for our *South Pole Yearbook*. In addition, one by one they began to shave off their beards. Earlier, McPherson had shaved his, then without warning Chet Segers shaved off his, which was one of the finest in camp. Then Earl removed his and was followed by Bob Benson. In typical Benson experimental style Bob only cut off half his beard the first day.

The result of this beard removal epidemic was startling. As each man made his appearance without his beard, the others gasped. For without a beard not only did each man's appearance change, but his personality seemed to alter as well. For instance, Bob Benson lost his studious mien with the disappearance of his beard and looked like a teen-ager. Doc Taylor looked much less severe without his. For a while it took time and conscious effort to recognize who the men were without their hairy adornments.

On November 7, an R4D started out from McMurdo for the Pole with two IGY and three Navy replacements aboard. Doc Taylor and Earl Johnson were alerted for departure. However, halfway up the Beardmore Glacier one of the plane's engines failed. Luckily they made it back to the Liv Glacier Depot in the Queen Maud Range, but only after the pilot jettisoned the special tools and hoists needed to enable us to remove the prop and engine of the crippled P2V still with us at the Pole.

"There is a conspiracy against us," Doc Taylor exclaimed to me worriedly, for he was anxious to get back to the States and begin a special surgery internship at the Yale Medical School. Perhaps an ill wind did blow because the very next day the starboard engine of another P2V with five IGY men aboard caught fire on its way to the Pole. The pilot of course turned back, and the engine was still burning when he set the plane down on the McMurdo runway.

Weakened by illness, crowded by the newcomers, and restless to leave, many of the old crew men were at loose ends by the weekend and found it difficult to while away the evening hours. Nor did it help that the men were kept on departure alert.

Several more Globemasters were due overhead to complete the required airdrops and I hoped this would occupy the men somewhat. However, I did not count on the airdrops themselves to add to our hazards. For instance, on Sunday, November 10th, two C-124's arrived together.

It had been decided to provide the Pole Station with a second D-2 tractor. Stripped down it would still weigh 7 tons when parachuted from the dropwell of a Globemaster. Since this was the heaviest object the planes had dropped at the Pole, the Air Force sent along a second Globemaster to photograph the historic event. In the process of lightening the basic load of the tractor, they removed the bulldozer's blade and the arms by which it was attached to the tractor, planning to drop this separately from the second plane. In order to strengthen the arms for the drop, a beam was attached across the open end of the U formed by the blade and arms. This assembly was placed on a platform to be dropped from the second C-124. It must have looked so much like a basket that the riggers were tempted into filling the space with parts disassembled from the tractor as well as the treads removed from the track. Each of these steel plates weighed about 25 pounds and were two feet long. By removing these, the McMurdo riggers had greatly lightened the weight of the heavy tractor.

Unfortunately, as the platform "basket" was released through the dropwell of the first Globemaster, we saw it turn in the air so that the unlocked plates fell free and came hurtling down over a half-mile-square area of snow. From a distance the bright orange plates twirling through the air reminded us of confetti. Willie and Bob out on the drop zone were narrowly missed as the plates sliced down into the snow all about them. As soon as we realized what they were, all who were free to do so went scrambling over the snow to retrieve them, since it was essential that we have them on hand to be able to reassemble the tread and attach it to the tractor as soon as it landed so that we could get it in operation and move it to the garage before the cold made this difficult if not impossible. Some of the rectangular plates had landed flat and were easily retrievable. Others had sliced their way into the snow like a knife and were more difficult to find and dig out.

We were all scattered about the drop area at work digging out the plates as the second Globemaster began its drop run and I saw the orange tractor on its 12 x 8-foot red platform gradually emerging from the dropwell of the plane. The plane was about 2,000 feet above the surface and no more than that distance away when the release began. The plane was flying in a line directly over Ed Flowers and myself. We watched fascinated as the tractor and platform began to tumble. Momentarily three huge 100-foot chutes billowed behind it, then drooped lifelessly as the turning tractor severed the shroud lines. My horrified eyes watched as the huge orange object came hurtling end over end down toward us. For an instant I feared it would drop on us, but the C-124's 200-mile-per-hour forward momentum carried it beyond us and it landed in the open snow fields like an exploding bomb, causing the icecap to shake as if from an earthquake. Herb Hansen, less than 200 feet from the impact, was lost from sight in the billow of snow rising high in the air.

The boards and the fifteen-pound felt and canvas crash pads which had been attached to the tractor at places in an effort to prevent the shroud lines from being severed had been liberated on their own. And being lighter, they did not carry as far. Now they came pounding down around all of us. I turned to speak to Ed Flowers, who had been standing only four or five feet away. I found him struggling to rise from the ground. One of the pads had struck him squarely on the head. Had he been looking up at the plane the force of the blow would certainly have snapped his neck, but since he had been looking toward where the tractor had crashed, the blow caught him squarely on top of the head and only knocked him down and almost out. The only permanent damage he suffered was a broken tooth.

When I reached the point where the tractor had landed, I found only a 10-foot-deep, 20-foot-wide crater, the snow bottom of which showed no signs of the tractor's presence. Later, after several days of digging, we found it down 30 feet, shattered beyond all hope of salvage and repair.

A number of us who thought we were recovered from our colds and thus went out to dig up the treads and the tractor, suffered relapses. Apparently, breathing the cold air while we were still infected had a lot to do with it. I myself stayed outside digging for several hours the day after the stream-in trying to find the tractor. When I went back indoors I found my voice down to a whisper.

I tried to carry on duties as usual, for there was much to be done, but it seemed such an effort to speak. This was especially so when I tried to carry on a radio conversation with a number of U.S. Congressmen who flew over us in a C-124. It was this visit, incidentally, which made me realize that the South Pole Station was on the map to stay.

On November 13th we had the first clear indications of the sun's warming effect. For the first time in 169 days—since May 27th— the temperature rose above −40° F.

Three days later at 2130 on November 16th, another P2V that had flown in from New Zealand reached the Pole. Taxiing halfway down the runway coming in, the plane stopped and as it did, the port engine stalled. Watching from a distance, several of our men groaned and someone said, "We'll have several more coming to dinner for a long stay." *

Fortunately, the engine started up again and the pilot kept it running while Doc Taylor and Earl Johnson, the only members of our winter party to leave, climbed aboard. "You don't need to depend on luck, Howard," I told Doc. "It has been my great pleasure to have known you."

---

* The South Pole Station is being continued indefinitely. As of this writing, the fourth wintering-over party is being readied for the field. Edward Flowers will serve as its Station Scientific Leader as well as again head the Meteorology Unit.

Farewells are always apt to be sticky. "Paul," he said, and then he hesitated, "it really has been a grand year."

Earl was sad when he took his leave, though he was anxious to get home and marry. He also wanted to use his GI student rights, planning to become a veterinarian or a wildlife specialist. I felt like a father to him. He had come originally to the Pole with a somewhat negative attitude caused by an occasional lack of confidence in his own abilities. "Remember, Earl," I told him. "No more 'Can't do's.' The motto of the Seabees is 'Can do.' "

"I'll remember," he said. And then they were gone.

The new arrivals on the plane that took out Taylor and Earl included four IGY replacements and a new Navy radio operator. The old crew was still in the majority, but they would not be for long! I alerted Bob, Arlo, John Guerrero and Floyd to leave on the next plane, which was expected during the next few days. It had been my hope that Jack Tuck and I would remain until the final airlift back to McMurdo. But almost as if he could read my thoughts, Admiral Dufek sent a message ordering Jack back on the next plane.

There was no way to delay his departure and the fateful day came on November 20th. The day before, Jack had turned over the Naval operation of the Station to Lieutenant Houk, and we had gone to the Pole to fly several special flags including the replica of Shirase's 1912 South Pole flag airdropped last February and Jack's Dartmouth Outing Club pennant.

John Guerrero was to leave with Jack and we passed considerable time joking. It was easily apparent to me that John had matured a great deal during his stay. The boy who had arrived in a Hawaiian Aloha shirt seemed to have more purpose now. I thought of old Art Walden, that colorful sourdough in charge of the dog teams on Byrd's first expedition. "The Antarctic is an intensifier of personality," Art had told me. "If a man has good qualities these may be the ones that intensify."

When Jack left, we both found it hard to talk. He looked at me with his deep-set, penetrating eyes and finally said it had been a wonderful year. I agreed. "Especially because I had the chance to work with you," he blurted. Jack was neither a sentimentalist nor emotional by nature and I knew he meant what he said. "That is exactly the way I feel about you," I told him.

There seemed to be so little time to say anything that we were almost totally silent from then until his plane's take-off. "Doc," he confided to me shortly before he climbed into the plane, "I've got more butterflies in my stomach right now in leaving than when I first came here with Dick Bowers and the dog team, or at any time during the year." I nodded with what I hoped was understanding. It was Jack's plan to do graduate work in polar geography.* When we would meet again was problematic.

I was glum now when I returned to camp. But I was not the only one who missed Jack. We had left Bravo with Chet in the mess hall and now Bravo went off in a wild search for Jack, barking at everyone. All evening then he lay in my doorway apprehensive and touchy. It was Jack's hope that Palle Mogensen, who was to succeed me, would retain Bravo as mascot. But there was evidence that the new station leaders preferred raising their own puppy.

Task Force orders were for five more of the men to leave on the next plane in a few days. Then I would leave with others on the following flight. It was difficult to believe that only a year before Jack's departure the pioneer construction crew had landed at the Pole, or that our going scientific program was of such recent vintage.

While we waited, we continued to retrieve airdrops that came in at regular intervals, and helped stow the supplies inside the camp. It was quite an operation rolling a new supply of full fuel drums back into the caches beside the garage and along Main Street. I thought of Slats and his two-man crew who had built the cache originally a year ago before the tunnels had been erected to enclose them.

I also spent considerable time briefing Mogensen, the new IGY leader. A former Army Major of Danish extraction, he had a good polar background in Greenland as well as last year's traverse to Byrd Station. I told him and Houk the reasoning back of some of our procedures and construction concepts. Their attention was most polite and yet I could sense their impatience to be on their own. I could not really blame them.

We were not quite down to the hundred-foot depth in the snow mine—our goal for so many months. "We will finish it," they assured me. "Don't worry." But I noticed the newcomers were already taking snow for the melter from where it was much easier to excavate. I stressed the importance of never letting any snow drift over the camp's flat roof. The construction crew a year ago had not only

---

* Lieutenant Tuck went on inactive status in the Navy shortly after returning home. He spent the following summer on an Arctic expedition, then was admitted to study for doctoral candidacy at Scott Polar Research Institute in Cambridge, England, in 1958.

been forced to leave out every other roof girder because of drop losses and air freight economy, but the lumber, chicken wire, and burlap tunnel structure joining the buildings together could not stand a heavy snow load. We had shoveled off the small drifts of snow created downwind from the Met dome and the Aurora Tower. This I stressed must be done each year.

Drift will normally accumulate rapidly to the top of large massive structures, like buildings, and then remain flush with the surface until the surrounding snow level catches up due to normal snow accumulation. This meant that at a snowfall rate of half a foot per year, the station's flat roof might remain bare for ten or fifteen years. But, I cautioned, if the snow should start to drift higher due to the camp's superstructures, the station's life might be cut short. Already the warming snowdrifts our own crew had left over our Grid South salvage area were beginning to slump and put their full weight on the random spanners, straps, and parachutes that had held up remarkably well all winter. I was amazed how, at air temperatures now averaging in the minus thirties, the hard winter surface snow which for the past six months had remained continuously below −60° F. was beginning to change character and lose its strength. It would require considerable effort if the cache were to be saved, although it contained little of value save the gleanings from construction days.

Certainly the new crew would have their own fresh crop of problems. They were acclimatizing well and taking over responsibility for their parts of the program from the last of our soon-to-depart first-year men. The new IGY staff was friendly and eager to gain purpose and understanding. They asked many questions concerning the value and accomplishments of our first year at the Pole and what lay ahead.

The answers I gave to accomplishments did not all deal with science. Certainly the biggest achievement was the technological advancement required to place a station at the Pole. For it was a national achievement of no mean stature to have established a station at the very bottom of the world. The effort had involved hundreds if not thousands of persons to varying degrees in the planning and execution of the operation. Our Defense forces, the Navy, the Air Force, and the Army, had accomplished on schedule a logistics and technical operation which would have been virtually impossible a few years earlier.

The task was not achieved without sacrifice of human life. It was costly and at times reckless, but it was bold. And while we who had spent the first winter had taken uncommon risks, essentially we had brought to bear the lessons begun by Byrd more than a quarter century earlier. As I looked back at the relatively comfortable year, I realized that most of our men never realized the adventures they might have experienced had we been less well prepared. As it was, the men for the most part had come to the Pole and carried out their assigned technical and scientific missions.

It is usually not possible to place an immediate evaluation on a scientific accomplishment. It often takes a matter of years to process the data gathered and an even longer time to analyze its significance. Still, already certain accomplishments were obvious. As a result of all the co-operating IGY stations in and surrounding Antarctica, daily weather maps were now available to permit forecasters to understand the mechanism of weather over the last large unknown segment of the world's surface. Each of the Antarctic stations ringing the continent had bridged a significant portion of the long water gaps between the temperate continents and islands. We, at the Pole, had in effect bridged the big inland gap by furnishing the tie across the continent in all directions.

Although the findings we had made in this hard-to-reach spot of which science was almost totally ignorant were important new facts, their value lay more as bits and pieces of a much larger picture—one, in fact, global in scope. Examined individually, the pieces of a jig-saw puzzle give little clue to the completed picture. Therefore, the gleanings of our hard-fought struggle would move on to the IGY data processing centers. Here in due course they would emerge in new physical concepts of the earth as a whole. Our Pole Station bricks of knowledge would be lost in the immensity of the scientific edifice under construction, but if they had not been available, the structure would be less sturdy and less complete.

The newcomers' role was also vital. They faced no struggle to complete the building of a station nor any apprehension as to the winter night. Therefore, they could be expected to accumulate considerably more complete scientific data.

Someone asked, "Who does this station here at the Pole belong to?"

"The U.S. taxpayers paid for the buildings, of course," I replied. "But six countries' claims intersect that ring of barrels out there on the drop zone."

I had participated in the IGY with a feeling of pride. Some sixty nations had worked together in harmony and unselfish purpose. For the most part nations had done their studies in their own back yards. However, here in Antarctica twelve nations were carrying on work without primary concern as to the sovereignty of the territory. A few feathers had been ruffled when the U.S. and the USSR went into Wilkes Land, an area claimed by Australia, to establish some of their bases. The U.S. had long occupied the Little Americas in New Zealand's Ross Dependency and now had McMurdo Station there as well. Ellsworth Station was located in a region claimed jointly by both Great Britain and Argentina. Japan and Belgium had their stations in Norwegian-claimed territory, while on the Graham-Palmer Peninsula Chilean, Argentine, and British stations ceased their open acts of dispute over sovereignty in the interest of international harmony during IGY. Would and could this peaceful international attitude continue after IGY was over?

It is understandable why a man like myself who has been intimately involved in Antarctic affairs for so many years would have mixed nationalistic and internationalistic views. Back in the sailing ship-dog team-primitive aircraft era twenty or thirty years ago, we who ventured into the unknown wastes of Antarctica with Byrd had felt impatient with our government and the public for failing to lay claim to new territory we saw for the first time. True, its usefulness was not readily apparent to most people but neither was that of Alaska nor of northern Greenland when the United States made the fortunate decision to buy the former and the less fortunate decision to sell the latter. Certainly, we thought, if other nations were laying claim to areas of the Antarctic continent they had never seen, why should we hesitate to claim those portions we had actually been first to see?

As time has passed, the question of our national position has become more difficult. We have actually viewed more and more of the continent while other nations—all good friends of ours—lay claim to it sight unseen. Yet if the U.S. were to assert its claim on the basis of the rights of first discovery to the segment including the Graham-Palmer Peninsula, lying between Longitude 40° W and 90° W, claimed throughout in overlapping wedges by the United Kingdom, Argentina, and Chile, we would possess the lion's share of the area.

American authorities are divided into those who would stick up for our rights at all costs; those who would refrain from claiming on the grounds of not offending our friends; and those who would refrain from showing any interest in claiming at all.

Still, time and world conditions will not stand still. The IGY experiment with twelve out of sixteen claiming nations working together on a common world problem is encouraging. It is axiomatic and inevitable that all world problems will eventually have to be dealt with in a harmony which will require greater international co-operation and less nationalism. If the world has at present grown sufficiently mature so that it can begin to administer trusts for common global good, certainly no better experimental area could be selected than Antarctica which is without a native population and possesses a minimum of currently desirable economic resources. Perhaps the nations which have worked together in Antarctica so harmoniously to develop a fund of geophysical knowledge could be entrusted to develop it for the scientific and economic welfare of the world.

Such a decision is more easily made by the U.S. which has done so much work in Antarctica without claiming territory than by smaller nations that have done less field work and claimed large tracts of land with questionable justification. Their pride of possession may stand in the way of logic.

Yet if it is not readily possible for ten or twelve nations to agree, perhaps the experiment could begin with two or three at first. For example, the U.S. and New Zealand have reached so high a degree of agreement on the Antarctic, that it would probably take little diplomatic skill to establish a single condominium or protectorate merging both nation's interests. The U.S. operations into the Ross Sea quadrant have depended upon New Zealand as a staging area since 1928, and during the IGY this dependence increased, and now the U.S. Navy and the U.S. Air Force have large personnel contingents in New Zealand to handle the traffic in and out. New Zealand, who was given the territory she claims by Great Britain, never visited her own claim territory officially until the IGY and the U.S. ship and air transport permitted scientists and government officials to travel south and return in a week or two. Hallett Station, manned jointly by U.S. and New Zealand personnel, has apparently functioned smoothly as witnessed by our "ham" chatter.

If New Zealand and the United States continue their interests after IGY, their mutual co-operation will be beneficial to both countries, with U.S. ship and air connections to Antarctica automatically giving the New Zealanders access in exchange for staging accommodations.

With such stimulus, tourist trade by ship and air would soon follow; with broad implied economic advantages to New Zealand.

But how far could such a merger go? I personally felt the pulse in semi-official quarters in both countries in 1947 and again in 1955 and 1956. The answer I got both times was simple. Interested citizens and government officials of both countries informally recognized the advantages of close U.S.-N.Z. co-operation, including even possible joint administration of the Antarctic territory from the French claim along Longitude 142° E across West Antarctica to the Weddell Sea, save for the hotly contested northern half of the Graham-Palmer Peninsula. But there was a problem labeled as unsolvable by both groups. The New Zealanders agreed that their own government would never offer the proposal because they would not want to give an impression of imposing on the generosity of the United States. American informal spokesmen, on the other hand, were equally certain that the United States would not initiate such a proposal because the United States would not want to risk an impression of pressuring a smaller nation. When both countries recognize that they can jointly demonstrate international co-operation to the whole world and at the same time obtain maximum mutual benefits, the reticence to propose such a treaty will lessen. Then perhaps such bilateral agreements might spread to other nations.

However, for the present Antarctica is an occupied continent to be reckoned with in world affairs from this time onward.

Such serious discussions as these made us realize that while we might be at the end of the world, we were still very much part of it. In fact, we wondered if we had been living in a no man's land or in the first truly federated land.

Thursday the 28th did not much seem like Thanksgiving Day although the new crew was celebrating its first holiday at the Pole, for Bob Benson, Arlo Landolt, Floyd Johnson, McPherson and Osborne departed that day. Mac and Oz planned to stay in the Navy. Bob and Arlo would return to college for graduate work and Floyd was to return to the Weather Bureau.* It was hard to see them leave.

---

* W. Floyd Johnson returned to the Antarctic at the close of IGY in 1959 to spend a year as meteorologist at Ellsworth Station operated by Argentina. The same year Herbert Hansen returned to the Wilkes Station operated by the Australians. Melvin Havener returned as a Seabee to winter over at McMurdo Sound, still a U.S. Navy support base.

After they were gone I suddenly felt that I was again a stranger in my own home. We of the first wintering party were now in the minority and only hours remained until another plane would be coming. This time for me. Most of my personal gear had already been shipped out.

The next day was beautiful and nearly calm. The annual resupply drops were nearly all completed, and now there were two tractors and two Weasels at the Pole. We could safely make a short journey out of camp, but we dared not go very far since we had to be available in the event a plane should start for the Pole.

We put a few supplies in a sled behind the Weasel and Ed Flowers, Willi Hough, Herb Hansen, Moose Remington, Mel Havener and I headed to Grid North to visit the snow stakes first. One near the camp showed no change in the snow surface level since before the March sun set, but the next six, running three miles farther to windward, all showed a six-inch rise on the eight-foot stakes. But since the surface irregularities were nearly that great, we didn't have too much faith in a one-season record. Next we headed more to the east up a slight slope toward what appeared to be a near horizon. Within less than a mile we found ourselves on top of the rise that we had noted in this direction from camp. All horizons seemed to lie far from us: I estimated that it was at least five miles to the next slight rises in other directions. We made a snow cairn to mark the crown of the high area, and noted that the snow was firmer than back at camp, hard and rough as right after the windy winter night. Looking toward the sun the wind-polished surface glistened in patches where it was not covered by softer, newer drift snow.

As we rode back to camp we recalled that this was the twenty-eighth anniversary of Byrd's flight to the Pole. We were also conscious of the relaxed feeling of comradeship we had known before the visitors and our replacements arrived at the Pole. I wished the rest of our remaining twelve men were with us to enjoy the sunny calm mildness some of them had never experienced during the months they had lived at the Pole.

We so enjoyed our morning excursion that after lunch we headed out toward Grid South, the "downhill" direction that was our longer vista from camp. At six miles we lost sight of the camp except for the higher antennas. But we recalled that Jack and Willi had seen the camp from as far out as seventeen miles in this direction and realized that we were in a slight hollow of some sort. The surface here was much smoother and softer than the snow on the higher ground north of camp we had visited earlier in the day. If there were any wind-glazed surfaces, they were covered by newer snow.

Certainly, these two short trips offered proof that there were decided local variations in the surface and possibly in the winds that created them. We regretted so little time to explore further.

We headed northeast until we could line up the camp flagpole and the South Pole flag to give us a positive bearing on our location. And here we built another snow cairn. What an amazing difference we discovered in the snow compared with that we had used earlier in the day. Here the snow was sugary, and we couldn't dig out the blocks of hard snow that make snow cairn building easy. We had to virtually scoop the snow into a soft heap, although down a foot or two we found somewhat firmer snow. We returned to camp tired and pleased with our first and last day of exploration outside the city limits of the South Pole city.

I rose at five A.M. on November 30 after three hours of sleep, took my last shower in camp and dressed in clean clothing. Partly because Herb Hansen had shaved his luxuriant beard the night before and partly because Chet, Moose, Cliff and Junior, who would be staying awhile, wanted to see me without my beard, I cut it off on its exact anniversary. "I wouldn't have known you," Chet said, his eyes wide, when I walked into the mess hall. "You look so much younger and different, too."

I spent the morning and afternoon packing my last few belongings and cleaning my room. As I did so, I realized I would carry away with me many memories of the hundreds of hours I had spent in this windowless, golden-yellow, parachute-shrouded cubicle. Willi Hough, Ed Flowers, Herb Hansen and Mel Havener were busy packing, too, for they were to leave with me. I packed one last sentimental souvenir. I had brought along two of those silvered glass balls. Now I exchanged the spare one with the one that had been on top of the flagpole on the garage roof all year.

A radio message came during the day: Bravo was to leave with us. I resented this officious treatment of the poor animal as I knew Jack did also. The poor pup knew no other life and really belonged at the Pole. Why did he have to suffer such a fate? "I won't be partner to taking him out," I told Willi. "It's like signing his death warrant to take him from this place."

Willi appointed himself Bravo's caretaker and braided a special leash for him.

The plane came in and our departure time was set at ten P.M.

Shortly before we were to leave, I walked out a short distance from camp and turned to examine the place I had called home during the preceding year. I breathed a thankful prayer that our first year at the end of the earth had been successful and without mishap. How fortunate I had been that Dick Bowers and Jack Tuck had been flexible and intelligent enough so that we had been able to develop a camp free of most of the impossible construction features the original planners had provided for us. Although I had not been sent fully mature scientists to carry out our task, thank heavens they had been eager and willing young men who had been full of the drive to make the most of their opportunity and had possessed remarkable talents for improvising. Certainly this had compensated for what they may have lacked in age, training, or experience. How good Providence had been that we had been able to live as a single unit and not as separated goats and sheep the way our parent organizations had cast our lot. We had come into a land of apparent hostile nothingness but we had survived. We had gradually discovered that this white austere country was a fascinating new world with a special character all its own.

Yet, as I sauntered out to the plane I took a last long look at the polar plateau. And as I gazed about me, the words of Scott came to my mind: "We see only a few miles of ruffled snow bounded by a vague wavy horizon, but we know that beyond that horizon are hundreds or even thousands of miles which can offer no change to the weary eye.... One knows there is neither tree, nor shrub, nor any living thing, not even inanimate rock—nothing but this terrible limitless expanse of snow. It has been so for countless years, and it will be so for countless more. And we, little human insects, have started to crawl over this awful desert.... Could anything be more terrible than this silent, wind-swept immensity...?"

But we are conquering it, I told myself, thanks to men like Scott, Amundsen, Shackleton and Byrd, all brave pioneers who paved the way for those of us who followed. If only Dick Byrd had been able to stand where I stood and look at the village at the Pole. This was indeed the legacy of his many efforts to bring the throb of humanity to this unknown continent.

He would have been proud, too, of the truly heroic effort of Dick Bowers and his valiant construction crew in creating a bit of America at the Pole. Bowers was indeed an explorer in the finest tradition of those who ventured into the unknown.

Twenty-seven hours after I left the Pole I was in New Zealand. Departure had been sad, though I was glad to be returning to my family and friends. I was pleased that Gus Shinn, who had been flying this polar run since Highjump days, was our pilot. We had landed at the foot of the Liv Glacier where we refueled, blasted off with the aid of JATO bottles and flew into McMurdo. After a brief rest, a quick meal and a talk with transient IGY friends, including Sir Hubert Wilkins, Linc Washburn, Bill Field, Dick Goldthwait and Paul Dalrymple, we climbed aboard a C-124 bound for Christchurch. We were glad to be out of earshot of poor Bravo. Restrained by a chain for the first time since early puppyhood, he was alternately crying and howling, abandoned in his new and strange surroundings according to orders.

It was past midnight and the rain was pelting down when I left the plane at the airport outside Christchurch. I felt strangely alone back in civilization. Then suddenly in front of me I saw a familiar face and pressed a firm hand in a hearty shake. It was Jack Tuck.

"Sorry I couldn't greet you with some minus one hundred and two degrees," he grinned, and we walked away.

Appendix 1

SOUTH POLE ROSTER

Those Who Came First

Ninety-seven miles from the pole at Lat. 88° 23′, January 9, 1909, a party on foot was forced to turn back. (British)

Jameson B. Adams
Eric Marshall, M.D.
Ernest H. Shackleton, leader
Frank Wild

First to arrive at the exact vicinity of the South Pole December 14–17, 1911, using dog transport. (Norwegian)

Roald Amundsen, leader
Olav Bjaaland
Helmer Hanssen
Sverre Hassel
Oscar Wisting

Second by only a month on January 18, 1912, a party on foot lost their lives in retreat from the Pole. (British)

H. R. Bowers
Edgar Evans
L. E. G. Oates
Captain Robert F. Scott, leader
Edward A. Wilson, M.D.

Of four parties supporting Scott, the last three men turned back at Lat. 87° 32′ on January 4, 1912, less than 150 miles from the Pole.

T. Crean
Edward R. G. R. Evans, Lt. R.N., leader
W. Lashly

Those Who Flew First to the South Pole

The first flight November 29, 1929, in the *Floyd Bennett,* a tri-motored Ford plane. (American)

Bernt Balchen, pilot
Commander Richard E. Byrd, leader and navigator
Harold I. June, pilot and radioman
Ashley C. McKinley, photographer

The second flight by two U. S. Navy twin-engine R4D aircraft on skis February 15, 1947.

Plane 1	*Plane 2*
Lt. George H. Anderson, pilot	George E. Baldwin
Rear Adm. Richard E. Byrd, senior officer	Raymond J. Butters
	Comdr. Clifford M. Campbell
Robert P. Heekin	Capt. Eugene C. McIntyre, co-pilot
Lt. Comdr. J. C. McCoy, co-pilot	A. V. Mincey
K. C. Swain	Maj. Robert R. Weir, pilot
J. E. Valinski	

The first 45-minute test landing was made by a U. S. Navy crew in an R4D *Que Será Será* on 31 October, 1956.

Capt. Douglas L. Cordiner, observer
P. O. 2/c William A. Cumbie, Jr., radioman
Rear Adm. George J. Dufek, C.O., Task Force 43
Capt. William M. Hawkes, co-pilot
Lt. Comdr. Conrad S. Shinn, pilot
P. O. 2/c John P. Strider, crew chief
Lt. John Swadener, navigator

The pilots of the first two R4D aircraft to land near the Pole with the 8-men Advance Party and one dog team on November 20, 1956.

Lt. Comdr. Conrad S. Shinn
Lt. Comdr. Roy E. Curtis

Those Who Constructed the Station

The Advance Party landed on November 20, 1956, 8 miles from the Pole.

Richard A. Bowers, Lt. (jg), leader
William W. Bristol, PMC
Thomas T. Montgomery, RM
Jerry L. Nolon, AG2
Dale L. Powell, RM2

John A. Randall, CM3
* John Tuck, Jr., Lt. (jg)
Floyd A. Woody, HM1

* Returned temporarily to McMurdo between December 1 to 29, 1956.

Additional construction party personnel landed at the South Pole on or before December 1, 1956.

Charles A. Bevilacqua, BUC
Robert L. Chaudion, YN1
William R. Goodwin, AE3
Howard A. Hisey, BU2
Edward H. Hubel, UTC
Patrick D. McCormick, BU3
Harold C. McCrillis, CE2
* Richard J. Patton, Sgt., USAF
Richard Prescott, BU2
Colon H. Roberts, SW3
Donald J. Scott, UT3
Dr. Paul A. Siple (representing IGY)
Charles M. Slaton, CMC
Raymond R. Spiers, CS1
Gordon C. Tyler, AD3
Clarence A. Wagner, UT1
Parry R. Williamson, BU1

* Parachuted in on November 22, 1956.

Those Who Manned the Station

The First Wintering-Over Party, 1957

IGY Personnel

Robert F. Benson, seismology
Edwin C. Flowers, meteorology
John F. Guerrero, meteorology
Herbert L. Hansen, meteorology
William S. Hough, ionosphere
William F. Johnson, meteorology
Arlo U. Landolt, aurora
Edward W. Remington, glaciology
Paul A. Siple, scientific leader

Navy Support

Clifford R. Dickey, Jr., ET1, electronics
Melvin C. Havener, CM2, mechanic
Earl F. Johnson, UT1, utilities man
William C. McPherson, Jr., RM1, radioman
Thomas M. Osborne, BU1, builder
Chester W. Segers, CS1, cook
Howard C. Taylor, III, Lt., medical officer
John Tuck, Jr., Lt. (jg), Navy support leader
Kenneth L. Waldron, CE2, electrician

The Second Wintering-Over Party, 1958

IGY Personnel

D. M. Baulch, meteorology
James B. Burnham, ionosphere
P. C. Dalrymple, micrometeorology
John A. Dawson, aurora and airglow
Stephen P. Fazekas, meteorology
M. B. Giovinetto, glaciology
Charles R. Greene, Jr., ionosphere
Kirby J. Hanson, meteorology
Arthur E. Jorgenson, meteorology
Palle Mogensen, scientific leader

Navy Support

Louis B. de Wit, CSC, cook
Gerald R. Du Bois, CMC, mechanic
Stanley C. Greenwood, Jr., RMC, radioman
John D. Hasty, RM1, radioman
Vernon N. Houk, Lt., MC, medical officer, Navy support leader
Ronald E. Mozetic, ET1, electronics
Donald Norman, CE1, electrician
Edward L. White, UT1, utilities man

The Third Wintering-Over Party, 1959

IGY Personnel

Luvern R. Bauhs, ionosphere
Edward J. Fremouw, aurora
Willis Jacobs, seismology
Fred S. Mayeda, meteorology
Clarence D. McKenny, meteorology
Julian W. Posey, meteorology, scientific leader
Howard D. Redifer, meteorology
Benjamin F. Remington, meteorology

Navy Support

Nello A. Bambini, UT1, utilities man
Clarence N. Engel, Jr., BU1, builder
Donald A. Finlayson, RM1, radioman
Jerry W. King, CE1, electrician
Donald A. Kitchen, CS1, cook
Norman E. Owens, RM2, radioman
Thomas E. Smith, ET2, electronics
Jack Stroud, CM1, mechanic
Sidney Tolchin, Lt., MC, medical officer

Appendix 2

IGY, NATIONAL AND INTERNATIONAL GROUPS ASSOCIATED WITH CURRENT ANTARCTIC ACTIVITIES

Countries Participating in IGY

* Argentina
* Australia
  Austria
* Belgium
  Bolivia
  Brazil
  Bulgaria
  Burma
  Canada
  Ceylon
* Chile
  China: Taipei
  Colombia
  Cuba
  Czechoslovakia
  Denmark
  Dominican Republic
  East Africa
  Ecuador
  Egypt
  Ethiopia
  Finland
* France
  German Democratic Republic
  German Federal Republic
  Ghana
  Greece
  Guatemala
  Hungary
  Iceland
  India
  Indonesia
  Iran

Ireland
Israel
Italy
* Japan
  Korea, Democratic Republic of
  Malaya
  Mexico
  Mongolian Peoples Republic
  Morocco
  Netherlands
* New Zealand
* Norway
  Pakistan
  Panama
  Peru
  Philippines
  Poland
  Portugal
  Rhodesia, Southern
  Rumania
  Spain
  Sweden
  Switzerland
  Tunisia
* Union of South Africa
* Union of Soviet Socialist Republics
* United Kingdom
* United States
  Uruguay
  Venezuela
  Vietnam (Republic)
  Vietnam Democratic Republic
  Yugoslavia

* Countries that have Antarctic or Sub-Antarctic Stations.

CSAGI

Comité Spécial De L'Année Géophysique Internationale
Special Committee For the International Geophysical Year

BUREAU

Professor S. Chapman, President
Dr. L. V. Berkner, Vice-President
Professor V. V. Beloussov, Member
Professor J. Coulomb, Member
Professor M. Nicolet, General Secretary

United States National Committee For the International Geophysical Year

Chairman: Joseph Kaplan, National Academy of Sciences
Vice-Chairman: A. H. Shapley, National Academy of Sciences
Executive Director: Hugh Odishaw, National Academy of Sciences
Members:
Leason H. Adams, Carnegie Institution of Washington
Allen V. Astin, National Bureau of Standards
H. G. Booker, Cornell University
Lyman J. Briggs, National Bureau of Standards
G. M. Clemence, United States Naval Observatory
Earl G. Droessler, Department of Defense, Research and Development
Hugh L. Dryden, National Advisory Committee for Aeronautics
C. T. Elvey, Geophysical Institute, University of Alaska
Laurence M. Gould, Carleton College
E. R. Piore, International Business Machines Corporation
F. W. Reichelderfer, United States Weather Bureau
E. B. Roberts, United States Coast and Geodetic Survey
J. A. Simpson, the Enrico Fermi Institute for Nuclear Studies, The University of Chicago
Paul A. Siple, Department of the Army
Athelstan F. Spilhaus, University of Minnesota
Merle A. Tuve, Carnegie Institution of Washington
A. Lincoln Washburn, Dartmouth College
Harry Wexler, United States Weather Bureau
Ex officio and liaison:
Wallace W. Atwood, Jr., National Academy of Sciences
Lloyd V. Berkner, Associated Universities, Inc.
Robert Brode, University of California, Berkeley

Maurice Ewing, Lamont Geological Observatory
Leo Goldberg, University of Michigan
J. Wallace Joyce, National Science Foundation
Walter M. Rudolph, Science Advisor's Office, Department of State
H. W. Wells, Carnegie Institution of Washington

USNC Executive Committee

W. W. Atwood, Jr.
L. V. Berkner
L. M. Gould
Joseph Kaplan, Chairman
Hugh Odishaw
F. W. Reichelderfer
A. H. Shapley, Vice-Chairman
A. F. Spilhaus
M. A. Tuve

Ex officio

J. W. Joyce

USNC Antarctic Committee

Richard B. Black	John Jones, Secretary
Bernt Balchen	Hugh Odishaw
Albert P. Crary	A. H. Shapley
George Dufek	Paul A. Siple
Laurence M. Gould, Chairman	A. Lincoln Washburn
John Hannessian, Jr.	Harry Wexler, Vice-Chairman

Consultants

J. Glenn Dyer
William O. Field
Finn Ronne

USNC Antarctic Program Direction

L. M. Gould, Director	N. J. Oliver, aurora
Harry Wexler, Chief Scientist	M. J. Rubin, weather central
Albert P. Crary, Deputy Chief Scientist	Harry Sellery, ionosphere
D. S. Carder, seismology	J. A. Simpson, cosmic rays
Albert P. Crary, glaciology	S. F. Singer, cosmic rays
P. A. Humphrey, meteorology	J. A. Van Allen, rocketry
J. H. Nelson, geomagnetism	G. P. Wollard, gravity

Scientific and Navy Support Leaders at U. S. IGY Stations

Scientific Leaders   Navy Support Leaders

AMUNDSEN-SCOTT SOUTH POLE STATION

1956–57: Dr. Paul A. Siple   Lt. (jg) John Tuck, Jr.
1957–58: Palle Mogensen   Lt. Vernon N. Houk, MC, USN
1958–59: Julian W. Posey   Lt. Sidney Tolchin, MC, USN

BYRD STATION

1956–57: G. R. Toney   Lt. Brian C. Dalton, MC, USN
1957–58: S. Barnes   Lt. Peter P. Ruseski, MC, USN
1958–59: John Pirrit   Lt. Edward J. Galla, MC, USN

ELLSWORTH STATION

1956–57: Capt. Finn Ronne, USNR   Capt. Finn Ronne, USNR
1957–58: Dr. Matthew J. Brennen   Lt. Paul Tidd, USNR
1958–59: Being operated by Argentina—Wm. Floyd Johnson, U.S. Rep.

HALLETT STATION

1956–57: Dr. James A. Shear   Lt. Juan Tur, MC, USN
1957–58: Kenneth J. Salmon   Lt. R. C. Bornmann, MC, USN
1958–59: Charles L. Roberts   Lt. Albert H. Bridgeman

LITTLE AMERICA STATION

1955–56:   OIC LCDR R. G. Graham, USN
1956–57: A. P. Crary   OIC LCDR H. J. Orndoff, USN
1957–58: A. P. Crary   OIC LCDR T. N. Thompson, USN
1958–59: Not being operated

WILKES STATION

1956–57: Carl R. Ecklund   Lt. (jg) D. R. Burnett
1957–58: Dr. W. L. Tressler   Lt. R. S. Sparks
1958–59: Being operated by Australia—Herbert Hansen, U.S. Rep.

NAVAL AIR FACILITY McMURDO SOUND *

1955–56: OIC LCDR D. W. Canham, Jr., USNR
1956–57: OIC LCDR S. W. Marshall, USN
1957–58: OIC LCDR E. E. Ludeman, USN
1958–59: OIC Comdr. William A. Lewiston, USN

* Not an IGY Station.

*United States Government Agencies Participating in
or Interested in the Antarctic*

1. Department of Defense: Joint Chiefs of Staff, Office of Special
   Operations:
   a. Department of the Navy: (1) Task Force 43, (2) Office of Naval
      Research, (3) Hydrographic Office, (4) Bureau of Medicine and
      Surgery, (5) Bureau of Aeronautics, (6) Bureau of Yards and
      Docks, (7) Bureau of Supplies and Accounts.
   b. Department of the Army: (1) Office of Chief of Staff for Re-
      search and Development, (2) Corps of Engineers (SIPRE),
      (3) Signal Corps, (4) Quartermaster Corps, (5) Transportation
      Corps.
   c. Department of the Air Force: (1) Director of Research and
      Development, (2) Air Force Cambridge Research Center, (3)
      Arctic, Desert, Tropic Information Center.
2. Department of State
3. Department of the Interior:
   a. United States Geological Survey
   b. United States Fish and Wildlife Service
4. Department of Commerce:
   a. National Bureau of Standards
   b. United States Coast and Geodetic Survey
   c. United States Weather Bureau
5. National Science Foundation: Office for International Geophysical
   Year
6. United States National Academy of Science
7. Central Intelligence Agency
8. Atomic Energy Commission
9. Office of Defense Mobilization
10. Department of Health, Education, and Welfare:
    a. Food and Drug Administration
    b. National Institutes of Health
11. National Archives
12. Library of Congress
13. Smithsonian Institution:
    a. United States National Museum
    b. National Zoological Park
14. United States Board on Geographic Names

U. S. Antarctic Programs (1955, up to August 15, 1957)

* Rear Adm. Richard E. Byrd, U. S. Antarctic Programs Officer
Capt. Richard B. Black, Acting Chief of Staff

* Deceased.

Lt. Richard E. Byrd, Jr., Assistant
Dr. Henry M. Dater, Historian
Chief J. H. De Loach, Yeoman 1st cl., USN
Mary E. Diffley, Secretary
Roberta Graham, Secretary
* Capt. Charles Lanman, Chief of Staff
Lt. Comdr. Frank Loveless, Public Information Officer
Capt. Stevan Mandarich, former Chief of Staff
David Martin, Personal Aide to Adm. Byrd
Dr. James E. Mooney, Consultant
Dr. John Roscoe, Research
Lt. Comdr. Viola Sanders, Administration Officer
Dr. Paul A. Siple, Deputy to Adm. Byrd
Elizabeth A. Statton, Secretary
Maj. Murray A. Wiener, USAF Assistant

* Deceased.

U. S. Antarctic Projects (August 15, 1957–April 14, 1959)

Rear Adm. George J. Dufek, U. S. Antarctic Projects Officer
Lt. Barry C. Bishop, USAF Assistant
Raymond A. Butler, Map Curator
Dr. Henry M. Dater, Historian
Chief J. H. De Loach, YN1, USN
 relieved by Charles R. Vonderheide, YN1, USN
Mary E. Diffley, Secretary
Roberta Graham, Secretary
Capt. Edwin A. MacDonald, Chief of Staff
 relieved by Comdr. Paul W. Frazier
 relieved by Capt. J. M. Hermanson
Dr. James E. Mooney, Consultant
Lt. Comdr. Viola Sanders, Administration Officer
 relieved by Lt. Comdr. Ruth M. Streeter
Elizabeth A. Statton, Secretary

U. S. Antarctic Projects (from April 14, 1959)

Rear Adm. David M. Tyree, U. S. Antarctic Projects Officer
Raymond A. Butler, Map Curator
Capt. John Cadwalader, Chief of Staff
Dr. Henry M. Dater, Historian
Mary E. Diffley, Secretary
Roberta Graham, Secretary

Ens. George F. McCleary, Jr., Public Information Officer
Dr. James E. Mooney, Deputy
Elizabeth A. Statton, Secretary
Lt. Comdr. Ruth M. Streeter, Administration Officer
Charles R. Vonderheide, YN1

Foreign Polar Organizations

Country: Argentina
Title: Instituto Antartico Argentino
Established: 1951

Country: Australia
Title: Antarctic Division of the Department of External Affairs
Established: 1948

Country: Chile
Title: Antarctic Department, Ministry of Exterior Relations
      Antarctic Department, General Staff of the Armed Forces

Country: Denmark
Title: Arktisk Institute
Established: 1954

Country: France
Title: Expéditions Polaires Françaises: Missions Paul-Emile Victor
Established: 1947

Country: New Zealand
Title: New Zealand Antarctic Society
Established: 1933; suspended during World War II, revived 1949

Country: Norway
Title: Norsk Polarinstitutt
Established: 1948

Country: Union of Soviet Socialist Republics
Title: The Arctic Institute of the Soviet Union
Established: 1930

Country: United Kingdom
Title: Scott Polar Research Institute
Established: 1926

Country: Canada and U.S.A.
Title: Arctic Institute of North America

Index